ENERGIES FOR TRANSITION

**Proceedings of the Fourth National Conference of the Association of College and Research Libraries
Baltimore, Maryland, April 9–12, 1986**

Edited by: Danuta A. Nitecki
Associate Director for Public Services
University of Maryland Libraries
College Park, Maryland

**Association of College and Research Libraries
A Division of the American Library Association**

Chicago, 1986

Printed by: **OMNIPRESS . . . *"The Proceedings Printer"***
Madison, Wisconsin

Copyright © 1986 by the American Library Association.
All materials in this book subject to copyright by the
American Library Association may be photocopied for the
noncommercial purpose of scientific or educational advancement
granted by Sections 107 and 108 of the Copyright Revision Act
of 1976. For other reprinting, photocopying, or translating,
address requests to the ALA Office of Rights and Permissions,
50 E. Huron St., Chicago, IL 60611.

ISBN 0-8389-6976-3

CONTENTS

List of Contributors	vii
ACRL Who's Who	xii
Readers of Contributed Papers	xiii
Preface	xv

SECTION I: ACADEMIC AND RESEARCH LIBRARIANSHIP

RESOLVED: LIBRARY SCHOOLS DO NOT MEET THEIR GOALS AND OBJECTIVES IN TRAINING ACADEMIC LIBRARIANS TO PERFORM RESEARCH
  David G. Anderson and Christina Landram   3

THE ACADEMIC LIBRARY'S CHANGING ROLE IN THE UNIVERSITY SETTING
  Stephen E. Atkins   8

FREEDOM OF ACCESS TO INFORMATION IN MACHINE READABLE FORM: THE LIBRARIANS ROLE
  Samuel G. Demas   11

* CURRICULUM CHANGE: TRANSITIONS IN TIME
  Michael Haeuser   13

ACADEMIC LIBRARY CENSORSHIP IN A CONSERVATIVE ERA
  Elizabeth Hood   15

THE BENEFITS OF RESEARCH FOR ACADEMIC LIBRARIANS AND THE INSTITUTIONS WHICH THEY SERVE
  Dale S. Montanelli and Patricia F. Stenstrom   18

SECTION II: BIBLIOGRAPHIC CONTROL

HANDLING OF SERIALS IN MICRO-REPRODUCTION: SINGLE BIBLIOGRAPHIC RECORD/MULTIPLE FORMATS--AN OHIO STATE UNIVERSITY EXPERIENCE
  Marjorie E. Adams and Daphne C. Hsueh   23

ERROR DETECTION IN BIBLIOGRAPHIC RECORDS: CAN THE COMPUTER DO IT ALL?
  Jaye Bausser, Jinnie Y. Davis and David Gleim   27

BORN AGAIN CATALOGING IN THE ONLINE NETWORKS
  Ruth Hafter   30

* SHARING SERIAL COLLECTIONS
  Carol Marie Kelley   34

ACCESS POINTS AND BOOK USE: DOES THE CATALOG RECORD MAKE A DIFFERENCE?
  Gunnar Knutson   35

QUALITY CONTROL OF ONLINE CATALOGS: AUTOMATION VS. HUMAN CONTROL
  Ichiko Morita   44

SECTION III: BIBLIOGRAPHIC INSTRUCTION

CONCEPTS FOR BIBLIOGRAPHIC INSTRUCTION IN THIS TIME OF TRANSITION
  Deborah Fink   49

BUILDING A BRIDGE: ARTICULATION PROGRAMS FOR BIBLIOGRAPHIC INSTRUCTION
  Barbara E. Kemp, Mary M. Nofsinger and Alice M. Spitzer   52

* END-USER INSTRUCTION--WHAT ARE YOU DOING?
  Sharmon H. Kenyon   55

TEACHING MICROCOMPUTER LITERACY: NEW ROLES FOR ACADEMIC LIBRARIANS
  Linda J. Piele, Judith Pryor and Harold W. Tuckett   56

* THE EFFECT OF AN ENDUSER TRAINING PROGRAM ON AN ONLINE SEARCH SERVICE
    Judith G. Robinson and Julia R. Shaw   59

SECTION IV: COLLECTIONS MANAGEMENT

BREAKING ROLE AND SPATIAL BARRIERS: THE SYLLABUS EXCHANGE IN BIOETHICS FOSTERS COLLABORATION BETWEEN A RESEARCH LIBRARY, INTERDISCIPLINARY SCHOLARS AND CLINICAL PRACTITIONERS
    Judith A. Adams and Mary Carrington Coutts   63

COMPUTER ACCESSIBLE MATERIAL IN THE ACADEMIC LIBRARY: AVOIDING THE KLUDGE
    Katherine S. Chiang   67

* A MODEL INTERACTIVE AUTOMATED ACQUISITIONS SYSTEM
    Colleen Cook   70

HARDCOPY IN TRANSITION: THE PLAN FOR A PROTOTYPE AUTOMATED STORAGE AND RETRIEVAL FACILITY FOR LOW USE LIBRARY MATERIALS AT CALIFORNIA STATE UNIVERSITY, NORTHRIDGE
    Norma S. Creaghe and Douglas A. Davis   76

* DEVELOPING-WORLD IMPRINTS IN ACADEMIC LIBRARY COLLECTIONS
    David L. Easterbrook   80

ASSESSING COLLECTION DEVELOPMENT ORGANIZATION IN A SMALL ACADEMIC LIBRARY
    Lynne Gamble   82

INTEGRATING MICROFORMS WITH GOVERNMENT DOCUMENTS: A THIRD ALTERNATIVE
    Edward Herman   86

BEYOND THE BOOK: COLLECTION DEVELOPMENT AND THE SPECIAL COLLECTIONS LIBRARIAN
    Gretchen Lagana   90

CAPTURING THE MAINSTREAM: AN EXAMINATION OF PUBLISHER-BASED AND SUBJECT-BASED APPROVAL PLANS IN ACADEMIC LIBRARIES
    Karen A. Schmidt   93

SECTION V: LIBRARY ADMINISTRATION

THE DEVELOPMENT TEAM
    Dwight F. Burlingame   99

FINANCING ACADEMIC LIBRARIES: MAKING THE TRANSITION FROM ENROLLMENT GROWTH TO QUALITY ENHANCEMENT
    John M. Cooper   101

MANAGING VALUES IN AN ACADEMIC LIBRARY
    Mary Ann Griffin   105

STRATEGIES FOR CHANGE
    Carol A. Johnson and Michael D. Kathman   108

TECHNICAL SERVICES: PUBLIC SERVICES BEHIND CLOSED DOORS
    Georgene A. Timko   112

SECTION VI: PERSONNEL

THE PLATEAUED LIBRARIAN: SOLUTIONS FOR IMPROVING PERFORMANCE LEVELS
    James F. Comes   117

PAY FOR PERFORMANCE: THE TE*MS EXPERIMENT
    Constance Corey and Virginia Steel   122

JOB DESIGN FOR THE AUTOMATED TECHNICAL SERVICES ENVIRONMENT
  Kathleen M. Hays   130

ACADEMIC LIBRARIANS' WORKLOAD
  Eileen E. Hitchingham   133

* THE FLOW OF HUMAN RESOURCES: A TURNOVER AGENDA FOR ACADEMIC LIBRARIANSHIP
  James G. Neal   139

A LIBRARY MIDDLE MANAGER LOOKS AT PERFORMANCE APPRAISAL
  Barbara P. Pinzelik   141

STAFF UTILIZATION IN BRANCH LIBRARIES: A RESEARCH REPORT
  Carolyn A. Snyder and Stella Bentley   146

SUGGESTED GUIDELINES FOR SALARY DETERMINATION IN AN ACADEMIC LIBRARY
  Jeanie M. Welch   152

SECTION VII: READER SERVICES

INTEGRATION OF AN ONLINE SEARCH SERVICE INTO THE REFERENCE DEPARTMENT
  Sandra E. Belanger and Rosemary Thorne   159

EARS--THE PHOTOCOPY SOLUTION
  Marilyn Borgendale   165

LIBRARIAN SATISFACTION WITH COMPUTER BIBLIOGRAPHIC SEARCHING
  Kevin Carey   168

PSYCHOLOGICAL NEEDS AND SOURCE LINKAGES IN UNDERGRADUATE INFORMATION-SEEKING BEHAVIOR
  Kathleen Dunn   172

REFERENCE BEYOND (AND WITHOUT) THE REFERENCE DESK
  Barbara J. Ford   179

AN EVALUATION OF DELIVERY TIMES AND COSTS OF A NON-LIBRARY DOCUMENT DELIVERY SERVICE
  Douglas P. Hurd and Robert E. Molyneux   182

USER DEMAND FOR LIBRARY SERVICES: AN UNDERGRADUATE LIBRARY MODEL
  Elaine McPheron   186

A LIBRARY RESEARCH APPLICATION OF FOCUS GROUP INTERVIEWS
  Meg Koch Scharf and Jeannette Ward   191

REDUCTION OF NOISE IN TWO CAMPUS LIBRARIES OF A MAJOR UNIVERSITY
  Sally S. Small and Maureen E. Strazdon   194

ROBOT AT THE REFERENCE DESK?
  Karen F. Smith   198

ONLINE SEARCHING AND THE RESEARCH PROCESS
  Patricia Tegler and Connie Miller   202

* LIBERAL ARTS COLLEGES, ONLINE SEARCHING AND ECONOMIC SURVIVAL
  Celia Wall   205

SECTION VIII: TECHNOLOGY

THE OPEN SYSTEM INTERCONNECTION AS A BUILDING BLOCK IN ELECTRONIC NETWORKING
  Richard W. Boss   209

CD-ROM OPTICAL DISC TECHNOLOGY IN LIBRARIES: ACCEPTANCE AND IMPLEMENTATION
  Nancy L. Eaton and Julie B. Schwerin   214

THE USE OF AN ELECTRONIC CONFERENCING SYSTEM AS A MIDDLE AND UPPER MANAGEMENT TOOL
IN AN ACADEMIC LIBRARY
  Virginia Gillham   218

A POPULIST APPROACH TO AUTOMATION: DEVELOPING LOCAL SYSTEMS IN A MAINFRAME CONTEXT
  David F. Kohl   222

CONSERVATION, PRESERVATION AND DIGITIZATION
  Clifford A. Lynch and Edwin B. Brownrigg   225

THE LIBRARY OF CONGRESS OPTICAL DISK PRINT PILOT PROJECT STAFF EVALUATION
  Victoria Ann Reich and Melissa Ann Betcher   229

MOVING FROM A FIRST GENERATION TO A SECOND GENERATION ONLINE CATALOG DATABASE
  Judith Sessions and William Post   236

* ACCESS TO INFORMATION IN THE ONLINE LIBRARY
  Joe Santosuosso   239

THE EFFECT OF AUTOMATION ON THE RATE OF CHANGE IN PROCEDURES
  Pat Weaver-Meyers and Nedria Santizo   240

Author Index   245

Subject Index   246

* designates an idea brief, # designates a research report, all others are position papers.

LIST OF CONTRIBUTORS

Judith A. Adams
Head, Humanities Division
National Reference Center
for Bioethics Literature
Oklahoma State University
Stillwater, Oklahoma

Marjorie E. Adams
Head, Continuation Acquisitions
Main Library
The Ohio State University
Columbus, Ohio

David G. Anderson
Head, Monograph Unit
Catalog Department
Pullen Library
Georgia State University
Atlanta, Georgia

Stephen E. Atkins
Political Science Subject Specialist
Education and Social Sciences Library
University of Illinois at Urbana-Champaign
Urbana, Illinois

Jaye Bausser
Head, Post Cataloging Operations Section
Perkins Library
Duke University
Durham, North Carolina

Sandra Belanger
Reference Librarian
Reference Department
Clark Library
San Jose State University
San Jose, California

Stella Bentley
Planning and Budget Officer
Indiana University Libraries
Indiana University
Bloomington, Indiana

Melissa Ann Betcher
Planning Assistant
Office of Planning and Development
Library of Congress
Washington, D.C.

Marilyn Borgendale
Head, Circulation Services
Health Sciences Library
University of Maryland at Baltimore
Baltimore, Maryland

Richard W. Boss
Senior Consultant
Information Systems Consultants Inc.
Bethesda, Maryland

Edwin B. Brownrigg
Director
Division of Library Automation
University of California
Berkeley, California

Dwight F. Burlingame
Dean of Libraries and Learning
Resources
Bowling Green State University
Bowling Green, Ohio

Kevin Carey
Assistant Reference Librarian
Main Library
University of Illinois at Chicago
Chicago, Illinois

Katherine S. Chiang
Computerized Data Services Librarian
Albert R. Mann Library
Cornell University
Ithaca, New York

James F. Comes
Health Science Librarian
Ball State University
Muncie, Indiana

Colleen Cook
Head, Circulation and Automation
Sterling C. Evans Library
Texas A & M University
College Station, Texas

John M. Cooper
Doctoral Candidate
Harvard Graduate School of Education
Harvard University
Cambridge, Massachusetts

Constance Corey
Assistant University Librarian
for Management Services
Hayden Library
Arizona State University
Tempe, Arizona

Mary Carrington Coutts
Kennedy Institute of Ethics
Georgetown University
Washington, D.C.

Norma S. Creaghe
Associate Director of Libraries
University Libraries
California State University, Northridge
Northridge, California

Douglas A. Davis
Physical Planning Coordinator
California State University, Northridge
Northridge, California

Jinnie Y. Davis
Library Planning and Online Systems
Specialist
Hill Library
North Carolina State University
Raleigh, North Carolina

Samuel Demas
Associate Director
Albert R. Mann Library
Cornell University
Ithaca, New York

Kathleen Dunn
Chairman, Department of Public Services
La Sierra Campus Library
Loma Linda University
Riverside, California

David L. Easterbrook
Bibliographer for Professional Studies
Collections Development Department
University of Illinois at Chicago
Chicago, Illinois

Nancy L. Eaton
Director of Libraries
Howe Library
University of Vermont
Burlington, Vermont

Deborah Fink
Instructional Services Librarian
University of Colorado Libraries
University of Colorado
Boulder, Colorado

Barbara J. Ford
Assistant Director for Public Services
Elizabeth Coates Maddux Library
Trinity University
San Antonio, Texas

Lynne Gamble
Assistant to the Director
Robert E. Kennedy Library
California Polytechnic State University
San Luis Obispo, California

Virginia Gillham
Assistant Librarian for Reader Services
McLaughlin Library
University of Guelph
Guelph, Ontario

David Gleim
Assistant Head, Catalog Department
Davis Library
University of North Carolina at Chapel Hill
Chapel Hill, North Carolina

Mary Ann Griffin
Director, Falvey Memorial Library
Villanova University
Villanova, Pennsylvania

Michael Haeuser
Director of Learning Resources
Gustavus Adolphus College
Saint Peter, Minnesota

Ruth Hafter
Library Director
The Ruben Salazar Library
Sonoma State University
Rohnert Park, California

Kathleen M. Hays
Head of Cataloging
Milton S. Eisenhower Library
Johns Hopkins University
Baltimore, Maryland

Edward Herman
Government Documents Department
Lockwood Library
State University at New York at Buffalo
Buffalo, New York

Eileen E. Hitchingham
Automation Project
Kresge Library
Oakland University
Rochester, Michigan

Elizabeth Hood
Serials Cataloger
Elizabeth Coates Maddux Library
Trinity University
San Antonio, Texas

Daphne C. Hsueh
Head, Serials Cataloging
Main Library
Ohio State University Libraries
Columbus, Ohio

Douglas P. Hurd
Public Services Librarian
Science and Engineering Library
University of Virginia
Charlottesville, Virginia

Carol A. Johnson
Alcuin Library
St. John's University
Collegeville, Minnesota

Michael D. Kathman
Director of Libraries and Media
Alcuin Library
Saint John's University
Collegeville, Minnesota

Carol Marie Kelley
Assistant Head, Acquisitions Department
Texas Tech University Libraries
Texas Tech University
Lubbock, Texas

Barbara E. Kemp
Head, Humanities/Social Sciences
Public Services
Holland Library
Washington State University
Pullman, Washington

Sharmon H. Kenyon
Business/Economics Librarian
Humboldt State University
Arcata, California

Gunnar Knutson
Assistant Catalog Librarian
Cataloging Department
University Library
University of Illinois at Chicago
Chicago, Illinois

David F. Kohl
Assistant Director for
Undergraduate Libraries and
Instructional Services
Undergraduate Library
University of Illinois at Urbana-Champaign
Urbana, Illinois

Gretchen Lagana
Special Collections Librarian
Main Library
University of Illinois at Chicago
Chicago, Illinois

Christina Landram
Head, Catalog Department
William Russell Pullen Library
Georgia State University
Atlanta, Georgia

Clifford A. Lynch
Manager, Computing Resources
Division of Library Automation
University of California
Berkeley, California

Elaine McPheron
Head, Bibliographic Instruction
Silverman Undergraduate Library
State University of New York at Buffalo
Buffalo, New York

Connie Miller
Acting Science Librarian
University of Illinois at Chicago
Chicago, Illinois

Robert E. Molyneux
Decision Support Librarian
Alderman Library
University of Virginia
Charlottesville, Virginia

Dale S. Montanelli
Director of Administrative Services
University of Illinois Library
University of Illinois at Urbana-Champaign
Urbana, Illinois

Ichiko Morita
Associate Professor and
Head, Automated Processing Department
The Ohio State University Libraries
Columbus, Ohio

James G. Neal
Assistant Dean and Head,
Reference and Instructional Services
Division
University Libraries
The Pennsylvania State University
University Park, Pennsylvania

Mary M. Nofsinger
Public Services Librarian III
Holland Library
Washington State University
Pullman, Washington

Linda J. Piele
Head, Public Services Division
Library/Learning Center
University of Wisconsin-Parkside
Kenosha, Wisconsin

Barbara P. Pinzelik
HSSE Public Services Librarian
Purdue University Libraries
Purdue University
West Lafayette, Indiana

William Post
Assistant University Librarian
Meriam Library
California State University, Chico
Chico, California

Judith Pryor
Coordinator of Instruction
Library/Learning Center
University of Wisconsin-Parkside
Kenosha, Wisconsin

Victoria Ann Reich
Planning Librarian
Office of Planning and Development
The Library of Congress
Washington, D.C.

Judith G. Robinson
Reference Librarian, Online Coordinator
Tompkins-McCaw Library
Virginia Commonwealth University
Richmond, Virginia

Nedria Santizo
Online Processing Supervisor
University of Oklahoma Libraries
University of Oklahoma
Norman, Oklahoma

Joe Santosuosso
Marketing Analyst
CLSI, Inc.
West Newton, Massachussets

Meg Koch Scharf
Coordinator, LINE
University Library
University of Central Florida
Orlando, Florida

Karen A. Schmidt
Acquisitions Librarian
University of Illinois at Urbana-Champaign
Urbana, Illinois

Julie B. Schwerin
President
Info Tech
Pittsfield, Vermont

Judith Sessions
University Librarian
Meriam Library
California State University, Chico
Chico, California

Julia R. Shaw
Reference Librarian
Enduser Training Program Coordinator
Tompkins-McCaw Library
Virginia Commonwealth University
Richmond, Virginia

Sally S. Small
Associate and Head Librarian
Berks Campus Memorial Library
The Pennsylvania State University
Reading, Pennsylvania

Karen F. Smith
Head, Documents and Microforms Department
Lockwood Library
State University of New York at Buffalo
Buffalo, New York

Carolyn A. Snyder
Associate Dean for Public Services
Indiana University Libraries
Indiana University
Bloomington, Indiana

Alice M. Spitzer
Public Services Librarian III
Holland Library
Washington State University
Pullman, Washington

Virginia Steel
Assistant to the University Librarian
Hayden Library
Arizona State University
Tempe, Arizona

Patricia F. Stenstrom
Library and Information Science Librarian
University of Illinois at Urbana-Champaign
Urbana, Illinois

Maureen E. Strazdon
American International Group
Research and Development Department
New York, New York

Patricia Tegler
Kirkland & Ellis
Chicago, Illinois

Rosemary Thorne
Reference Department Head
Clark Library
San Jose State University
San Jose, California

Georgene A. Timko
Technical Services Director
John Vaughan Library/Learning Resources Center
Northeastern State University
Tahlequah, Oklahoma

Harold W. Tuckett
Coordinator of Data Base Searching
Library/Learning Center
University of Wisconsin-Parkside
Kenosha, Wisconsin

Celia Wall
Reference Librarian
Waterfield Library
Murray State University
Murray, Kentucky

Jeannette Ward
Technical Services
University of Central Florida Libraries
University of Central Florida
Orlando, Florida

Pat Weaver-Meyers
Head, Access Services
University of Oklahoma Libraries
University of Oklahoma
Norman, Oklahoma

Jeanie Welch
Head, Reference Department
Mary and John Gray Library
Lamar University
Beaumont, Texas

ACRL WHO'S WHO

ACRL FOURTH NATIONAL CONFERENCE

H. Joanne Harrar, Chair

Contributed Papers:
Danuta A. Nitecki, Chair
Arnold Bellefontaine
Keith Russell
Kris Benitez, Secretay
Karen Nelson, Secretary

Consultant:
Gary L. Menges
Vicki Kreimeyer

Exhibits Manager:
Sandy Donnelly

Local Arrangements/Hospitality
Suzanne P. Hill, Chair
Ruth E. Kifer
Susan Mower
Simmona Simmons
Joyce Tenney

Program:
Bonita Perry, Chair
Martin Smith
Sister Mary Ian Stewart
Thomas Strader

Publicity:
Charmaine S. Boyd, Co-Chair
William G. Wilson, Co-chair
Marianne C. Rough

Special Events:
Diana Cunningham, Chair
Susan J. Arrington
Dara Cook
Bonnie Preston
Larry Wilt

ACRL Conference Staff:
Cathleen Bourdon, ACRL Deputy Director
Elaine T. Opalka, Secretary
JoAn S. Segal, ACRL Executive Director

ACRL BOARD OF DIRECTORS

1985/1986

President
Sharon A. Hogan

Vice President/President-Elect
Hannelore B. Rader

Past President
Sharon J. Rogers

ACRL Councilor
Millicent P. Abell

Chair, Budget & Finance
Robert Almony

Directors-At-Large
Bob D. Carmack
B. Anne Commerton
Mary Sue Ferrell
W. Lee Hisle
Edward J. Jennerich
Jean A. Major
Alexandra Mason
Rochelle Sager

READERS OF CONTRIBUTED PAPERS

The following individuals refereed papers submitted to the Conference

Pamela J. Andre
Joyce Ball
Wendell A. Barbour
Alan R. Benenfeld
Scott Bennett
Bella Berson
David F. Bishop
Florence Blakely
Julia C. Blixrud
Carol Boast
Martha A. Bowman
B. J. Busch
Dale B. Canelas
Bob D. Carmack
Norma Carmack
Ruth C. Carter
Joan L. Chambers
Hendrik Edelman
Mary Farrell
Jill B. Fatzer
Sara Fine
Selma Foster
Martha Friedman
Mary W. George
Nancy B. Gwinn
Carolyn L. Harris
Norman Horrocks
Willis M. Hubbard
Betsy Humphreys
C. Lee Jones
Catherine Jones
David Kaser
Nancy C. Kranich
Gary E. Kraske
Christian Larew
Signe E. Larson
Ronald G. Leach
Mary Jo Lynch
Nancy R. McAdams
Jean A. Major
Carol Mandel
Leslie Manning
Gary L. Menges
Joseph J. Mika
William Miller
James E. Morgan
Carol Mueller
Marcia J. Myers
Janice Bonneville Olsen
Richard W. Oram
Maureen D. Pastine
Anna H. Perrault
Jay Martin Poole
Gail A. Schlachter
James C. Schmidt
Beth J. Shapiro
Thomas Shaughnessy

Jessie C. Smith
Carla J. Stoffle
Susan Tarr
James L. Thompson
Philip Tompkins
David B. Walch
Patricia Wand
Peter G. Watson
C. Brigid Welch
Richard Hume Werking
Sara Lou Whildin
Myra Jo Wilson
William G. Wilson
Jennifer A. Younger

Preface

Academic and research libraries, the institutions of which they are a part, the environments in which they function, and the constituencies they serve, are all swept up in transitions of numerous kinds and dimensions. Trends in higher education, including new methodologies in instruction, new directions for research and the rise of the information society, all place varied and vastly different demands on libraries from those traditionally anticipated. Library management techniques are being altered in order to accommodate both austerity and affluence, the high rate of technological change and emerging organizational structures. Campuses are being wired to utilize new technologies for data and video transmission and to permit necessary telecommunication linkages. Automation continues to find new applications, transforming libraries in their relations to each other, to other institutions, and the their evermore diverse clientele in hitherto undreamed-of ways.

These developments are forcing librarians to assume new attitudes, to seek appropriate strategies, and to exploit finite resources in new ways so as to fulfill missions which necessarily are shifting as well. The focus of the 1986 ACRL National Conference in Baltimore was to explore the theme, Energies for Transition. The Conference attempted to identify the nature of many of the transitions facing librarians and to suggest energies by which to respond effectively to them, through both formal programs and the informal gathering of colleagues.

Contributed papers were a major feature of the conference. Expectations for research findings were high among some of the ACRL leadership, while at the same time the desire to share practical experiences from the field was high among others. In addition an applauded feature of previous conferences was the various forums offered for discussion. An attempt was made to address these different objectives in planning of this conference. As a result, new to the Fourth National ACRL Conference was the invitation for authored contributions in any of three categories identified as follows:

1) Research reports (descriptions of studies which utilize rigorous research methodology and which include identified hypotheses and clearly stated conclusions);

2) Position papers (descriptions of locally implemented experiences, theoretical models, or state of the art reviews in which problems are clearly identified and solutions proposed);

and 3) Idea Briefs (short introductions of possible research ideas, evolving concepts or programmatic concerns which are intended to stimulate discussion).

The call for contributions resulted in receipt of one hundred ninety-five manuscripts. Each was sent to two reviewers who were persons selected by the Contributed Papers Committee from among distinguished researchers and leaders in the profession. The identity of the author was of course kept anonymous during the review process. Due to the need to limit the number of conference presentations, the committee members relied completely on the reviewers' recommendations and accepted no paper which either reviewer recommended be rejected.

The idea brief was a totally new category of contribution for this conference. More traditional as a conference contribution, the research reports and position papers both were formal, developed arguments, presented at the conference within twenty and fifteen minutes, respectively. In contrast, the idea briefs were well stated problems or questions with appropriate background and were presented at the conference within ten minutes followed by twenty minutes of discussion among those attending the session. A different selection procedure was used for this new approach whereby each contributed idea brief was reviewed by two committee members. Only those which both readers recommended to be accepted without modification were included.

The selection process culminated in the acceptance of sixty papers - seven research reports, forty-four position papers and nine idea briefs. Reviewers' comments were sent to authors. The revised papers prepared by the authors, are offered in this printed proceedings and each was presented twice during the conference.

This published proceedings includes only the accepted contributed research reports, position papers, and idea briefs. Theme papers presented by invited speakers are not included here; these feature speakers were invited to publish their presentations in future issues of College and Research Libraries.

No editorial work was done on the papers included here. The camera-ready copies were prepared by the authors. The diversity of typeset is accepted in exchange for the timeliness of producing the printed proceedings in time to be distributed at the conference. The contributions are grouped into eight subject areas and are arranged alphabetically by first author's last name within each category. An author index and a subject index conclude this volume. Committee members created the subject index using keywords assigned by the authors or wherever not offered by the authors, assigned by a librarian assistant. Slight modifications were made for clarity and consistency. Numbers appearing after subject headings refer to the number of the first page of the associated article.

Production of this proceedings consumed the valued time of many persons, all of whom deserve a special word of thanks. The authors' efforts are well appreciated as are the volunteered time contributed by the reviewers. Working with Keith Russell and Arnold Bellefontaine - the other two members of the Contributed Papers Committee - was perhaps the most enjoyable part of this project. Both gentlemen matched their insights to trends in librarianship and their knowledge of its leaders to provide valuable advice, hard and often tedious work, and good humor. We all wish to thank our respective institutions for supporting our involvement in this undertaking and to acknowledge the helpful coordinating efforts of the ACRL staff. The conference would not have occurred and these papers not published without the unselfishly volunteered work during the past eighteen months of members of the Conference Planning Committee, chaired by Dr. H. Joanne Harrar, and the many members of each subcommittee. To all of these people who gave their own energies for the preparation of this event and its published record, a salute of gratitude is extended.

Finally, my personal thanks are added to the traditional appreciation offered to the secretaries who kept the correspondence and records correctly moving, both in paper and electronically. Kris Benitez and Karen Nelson met the challenges of the conference deadlines, with tons of typing and with continual good spirit amidst several other stressful demands occurring in our office during the transition to finalize these conference proceedings.

Danuta A. Nitecki, Chair
Contributed Papers Committee

February, 1986

ACADEMIC AND RESEARCH LIBRARIANSHIP

RESOLVED: LIBRARY SCHOOLS DO NOT MEET THEIR GOALS
AND OBJECTIVES IN TRAINING ACADEMIC LIBRARIANS
TO PERFORM RESEARCH

David G. Anderson
Christina Landram
William Russell Pullen Library
Georgia State University
Atlanta, Georgia

Abstract. Since academic librarians have gained faculty status, they must meet the same criteria for promotion and tenure as other faculty members. These criteria include research together with job performance and service. Our position is that library schools in the United States do not meet their stated goals and objectives in regard to training librarians for entry level academic positions. Current library school catalogs are examined for their statements of goals and objectives and these are then compared to courses taught in research and statistical methods as well as the availability of a thesis option.

Key Words and Phrases. Academic Librarians; Library School Courses; Goals; Objectives; Research; Statistical Methods.

There has been much discussion in the past decade or two concerning whether or not librarians should be classified as faculty in academic institutions. That debate has pretty well been resolved. The "Statement on Faculty Status of College and University Librarians,"[1] which was issued in 1974 asserts that librarians in academic institutions should have faculty status. By 1978 it had been endorsed by fifty-eight state and national library organizations.[2] How many academic librarians have faculty status? Surveys in the literature in 1981 and 1983 indicate that forty-four to forty-six percent of academic librarians have faculty status. We are not debating faculty status for librarians. The fact is that many are on the faculty--and if librarians are on the faculty, are they required to do research?

In order for faculty to be promoted in rank, to achieve tenure, and possibly to receive merit raises, they are frequently judged on the basis of three criteria: teaching, research, and service. Reports in the literature indicate that librarians given faculty status are often subject to the same criteria. The policy statements compiled by the Committee on Academic Status of ACRL indicate that evidence for promotion in rank may include activities related to inquiry and research.[3] For example, Thomas English, in a 1983 survey found that librarians with faculty status were required to meet two distinct sets of criteria. One set was designed to measure performance as librarians and the other set was designed to measure performance as faculty, that is, research, scholarly achievement, and publication.[4] Other surveys indicate that while for some librarians research is required, others are "encouraged" to publish.

Librarians have faculty status and are expected to do research. Whether it is required or encouraged, there is pressure to perform the task. Are academic librarians prepared to perform? Thomas Childers has reported "that the people who enter the library and information science profession are less than optimally skilled in and oriented to research."[5] If preparation for librarianship is based on a degree from a library school, what are library schools doing to prepare librarians? First of all, what are the schools' goals and objectives? Are they even attempting to train academic librarians? If not, we have no argument; if so, what are they doing to meet their stated goals and objectives? Are courses offered or required that teach research? Do they emphasize evaluation of research or performance? Are statistics courses available and do they teach performance? Is a thesis required or are independent study courses offered? What are the schools' admission requirements? If a research capability is required for admittance, there is no need to teach research.

METHODOLOGY

In order to answer these questions we decided to look at catalogs or bulletins of the sixty graduate library education programs in the United States accredited by the American Library Association as of October 1984. We wanted to determine whether library school courses carried out the schools' goals and objectives in relation to academic librarians and research. The information for each school was tabulated on a chart and the coded information from these charts was input into a microcomputer using PC File. Results were sorted and tabulated using the same program. Graphs were obtained using Lotus 1-2-3. A summary of the coded information from the bulletins is presented in Appendix I.

RESULTS

Our first question concerned admission standards and whether any kind of research experience was required. If that was the case, we didn't feel it was necessary for the school to teach research. For two schools: Southern Connecticut State University and University of California, Los Angeles, this was true. For the other fifty-eight we need to continue our quest.

Do the goals or objectives state or imply that academic librarians are trained? Forty-five schools, or seventy-five percent, make some statement in their bulletins to the effect that they train academic librarians. This is either stated explicitly or it is implied through statements that they train all librarians, beginning or entry level librarians, or provide skills necessary for the profession. Graph 1 illustrates this. One might ask why <u>all</u> library schools do not state in some way that they train academic librarians. Perhaps they feel this is self evident and need not be stated.

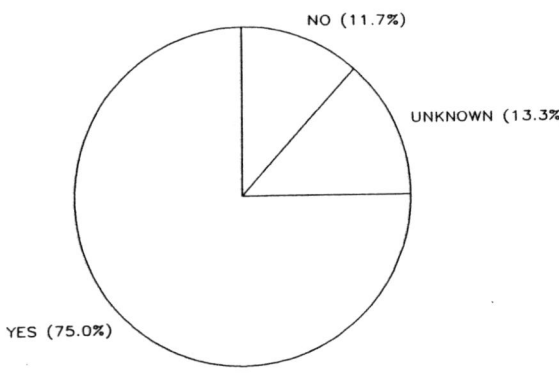

GRAPH 1

Are library schools committed by their goals or objectives to training librarians in the area of research? Graph 2 shows that slightly over half (53%) state that they are. If academic librarians are expected to do research and almost half the library schools do not see teaching research as one of their objectives, one must question whether these schools do train academic librarians.

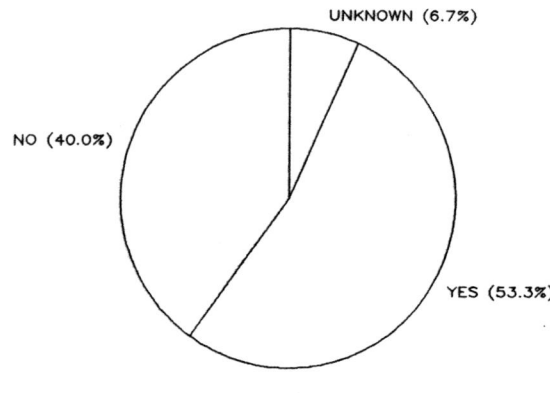

GRAPH 2

It is clear then that the goals and objectives of most library schools in the United States state or imply that academic librarians are trained while over half state that they train in the area of research. What do the schools do to accomplish their goals? How well do they fulfill their objectives? Are there courses offered to help train students in the areas of research and statistics? Thirty-five of the sixty schools, or fifty-eight percent, offer a course in research methods at the master's level, twenty-five do not. Of those thirty-five which offer a course, what is the content of that course? Promotion and tenure are based on performing research, which is quite different from evaluating what someone else has done. Almost half of the courses offered teach performance while the remainder either teach only evaluation or do not describe which aspect is taught. How much weight or importance do library schools give these courses? One way to determine this might be to consider whether or not a research course is required. Only twenty-three of the thirty-five schools which offer a research course require that it be taken. Of those only eleven teach performance.

The most interesting results are obtained when the schools' goals and objectives are compared to what they offer. Graph 3 shows a comparison of the forty-five schools which claim to train academic librarians with whether research courses are offered or required and whether or not those courses teach performance. Twenty-seven offer a research course, fourteen of which teach performance. Only seventeen require the course, of which eight teach performance.

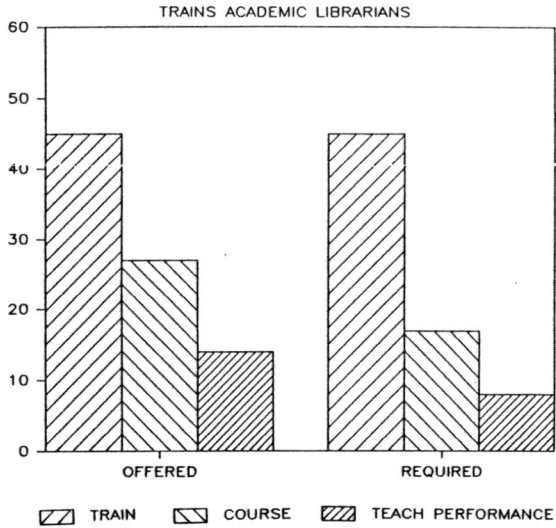

GRAPH 3

Looking at those whose goal or objective is to train in the area of research, Graph 4 illustrates the relationship of courses which are offered or required as well as whether the course requires performance. Of the thirty-two schools which train in research, twenty-one offer a course in research, twelve of which teach performance. Only eleven require the course, seven of which teach performance.

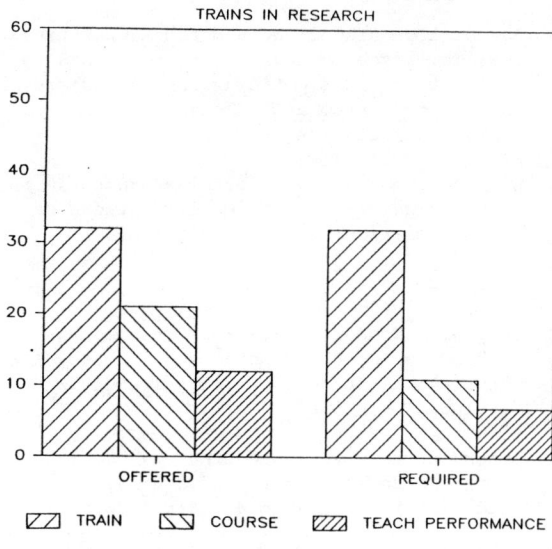

GRAPH 4

A necessary component of much research is the ability to create and use statistics. One might reason that a course in statistics would be preferable to one in research methods--or at least should be offered in addition to research methods courses. Statistics courses are almost as elusive as Clara Peller's famous "beef." Only eleven schools, or eighteen percent, even offer courses in statistical methods. Of those, four teach performance, four teach evaluation, and three do not describe which aspect they teach. Of the eleven schools that offer a statistics course, only, six, or ten percent of the sixty, require the course to be taken.

Again, we think it is important to compare the schools' intentions with what they offer. Of the forty-five schools which claim to train academic librarians, eight offer a course in statistics, three of which teach performance. Only five schools require the course. This comparison is shown in Graph 5.

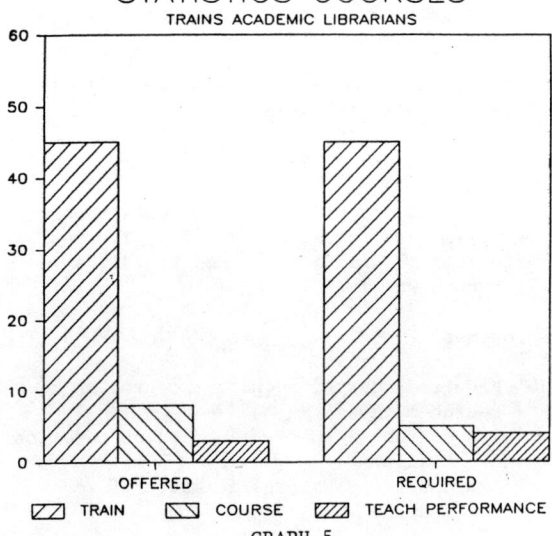

GRAPH 5

Graph 6 covers those thirty-two schools which claim to train in research. Only six offer a course in statistics, and of those six only three teach performance. Of the same thirty-two schools only four require a course and of these four, three teach performance.

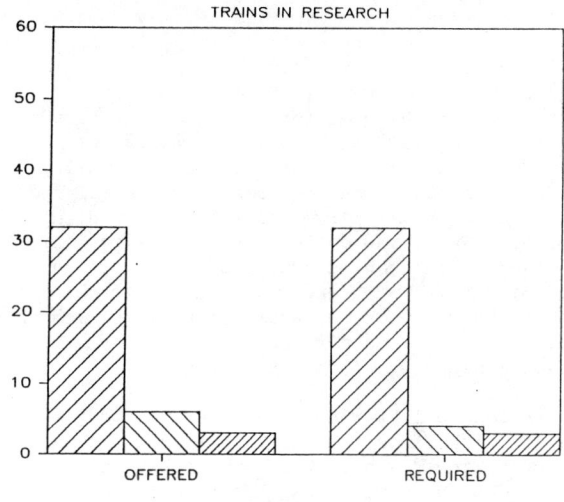

GRAPH 6

We would like to make two more short comparisons before we state our conclusions. It is possible that if a school requires a thesis, librarians would get experience in research in library school. So, let's examine those institutions which state that they train academic librarians and train in research. Graph 7 illustrates first that of the forty-five schools which claim to train academic librarians twenty-six do offer a thesis option but only six require it. As for the thirty-two schools which claim to train in the area of research, only ten offer a thesis, and only five require it. Requiring a thesis would provide research experience irrespective of other courses offered.

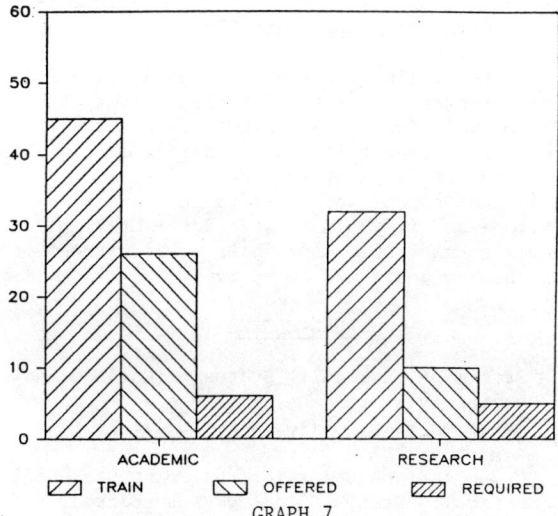

GRAPH 7

CONCLUSION

It is clear to us that some few library schools accomplish their goals and fulfull their objectives laudably. However, most library schools do not meet their stated goals and objectives in training academic librarians in the area of research. Library schools should critically examine whether the programs offered meet their goals and objectives and if they do not, they should either re-state their goals or change their programs. Either library schools should require prior training in research methods and statistical techniques for admittance or persons entering the field of academic librarianship should be required to take such courses while in library school. These courses could be offered in the graduate library school or obtained in another area of the college or university. Librarians would then be equipped to work in an academic environment and would be better able to support the role of colleges and universities in their research endeavors and to accomplish those pursuits expected of faculty members.

Academic librarians are entering the profession with almost no experience in a growing aspect of their jobs. Where will they get this experience? Who will take the first step? Beverly Lynch has stated that "the role of the academic librarian being forged in the field is not yet the role adopted by those teaching in library schools."[6] Library schools should be the leaders and not the followers in preparing academic librarians.

Some library schools are aware of the problem and are taking action now. Here are two things that are already being done. The March 15, 1985 Library Hotline reported that the University of Michigan School of Library Science is going to a two year degree with more emphasis on such things as quantitative analysis in order to help students who are going to work in research libraries.[7] Another thing that would be very helpful to students is a statement such as is in the Kent State University library school bulletin: "A thesis is strongly recommended for students preparing to work in academic libraries. Large university libraries, in particular, often require that prospective employees submit evidence of research capability."[8]

Academic librarians need to understand and be prepared for the realities of academe. It would be well for library students anticipating careers in academic institutions to look closely at courses provided by library schools and choose that school which offers the best preparation--and it would be well for library schools to make sure that their curriculums meet their stated goals and objectives.

REFERENCES

1. "Statement on Faculty Status of College and University Librarians," College & Research Libraries News 35 (February 1974): 26.

2. "Organizations Endorsing the Joint Statement on Faculty Status," College & Research Libraries News 39 (February 1978): 39.

3. Association of College and Research Libraries, Committee on Academic Status, Faculty Status for Academic Librarians: a History and Policy Statements. (Chicago: American Library Association, 1975), p. 41.

4. English, Thomas G., "Librarian Status in the Eighty-Nine U.S. Academic Institutions of the Association of Research Libraries: 1982," College & Research Libraries 44 (May 1983): 204.

5. Childers, Thomas, "Will the Cycle be Unbroken? Research and Schools of Library and Information Studies," Library Trends 32 (Spring 1984): 530.

6. Lynch, Beverly P., "A Comment on the Role of the Academic Librarian," Journal of Academic Librarianship 4 (July 1978): 134.

7. Library Hotline 14, no. 11 (18 March 1985): 5.

8. Introducing Library Science 1983-1985, Kent State. (Kent, Ohio: School of Library Science, Kent State University), p. 7.

APPENDIX I

Coded Information from Bulletins

1 = Identification number of institution: (60 institutions)

2 = Do admission standards require a research methods course or statistical methods course?
1 = yes: 2 (2%), 2 = no: 55 (92%), 3 = unknown: 3 (5%)

3 = Goals and objectives

3.1 = Goals or objectives state or imply that academic librarians are trained: e.g., train all librarians, train beginning or entry level librarians, train academic librarians, provide skills necessary for the profession
1 = yes: 45 (75%), 2 = no: 7 (12%), 3 = unknown: 8 (13%)

3.2 = Goals or objectives state they train librarians in the area of research
1 = yes: 32 (53%), 2 = no: 24 (40%), 3 = unknown: 4 (7%)

4 = Thesis program offered or master's report
1 = yes, not required: 27 (45%), 2 = yes, required: 7 (11.7%), 3 = no: 25 (41.7%), 4 = unknown: 1 (1.7%)

5 = Courses

5.1 = Required courses require a course on research methods
    1 = Course teaches evaluation of research: 9 (15%)
    2 = Course teaches performance of research: 7 (11.7%)

3 = Course teaches both evaluation and performance: 4 (6.7%)
4 = Course does not describe which aspect: 3 (5%)
5 = No course required: 37 (61.7%)

5.2 = Required courses require a course on statistical methods
1 = Course teaches evaluation of statistics: 1 (1.7%)
2 = Course teaches performance using statistics: 3 (5%)
3 = Course teaches both evaluation and performance: 1 (1.7%)
4 = Course does not describe which aspect: 1 (1.7%)
5 = No course required: 54 (90%)

5.3 = Independent study course offered
1 = yes: 36 (60%), 2 = no: 24 (40%)

5.4 = Course in research methods offered at the master's level but not required
1 = Course teaches evaluation of research: 11 (18.3%)
2 = Course teaches performance of research: 8 (13.3%)
3 = Course teaches both evaluation and performance: 9 (15%)
4 = Course does not describe which aspect: 7 (11.7%)
5 = No course offered: 25 (41.7%)

5.5 = Course in statistical methods offered at the master's level but not required
1 = Course teaches evaluation of statistical methods: 4 (6.7%)
2 = Course teaches performance using statistics: 4 (6.7%)
3 = Course teaches both evaluation and performance: 0 (0%)
4 = Course does not describe which aspect: 3 (5%)
5 = No course offered: 49 (81.7%)

THE ACADEMIC LIBRARY'S CHANGING ROLE IN THE UNIVERSITY SETTING

Stephen E. Atkins
University of Illinois Library
Urbana, Illinois

Abstract. The academic library survived the university financial difficulties in the 1970s with the certainty that the library would be vulnerable during the university's next financial downturn. Unless libraries and librarians improve their political base within the university the next period of financial shortfall will damage the library. A solution is for librarians to play an active role in university governance, but this means that librarians have to be considered equal to the teaching faculty. Only by this means can the library be protected from those university administrators who consider the library a bottomless pit for funds.

Keywords and Phrases. faculty governance, faculty status, governance, library directors, library research, university governance.

The academic library survived the university financial difficulties in the 1970s with the certainty that the library would be vulnerable during the university's next financial downturn. After all, some universities during this period used the excuse of financial funding loss to cut costs by lowering library services and by stripping librarians of rank and benefits.[1] Today the academic library is in an era of balancing growth with fiscal restraint, but behind this appearance of stability there is pressure from university administrations to plan for the eventuality of another financial downturn. The library remains a natural target, because on a national average libraries consume between two and seven percent of an university's budget.[2] This financial concern on the part of university planners hides a profound difference of opinion among the various constituencies of the university community on the role and the function of the academic library. Such a difference of opinion could be a favorable omen for change except that the academic library now has a rival for funds in university computer centers.[3] Unless there is better understanding between university administrators, faculty and librarians on the library's place in the university there is the distinct possibility that during the next financial crunch the university library will lose out to the computer center in a competition for funding.[4] Now is the time for librarians to understand the role of the library in the university setting and for them to make preparations before the next budgetary crisis hits the university scene.

A major criticism of academic libraries has been their lack of goals. Indecision on whether academic libraries are an integral part of the educational mission of the university, or merely a service component, has made the library's role unclear. But universities, in general, have had the same problem of indistinct goals. Universities have never been able to reconcile their two competing roles: the university with the special function of searching for truth and evaluating society, and the university with the goal of service to society.[5] Goal ambiguity has brought conflict to many universities, and such crises have often served as a catalyst for educational reform.[6] Universities, however, acknowledge that there is a strong public service element in their educational mission. Since universities are "client-serving institutions", they need highly trained professionals able to cope with uncertain goal.[7] Traditionally, these professionals have been called teaching faculty, but the term can be expanded to include administrators, librarians and scientific researchers. Each fits the criterion of a professional as a self-sustaining, highly motivated individual with a specialized body of knowledge.

University administrations have nominal control over the library by means of administrative channels and budgetary controls. Most universities have a special staff, often called the Office of Institutional Research, or a faculty committee, whose function is to assemble information from each part of the university and to study how the management of the university can be made more efficient.[8] These bodies have shown interest in management systems which would include the library. Among the systems under consideration now and in the immediate past have been mathematical oriented management systems, Planning, Programming, Budgeting Systems (PPBS), and self-assessment studies.[9] While none of these systems have had more than limited success in either the university-at-large or the library, they are attempts to bring an unwieldy administrative apparatus under control.[10] The underlying assumption of these systems is the belief of university administrations that libraries, and, other comparable parts of the university, must be transformed to meet current and future obligations at an acceptable cost. Although the library remains a source of pride to the university, many administrators believe that it is also "at times an uncontrollable drain on the university's budget."[11] Much of past retrenchments have come in library personnel and services rather than in the acquisition budget, but there is concern that in the future all library appropriations will be affected.[12] Rather than capitulating before another cost cutting phase, the library needs to mobilize its defenders and prepare viable alternatives. But at present the library's primary defenders, the library professionals, have little influence or power in the university.

A major weakness of the library in the university administrative structure is the lack of participation by librarians in university governance. Governance has been defined variously as the act of governing, or as "the process of direct control by groups or individuals over university policies."[13] During the last twenty-five years university governance has fallen into the hands of three bodies: governing boards, the university administration and the faculty.[14] Each of these groups are part of a compromise on governance obtained only after years of political infighting. But it has been the emergence of the professional manager that has changed the governance balance of power. These managers have been able to relieve the university president of onerous administrative duties, but they have also imposed a bureaucratic barrier in the governance process. This assortment of vice-presidents, deans, directors and business managers have formed a cabinet style of university government where they advise the president on policies and procedures.[15] Although nearly all of these administrators have backgrounds in university teaching, no two administrators view the university library in the same way.[16]

The teaching faculty has always had a vested interest in governance, but its role in the past has been ill-defined. Early in the history of the American university faculties played an active role in university affairs, but as the institutions grew more complex and administrative layers began to appear the faculty concentrated mostly on their teaching duties.[17] Only during the political turmoil of the 1960s did the faculty reestablish its prerogatives in governance. But faculty governance is characterized by numerous committees and study panels many of which prove to be tedious and unrewarding. In the end, only a small number of faculty participate actively in the governance process, but the teaching faculty, nevertheless, want a role in it and believe that university administrators should be held accountable to them for their decisions.[18]

Librarians have only recently begun to enter into the governance picture. Most contact between the university administration and the library has come through the library director, or the university librarian. This position is administrative rather than faculty, and most appointments are at the will of the university administration rather than as a part of a peer review process. The modern library director position has grown to include the roles of "fundraiser, a campus politician, a learned person and a reader of books, an expert on electronics, and an expert in the science of management."[19] Despite this impressive array of abilities and responsibilities, the library director remains outside the mainstream of university decision making, and, instead, ends up representing the library as a special interest advocate. There are, of course, exceptions when library directors are able to transcend organizational limits and make personal contacts with university administrative leaders, but these individuals are exceptional. This has left the library vulnerable to the interplay of personal relationships among top-level library and university administrators.

Librarians have been slow to recognize the precariousness of their position within the university structure. Outside regular administrative channels and with only a few spokespersons representing their views before the university administration, librarians have been treated as inferior to the teaching faculty. This has led to the feeling by librarians that administrators perceive librarians to be "somewhere between secretaries and warehouse supervisors."[20] Only political support from the teaching faculty saved the library from further damage during the financial difficulties in the 1970s. While the teaching faculty has been a natural ally of the library since the library provides them with resources for success in research and teaching, this support has not translated into acceptance of librarians as equal partners in the educational process.[21] Much of the fault resides within the library profession. Librarians have wasted their energies in arguments about faculty status and professionalism without realizing that librarian participation in university governance is the key to success for both the library and the library profession. Faculty status for librarians is part of the solution, but only if librarians have equal faculty status with the teaching faculty.[22] While a growing number of universities have adopted faculty status for librarians, only a small number require their librarians to meet the standards for research and tenure of the teaching faculty.[23] Such separate but equal standards hurt the library when time comes for librarians to compete with the teaching faculty in the university political arena.

Librarians have advantages for both the university and themselves in governance activities. Isolation from departmental and division politics makes librarians desirable for committee duty. This point is reinforced by the comments of a veteran of many faculty committess:

> Librarians often see education issues from the perspective of the entire institution, and, particularly, if they are respected by their colleagues, can convince their colleagues of the importance of this perspective.[24]

The key concept here is colleague respect. Respect can only be earned by accomplishment. Expertise in research and teaching is the basis of the teaching faculty's influence and power, and the higher the degree of expertise the more power and autonomy.[25] Librarians have expertise in the daily operations of the library and the knowledge of current developments in library scholarship, technology and management, but there has been a reluctance to capitalize on this expertise. Only about twenty-five percent of academic librarians engage in any form of publishing activity.[26] But high-grade research provides the avenue for librarians to promote their careers, and, at the same time, to advance the cause of the library. Resistance toward research librarianship is to be expected from librarians unused to research demands, but efforts must be made in library science schools and on-the-job to train and to support librarians for research and operations analysis.[27] A benefit will be that the relationship between librarians, administrators and teaching faculty will improve in proportion to the increase in status for librarians.

The university is in the middle of a self-examination phase and librarians need to participate in the decision making. Librarians have to assert themselves and to become equal partners with the teaching faculty in university governance both for the sake of the library and for themselves. While there is still time for librarians to take the steps necessary to earn respect from administrators and the teaching faculty by service and research, the university is busy making continguency plans, which include the library, for the next financial crunch. Librarians must realize that decisions concerning the library will continue to be made without their input unless they start participating in university governance.

REFERENCES

1. "Association of College and Research Libraries," American Libraries 9, no. 2 (December 1978): 635.

2. Richard J. Talbot, "Financing the Academic Library," New Directions for Higher Education: Priorities for Academic Libraries, no. 39 (September 1982): 36.

3. Robert M. O'Neil, "The University Administrator's View of the University Library," New Directions for Higher Education: Priorities for Academic Libraries, no. 39 (September 1982): 3-9.

4. D. Kaye Gapen, "Myths and Realities: University Libraries," College and Research Libraries 45, no. 5 (September 1984): 359.

5. Daniel Bell, "By Whose Right?" in Power and Authority, ed. Harold L. Hodgkinson (San Francisco: Jossey-Bass, 1971), p. 165.

6. J. Victor Baldridge et al., Policy Making and Effective Leadership (San Francisco: Jossey-Bass, 1978), pp. 21-2.

7. Ibid.

8. John J. Corson, The Governance of Colleges and Universities (New York: McGraw-Hill, 1975), pp. 156-7.

9. New Directions for Higher Education: Successful Responses to Financial Difficulty, no. 38 (June 1982): 1-119.

10. Talbot, "Financing the Academic Library," pp. 37-8.

11. O'Neil, "The University Administrator's View," p. 5.

12. Paul Olum, "Myths and Realities: the Academic Viewpoint I," College and Research Libraries 45, no. 5 (September 1984: 365-6.

13. Walter Schenkel, "Who Has Been in Power?" in Power and Authority, p. 2.

14. Ibid., p. 12.

15. L. Richard Meeth, "Administration and Leadership" in Power and Authority, p. 42.

16. O'Neill, "The University Administrator's View," p. 5.

17. Mary F. Berry, "Faculty Governance," in Leadership for Higher Education, ed. Roger W. Heyns (Washington, D.C.: American Council on Education, 1977), p. 27.

18. Ibid., p. 29.

19. Ralph E. Ellsworth, "The University in Violent Transition," in The Library in the University, ed. William H. Jesse (Hamden, Conn.: Shoe String Press, 1967), pp. 281-5.

20. William A. Moffett, "What the Academic Librarian Wants from Administrators and Faculty," in New Directions for Higher Education: Priorities for Academic Libraries, no. 39 (September 1982): 16.

21. Gresham Riley, "Myths and Realities: The Academic Viewpoint II," College and Reaearch Libraries 45, no. 5 (September 1984): 367.

22. Thomas G. English, "Librarian Status in the Eighty-Nine U.S. Academic Institutions of the Association of Research Libraries: 1982," College and Research Libraries 44, no. 3 (May 1983): 203.

23. C. James Schmidt, "Faculty Status in Academic Libraries: Retrospective and Prospect," in New Horizons for Academic Libraries, ed. Robert D. Stueart and Richard D. Johnson (New York: K.G. Saur, 1979), pp. 412-3.

24. Joe E. Elmore, "Developing Faculty Leadership," in Leadership for Higher Education, p. 33.

25. Baldridge, Policy Making, p. 150.

26. Joyce Payne and Janet Wagner, "Librarians, Publication and Tenure," College and Research Libraries 45, no. 2 (March 1984): 138.

27. Millicent D. Abell and Jacqueline M. Coolman, "Professionalism and Productivity: Keys to the Future of Academic Library and Information Services," in New Directions for Higher Education, no. 39 (September 1982): 30.

FREEDOM OF ACCESS TO INFORMATION IN MACHINE READABLE FORM:
THE LIBRARIANS ROLE

Samuel G. Demas
A. R. Mann Library
Cornell University
Ithaca, NY 14853

Abstract. In exploiting the incredible potential of new technologies for improving information access, we must not overlook their potential for restricting freedom of access to information. As powerful economic forces define the dynamics of the emerging information society, information is increasingly handled and regulated as a commodity rather than as an entitlement. I believe the question of access to information in machine-readable form is one of public policy as much as it is one of economics. As with our societal role in intellectual freedom issues, librarians have a unique and pivotal role to play in this new intellectual property struggle. This paper outlines the potential threat to freedom of information access, and describes the role I think librarians should play in defining the changing patterns of information access which result from new technologies.

Keywords and phrases. Copyright and machine-readable formats. Copyright. Freedom of access to information. "Fair Use" of computerized information.

Democracy is based on the participation of an informed citizenry in the governmental process. The principle of freedom of access to information, regardless of ability to pay, finds its most concrete expression in the remarkable system of public libraries and in cooperation among libraries of all types.

In making information freely available through libraries the property rights of authors and publishers are protected to assure an adequate financial incentive to the producers of published knowledge. This is accomplished through Copyright Law. Unlike European copyright law, which is based on protection of the rights of authors, U.S. copyright legislation stems from the constitutional mandate to promote science and the arts. The concept of "fair use" of copyrighted material essentially provides an entitlement of citizens to free access to information.

One can argue that questions of control of machine-readable information, such as copying microcomputer software and downloading from online data bases, are simply variants of the classic copyright issues. In addressing the special problems posed by photocopy machines and VCR's the copyright law has already responded to intellectual property issues which are conceptually the same but technologically different. But the copyright law as currently written is inadequate to the task of regulating control and access to machine-readable formats. In order to protect their enormous investments and assure sizable profit margins, producers of software and online database are increasingly turning to other bodies of law: contract, patent and trade secret law. In so doing they are taking the questions of access to information out of the realm of public policy and entitlement and framing patterns of access based purely on business interests and principles applied to commerce in commodities. For example, software publishers affix site licenses to their shrink wrap packaging which restrict use of a disk to one machine and prohibit creation of an archival copy. Database producers routinely insert contract clauses which prohibit any form of downloading from their database. None of these restrictions has any basis in copyright law; but if we agree to the terms of such site license and contracts we should be prepared to live with the restrictions they stipulate. The problem is that in these transactions the patterns of power, control, dependency, and domination are being forged in the establishment of institutional structures to accomodate the transfer and control of computerized information. If the present trend continues, there is a real danger that a class of "information poor" citizens will be created. Many citizens may not be able to afford the high cost of computerized information. Libraries may not only be unable to afford to subsidize access to all types of information, but may also be constrained by business law in performing their mission of freely providing information access.

Just as librarians have worked to protect the public's right to uncensored information, so we must serve as advocates for access to information resources on an equitable basis. Librarians are the only organized, institutionalized voice speaking for the rights of end users. As the single largest group of online database customers, libraries have an economic leverage far greater than that of the individual information seeker. I believe librarians have an urgent professional obligation to help shape the evolving laws and arrangements concerning access to computerized information. We can insert ourselves into this process in the following ways:

1. By using the popular media to create public awareness of the issues around free access to information. Articles in newspapers and popular periodicals are needed as much or more than articles by librarians for librarians.

2. Labraries can organize lecture/discussion groups to stimulate interest in the social, political role of libraries as information centers.

While we should not limit our approach to pleading our worth as socially useful institutions, this is a time in our history when we must clearly articulate some of the fundamental principles of freedom of access to information, for they may be overlooked in the "information revolution".

3. The profession should gear up to conduct quantitative research on the financial aspects of the information industry. We must do our homework in preparation for the arguments that the financial incentive for corporate investment in information systems is destroyed by freedom of access to information.

4. Through our professional organizations we should flex our collective economic muscle to negotiate equitable pricing structures for library access to information systems. As big customers we would qualify for quantity discounts on an annual flat fee for unlimited searching. If we don't lobby for special price structures, we'll end up paying _more_ than individual users, as we do for periodicals.

5. Our professional organizations must lobby at the state and federal level for legislation which protects the public against unnecessarily restrictive regulations on information transfer. Federal copyright legislation continues to be a key consideration, but it is no longer the only arena in which we should be active.

6. And finally, as a profession we should take the offensive through the judicial system on this issue. Rather than wait around for the industry to take some library to court to establish a case law precedent, we should seek out the ideal test case from our viewpoint, and bring the issues to the courts on our own terms.

On that note, I open the floor to questions, comments and discussion.

CURRICULUM CHANGE:
TRANSITIONS IN TIME

Michael Haeuser
Gustavus Adolphus College Library
St. Peter, Minnesota

Keywords and Phrases. Curriculum Reform, Libraries-Curriculum Reform, Librarians-Curriculum Reform, Liberal Arts.

In the Twelfth Century the French grammarian and philosopher Bernard of Chartres wrote: "We are like dwarfs seated on the shoulders of giants; we see more things than the ancients and things more distant, but this is due neither to the sharpness of our sight nor to the greatness of our stature, but because we are raised and borne aloft on that giant mass."[1]

This "giant mass" is all our history, our literature, our theologies, our political ideals, our slogans, values, ideas, and habits of thought. In short, the study of our Western heritage to better understand and appreciate all knowledge was, until recently, the matrix and the norm of an education for life.

In the 1980's, however, dwarfs do not sit on giant's shoulders. Liberal education and the educational values it represents have been replaced by a curriculum given to a marketplace philosophy. It is a supermarket where students are shoppers and professors are merchants of learning. Fads and fashions, the demands of popularity and success enter where wisdom and experience should prevail. The marketplace philosophy refuses to establish common expectations and norms. General education, education for life, lacks a rationale and cohesion.

The educational failures of the United States are emerging as a major concern of the 1980's. The theme of this conference, Energies for Transition, suggests change and adaptation -- and implies it will require effort. These energies are to be applied to transitions that we recognize. The abundance of reports (for example the National Commission on Excellence in Education, A Nation at Risk; the National Endowment for the Humanities, To Reclaim a Legacy; and the Association of American Colleges, Integrity in the College Curriculum, that diagnose and prescribe for our colleges, the urgency with which they are argued, the evidence they summon, and the analysis that they offer are persuasive evidence there is a profound crisis.[2]

What energies have colleges brought to bear on this crisis, and how can we in the Library world respond? A recent American Council on Education Report says that six in ten U.S. colleges are reviewing the quality of their curricula by focusing on general education requirements and the communication skills that graduates should possess.[3] In a recent New York Times article representatives of some twenty selected colleges and universities were questioned to see what curriculum change meant to them.[4] Based on that article, questionnaires were sent to librarians inquiring to what extent they have influenced the curricular change and what changes, if any, have affected library service. The answers ranged from "no influence -- no change" to "some influence -- considerable change." In my own library's case, where planning for curriculum change went on for four years and was implemented in September of 1985, a librarian served on the committee overseeing the complete review of the entire curriculum. A librarian was appointed to lead a committee that assisted each department head to bring the requirements for the program for their majors in line with committee-stated guidelines. A librarian serves on each twelve person team that directs the most exciting innovation -- an integrated group of courses and activities that feature librarian-led common readings and a capstone seminar with librarians participating. Finally, a library friends group is raising $125,000 to match an National Endowment for the Humanities Challenge Grant that will provide an endowment for materials to support this innovation.

Curriculum reform and efforts to move teaching and learning to a more traditional model clearly have a role for librarians. We must support efforts to create firmer means of education and involve our energies to support excellence. We must recognize and support those curricular reforms which will make our libraries the giants that support the shoulders of learning.

REFERENCES

1. The Metalogicon of John of Salisburg; A twelfth-century defense of the verbal and logical arts of the trivium, III, 4, trans. Daniel D. McGarry (Berkeley: Univ. of Cal. Press, 1955), p. 167.

2. See National Commission on Excellence in Education, A Nation At Risk: The Imperative For Educational Reform (U.S. Dept. of Education, 1983). Other recent studies include that of the Study Group on the Conditions of Excellence in American Higher Education entitled "Involvement in Learning: Realizing the Potential of American Higher Education," Chronicle of Higher Education, v. 29, no. 9 (Oct. 24, 1984), p. 35-49; the National Endowment for the Humanities Study Group on the State of Learning in the Humanities "To Reclaim a Legacy", Ibid, v. 29, no. 14 (Nov. 28, 1984), p. 16-21; and the Association of American Colleges, "Integrity in the College Curriculum", Ibid, v. 29, no. 14 (Nov. 28, 1984), p. 16-21; and the Association of American Colleges, "Integrity in the College Curriculum", Ibid, v. 29, no. 22 (Feb. 13, 1985), p. 12-30.

3. Elaine El-Khawas, <u>Campus Trends, 1984</u>, (American Council on Education, 1985).

4. "Wave of Curriculum Change Sweeping American Colleges," <u>New York Times</u>, 10 March 1985, sec. 1, p. 1.

ACADEMIC LIBRARY CENSORSHIP IN A CONSERVATIVE ERA

Elizabeth Hood
Trinity University
San Antonio, Texas

Abstract. It is often assumed that the censorship question is a moot point in academic libraries, where support of curriculum and research interests are deemed the primary responsibility of the library. However, studies of censorship have almost completely ignored the attitudes of academic librarians. An informal survey of the staff of one medium size college library revealed that personal agreement with controversial material was influential in determining selection. If this observation is accurate for many academic librarians, a conservative political climate and less affluent circumstances could bring an increase in the incidence of self-censorship.

Keywords and Phrases. Censorship; Book selection; Book selection -- Policy statements

In 1970 Professor Ross H. Moore, longtime chairman of the History Department at Millsaps College, reminded a group of fledgling liberal senior majors, us majors who had just discovered the evils of the racist, sexist, militaristic, conservative society in which we lived, "You must not forget, the conservative position is always respectable." The American library profession, young as professions go, whose self-consciousness is as youthful as those college seniors', discovered not long ago the evils of censorship. Richard L. Darling points out that before the 1930's librarians were as likely as not to side with the censor, seeing their libraries as forces for public improvement.[1] From a political and philosophical perspective, our First Amendment guarantees are truly radical, and ALA's defense of them is less than half a century old. On the other hand, censorship in the academy, with noteworthy philosophical defenders even today, can trace its venerable heritage to Plato's *Republic*.[2]

Just as there were many members of my college class who did not share my friends' liberal indignations, many of our fellow professional librarians do not share ALA's present position on censorship. Only a decade ago *Library Journal* devoted five full pages to Leo N. Flanagan's highly critical review of the introduction to the *Intellectual Freedom Manual*, then recently published by the ALA Office for Intellectual Freedom.[3] Not so long out of fashion, censorship's conservative advocates are still living perfectly respectable if usually quiet professional lives.

Librarians have not failed to study their own censorious attitudes and methods. As early as 1881 ALA's Cooperation Committee conducted a checklist study of literature of a sensational nature. Checklist studies, attitude surveys, and theoretical arguments have continued to appear for the last century, particularly since World War II. In 1982 Judith Serebnick surveyed checklist-based research and commented on major studies, their compilation, interpretation, usefulness, and short-comings.[4] Of the studies Serebnick analysed, only two, Leon's survey of libraries in the Philadelphia area[5] and Pope's doctoral dissertation,[6] included academic libraries. The remainder of the studies were concerned with public and school libraries. The implicit assumption seems to have been that censorship is not a problem for academic libraries, perhaps because the first purpose of an academic library is to support the curriculum, and higher education is regarded traditionally as a bastion of intellectual freedom.

Not long ago I conducted an informal exercise which pointed out to me the fallacy of this assumption. I purchased a personal copy of a controversial book and asked academic librarians at one library if they would add the title to their collection. The library chosen was that of a medium size state supported institution in the Southeast. Primarily undergraduate, the institution had several graduate programs and was encouraging their growth: master's, specialist, and doctoral programs in education and masters programs in clinical nursing, psychology, and criminal justice. The school had an excellent record for placing its pre-medical graduates in the state medical college also. Although the faculty recommended almost all the library's purchases for their disciplines, each professional librarian assumed collection development responsibilities for from three to five academic departments, supervising collection growth, suggesting to the faculty titles to fill gaps in the collections, and making final approval of all orders. The materials budget was not awash in money, but neither was it strapped for funds. The library had a clearly written collection development policy which reflected the principles of the Library Bill of Rights.

The book selected for this project was Derek Humphry's *Let Me Die Before I Wake: Hemlock's Guide to Self-Deliverance for the Dying*.[7] With a title reminiscent of a child's bedtime prayer and a bright yellow paperback binding with a butterfly, the book was obviously designed for popular appeal. The Library of Congress assigned the subject headings "Euthanasia--Case studies" and "Right to die--Case studies." But the book goes beyond these two controversial topics. What makes this book particularly provoking is that it describes precisely the least painful methods of suicide. It gives the reader brand names of frequently prescribed barbituates, lethal dosages of various drugs, the most effective combinations of drugs and alcohol, and shelf life if one must accumulate drugs over a long period of time. It suggests ways to persuade a doctor to prescribe particular medications, ways to reduce nausea, a common side-effect of drug overdose, and ways to secure drugs outside the U.S. The book also gives street names of drugs, in case one's physician resists giving him a prescription.

I presented the book to each librarian independently and rather casually, gave them a little time to look at the book, and asked to come back later to talk with them about it. I asked each one if he or she would add the book to the collection and why. Everyone had an opinion, but not one cited the collection development policy. Of the eight librarians, there was a full and nearly evenly-spread range of reaction. One person, interested in collection growth, told me immediately without further consideration that he would add it. Another wanted to add it because he found the topic interesting. One would have added the title because she knew a psychology professor who would be interested in seeing it. Still another found the book dangerous, but would add it to the collection anyway, because she could see a demand for it. Two librarians would have added the book after consultation with library or institutional administration but would restrict its circulation by placement in Special Collections or reserve. One librarian said that if a certain professor wanted his students to read the book, he could buy a copy and place it in reserve, but the library should not own the book. Finally, one librarian would not add the book and would prefer not to circulate it as a personal copy reserve.

Somewhat surprised by the range and strength of reactions, I played the devil's advocate in all cases, trying to dissuade each person from his or her original position. I pointed out that the drug dosage information was available in other sources at that library, but not in a popularly written account with persuasively sympathetic case histories. I reminded the selectors that the institution served a suicide-prone population by age group, that the information could easily be misused, and that the insitution sometimes fostered an *in loco parentis* expectation on the part of students' families. On the other hand, I noted that the first purpose of a college library is curriculum support, that classes in nursing, medical ethics, and sociology of dying would find the book stimulating, that graduates of the nursing program would confront patients facing the dilemma of terminal illness, and that euthanasia was one of the most frequently queried topics for freshman composition and communications classes. I argued that the book specifically and persuasively decries "emotional suicide" and suggests sources where a suicidal person can find help. I also noted that the book is well researched, accurate, and clearly written. After the discussions one person changed his opinion from exclusion to addition with restrictions.

Though I had expected to keep the discussions on a purely professional level, analysing principles of librarianship, the library's collection development policy, and the practi-

calities of institutional politics, the conversations inevitably turned to the moral rectitude of euthanasia and suicide. With little exception, these librarians were making a selection decision based upon their own social, moral, and political interests and their feelings of personal responsibility for the use of their library's collections.

A study of public librarians' attitudes reflected somewhat similar findings in 1982. Mary Lee Bundy and Teresa Stakem surveyed "rank and file" librarians by means of a questionnaire sent to a sample of ALA's membership list.[8] While 94% of these librarians strongly supported the principle of intellectual freedom as a chief commitment for librarians, questions describing narrower situations with specific circumstances produced less unanimity. The survey analysed attitudes by sex, age, race, and political orientation of the respondents. Age did not markedly affect response, and sex even less. Only a small percentage of the sample identified themselves as black. Therefore conclusions about differences of response based on race were tentative. However, with the exception of attitudes toward material characterized as "hate group" literature, significant differences were found to conform to political orientation. The study also concluded that censorial influences such as heavy dependence on selection tools that largely exclude non-establishment literature were not well recognized. The authors suggested that many librarians do not have a consistent philosophical base for their views on intellectual freedom.

No one expects censorship to disappear completely. However, we have experienced a period of increased access to information, a written code of ethics "specifically committed to intellectual freedom,"[9] and considerable attention paid in the professional literature to the self-censorship phenomenon, and we have come to assume that almost all librarians recognize their inclinations to censor and make efforts to compensate for them, especially in academic libraries. But if our sensitivity rests more on our personal political orientation than on philosophical foundations, we will fail to recognize the forces that limit access to information. As our materials budgets shrink in an age of retrenchment for higher education, we will find it easy to argue that we cannot buy everything. If our users adopt more conservative attitudes, we will find it easier to argue that there is little interest in the "fringe" publications. Our own increasing conservatism might lead us to exclude controversial materials. We will be less inclined to trouble ourselves to collect materials from alternative, dissident, or independent publishers.

If we are to begin to live up to our professional principles, we must first discover what we practice. Methodical research should be conducted to determine the extent of censorious attitudes among academic librarians. For years we have failed to study censorship in relation to libraries serving academic communities.

Many librarians, settled in their own acceptance of the principles of intellectual freedom, presume that academic librarians are monolithic and unanimous in a similar attitude. That presumption is false. If we are to serve our users, we must recognize and examine our practices with regard to this issue.

There is virtually no area of modern higher education that is untouched by the question of access to controversial library materials, be they literary and artistic expression, sensitive technical and medical information, potentially explosive social and political issues, or religious controversy. The library profession must not rest too easily upon its statements, its bills of rights, and its collection development policies. In an era that once again recognizes the respectability of the conservative opinion, academic librarians must clearly understand the motivations and the implications of their selection practices.

REFERENCES

1. Richard L. Darling, "Access, Intellectual Freedom and Libraries," Library Trends 27, (1979): 315.

2. Plato, Republic 376E-392C.

3. Leo N. Flanagan, "Defending the Indefensible: The Limits of Intellectual Freedom," Library Journal 100, (1975): 1887-1891.

4. Judith Serebnick, "Self-Censorship by Librarians: An Analysis of Checklist-Based Research," Drexel Library Quarterly 18, (1982): 35-56.

5. S. L. Leon, "Book Selection in Philadelphia," Library Journal 98, (1973): 1081-1089.

6. Michael J. Pope, "A Comparative Study of the Opinions of School, College, and Public Librarians Concerning Certain Categories of Sexually Oriented Literature" (Doctoral dissertation, Rutgers University, 1973).

7. Derek Humphry, Let Me Die Before I Wake: Hemlock's Guide to Self-Deliverance for the Dying (Los Angeles: Hemlock, 1981).

8. Mary Lee Bundy and Teresa Stakem, "Librarians and Intellectual Freedom: Are Opinions Changing?" Wilson Library Bulletin 56, (1982): 584-589.

9. "Statement on Professional Ethics 1981," American Libraries 12, (1981): 335.

THE BENEFITS OF RESEARCH FOR ACADEMIC LIBRARIANS AND THE INSTITUTIONS WHICH THEY SERVE

Dale S. Montanelli & Patricia F. Stenstrom

University of Illinois at Urbana-Champaign
230 Library
1408 West Gregory Drive
Urbana, IL 61801

Abstract. Although some academic librarians, administrators, and teaching faculty have expressed concern that librarians cannot or should not do research, there is a growing body of literature which supports research by librarians as carrying significant benefits both to the individual librarian and to the institution served. The benefits of research include job advancement, personal recognition when no advancement is possible, improved relationships with teaching faculty, increased responsiveness to change and innovation, and better library service through shared knowledge and experience.

Since the end of the second world war there has been a continuing, active discussion of the appropriateness and benefits of academic status for librarians in academic and research institutions. With the adoption of the ACRL standards for faculty status for research librarians in 1971[1], increasing concern for and emphasis on the requirement for librarians to conduct research and write scholarly articles has been expressed. In surveys of librarians in academic institutions such as those by Russ Davidson et. al. in 1981[2] and 1983[3], a fear or reluctance on the part of academic librarians to become involved in the research process has been reported. Librarians argue that the twelve month, forty hour per week structure of their jobs does not allow for research initiatives. Thomas English in his 1984[4] survey of administrators' views of library personnel status has found similar concerns. Not only do administrators see the work of librarianship as different from that of the rest of the faculty, they see librarians as having fewer degrees of freedom, less independence, and different basic responsibilities. In an article more positive toward faculty status, M. Kathy Cook (1981)[5] also presented the concern of some teaching faculty that librarians do "insufficient research". In contrast to these survey findings, there is a strong and growing body of literature which supports research by librarians as carrying significant benefits, both for the librarians and the institutions in which they serve.

This paper will focus on those benefits which may be considered to be of greatest importance. They include: job advancement, personal recognition when no advancement is possible, improved relationships with teaching faculty as a result of better understanding of the research process, increased responsiveness to change and openness to innovation, and better library service through shared knowledge and experience. The discussion will touch briefly upon two related topics: faculty status and librarian autonomy. While both faculty status and autonomy are desirable, the value of research should be seen as independent of either of these issues.

There are two reasons that research is beneficial to the individual librarian. First research promotes advancement and second, it provides recognition when advancement is not possible. Watson (1977)[6] commented on the preponderance of administrative, branch librarians, and department heads as library publishers. She stated that "it was possible that most librarians in the study: administrative, branch librarians, and the department heads have gained their positions of responsibility because they are more competent and motivated than other professionals. It may also be due to the autonomy which librarians in these positions have traditionally enjoyed." Whatever the reason, study after study indicates that successful librarians, as measured by professional advancement, publish more than their less successful counterparts. Anderson (1984)[7] compared Council on Library Resources senior fellows (who were defined as being library leaders) with both a matched group and a control group of ACRL members. She found that senior fellows reported more than twice as many publications, speeches, and courses taught as the ACRL matched group and nearly three times as many as the ACRL control group. This study showed "those academic librarians considered successful by their selection as senior fellows published dramatically more than a control group of academic librarians." The study found that leaders in academic librarianship, whether male or female, started earlier, published more, spoke and taught more, and moved more often than their peers. These findings suggest that publishing is viewed by librarians themselves as important in obtaining promotion and job advancement. Librarians become leaders because they publish more rather than the other way about.

In a recent study contracted by the Office of Library Personnel Resources, Berstein and Leach[8] found that librarians indicated that recognition meant more to them than financial reward. The same study revealed a concern for lack of job mobility and advancement. Publishing provides an alternative route to hierarchical advancement for recognition. In those academic libraries with faculty status this recognition may take the form both of financial and status rewards.

Veaner (1985)[9] worried that librarians are leaving the profession because of frustration and boredom, "burning out" as a result of the repetitive, nature of their jobs. He hypothesizes that what is missing is autonomy and opportunity to develop creatively. Charles Martell (1985),[10] writing on the quality of work life identified six characteristics which should be included in the employee's work:

- autonomy
- challenge
- expression of creativity
- opportunity for learning
- participation in decision-making
- use of variety of valued skills and abilities

The inclusion of research into the work life of academic librarians satisfies all of these requirements and provides the stimulus that Veaner claims is missing.

In addition to the benefits reported for the individual librarian, there are clear advantages for the institution and the profession; chief among these are improved relationships with teaching faculty, increased responsiveness to change, and better library service.

Biggs, in a 1981 analysis of the relationship between librarians and teaching faculty, points out that: "present day advocacy of 'subject specialists' and 'second master's degrees' implicitly recognizes the problem of a library staff without knowledge of, and respect for, books and methods of scholarly investigation."[11] While this statement may be too strong an indictment library education, it does serve to identify a problem of credibility which often confronts librarians. Other studies, such as the previously mentioned one by Cook, reveal an ambiguous attitude on the part of teaching faculty toward librarians. Even those faculty of the greatest goodwill are not strongly convinced of the importance of the librarian in their use of the library. Halsey, (1982)[12] while urging the need for a changed image for librarians, defined the profile of the twentieth century librarian as that of a "docile golden retriever". Veaner (1985)[13] also cites the image of the librarian as a passive keeper or custodian of materials rather than as a dynamic force in the creation and organization of knowledge. How much better in combating this image of passive, docile inactivity to have proof of knowledge of methods of scholarly investigation and an image which shows dynamic organization and leadership developed through a record of research and publication. Whether such publication occurs in the field of librarianship or in the subject field in which the librarian chooses to work, this knowledge of research methods will translate into better service to the other scholarly users of the library.

One of the hallmarks of librarianship in the 1980s is the need for dynamic reaction to change. John Naisbitt reports that "change is occurring so rapidly that there is no time to react; instead we must anticipate the future."[14] JoAnne Hall (1984)[15] has suggested that librarians who are involved in research perceive themselves to possess managerial and leadership skills, and, in fact, research activity was found to be a significant factor in receptivity to change. Hall speculates that reading of library literature might achieve the same results as doing research. But what are the incentives to read library literature and once read, to apply rigorous evaluative and analytic judgments to the reading? Research requires an active questioning approach, exactly the approach needed to anticipate change.

It is clearly the case that research in many areas of librarianship is needed as a number of our library "seers" have mentioned when looking into future issues.. Biggs herself pointed out that in the increasingly complex nature of library activities require research. And Martell (July, 1985)[16] called for creative responses to the dramatic changes we are encountering in the "knowledge society". He suggested that library bureaucracies make room for the research and development function which is clearly necessary for libraries to be able to deal with change and requirements which campuses will place on them in the future. Academic libraries need active programs of research and publication, to share their experience and gain from each other? How much better can these topics be handled by professional librarians working in academic environments with patrons and administrations than for outside research agencies to be hired on contract to do work that librarians should be doing for themselves and can do better for themselves.

One of the excuses frequently given as a reason why librarians cannot be expected to carry out research is because they do not have the flexible schedules which members of the teaching faculty are likely to have. In a dynamic library environment, no professional librarian is chained to a work station in the manner that books were chained to tables in the twelfth century. The conception that teaching faculty have unlimited free and flexible time is, in fact, a misconception. Studies of faculty use of time conducted at major research universities indicated that faculty spend between fifty and sixty hours a week in teaching and research-related activities.[17] Work in the academic community is not a time clock oriented, forty hour a week job. Academic librarians should have freedom to manipulate their schedules such that all aspects of the work get done and all responsibilities are met.

The other negative myth surrounding research is that service will suffer because excellent librarians will not receive tenure. English refers to the superb reference librarian who has been terminated for failing to meet traditional faculty requirements. Substitute political science professor or education professor for reference librarian, and you will have campus newspaper headlines from every research university in the country in the 1970s. Requirements for research for librarians will vary depending on comparable levels of research in the institution which the library serves. There will always be the outstanding librarian who cannot or will not conduct research, but as is true with the teaching faculty -- research and good teaching are not mutually exclusive.

We live in an era which emphasizes both competition and competency. These are difficult but exciting times. Research can help us.

REFERENCES

1. "Standards for Faculty Status for College and University Librarians," College and Research Libraries News, 8:210-212 (Sept. 1972).

2. Russ Davidson; Connie Capers Thorson; and Margo C. Trumpter, "Faculty Status for Librarians in the Rocky Mountain Region: A Review and Analysis," College and Research Libraries, 42(3):203-213 (May 1981).

3. Russ Davidson; Connie Capers Thorson; and Diane Stine, "Faculty Status for Librarians: Querying the Troops," College and Research Libraries, 44(6):414-420 (November 1983).

4. Thomas G. English, "Administrators' Views of Library Personnel Status," College and Research Libraries, 45(3):189-195 (May 1984).

5. M. Kathy Cook, "Rank, Status and Contribution of Academic Librarians as Perceived by the Teaching Faculty at Southern Illinois University, Carbondale," College and Research Libraries, 42(3):214-223 (May 1981)

6. Paul DeSimone Watson, "Publication Activity Among Academic Librarians," College and Research Libraries, 38(5):375-384 (Sept. 1977).

7. Dorothy J. Anderson, "Comparative Career Profiles of Academic Librarians: Are Leaders Different?," The Journal of Academic Librarianship, 10(6):326-332.

8. Ellen Bernstein and John Leach, Career Perceptions of American Librarians, Chicago: American Library Association, Office for Library Personnel Resources, 1985.

9. Allen B. Veaner, "1985 to 1995: The Next Decade in Academic Librarianship, Part I," College and Research Libraries, 46(3):209-229 (May 1985).

10. Charles Martell, "QWL Strategies: People are the Castle, People are the Walls, People are the Moat," Journal of Academic Librarianship, 10(6):350-354 (January 1985).

11. Mary Biggs, "Sources of Tension and Conflict Between Librarians and Faculty," Journal of Higher Education, 1981, 52(2):182-201.

12. Halsey, Richard S. "Recall-Research-Renewal: A Message of Necessity for the University Library." In: Future of Libraries. Panel discussion by librarians, administrators, faculty and students; papers from the Millionth Volume Celebration, University Libraries, State University of New York at Albany, 1982.

13. Allen B. Veaner, "1985 to 1995: The Next Decade in Academic Librarianship Part II," College and Research Libraries, 46(4):295-308 (July 1985).

14. John Naisbitt, Megatrends. New York: Warner Books, 1984.

15. JoAnne Hall, The Relationship Between Innovation or Change Agent Characteristics of Academic Librarians in the Southeastern United States. Ph.D. Thesis: University of Michigan, 1984.

16. Charles Martell, "Editorial: Creative Behavior in Libraries," College and Research Libraries, 46(4):293-294 (July 1985).

17. John Terwilliger, Office of Administrative Studies, University of Illinois at Urbana-Champaign. Personal Communication, (July 1, 1985).

BIBLIOGRAPHIC CONTROL

HANDLING OF SERIALS IN MICRO-REPRODUCTION:
SINGLE BIBLIOGRAPHIC RECORD/MULTIPLE FORMATS--
AN OHIO STATE UNIVERSITY EXPERIENCE

Marjorie E. Adams, and Daphne C. Hsueh
Ohio State University Libraries
Columbus, Ohio

Abstract. This position paper describes the problems created by the national policy for cataloging multiple formats of a serial title, in which the format of a work is emphasized over the content.

It details a solution successfully practiced for five years in an academic library's online catalog which lists together, under a single title record, all holdings of a serial regardless of format. It further proposes a departure from traditional bibliographic description and advocates the concept of describing the intellectual content in the primary record with attached records showing physical formats and detailing holdings.

Keywords and Phrases. Access to serials in micro-reproduction; bibliographic control of serials in micro-reproduction; cataloging of micro-reproductions; micro-reproduction, serials in; Ohio State University Libraries; serials in multiple formats.

INTRODUCTION

In keeping with the theme of this conference, this position paper discusses a transition taking place in the library community's view of the bibliographic control of micro-reproductions. It describes an experience at Ohio State University Libraries in the ever evolving search for better bibliographic control and access for serials in micro-reproduction; it traces a passage from where we were (the problem), to where we are (the solution) to where we want to go (a model for the future).

Before stating the problem, let us regress in time to 1980 and look at the environment which nurtured it. Ohio State University Libraries (hereafter referred to as OSUL) has in place an online public-access catalog, which lists serial holdings at the volume level for 41 holding locations. A program of acquiring microforms in lieu of binding the original paper copy of heavily used periodicals has been instituted; one of its goals is to improve patron access to periodical back volumes.[1] National cataloging rules, which it is our policy to follow, prescribe that each format of a title be cataloged separately. The Cataloging Department has been understaffed for years and will probably go under for the last time if it has to deal with all the newly acquired microform titles. And last but not least, our library users in keeping with the times, have an unquenchable thirst for instant information.

DESCRIPTION OF PROBLEM

The combination of factors just outlined bring us face to face with the problem to be examined in this paper. Simply stated it is: cataloging rules for micro-reproductions emphasize the format of a work over the content; library patrons (except in rare cases) are seeking the content of the work, not the format.[2] In practical terms the problem manifested itself as follows: if OSUL conforms to national policy and catalogs microform replacements separately from the originals in paper, each format would receive a separate entry in the online catalog. This would splinter the holdings of a given serial title into several records. The library user in search of a particular volume, or the complete holdings of a given serial, could be faced with retrieving and examining as many as four separate records. This definitely would not improve patron access to periodical back volumes and would be economically and practically unfeasible.

Before revealing our solution to this quandry let us briefly analyze the problems presented by the cataloging rules pertaining to micro-reproductions and examine the results of their implementation.

PROBLEMS IN BIBLIOGRAPHIC DESCRIPTION

AACR II rule 0.24 dictates that bibliographic description be based on an item in hand, it makes no distinction in whether the piece is a micro-reproduction of a previously published work or an original publication.[3] Furthermore, the chief source of information for description of microforms specified by Chapter 11 is not the intrinsic part of the literary unit, i.e., the work itself. Instead, it comes from the title frame, i.e., the information provided by the micro-publisher. Following AACR II and describing piece in hand has a profound impact on collocation, or, the logic governing the organization of a catalog, be it manual or online. For instance in the case of a generic title, when a unique title is needed to distinguish it from a similar one, the qualifying elements such as place of corporate body (or both) will be those of the micro-publisher; thus the record for the micro-reproduction will be separated from the record for the original.

Description based on a microform's title frame has other limitations. Micro-publishers do not manufacture with current cataloging rules in mind. The title they pick often is not the title proper of the serial. And, the amount of information that can be provided is often limited by space. What are catalogers to do when the title frame and the outside of the containers all proclaim a seemingly innocent title when in fact the 50 some boxes of microfilm represent three title changes? In the absence of a title frame, are we going to use only the chronological designation appearing on the eye-readable portion of a fiche, when we know quite well that there is a corresponding numeric one in the work, or vice versa? And to make the situation more interesting, are we going to use the fiche number in the absence of chronological/numeric designations in the prescribed source of information?

Since AACR II requires description based on the physical piece in hand a separate record must be created for a work in reproduction that the library might already have in the original. One consequence of this requirement is to crowd a data base with seemingly different, but in reality duplicate, records making searching a time consuming process. A second is to increase the cost of processing library materials. The third and the most serious consequence of separate records for each format is that the records may not be displayed together and frequently it is the combined holdings of the micro-reproduction and the paper original that represent the complete run of a serial title. This problem is further aggravated in those online catalogs which require different call numbers for each record (OSUL's LCS is one of those systems). In situations such as those, unified access to all the records for one title is impossible when searching by a single call number.

Due to the problems in the process of description and entry under AACR II, the Library of Congress made, in 1981, its now famous (or, infamous) decision to not follow AACR II in its cataloging of micro-reproductions.[4] That decision restored to a position of primacy the description of the original imprint; the information on micro-reproduction was relegated to a note field. This LC "interim policy" corrects a great many problems created by the demands of AACR II, but it still requires a separate record for each format of a title, a requirement with inherent problems as previously mentioned.

SOLUTION AT OSUL

The solution that OSUL found to the problems posed by the cataloging rules for micro-reproductions departs from national policy. Its purpose, however, is one and the same with a major theme throughout the literature of the past ten years -- bibliographic control of microforms.[5] In the literature there is also support for the specific concepts undergirding our solution: "microform materials [should be] as equally accessible as paper materials of the same type";[6] "entry... in the catalog is the only procedure that guarantees user access";[7] and "microforms do not derive special significance from their format".[8]

Our solution to the problem of representing micro-reproductions in the catalog is to emphasize the intellectual entity, or content, of the title, rather than its physical manifestation, or format. All holdings of a serial title regardless of format are combined into one unified holdings display in the online catalog, LCS. The bibliographic record describes the original work and a format designator in the holdings record indicates the format. Microform holdings are added to the online catalog in an online maintenance mode as volumes are received in Acquisitions and are sent immediately to the location; no additional handling or cataloging is required.

Illustration 1 shows two types of title displays: the full bibliographic display and the short title display, which is the default in general searches. The short title display lists only a short title, and within each location lists holdings by volume. No format designator implies paper, with microformat indicated in parenthesess.

ONLINE CATALOG— TITLE DISPLAYS

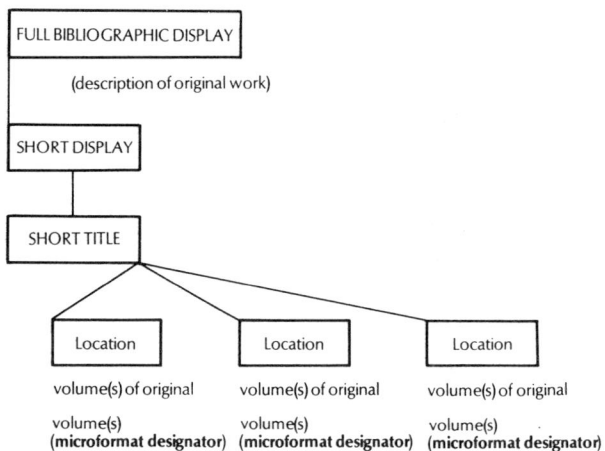

Illustration 2 shows an actual LCS short title display containing: short title, call number, copies, locations, volumes, format designator and year. The notes explain that the title is currently received in both the original paper and in microfilm, and indicate the retention of the paper.

LCS DISPLAY

HN51J8		SOCIAL FORCES	NOLC	291665	1922	3	SER
01	001	MAI					
02	002	NOCIR SOC					
03	003	NOCIR UND					
04	MAI 001	S	CURRENTLY RECEIVED IN PERIODICAL ROOM				
05	MAI 001	S	MICROFORM RECEIVED IN SPECIAL MATERIALS RM(SPE)				
06	MAI 001	S	PAPER COPY RETAINED UNTIL REPLACED BY MICROFORM				
07	MAI 001		1984	V63NO1-2			
11	SPE 001	NOCIR	1983-1984	V62 (MICROFILM)			
14	SPE 001	NOCIR	1982-1983	V61 (MICROFILM)			

PAGE 1 MORE ON NEXT PAGE. ENTER PD2

The solution that OSUL has derived has worked for six years, almost without flaw. The flaw in the solution (or the fly in the ointment) is not in the effectiveness of the solution, but is in its theoretical underpinnings. By not providing in the catalog physical descriptions for microforms held also in the original, we are deviating from the national standard for representation of micro-reproductions. Since OSUL is a large research library belonging to OCLC, it cannot totally deviate from national standards and network requirements. What we have been doing to create the system that works for us, and yet does not conflict with OCLC network requirements, is to create in the data base a bibliographic record for the original when the item in hand is a micro-reproduction; the microformat is indicated only in the holdings record of the online catalog.

PRACTICES IN OTHER ORGANIZATIONS

Others in the library community have explored similar departures from the traditional concept of bibliographic description. In order to facilitate union listing OCLC digressed from the ANSI standard for reporting holdings by incorporating microform volumes into records for hard copy serials. They reasoned that this exception avoids delays in cataloging and provides more unified displays.[9] To cope with problems presented by the U.S. Newspaper Project, the Library of Congress "is using the master record convention to account for the various physical forms in which a newspaper may be held. The bibliographic record describes the newspaper as it was originally published. Other physical forms, whether hard copy, film, photo-reproduction, etc., are indicated in local data records listing the holdings of participant institutions."[10] At ALA midwinter and summer meetings in 1985 two groups of the RTSD Serials Section dealt with the topic of cataloging serials in micro-reproduction and reprint. It was evident in those discussions that there is overwhelming interest in modifying the cataloging rules for serial reproductions. Some libraries have, like OSUL, merged holdings of micro-reproductions with the original in online catalogs or union lists.[11]

PROPOSED SOLUTION

In our view, the ultimate solution to the problem of bibliographically controlling micro-reproductions of serials in a user-oriented, cost-effective fashion, moves one step further. The record structure we envision consists of a core bibliographic record describing the intellectual content of a work and a cluster of satellite records describing all of the various physical manifestations that the work may take, including the original. There would be the potential for two types of holdings record: one, a "composite" record directly linked to the core record showing the entire holdings of that particular intellectual entity; and two, a "format specific" holdings record attached to each satelite record.

Illustration 3 is our concept of such a record structure. The user would have the capability of calling up the core record, or, the composite record which could indicate not just holdings but also their formats, or, a specific format record with physical description and holdings.

MODEL OF "IDEAL" RECORD STRUCTURE

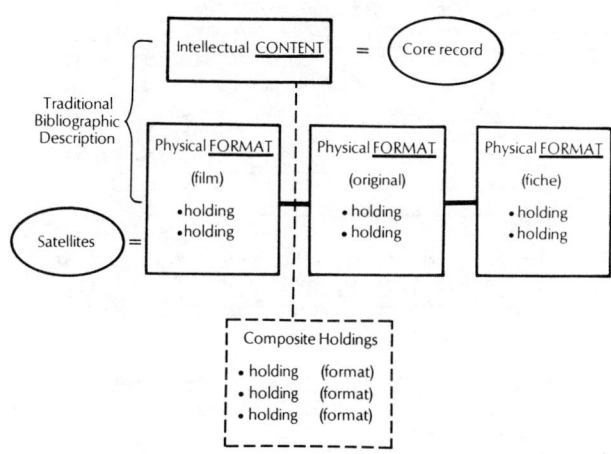

A record structure such as this with flexible record elements is the model we are proposing for future bibliographic description. In an automated environment various levels of information could be retrieved in various combinations depending on the end use of the record. Such a record will require modification of the traditional concept of bibliographic description. We see it as the final step in the transition we have been describing. Transition implies movement, change, process, an idea not yet finished but developing. We hope that we have left you with an idea for transition in the handling of serials in micro-reproduction.

REFERENCES

1. For a fuller description see: Marjorie E. Adams, "On-Line Public Access to Serial Holdings," in Nancy J. Melin, ed., Serials and Microforms: Patron-Oriented Management - Proceedings of the Second Annual Serials Conference and Eighth Annual Microforms Conference; Columbus, Ohio, October 22-23, 1982 (Westport, Conn.: Meckler, 1983), p.63-77; Lawrence J. Perk, "Microforms at Ohio State University," Ibid., p.79-86.

2. For this concept consult: Diane Stine, "The Cataloging of Serials in Microform under AACR II Rules," Serials Librarian 5, no. 3: 19-23 (Spring 1981); Louis Charles Willard, "Microforms and AACR 2, Chapter 11: Is the Cardinal Principle a Peter Principle?" Microform Review 10:75-78 (Spring 1981).

3. Anglo-American Cataloguing Rules, 2nd ed. (Chicago: American Library Association,

1978) p.8.

4. Cataloging Service Bulletin, no. 14 (Fall 1981), p.56-57.

5. A number of articles have addressed this topic: Edward C. Carroll, "Bibliographic Control and Microforms: Where Do We Go from Here?" Microform Review 7:321-326 (Nov./Dec. 1978); Dale E. Cluff, "Determining National Interest and/or Activity Relating to Bibliographic Access of Microforms," Microform Review 4:266-269 (Oct. 1975); Susan Cates Dodson, "Bibliographic Control of Microforms: Where Are We Today?" Microform Review 12:12-18 (Winter 1983); Nancy Hyde, "Bibliographic Control: A British View," Microform Review 10:166-169 (Summer 1981); Carl W. Jackson, "Bibliographic Access to Microforms: On the Threshold?" Microform Review 9:28-31 (Winter 1980); Felix Reichman and Josephine M. Tharpe, Bibliographic Control of Microforms (Westport, Conn.: Greenwood Press, 1972), 3-33.

6. Robert Grey Cole, "Bibliographic Control," Illinois Libraries 58:212 (March 1975).

7. Marcia Jebb, "Bibliographic Control of Microforms," Drexel Library Quarterly 11, no. 4:34 (Oct. 1975).

8. Gloria Hsia, "Library of Congress Contribution to the Bibliographic Control of Microforms," Microform Review 6:13 (Jan. 1977).

9. OCLC, Serials Control: User Manual (Dublin, Ohio: OCLC, 1983), Appendix E: A 28-29.

10. Robert Harriman, Newspaper Cataloging Manual (Washington, D.C.: Library of Congress, 1984), p.5.

11. These topics were discussed in : Presentations by Linda Bartley, Marjorie Bloss, Jeff Heynen, et al., at Midwinter Meeting of American Library Association, Resources and Technical Services Division, Serials Section, Large Research Libraries Discussion Group, coordinated by Crystal Graham, Washington, D.C., January 1985; Committee to Study Serials Cataloging, Annual Meeting of the American Library Association, Resources and Technical Services Division, Serials Section, Chicago, July 1985.

ERROR DETECTION IN BIBLIOGRAPHIC RECORDS: CAN THE COMPUTER DO IT ALL?

Jaye Bausser
Duke University

Jinnie Y. Davis
North Carolina State University

David Gleim
University of North Carolina
at Chapel Hill

Abstract. The authors explore the shifting roles of automatic and manual error detection during the transition from card to online bibliographic catalogs. Using the TRLN validation system as an example, the authors find that existing automatic systems cannot detect all important errors. They suggest that greater sophistication of automatic error detection will be needed as online systems develop. The authors describe the impact on catalog management activities as the balance between manual and automatic error detection shifts in favor of the computer.

Keywords and Phrases. TRLN, error detection, automatic validation, online catalog maintenance, catalog maintenance, tape processing.

ERROR DETECTION

A clean, usable database is the foundation for an online catalog and can be insurance against early obsolescence. Achieving such a database is not an easy process, but it is facilitated if the principles of creation and maintenance include a commitment to creating records that are complete and maintaining them so they are up-to-date and as error free as possible. It is further expedited if the system itself can be used to assist in the process of detecting and correcting errors. As we evolve from manual to online systems, we find that our process of detecting and correcting errors also evolves from a reliance on manual processes to use of automated techniques and that, as a result, catalog management activities will change. This has been the experience of the libraries involved in the cooperative development of an online integrated library system through the Triangle Research Libraries Network (TRLN).

TRLN

TRLN comprises the libraries at Duke University, North Carolina State University, and the University of North Carolina at Chapel Hill. Since 1979, the libraries have been working together to design and implement an online catalog as the first goal in the integrated system. Reaching that goal has been an evolutionary process. One of the first products was development of a system to process OCLC archive tapes and create a database for online maintenance of cataloging records. The Archive Tape System (ATS) is used to process OCLC archive tapes. Duplicate records are dealt with and records are validated. Validation includes detection of errors and flagging records that have conditions indicative of possible errors. Certain types of errors are automatically corrected. All of these activities result in reports sent to the individual libraries after each archive tape is processed. Used in combination with manual processes in the libraries for finding and correcting errors, the reporting system of ATS has enabled the libraries to ensure a consistent standard of quality for many aspects of the records created through OCLC.

As TRLN development has continued, a database has been created which provides online interactive maintenance of records. This is called the Online Editing System or OES.[1] Catalog maintenance staff at the libraries use this database to update bibliographic and holdings information. As changes are made online through OES, the system checks for errors. If an error is noted, the system will not allow updating until the terminal operator has corrected the error. Using the ATS and OES systems has enabled the TRLN libraries to develop a clean and usable database that is facilitating the development of the next phase: implementation of the online catalog. It is also presaging for us a future in which there will have to be a stronger reliance on automatic error detection or validation of records and in which significant changes in catalog management will occur.

ERROR DETECTION IN TRLN LIBRARIES

Currently the TRLN libraries are relying on a combination of traditional, manual means of error detection as well as on automated validation. Processes for manual detection in the three libraries vary, but basically filing, filing revision, and typical catalog maintenance activities result in the discovery of errors. Automatic error detection is accomplished through the Archive Tape System. New OCLC archive tapes are received every four weeks and records are validated in a process that generates printouts of errors (such as missing filing indicators), and warnings of possible errors (such as a missing 2XX field or imprint). All of these conditions are referred to as "errors" in this paper.

EFFECTIVENESS OF AUTOMATIC VALIDATION

As part of the validation process, a summary is produced which lists the frequency and types of errors. There are 124 different error messages, 88 of which are common to the three libraries. In an attempt to analyze the effectiveness of automatic validation and compare it to traditional manual error detection, the summary reports for the period from January 1983 to March 1985 were examined for answers to the following questions: (1) What kinds of errors are validated automatically? (2) What kinds of validation errors occur most frequently? (3) How important are these frequent errors? and (4) Are there important errors that are not validated automatically?

Analyzed as a single sample, the 88 messages for the three institutions reported a total of 9,616 errors in 360,717 records, for an average of .03 errors per record. The most frequent categories were filing indicator errors, which comprised 48% of all errors, and fixed field errors, which comprised 25% of all errors.

The importance of these top two categories is quite clear for filing indicators; it is less clear for fixed field errors. As anyone who searches the TRLN online catalog soon learns, a missing or incorrect filing indicator will cause a field to be indexed automatically under an article or, even worse, under perhaps the second or third letter of the leading word in a field. Thus a missing or incorrect filing indicator has a significant impact on the retrievability of records.

Most of the fixed field elements, however, have no current role in TRLN indexing. The extensive validation of these elements is based upon a belief in their potential value for enhancing access. For example, they may be used in the future to limit searches to specific publication dates or formats.

Are there important errors that the TRLN system does not validate automatically? An analysis of the TRLN error messages showed that 72% of validation is unique to the computer environment, that is, the errors validated cannot be found manually on catalog cards; only 28% of automatic validation duplicates manual error detection. What kinds of errors are detected manually? A one-year study conducted at North Carolina State University on errors caught by manually proofreading shelflist cards showed that the largest category of error (39%) was spelling mistakes. While hardly definitive, these findings do suggest that TRLN validation supplements rather than replaces manual error detection and that a sizeable portion of errors detected manually are spelling mistakes. Spelling mistakes, which could affect retrievability, comprise an important category of error that the TRLN system does not validate automatically.

Another study of cataloging done in 1981 by James Schoenung gives additional indirect evidence that bibliographic records contain numerous errors that cannot be validated automatically.[2] In a sample of more than 1000 OCLC records, Schoenung found an amazing average of 14.6 errors per record, many of which could not be caught by current validation techniques. Some examples are missing subject and author added entries. These findings indicate that automatic validation systems like that of TRLN need considerably more sophistication before they can replace manual error detection.

IMPLICATIONS FOR THE FUTURE

The TRLN experience with automatic validation is only the beginning in the transition from a manual to an automated environment and foreshadows a number of changes in error detection and catalog management. At present both automatic and manual methods of error detection are needed to ensure a clean database. This reliance on dual systems will be less and less feasible as cards give way to a totally online system. The implications are threefold: (1) there will be a heavier reliance on automated techniques of error detection; (2) there will be a move toward interactive, rather than batch, validation of records; and (3) as these changes occur, there may well be a shift in the role of cataloging personnel from error detection and correction as an end process to detection and correction at the time of record creation.

Increased Use of Automatic Validation

Our automated systems must take advantage of the greater sophistication of online catalogs and expand automatic validation into areas presently reserved for manual error detection. Some possibilities are the use of automatic shelflisting to prevent duplicate assignment of call numbers, automated authority control to ensure consistent use of headings, and validation of classification sequences used in departmental library collections to detect inappropriate call numbers. Automatic detection of spelling errors must also be part of the expanded role of validation. Another capability that might be exploited is that of having special programs written for error detection. For example, a validation program might report all articles indexed in fields that lack filing indicators.

These features can be built into an online system. It is important that systems designers be made aware of the need for incorporating validation techniques and that they be encouraged to develop ever more sophisticated capabilities.

In spite of the expansion of automatic validation into areas formerly left to manual error detection, there will exist a remainder of errors that cannot be found automatically or that can be found automatically but only at unacceptable cost. Some will be relatively insignificant, such as grammatical errors in notes. Others will have far-reaching ramifications in searching and retrieval, such as a missing entry for a joint author or incorrect spacing in the entry of a corporate name so that two words appear as one. How far into the transition to totally online systems will it be cost-effective to retain manual error detection schemes to find this residue of intractable errors? We may find that we cannot afford the luxury of manual review, or we may discover that we must provide for it.

Automatic Interactive Validation

The growing reliance on automated error detection will be paralleled by changes in the organization of catalog and data management functions and responsibilities. Interactive links between bibliographic utilities and local online catalogs will permit validation of new records against the entire local database at the moment of record creation. The TRLN institutions, for example, are planning an interactive, computer-to-computer link with OCLC which will allow edited OCLC records to be added directly to the TRLN database, instead of copied to archive tapes by OCLC. By validating new records at the time of creation, the TRLN online system will prevent any record from entering the local database until it is free of all errors that can be detected automatically.

Changes in Organization and Staffing

Such a link may signify a radical shift in the responsibility of catalog management activities from the catalog management staff, as a post-cataloging activity, to the record creation or inputting staff, as a cataloging activity. Inputting staff may require more cataloging training in order to deal with interactive validation. The cost of inputting may increase. Alternatively, we may have to limit the use of interactive validation. The computer may be so sophisticated in detecting errors that dealing with all of them at the inputting stage may be inefficient. Use of batch validation, "save files," and printouts, for example, may be a better approach for certain groups of errors.

Further complicating record input and management will be the relationships of cataloging records or data to other records or data, such as those for authority control, serials control, acquisitions, and in-process files. In order to use our future online systems effectively, a higher level of staff training will be required, not only in the traditional technical services specialties of cataloging or acquisitions, but also in a broader understanding of the interrelationships of all technical services activities. Finally, in cooperative, online ventures such as TRLN's, record creation and maintenance staff will not only be using records of participating institutions but will also be sharing responsibility for maintenance of the data.

THE CHALLENGE

Error detection and catalog management will continue to be a changing and growing area of technical services. The new problems posed by an online catalog are many, but online technology also offers many opportunities for improvements. These cannot take place without a price and must be balanced against the costs in time, money, and staff morale. The challenge will be to demonstrate creativity and flexibility in taking advantage of opportunities to replace manual error detection with systematic automatic validation, in order to create clean databases that can best support use of the online catalog.

REFERENCES

1. The TRLN libraries used the Online Editing System from May 1982 to July 1985. Its error detection and editing functions have since been incorporated into TRLN's online catalog, the Bibliographic Information System.

2. James Gerald Schoenung, "The Quality of Member-Input Monographic Records in the OCLC On-Line Union Catalog" (Ph.D. dissertation, Drexel University, 1981).

BORN AGAIN CATALOGING IN THE ONLINE NETWORKS

Ruth Hafter
Sonoma State University Library
Rohnert Park, California

Abstract. Participation in an online network means that the work of individual libraries and their catalogers becomes visible to, and utilized by, many other libraries. Network affiliated libraries and network quality control personnel thus become participants in evaluating each cataloger's work. Results of a 1983-84 case study of six academic libraries indicate that the shift from in-house to nationwide evaluation of catalogers' records creates enhanced status and influence for cataloging peer groups and provides both networks and individual libraries new opportunities to identify master catalogers by online inspection of their work.

GOING PUBLIC: BORN AGAIN CATALOGING IN THE ONLINE NETWORKS

One of the most important developments affecting library and information agencies in the past decade has been the growing reliance by individual libraries on the services of automated cooperative networks, also known as bibliographic utilities. These utilities offer a range of products designed to help libraries exploit the fact that work done at one institution can often be utilized by another library with little or no change being required. Since adherence to cataloging codes is a mandated professional requirement, catalogers everywhere are theoretically able to use each other's work. Thus, development of a huge online catalog, accessible to all member institutions, should result in a vast overall saving of catalogers' time without the dilution of quality inherent in most mass production activities.

Network participation also creates new ways to evaluate quality. Access to the network's communal catalog makes an immense public record visible nationwide on every participating library's terminal. Because cataloging departments and/or their individual catalogers attach identifying codes to these records, it is possible for peers, managers, critics and consultants to evaluate cataloging successes and failures. This remarkable increase in the groups concerned with evaluating an individual library's product has received little attention in the library research literature despite the fact that sociologists and other social scientists have developed numerous case studies indicating that increased work visibility tends to lead to decreased professional status and loss of ability to maintain professional quality standards.[1] Therefore, as part of my doctoral research at the University of California, I developed a case study designed to explore how catalogers adapted to work in an online environment, how this shift affected their work assignments and professional status, and whether countervailing strategies had been developed by these library professionals to retain control over cataloging standards and reinforce their professional authority.

Methodology

The case study was conducted during 1983-84 and focused on 68 in-depth interviews with catalogers, library administrators and network quality control personnel. In addition, I had an opportunity to attend the OCLC network sponsored Oglebay Conference on Quality Control and was able to interview many network indentified master catalogers at that meeting.

Six academic libraries were the sites for most of my interviews. One criterion for selecting these libraries was that they belong to a cataloging network (Online Computer Library Center [OCLC], Research Libraries Information Network [RLIN] or Washington Library Network [WLN]). They were also required to have a budget over one million dollars. This criterion was imposed in order to guarantee that they would have a cataloging department of sufficient size to be able to develop a sample group or quote without danger of improperly indentifying one's source.

Finally, geographic and financial considerations limited my research to a sample located on the West Coast of the United States. (Stanford University, University of California. Berkeley, University of Washington, San Francisco State University, Sonoma State University.) However, since librarianship is an occupation characterized by national norms, national networks, and national job markets, this regional sample should still reflect current American practice.

Results

In every library that I visited the catalogers, even the subject specialists, had extremely limited contact with students and with faculty. They tended to work alone in offices or in partitioned alcoves so that they could devote intense attention to the literature that they were describing. Since most of the catalogers interviewed were isolated from users, especially knowledgeable faculty members, their only sources for evaluating their cataloging work were the cataloging rules and the approval of other catalogers.

In an isolated work environment network visibility can provide potential benefits for catalogers who feel proud of their work and seek to enlarge the audience that is able to appreciate it. Many catalogers in the sample libraries, especially the three large research libraries, fall into this category. Thus Berkeley catalogers bemoan the fact that their initials are removed from the bibliographic record before it is input into RLIN. True, their quality work is still indentified as a Berkeley product, but their individual contributions to their institution's prestige will not be known to other catalogers.

On the other hand, all of the catalogers that I interviewed were aware of the potential negative effects of visibility. They mentioned the growing number of library blacklists of institutions whose cataloging was deemed to be unacceptable. At some of the sample libraries, catalogers were aware of these lists. Department members even admitted to creating these lists. On balance, however, catalogers showed far more interest in the white lists developed by their departments -- lists of libraries whose cataloging could be accepted with little or no revision or of libraries that were especially esteemed for some area of specialized cataloging (e.g. music scores). Although catalogers interviewed had not actually compared their lists with colleagues in other institutions, most felt confident that the same names would appear on the majority of library white lists.

Network quality control personnel were also aware of and used white lists to create spinoff products. Because OCLC, its regional networks, and its cataloging advisory groups, know where the high quality cataloging departments are located, they were confident in, and capable of, assigning these departments the task of revising errors in the data base. Project Enhance, inaugurated in December, 1983, with its initial designation of 20 revising libraries, is a direct offspring of network visibility, quality control and evaluation.

Both OCLC and WLN have compiled resource lists of catalogers knowledgeable about cataloging rules and network procedures and these lists are available to institutions seeking expert consultants. Of course, the lists also provide the source from which new members of network advisory committees can be drawn.

It is true that acknowledged nationwide cataloging experts existed in the library profession prior to networks. They were usually identified because of their rank (e.g. heads of cataloging departments of major research libraries), their articles in the library literature, or their membership in important state or national cataloging committees. Network participation has added two new posibilities for nationwide renown -- participation in network committees and/or quality of cataloging prepared by the individual or the department that he/she represents. In some ways the first of the new possibilities is simply a variation on the old requirements for approval by the Establishment. After all, being head of a catalog department, being selected to publish in refereed library journals, or being appointed to national committees, is a function of the cataloger's ability to meet the standards of the existing power structure of the library world. The second of the new paths to cataloging stardom, however, does not fit comfortably into the traditional mold. It stresses performance and peer evaluation rather than administrative approval and political alliances. While this phenomenon is much too new to be realistically assessed, interviews with catalogers reveal a great interest in, and approval of, working peers, especially those that are associated with the networks. In fact, among the catalogers interviewed there appeared to be a high level of consensus that peer group representatives are worthy leaders who have publicly proved their high ethical standards by adhering to quality professional cataloging standards, even when doing so sometimes becomes unpleasant. One cataloger at the Oglebay Conference saw things this way:

> "Quality control is a lot like cleaning a cat box. It is expected -- that is your fellow librarians expect you to keep their data base clean."[2]

But, of course, people who clean out cat litter boxes sometimes develop such strong aversions to their contents that they decide to get rid of the animals responsible for producing the mess. Discussions with network quality control personnel indiciate that master catalogers are characterized both by the high quality of their work and their tendency to report substandard cataloging done by others. In fact, error reporting is one way that OCLC regional networks identify resource people and potential members of their advisory groups. These networks analyze the error reports sent to them, examine the documentation that accompanies the report in order to establish that the record is indeed in error, and develop files of individuals dedicated to maintaining a "clean" data base. The regional networks then review online the work produced by each cataloger and if that work is ranked superior, the error-spotting cataloger will begin to be invited to participate in network committees. In time, this participation will often lead to invitations to join nationwide cataloging advisory committees.

While this process is favorable for the error reporter, what impact does it have on the individuals or departments that errors are assessed against? In general, in the sample libraries, some resentment at errors assigned the institution was expressed and, in at least three of them, serious effort was made to review the record and determine if substandard cataloging had actually occurred.

It was only when speaking to network quality control personnel, however, that the rage of the embattled cataloger against whom errors were assessed could be discerned. At all three networks, quality control personnel expressed some feelings of stress resulting from having to deal with librarians whose records allegedly contained errors.

Some of the catalogers felt personally compelled to develop huge and thoroughly indexed documentation justifying their innocence. If, despite these protests, their records were revised at the network office, they took personal affront at what they considered to be stains on their professional record. In one of the networks, the strain of dealing with this small, but outraged and vocal, constituency took a noticeable toll upon the entire quality control staff. Network administrators became so concerned that they ordered that group members use some company time to take classes in biofeedback and thus relieve their stress. Unfortunately, this enlightened management strategy was not totally successful. Several biofeedback students experienced additional stress worrying that their bosses would monitor their biofeedback performance and find them at fault for not having relaxed enough. Thus visibility doth make victims of us all!!!

At another network, the chief reviser separated catalogers into two groups -- "those that want to dance and those that want to fence". The dancers are willing to accept revisions for the sake of the consistency of the network data base. The fencers, usually the more renowned catalogers, are supremely confident of their own judgments and will contest every error call. The network revisor (obviously a natural born fencer) enjoys the contest, admires the combatants, and often makes mental notes that they possess the right stuff needed to become members of network committees.

All of the network quality control personnel commented on what they consider to be a statistically insignificant but fascinating aberration -- Some catalogers, aware of the visibility and publicity that network participation creates, are deliberately using error reports to disparage the work of colleagues in other institutions. Instances of this type occur most often when there are competing cataloging departments, especially in institutions that have had traditional football rivalries with each other. In this case, technology has made it possible for a new form of the Super Bowl to be played on video screens by competing catalog departments.

But, in general, maintaining standards is not a game to catalogers. It is serious and important work. One of the most striking impressions that emerges from reviewing cataloging literature is the judgmental and moral world view of catalogers, especially in the area of standard setting and enforcement. Moreover, during the course of my interviews phrases like "lapses from grace," "worthy peers," and "born again catalogers," appeared to form natural parts of the catalogers' vocabulary -- an in-group tone and use of language that an outsider would be more likely to associate with the ministry than with the technical experts catalogers pride themselves on being.

Because they are engaged in protecting the purity of cataloging standards, the emerging subgroups of master catalogers and cataloging peer groups appear to have, quite unconsciously, cloaked themselves in the mantle of the righteous. Like any group of the Elect they are sometimes disliked and resented, but no serious collegial challenge to their right to discover and assign error has yet emerged. In fact, network designation as resource consultants, as approved revisors (e.g. Project Enhance), as "buddies" for new or wayward cataloging departments, provides new cataloging peer groups with nationwide influence, power, and prestige. This same combination of factors then makes it possible for those groups to pressure networks for the retention of standards and the very detailed records so dear to catalogers' hearts.

This enhanced status is, of course, bestowed on a very small minority of catalogers through network participation. The vast majority of these librarians are threatened by loss of jobs and the many deprofessionalizing trends that standardized and routine network work processes create. Despite this, many catalogers expressed more hope for the survival of their professional ideals as a result of the work of peer groups, than through the continued activities of their individual departments.

In two of the libraries, comment was made about networks providing a new opportunity and a new forum to discuss standards. Moreover, as one San Francisco State cataloger noted, "...networks might be worrisome because they assign errors, but at least they have some interest in discovering them. Most libraries don't care anymore."

In "The Professionalization of Everyone?" Wilensky points out that the optimal knowledge base for professionals is "...neither too vague nor too precise, too broad or too narrow." [3] Cataloging work may well fall into the too narrow and too precise category which is susceptible to being broken into ever smaller components that can then be taught to workers with lesser skills. On the other hand, Wilensky also argues that:

> "...Many of us might construct a homemade bookcase, few would forego a clergyman at the grave. The key difference is that the clergy's tasks and tools, unlike the carpenter's, belong to the realm of the sacred - which reinforces a jurisdictional claim grounded in formal training and indoctrination. Occupations which successfully identify themselves with the sacred may achieve as much of a mandate by monopoly as those that identify themselves with science." [4]

Thus he charts many paths used by occupational groups in their ascent to the peak of professionalism. At present, there is certainly no evidence that catalogers are consciously trying to replace a diminished knowledge base with an expanded claim to moral superiority. Indeed, striving toward some abstract ideal has always characterized these professionals and turned them inward in a search for collegial approval. But with the rise of designated master workers and knowledgeable peer groups, catalogers appear to be developing a breed of colleagues whose knowledge base is expanding to include an overview of network systems and whose standard setting influence is acknowledged by network personnel as well as by other catalogers. These workers could possibly develop into new hybrid catalogers, possessing some measure of automation expertise, political clout, and devotion to traditional cataloging standards. If so, there is a chance that they are harbingers of the reprofessionalization of cataloging.

Thus while the network has sowed the seeds for the deprofessionalization of cataloging, it has also reaped the crop of the new breed of born again catalogers.

REFERENCES

1. I. Zola and S.J. Miller, "The Erosion of Medicine From Within," in The Professions and Their Prospects (Beverly Hills: Sage, 1972) pp. 153-172; Rose Laub Coser, "Insulation From Observability and Types of Social Conformity," American Social Review 26: (Fall, 1961): 28-39.

2. Oglebay Institute on Quality Control, Proceedings (Dublin, Ohio: Pittsburgh Regional Library Center and OCLC, 1983), p.4.

3. Harold Wilensky, "The Professionalization of Everyone?" American Journal of Sociology 70: (September, 1964): 148.

4. Ibid. p. 139.

SHARING SERIAL COLLECTIONS

Carol Marie Kelley
Texas Tech University Libraries
Lubbock, Texas

Abstract. What types of cooperation are being practiced among academic libraries due to the use of new technologies?

Keywords and Phrases. Cooperation. Automation.

As libraries move into new technologies, opportunities are arising for more cooperation. Cooperative cataloging is a common practice available to all sizes of libraries. Energy is now being poured into serials control and union listing. Both serial acquisitions vendors and integrated library system vendors are offering online serial control packages to customers. Is the technology for serials going to instigate steps for cooperative buying and loaning among libraries? If this is so, what steps are necessary within each library to allow for this cooperation? Are libraries going to be willing to share information and allow comparisons for cooperative collection development?

I am interested in investigating these questions. How will libraries use the technology to their advantage? How do consortia who do not own the same systems handle their cooperative functions? Have consortia with the same systems changed policies that were written before the systems became available?

Cooperative buying is possible if libraries allow vendors to run comparison invoice tapes. Libraries who share the same vendor can work together now to scrutinize buying within a geographic area.

What type of workflow changes are brought about after serials systems are installed? How do systems affect the staff of the departments involved with serials control, acquisitions, collection development, and service? Does an online union list shift responsibilities from different departments within the library and likewise change workflows between borrower and lendor?

What workflows will have to change to increase the cooperative efforts among libraries?

I believe these questions would allow librarians in interlibrary loan, acquisitions, and serials to bring up more problems and discuss solutions that are in progress now. If the discussion does elicit interest I would continue my investigation with a questionnaire that would circulate in college and university libraries in the Southwest. [New Mexico, Texas, Oklahoma, Arizona, and perhaps others.] The results could be tabulated and submitted for publication in a library periodical. All these states have universities with small enrollments, under 6,000, to large enrollments, over 23,000. Oklahoma has had a statewide union list for several years. The statewide union list in Texas is less than a year old. However, there are Texas consortia that have had union lists for years. SOAR (Serials Online in Arizona) is a new group that is attempting to display holdings for that state.

Because college and university libraries in the area are approaching cooperative operations in different ways, I believe their response to questions would provide a good sample to work with.

ACCESS POINTS AND BOOK USE:
DOES THE CATALOG RECORD MAKE A DIFFERENCE?

Gunnar Knutson
University of Illinois at Chicago
Chicago, Illinois

Abstract. This study builds on limited past research on correlations between catalog access points and circulation. The study examines 1105 catalog records in three LC classifications and one subclass, comparing number and type of access points with number of circulations by type of user. Results show no significant positive correlation between total numbers of subjects or other access points and total circulation. However, stronger correlations emerge when data are examined by type of subject and type of user. As we consider modifying or enhancing the catalog record, we must take into account such differences in users and subject areas.

Keywords and Phrases. Access points, added entries, bibliographic records, cataloging, circulation, subject headings.

INTRODUCTION

As libraries make the transition from manual to automated systems, more information about the effects of such changes is needed in order to make the best use of the new technologies. One area where more knowledge is required is in the relationship between cataloging and user behavior. We need to understand better the results of our past efforts to provide bibliographic access to academic library users. The current study provides further information on the question of whether circulation of library materials can be associated with elements of catalog records.

The central concern of this study is the relationship between access points on catalog records and circulation: specifically, is there a correlation between an increased number of subject headings, and/or other access points, and the number of recorded uses of the book described? In the course of trying to answer this question some other aspects of the bibliographic record which might affect circulation are also considered.

PAST RESEARCH

There is surprisingly little information linking catalog records and circulation. Margaret Tayler concluded after a literature search for her 1982 doctoral dissertation that "there appears to be very little research which truly relates the idea of bibliographic accessibility, or the provision of bibliographic information, to the use of materials."[1] Studies which have addressed the question have all concluded with calls for more research, as there are many ways of approaching the problem. Taylor studied circulation patterns in a public library using the Dewey Decimal System. Pal V. Rao confined his more limited study (100 records) to the Library of Congress education (L) classification section of an academic library.[2] An earlier study by William Carl Highfill was conducted in a college library using the Dewey system.[3] It examined subject access points only, and was done during the summer session when use patterns may have been atypical.

While Rao and Taylor found essentially no significant correlation between number of access points and circulation, Highfill did conclude that "those books which have been assigned a greater number of subject headings have a greater chance of being selected by users during subject searches."[4] Since type of library and type of collection, as well as the subject areas chosen for study, might have influenced these different findings, all of the authors called for further inquiry.

METHODOLOGY

The present study was conducted at a medium sized research library that uses the Library of Congress classification system. The library's cataloged collection of about eight hundred thousand volumes is housed on open shelves. A divided author/title and subject card catalog provides primary access to the collection; this is augmented by an automated circulation system with primary author and title search keys, but no added entries or subjects. There are no figures available on comparative use, but observation indicates that the card catalog is the primary source of bibliographic information.

A sample of one year's acquisitions in three different subject areas was studied and compared to circulation statistics for one academic year. The six months which elapsed between the date of the last acquisition and the beginning of circulation statistics was chosen to make certain that all books had been returned from the bindery and that all catalog cards had been filed.

The samples were taken from new book lists for the year 1981. Using a standard sample size formula provided by Taro Yamane,[5] systematic samples were drawn in three subject areas: law (class K, 232 records), fine arts (class N, 301 records), and social science (class H, 372 records). In addition, 200 records in the criminology section of social science (HV6001-9920, hereafter referred to simply as HV) were examined. (There was an overlap of 46 records which appeared in both the H and HV samples.)

Three broad classifications were chosen to check if separate patterns in correlations could be observed. By choosing these distinct classifications, all of which exhibited a fair degree of circulation activity, the study was able to look for both broad and unique characteristics. The criminology group (HV) was added to provide an in-depth analysis of all 1981 acquisitions in an area with exceptionally high circulation--more than twice that of the other classes in the sample.

For each record data were collected on the number and type of access points, plus date of publication, length, and language. To these were added circulation data derived from the library's automated circulation system for the academic year 1982/83. These data were entered by type of borrower: academic, graduate, undergraduate, and total. (The "academic" category includes all faculty, plus a small number of employees with faculty equivalent rank; the "total" category includes use by a small number of non-academic, non-student employees.) Books which had circulated to non-university users through interlibrary loan, etc., or had been placed on reserve during the year were removed from the study, because these circulations would probably not have occurred through use of the card catalog. Multi-copy and multi-volume sets were also removed because they had a greater potential for circulation. Only circulating items kept on open shelves in the main library were considered for the sample.

All data were entered into a Time Zero Software statistical program designed for the Macintosh computer.[6] Each research hypothesis was that a significant positive correlation existed between the number of subjects or other access points and the total number of circulations during the year. Each null hypothesis being tested was that there was no significant correlation between the number of subjects or other access points and the number of times the item had circulated during the year. A 95% confidence interval was set for the tests. No cause-effect relationship was posited; what was sought was a level of correlation between the two factors which could not be explained by chance.

Some limitations affecting the study must be acknowledged. Open shelving means that browsing will be a factor of unknown dimensions in circulation figures. Recent studies indicate that catalog users often use the subject catalog as a starting point to guide them to a shelf area where they can browse for the books they need,[7] and one portion of this study--class HV--seems to support this belief. The major reason for choosing the K classification as an area of study was to try to offset the browsing factor, as this classification is particularly difficult to browse. The size of the classified collection in the study library (ca. 800,000 volumes) would also tend to make browsing more difficult. Online author/title access to a majority of the collection through the automated circulation system surely had some effect on the non-subject statistics gathered, but would be of use only in known-item searching. This is discussed further in that section of the analysis.

FINDINGS

What follows is a summary of major findings and an attempt to apply such information to cataloging theory. Full statistical data are given in accompanying tables.

A central point of the study was to learn if items with more LC subject headings circulated more than items with fewer such headings. Subjects are the one area of a standard cataloging record which seem to offer the possibility of easy expansion. Most of the records in this study were unaltered MARC cataloging (over 90% in each classification, and 95% overall). The range of subject entries observed was between one and eight, with an average of 2.2 subjects per record. This is considerably higher than the average figures of 1.3 reported by McClure in 1976[8] and 1.4 reported by O'Neill and Aluri in 1981,[9] and can be attributed to the choice of non-literary classes with recent imprint dates.

Classes H, K, and N have low positive correlations with total circulation ranging from .046 to .088. HV has a negative correlation of -.072. In all cases the values are such that the negative hypothesis of no association cannot be rejected. That is, the figures are low enough that it cannot be stated that they could not have occurred by chance. The average number of LC subject headings per record, by itself, does not have a significant effect on circulation in the four areas studied. An interesting finding is that undergraduate circulation figures are exceptionally high in the criminology section, HV. This, coupled with the negative total subject-circulation correlation, makes it seem likely that browsing plays a larger role in high circulation areas, while the subject catalog is more important in less used areas of the collection. For high circulation areas the catalog may serve more as a guide to the general classification that to a specific work.

Subject heading data were recorded in two sub-categories as well as a combined figure. The sub-categories were labeled topical and specific.[10] "Specific" headings were any subject headings beginning with a personal or corporate name, or with a geographic name. One might expect that such "specific" headings would be easier for patrons to locate in the subject catalog and therefore might be correlated with more circulations. Other subjects--the "topical" headings--are not always represented in the LC subject vocabulary in the same terms as they may occur to a patron, and so conceivably might be associated with a lower correlation. Research shows that patrons rarely consult Library of Congress Subject Headings volumes for assistance.[11] As an example, a patron seeking a book on the art of Marcel Duchamp could locate it directly by a subject search under "Duchamp," but might have trouble seeking a work on modern French art, which could be sought by such terms as "French art," "modern art," "French modern art," etc., rather than under the LC form "Art, Modern--20th century--France."

Just the opposite interpretation is supported by the total circulation figures. In three of the four total circulation categories, topical subject headings were more strongly correlated with circulation than were specific subject headings. There may be other factors which account for this difference--for instance, the type of books represented by these headings might be less in demand for other reasons. Nevertheless, the aggregate figures do not support the idea that users are more likely to select a subject heading beginning with a proper noun.

When these statistics are broken down between types of users (see Table III) we see that there is a noticeable difference in the topical and specific correlations by undergraduates and other users. Undergraduate use correlates positively to topical subject headings, while the academic and graduate use correlation figures are mostly negative. With specific subjects, i.e., subject headings beginning with personal, corporate, or geographic names, the undergraduate correlations are the lowest of the categories in three of four cases. This difference might be caused by the type of materials sought by the different user groups, but that possibility is beyond the scope of the data gathered. What can be stated is that subject use to retrieve library materials is even more complex than indicated by previous studies.

Other access points are derived chiefly from the AACR2 rules by which a book is being cataloged. Although AACR2 gives some leeway in determining which access points to give a particular book, generally this is a standardized procedure. Depending on its descriptive cataloging, one work will receive only an author and a title entry, while another will also have access points for a series, joint author, and a prominent sub-title. It seems plausible that a patron approaching the catalog with an incomplete citation might have a slightly better chance of locating the book with more access points. Past research has shown that incomplete or garbled citations are common with library users,[12] and so it is possible that books with these extra access points might be charged out more often.

For three of the four classes examined (K, H, HV) there was a negative correlation between total non-subject access points and total circulation. Class N had a slightly positive correlation of .031. None of these figures disproved the negative hypothesis of no significant correlation. It is interesting to note that for non-subject access points the most negative statistics came from series and corporate author correlations, while three-fourths of both the personal author and title correlations were positive. This suggests the possibility that patrons access materials infrequently through series or corporate authors. The higher correlations for author and title entries may be accounted for in part by the existence of the library's automated circulation system with its title and principal author search keys.

Access points are only part of the reason a patron might locate and choose a particular book. Other factors were noted and analyzed. Date of publication, number of pages, and language were recorded as possible contributing factors. Correlation results were mixed but three noteworthy figures were seen. Date of publication did not vary widely because the sample was composed of all new additions from the same calendar year, with average dates of 1977 to 1979. Circulation correlations were positive in all cases (i.e., newer books circulated more often). With class HV the figure of .153 was high enough so that the null hypothesis of no significant association could not be rejected. As one might expect, there was also a positive correlation between English language and circulation, and again the HV class figure of .158 was beyond the range of the null hypothesis. These figures would probably have been higher if there had been more foreign language books in the sample, but they ranged from only 1% to 8% of the totals. With such a preponderance of English works there was not much opportunity to observe the language factor.

Length is a more problematical factor as it is not easily associated with positive or negative characteristics. The correlations between greater length and higher use ranged from negative to positive, with the H class figure of .137 being high enough to indicate a significant positive correlation.

CONCLUSION

These figures should be considered in the context of other studies dealing with cataloging. Use studies have indicated that certain types of materials, such as foreign language books, circulate less frequently than average.[13] A study of short entry catalogs done at Bath University showed that most patron needs could be met by brief entry records with no more than two access points.[14] The current study lends some weight to the idea that for certain types of cataloging the equivalent of a full MARC record is not cost efficient in terms of future circulation of the titles. If circulation is accepted as a valid measure of library performance, there is little to suggest that the time and expense of full local cataloging of older backlog items for which no MARC cataloging is available, such as many foreign language materials, is justified.

Given the contradictory evidence gathered in this study there does not seem to be a simple, ready solution to the question of increasing subject accessibility. While it is true that most MARC records offer few subject access points, this research shows that increasing the number of LC subject headings may have little or no effect on book retrieval and use. One intriguing possibility is that an incremental increase in subject headings, such as from one or two up to three or four, does not affect circulation, but that a very large increase up to ten or more may begin to affect use figures. Carol Mandel has compiled a number of possible methods for such subject enhancement.[15] However, the data presented here, which is based on traditional cataloging records, does not offer statistical evidence that a larger number of subject headings is significantly associated with increased circulation.

It has been suggested that added entries are rarely consulted and might be dropped from catalog records under certain circumstances, especially if key word title access were added.[16] In this study no type of added entry was positivley associated with circulation at a significant level. When one considers the authority work that is often necessitated by series and corporate entries, consideration must be given to simplifying certain types of cataloging--older imprints, foreign language materials, and various materials found in backlogs come immediately to mind.

More information, particularly protocol analysis and transaction log analysis which can be more directly correlated with circulation, is necessary before making any major adjustments to the catalog record. The research reported here indicates that use patterns are complex and that catalog use varies from one subject area to the next and from one user group to the next. The catalog of the future must be built on knowledge of actual user behavior, and should be keyed more to the institutional situation and less to traditional expectations. It is conceivable that a record with less description and fewer added entries will be combined with greater subject access of a type that will be simpler to use. As we move forward, creating new catalogs for a new generation of academic users, every assumption concerning access should be continually tested. The knowledge gained will serve us well in the quest for ever better access to our collections.

ACKNOWLEDGEMENTS

I would like to extend special thanks to Nancy John, Assistant University Librarian, and Stephen E. Wiberley, Jr., Bibliographer for the Social Sciences, both from the University of Illinois at Chicago, for their advice and criticisms during the writing of this paper.

REFERENCES

1. Margaret Ann Thomas Taylor, "The Effect of Bibliographic Accessibility Upon Physical Accessibility in a Public Library Setting" (Ph.D. diss., University of Michigan, 1982), p. 19.

2. Pal V. Rao, "The Relationship Between Card Catalog Access Points and the Recorded Use of Education Books in a University Library," College & Research Libraries 43, no. 4 (July 1982): 341-345.

3. William Carl Highfill, "The Relationship of Indexing Depth to Subject Catalog Retrieval Effectiveness" (Ph.D. diss., University of Illinois, 1969).

4. Ibid., p. 233.

5. Taro Yamane, Statistics: An Introductory Analysis 2nd ed. (New York : Harper & Row, 1967), p. 886.

6. Basic Statistics for the Macintosh. (State College, Pa. : Time Zero Software, 1984).

7. Karen Markey, Subject Searching in Library Catalogs: Before and After the Introduction of Online Catalogs. (Dublin, Ohio : OCLC, 1984), p. 57-61.

8. Charles R. McClure, "Subject and Added Entries as Access to Information." Journal of Academic Librarianship 2, no. 1 (March 1976): 10.

9. Edward T. O'Neill and Rao Aluri, "Library of Congress Subject Heading Patterns in OCLC Monographic Records," Library Resources & Technical Services 25, no. 1 (January/March 1981): 70.

10. This is an altered and much simplified use of subject categories inspired by Stephen E. Wiberley, Jr. in "Subject Access in the Humanities and the Precision of the Humanist's Vocabulary," Library Quarterly 53, no. 4 (October 1983): 420-433.

11. Markey, p. 108-109.

12. Renata Tagliacozzo, Lawrence Rosenberg, and Manfred Kochen, "Access and Recognition: From Users' Data to Catalogue Entries," Journal of Documentation 26, no. 3 (September 1970): 234-240.

13. Alan Kent and others, Use of Library Materials: The University of Pittsburgh Study. (New York : Dekker, 1979), p. 44.

14. Alan Seal, "Experiments With Full and Short Entry Catalogues: A Study of Library Needs," Library Resources & Technical Services 27, no. 2 (April/June 1983): 149.

15. Carol A. Mandel, "Enriching the Library Catalog Record for Subject Access," <u>Library Resources & Technical Services</u> 29, no. 1 (January/March 1985): 12.

16. Seal, p. 147.

TABLE I
DESCRIPTIVE STATISTICS

Variable (average)	K (Law) 232 records	N (Fine Arts) 301 records	H (Social Sci.) 372 records	HV6001-9920 (Criminology) 200 records
Year of pub.	1978	1977	1979	1979
No. of pages	312	220	264	251
English	96%	92%	99%	96%
Foreign	4%	8%	1%	4%
Topical subjects	1.80	1.61	1.88	1.97
Specific subjects	.25	.56	.38	.17
Total subjects	2.05	2.17	2.25	2.14
Personal authors	1.32	1.41	1.30	1.27
Corporate entries	.18	.23	.23	.17
Series entries	.47	.22	.37	.29
Title entries	1.02	.98	1.01	1.01
Total non-subject access points	2.98	2.83	2.91	2.73
Total access points	5.02	5.00	5.16	4.87
Average no. circulations 1982/83 academic year:				
Academic	.04	.07	.10	.12
Graduate	.15	.14	.24	.23
Undergraduate	.50	.61	.47	1.53
Total*	.70	.89	.85	1.92

*Includes local non-academic circulation

TABLE II
CORRELATION COEFFICIENTS

Correlation coefficients of <u>total</u> circulation and variables. Underlined values have significant correlation at .05 level.

Variable	K (Law) 232 records	N (Fine arts) 301 records	H (Social Sci.) 372 records	HV6001-9920 (Criminology) 200 records
Date	.068	.077	.041	<u>.153</u>
Length	-.015	.024	<u>.137</u>	.095
Language	.104	.093	.055	<u>.158</u>
Topical subjects	.050	.042	<u>.158</u>	.020
Specific subjects	.067	.006	<u>-.116</u>	<u>-.198</u>
Total subjects	.088	.046	.071	-.072
Personal authors	.016	-.007	.084	.050
Corporate entries	-.097	.078	-.094	-.107
Series	-.026	-.026	<u>-.155</u>	-.061
Titles	.066	.013	-.021	.077
Total non-subjects	-.042	.031	-.076	-.051
Total access points	.028	.054	-.002	-.093

TABLE III

CIRCULATION CORRELATIONS BY TYPE OF SUBJECT

A. Topical Subject-Circulation Correlations

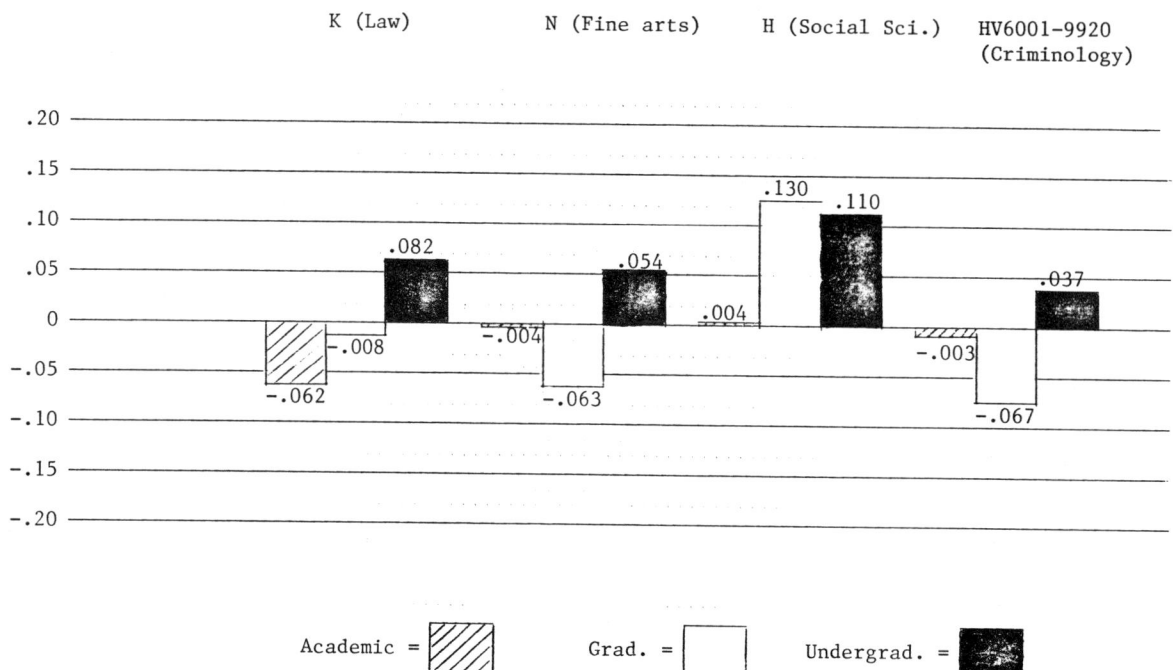

B. Specific Subject-Circulation Correlations

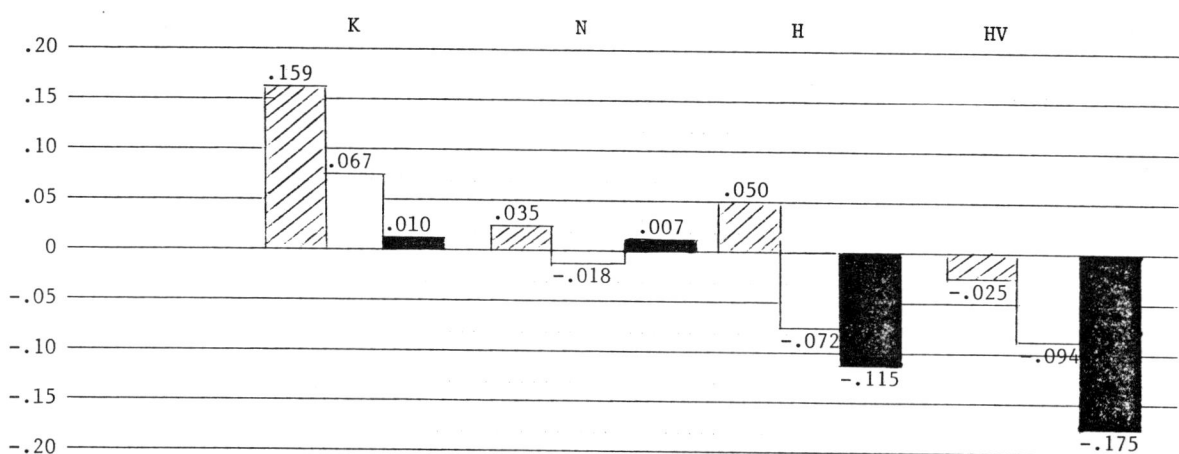

TABLE IV

CORRELATION COEFFICIENTS BY TYPE OF SUBJECT AND USER

(Note: Underlined values have significant correlation at .05 level)

	K (Law) 232 records	N (Fine arts) 301 records	H (Social Sci.) 372 records	HV6001-9920 (Criminology) 200 records
TOPICAL SUBJECTS:				
User group				
Academic	-.062	-.004	.004	-.003
Graduate	-.008	-.063	<u>.130</u>	-.067
Undergraduate	.082	.054	<u>.110</u>	.037
Total*	.050	.042	<u>.158</u>	.020
SPECIFIC SUBJECTS:				
User group				
Academic	<u>.159</u>	.035	.050	-.025
Graduate	.067	-.018	-.072	-.094
Undergraduate	.010	.007	<u>-.115</u>	<u>-.175</u>
Total*	.067	.006	<u>-.116</u>	<u>-.198</u>
TOTAL SUBJECTS:				
User group				
Academic	.045	.018	.039	-.015
Graduate	.036	-.075	.075	-.110
Undergraduate	.081	.059	.024	-.043
Total*	.088	.046	.071	-.072

*Total figures include local non-academic circulation

QUALITY CONTROL OF ONLINE CATALOGS: AUTOMATION VS. HUMAN CONTROL

Ichiko Morita
The Ohio State University Libraries
Columbus, Ohio, U.S.A.

Abstract. Quality here is concerned with both the intellectual content as well as the description of the catalog.

With the advent of the online catalog, we started automatic quality control, beginning with such activities as the detection of errors and duplicate entries.

As computer technology advances, the speed and magnitude of the shift from manual to machine control is increasing. Automated quality control is no longer limited to the descriptions of catalog records but is extending to their intellectual contents as well. The extent to which automated quality control of intellectual content might be taken must be given serious consideration.

Keywords and Phrases.

Automatic quality control.
Artificial vs. human intelligence.
Online catalogs.

The importance of maintaining high quality in library catalogs cannot be overemphasized. We have always made various efforts to maintain the quality of library catalogs as best we can. However, online catalogs, which have characteristics different from those of any of the traditional catalogs, introduced entirely new approaches. Offering greater precision and speed, computers now do what humans once did. Moreover, we are extending the capacity of computers to perform tasks humans could not do, with minimal time and effort.

Even at the dawn of the online catalog era, we were conscious of the quality of online catalogs, but not so conscious of the automatic quality control measures, though we had incorporated some into the then developing systems. A good example is that of the OCLC online shared cataloging system. It displayed error messages such as "E1," "E2," etc., indicating illegal tag, illegal 049 field, etc. when the operator input incorrect tags, codes, etc., rather than processing that erroneous information. This early type of quality control had the following characteristics:

1. Certain measures were necessary for the system to respond. For example, correct codes, tags, etc. were necessary in certain designated spaces. As a result, those measures worked as a kind of quality control.

2. Systems detected and warned of errors but did not correct errors. OCLC's system not only detected and warned, but prevented the input of erroneous information in one or two character spaces. In this respect, OCLC was a step ahead even at the very beginning.

3. Detection was very basic and simple. For example, in one or two character spaces, where the choice of the characters to be input was expected to be all numerals or all roman characters, if the wrong kind of character was input, the computer indicated this as an error. Systems made on-off type detections.

4. Systems did not need a large program, or series of programs. Their scope required neither dictionaries nor a large space in the file.

As systems developed, online catalogs became more sophisticated. Additional quality control measures were provided as systems added new programs. However, quality control measures were not the central part of the programming as online catalogs developed. They were accommodated with a little extra effort, usually as the by-products of efforts to develop programs for improving display formats of bibliographic records or to provide additional indexing.

In this manner, the Ohio State University Libraries, for example, have developed ways to detect errors automatically, though on a small scale. Some examples of what the Libraries have incorporated into their system are as follows:

1. For bibliographic records, the system detects duplicate entries, including duplicate call numbers and duplicate copy numbers, and rejects them. It also detects missing field information in fields like the 300 and call number fields. It rejects multiple information in an incoming record, such as multiple call numbers. It detects invalid codes or formats such as mistyped location codes or misformatted call numbers. In addition, some frequently recurring pattern information is processed automatically. For example, certain unnecessary information, such as book prices or w subfield information, is suppressed from displaying without manual deletion from the source tapes. Also, certain information may be displayed in various places, once it is provided, through automatic interpretation of the data. For example, if the collation indicates the size of a book as over 30 cm., the "oversize" code is displayed automatically.

2. For headings, the system reports headings new to the file, including the wrong form of an established heading, a heading with misspellings, etc. If an incoming heading is AACR2 LC form, it is coded as verified. If it is from a member library, it is entered as unverified.

Some of the above-mentioned mechanisms have been installed while developing additional programs for general improvements to the online catalog, and librarians have taken advantage of them to catch errors. Other mechanisms have been installed by special request, usually by adding a small program to the areas where programmers were working. Some requests have not yet been accepted because of priorities that the Libraries' Automation Committee has established for programming, as well as the cost of programming and the size of file the particular request requires. Although not all of them are incorporated yet, most requests are in a queue waiting to be incorporated as manpower and financial limitations allow.

Automatic quality control of systems has been drawing more attention recently. The reason, of course, is that rapidly developing technology makes it possible to program highly sophisticated transactions to detect errors and make corrections. At the same time, librarians are increasingly aware of computers' capabilities and potential. They have begun to entertain ideas of utilizing those capabilities to control and elevate the quality of online catalogs.

Ideas can be stretched much farther. In my thinking, I can at least say the following. If we create a large dictionary of vocabulary, we can correct spelling. This is already done by some software for word processors. The only difference is that libraries handle universal knowledge, and therefore, the size of vocabulary would have to be enormous to cover most records entered in online catalogs. However, if suitable conditions were met, this would not be impossible. Similarly, if we were to produce a list of call numbers and related subject headings for each call number, we could verify the appropriateness of the assigned subject headings for call numbers. A system might even suggest additional subject headings. Needless to say, one would have to compile a large and complicated list and the system would have to accommodate an enormous dictionary comprising such a list. This may not seem practical at this point, but theoretically and technically it is not impossible.

In summary, quality control of the online catalog initially consisted of the detection of forms, detecting whether forms were numerals or alphabets, whether they were present or not, and whether an incorrect form was input (the correct form was stored in the database as an established form for comparison). The errors that were detected or even corrected in the above situations occurred more often than not due to carelessness or typographical mistakes, and were by no means intentionally created as a result of conscious intellectual effort. Since those errors were created unintentionally, systematic detections, warnings and even corrections were most welcome.

However, if we advance our thinking in the direction I mentioned earlier, automatic quality control will grow from detection and warning to the prevention of erroneous information or wrongly entered information, and to correction according to predetermined rules and checking with provided dictionaries. Furthermore, we can expect to see the computer controlling the intellectual quality of the online catalog, distinguishing inappropriate subject headings from appropriate ones, or suggesting better call numbers for a title by scanning assigned subject headings. That is to say, computers will challenge our intellectual selection of information, no longer being limited to the correction of inadvertent human errors. I don't think these kinds of activities are being performed yet in any existing online catalogs because of the non-existence of such a profile and the expense of programming, as well as the size of files required. Besides, many imagine that LC or some major institutions will do original cataloging while local libraries will do almost none. Therefore, people may not yet fear the power of the machine. At any rate, the potential of automatic quality control must be recognized. When the development of online catalogs reaches the point where most objectives have been fulfilled and most functions are being satisfactorily performed, what will be the next challenge? Most likely more attention will be paid to the quality of information in those online catalogs. It is reasonable to assume that methods of cleaning up the records already existing in a system as well as those for verifying the appropriateness of the content of those records will be developed. Then, those methods will be quickly applied to what is currently being input.

One question arises here as to whether we want to control the quality of intellectual content of online catalogs or leave it to the computers. At least we should be able to decide what we want computers to do. It is an obvious statement, I think, isn't it? We have known and affirmed this all along. However, in practice there are many cases where we have compromised with what the computer might do or what we could temporarily live with because of financial limitations, a shortage of programmers or a lack of understanding of systems on the part of librarians.

Trends are difficult to resist and attention bias has brought many automation trends to develop in such a way, that we never recognize and consider the basic problems. Up to now, trends and attention bias have been affecting technical aspects of library functions. It is only a matter of time before artificial intelligence manipulates our intellectual portion of library activities. Before being too deeply influenced by or involved in those trends, we must forsee the potentials, whether advantages or dangers, and decide what we want. We should decide how far and in what way we want computers to control the intellectual content in online catalogs before others decide for us.

ACKNOWLEDGEMENTS

Author wishes to thank Darrell Peters for editing the manuscript.

BIBLIOGRAPHIC INSTRUCTION

CONCEPTS FOR BIBLIOGRAPHIC INSTRUCTION IN THIS TIME OF TRANSITION

Deborah Fink
University of Colorado Libraries
Boulder, Colorado

Abstract. The current transition of society to an information-based economy offers teaching librarians an opportunity to expand our conception of the library research process by introducing "information processing" in our instruction. Information processing is the operations which cycle information from communication to dissemination to acquisition and organization to access, manipulation and communication. A paradigm for this flow provides a conceptual framework for organizing and presenting the functions of authors, publishers, libraries, and researchers. The paradigm is also useful for exploring the political dimensions of information and to suggest strategies for integrating traditional and electronic modes of information access and manipulation.

Keywords and Phrases. Bibliographic instruction. Information processing. Research.

The current transition of society to an information-based economy offers teaching librarians a unique opportunity to expand our conception of the library research process by integrating the diverse aspects of "information processing" in our instruction. Information processing is the many operations which cycle information from communication to dissemination to acquisition and organization to access, manipulation and communication. The following paradigm for this flow provides a conceptual framework for organizing and presenting a variety of procedures and issues of particular interest to library users in this time of transition. It outlines the functions of authors, publishers, librarians, researchers, and writers (see figure 1).

This paradigm is useful for bibliographic instruction because it builds on current interest in the information age; and it focuses on information itself, not just access to it. As Frick maintains, "bibliographic instruction can help the student recognize that by understanding who generates information, who publishes it, who disseminates and classifies it, how, and for whom, he will develop a more subtle grasp of the value and limitations of that information."[1]

The paradigm can be used to overview the cycle of information processing, to provide context for any of the stages, and to explore the political dimensions of information. It can also be used to discuss current applications of emerging technologies and to suggest strategies for integrating traditional and electronic modes of accessing and manipulating information.

For example, the cycle of information processing can be traced to highlight the politics of information, with politics being defined simply as promoting a particular interest. The cycle begins when an author communicates some findings in writing and the information is disseminated. The decisions of whether to disseminate and how are political choices. The author may limit distribution to colleagues for immediate feedback or seek commercial publication for tenure or other purposes. A publisher will generally accept an item only if it appears to have market value and is consistent with the

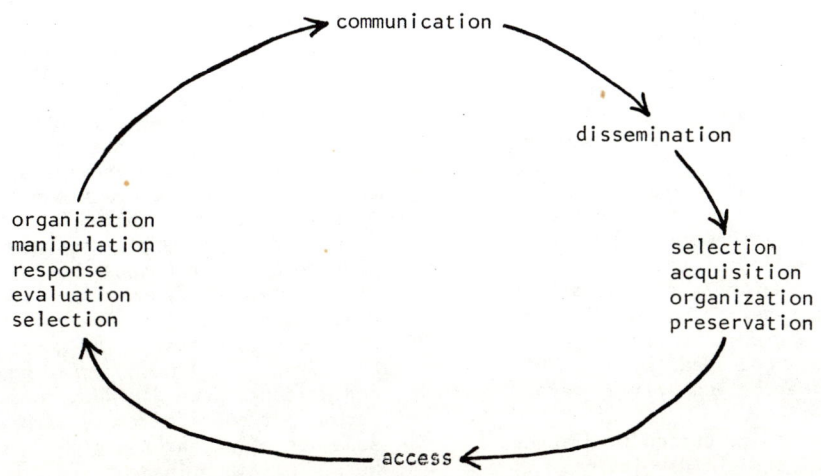

figure 1

publisher's public image.

Selection for acquisition is, of course, a politically charged process. Bookstores select those items which will bring a profit, organizations select those items which support their point of view, and, as institutions, libraries select those items which are congruent with their collection development policies. Institutions, however, do not select materials, individuals do. Within the parameters of the policies, individual librarians make choices based on their own interests and the perceived interests and needs of their constituencies.

The organization of library materials is less obviously a politically charged activity, but cataloging and classification tools are fraught with controversy: <u>The Library of Congress Subject Headings</u> has been labelled sexist, racist, and Anglo-Saxon. Even preservation efforts have political overtones, as decisions are made about what will be preserved, how, and where.

Access to information is the point of connection between the author and the researcher. This may occur without any intervening steps, but it is most likely to take place where published information has been collected and made available. Access is facilitated by organizational systems and reference sources and services, which make it possible for researchers to identify and locate sources of information. But bibliographic tools are not without politics, both in terms of the items selected for inclusion and their organization. As Frick asserts, "... reference structures both open and close certain information channels, [for example]... the rigidity of certain periodical indexes in regard to subject headings perpetuates certain views of the discipline."[2]

The processing of information by the researcher is prey to political perceptions from the outset. According to West, "The way a problem is stated or conceptualized may exert some influence on the solution and on the pertinent information which is gathered."[3] He also notes that, as research continues, there are "... potential distortive effects which emerge from preconceptions about previously gathered information; from prior knowledge; from emotional bias; from group norms; from particular items of information, and restrictions as to the sources of information."[4]

The paradigm provides a framework for considering censorship and selective publication, which hinder the flow of information; propaganda, which is a distorting device of the author and/or disseminator; and bias, which is the researcher's conscious or unconscious selection and distortion. With an active awareness of these concepts, students can be encouraged to approach topic formulation, research, and writing more critically.

The paradigm can also be traced to discuss issues raised by the electronic revolution. Electronic publishing offers a variety of applications, and electronic networks are already enabling writers to communicate without an intermediary publisher. Such developments threaten to create an information elite and have implications for copyright and preservation, not to mention the future of books and libraries. Libraries are not only using computers to perform routine functions, but also to take advantage of networking capabilities, and to provide new forms of access, notably the online catalog. Librarian intermediaries provide researchers with computer-based access to the online equivalents of printed indexes and other reference sources. Computer capabilities have spawned whole new types of reference sources (e.g., citation indexes) and can be used to decrease the time lag between publication and indexing. Individuals with access to a personal computer can directly search an expanding array of online resources, and software options are available for conceptualizing, organizing, writing, and editing research. Clearly, the computer has effected all aspects of manipulating and accessing information. However, in bibliographic instruction, it is important to present the computer not as a panacea, but as one component of the total search process.

At the point of access in the information processing paradigm, the rapid and prolific development of computer databases and software may be an overwhelming phenomenon; but search strategy, the foundation of contemporary BI, provides an approach to this situation. We can introduce our library users to the various types of online sources and packages (just as we now introduce them to the various types of printed reference sources) and teach them strategies to discover which types would be appropriate for their needs, as well as the advantages and disadvantages of particular sources. Pathfinders of online directories, bibliographies, and reviewing sources can supplement subject guides and enable researchers to fit together in a single strategy the sources, printed and electronic, which will satisfy their information needs.

It is also important to clarify relationships between conventional and computerized sources. Library users must know what holdings are reflected in an online versus a card catalog, when to use each and both. It is equally important that potential users of commercial databases understand to what extent a given field is covered online, what sources may be available only in printed form or only online. There are also aspects of manual searching which may make that approach a worthwhile preliminary step or adjunct to an online search. Users of computerized access are known to become so enthralled with that approach that they will exclude additional useful sources. The future may provide electronic access to all information, but in this time of transition, information seekers must be able to effectively integrate all available modes of information access.

Traditional methods of organizing research and writing, such as index cards and outlining, become outmoded for those with access to a personal computer and the growing selection of software. Although instruction librarians may not be teaching the mechanics of word processing or spread sheets, we will be called upon to teach appropriate applications of such techniques to the research process.

The information processing paradigm provides a framework for organizing and introducing concepts in bibliographic instruction. Applied to the credit course, the paradigm suggests a series of topics for discussion. The stages in the flow of information are explicit in the model, but the politics of information and the role of the computer in accessing and manipulating information are implicit. Although the library research course will concentrate on the point of access, the paradigm establishes a context which will enrich the research process. For example, a unit on indexing might include a look at what titles are included and excluded by a particular subject index, and how the coverage effects the dissemination of excluded titles or how the researcher's perception of the field is affected by those titles which are included. Applied to the one-hour lecture, the paradigm suggests a number of "hooks," that is, attention-catching and motivating introductions, which lead in to a brief look at the flow of information as a context for research strategies and sources. For example, a class might be asked why information is so important that it is the basis of a new age and how information becomes available to the researcher.

The electronic revolution has brought about a major transition in society and created general interest in the role and value of information. Teaching librarians can exploit this interest and bring about a transition in bibliographic instruction. Moving beyond the mundane view of library use instruction as merely procedural explanations of search strategy and the use of reference sources, we can introduce library users to the larger view of information processing.

REFERENCES

1. Elizabeth Frick, "Information Structure and Bibliographic Instruction," The Journal of Academic Librarianship 1, no. 4 (September 1975): 14.

2. Ibid.

3. Charles K. West, The Social and Psychological Distortion of Information (Chicago: Nelson-Hall, 1981), p. 78.

4. Ibid., pp. 80-81.

BUILDING A BRIDGE
ARTICULATION PROGRAMS FOR BIBLIOGRAPHIC INSTRUCTION

Barbara E. Kemp, Mary M. Nofsinger, and Alice M. Spitzer
Holland Library
Washington State University
Pullman, Washington 99164-5610

Abstract. This position paper addresses educational articulation, with emphasis on the transition of students from high school to college. These students frequently lack library/research skills which is a major problem for bibliographic instruction librarians in academic libraries. Based on models of school/college cooperation, current cooperative projects involving academic libraries are discussed. The relevance of articulation efforts between high school and university libraries is emphasized.

Keywords and Phrases. Articulation, educational; High school/college cooperation; Library skills; Cooperative programs; Bibliographic instruction.

EDUCATIONAL ARTICULATION

Several educational groups, including the American Association for Higher Education, the Carnegie Foundation for the Advancement of Teaching, and the Libraries and a Learning Society project have called recently for closer cooperation among the nation's high schools and colleges.[1,2,3] This desire for educational articulation, or the integration of educational experiences, takes many forms, but two common goals seem to be apparent: 1) to ease the transition of the student from one educational unit to another, and 2) to link the educational process into a lifelong learning continuum.

Unfortunately, programs and curricula often are developed or administered unilaterally. There is a "tendency of teachers and administrators to concentrate on the curriculum of their level to such extent that they ignore the learning goals of other levels"[4] while colleges frequently decide on admission requirements without consulting those most directly affected--the teachers and administrators in the secondary schools. The result is a poorly integrated, inefficient educational system, which has both gaps and unnecessary duplication in the curricula. Students and educators alike are frustrated by this discontinuity, and taxpayers are forced to bear the costs of remedial and duplicated programs.

To correct such problems, a Carnegie Foundation special report has urged that the nation's high schools and colleges "should join together to determine the content and specific skills considered essential requirements for entrance into college."[5] The same report lists five principles to follow in establishing collaborative projects: 1) "educators at both levels must agree that they, indeed, have common problems"; 2) "the traditional academic 'pecking order' must be overcome"; 3) "cooperative projects must be sharply focused"; 4) "those who participate must get recognition"; and 5) "cooperation. . . must focus on action--not machinery."[6]

ARTICULATION OF LIBRARY SKILLS

As educators, it is important for academic librarians to be aware of and understand this focus on articulation and to consider our bibliographic instruction efforts in relation to it. Like our colleagues in the subject disciplines, we must be prepared to establish cooperative programs with secondary schools to help students in their transition to college.

There are strong, practical arguments for collaborative efforts. Most academic libraries are requested to host classes from secondary schools or have high school students come to the reference desk for individual assistance. Since these classes and students are not always prepared or have poorly designed assignments, such requests often are not greeted enthusiastically by the academic librarians. Another drawback in this approach is that the timing often conflicts with heavy use by the academic library's primary clientele and is thus viewed as an intrusion.

By working to establish cooperative programs, the academic librarian can gain control over the situation. It can be made clear that classes are welcome when they are scheduled at times convenient to the rhythm of the academic calendar. Academic and school librarians need jointly to establish criteria for library assignments, define minimum library/research competencies, and establish methods of teaching them at the appropriate grade level. As a result, students are likely to be better prepared, and there would be less need for remediation. The development of mutual respect and understanding with our secondary school colleagues and a caring, welcoming attitude toward their students can also act as a strong marketing tool for the parent institution. This ultimately benefits the academic library's position within the college or university.

SCHOOL/COLLEGE LIBRARY PARTNERSHIPS

From our research it is apparent that there are several models of school/college library cooperative programs. Among these are: 1) high school class visits to academic libraries; 2) academic librarians working directly with high school students to provide instruction; 3) programs and privileges for special groups, such as gifted and advanced placement students; 4) academic librarians working with school librarians at a local or state level; 5) provision of materials designed to introduce high school students to the academic library. The following programs illustrate some of these models in use.

Washington State University, Pullman

At Washington State University, we had completed a bibliographic instruction needs assessment survey, and the data seemed to be contradictory. The vast majority of students indicated they had received instruction in library use when they were in secondary schools, yet most still had difficulty in answering basic questions about the library. Experience at the reference desk confirmed that many students lack understanding of fundamental library concepts.

In order to determine the cause of this discrepancy, we contacted the Washington Library Media Association to initiate preliminary discussions with school librarians. When invited to speak at their annual convention in 1984, WSU librarians presented a session on "Library Research Skills for College-Bound Students."[7] Participants discussed which library skills were most needed to be an effective library user and shared ideas on how to incorporate these skills into class assignments.

The enthusiastic response to the session resulted in an invitation to speak at the 1985 Washington Communication Conference (which included reading specialists, high school English, journalism and speech teachers, as well as librarians and media specialists). At the same time WSU librarians presented a pre-conference workshop entitled "Building the Library Bridge from High School to College: Strategies for Teacher-Librarian Cooperation". Here, teachers and librarians working in small teams designed class-related library projects covering skills needed for college and lifelong learning.

Chickasha Cooperative Bibliographic Instruction Project, Oklahoma

The Chickasha Cooperative Bibliographic Instruction Project was carried out by a team of librarians representing the Chickasha Public Library, the Chickasha High School Library, and the University of Sciences and Arts of Oklahoma Library.[8] The goal of the project was to make library users aware of the different library resources available to them in the Chickasha area and to make participants in the program more effective library users.

Instructional programs were presented to student and community groups. Several slide tape presentations and a workbook were prepared to assist in bibliographic instruction, and individual assistance was available during the programs. Participants benefited from increased understanding of library use and resources, and the libraries benefited from increased communication among themselves and greater public visibility.

University of South Carolina, Aiken

In the fall of 1979, librarians at the University of South Carolina, Aiken held a half-day seminar for city and county public school librarians, teachers, and language coordinators.[9] Its focus was on materials related to literature in the university library and joint, cooperative services which could be offered between the schools and the University.

An outgrowth of this seminar was the establishment of a gifted child program. Each secondary school in the Aiken area can select twelve outstanding children to participate in an annual library enrichment project in which they receive university library orientation, assistance in locating materials, and check-out privileges. In addition, university librarians provide guided tours and instruction to secondary school students upon the request of classroom teachers.

University of Massachusetts, Amherst

Also in 1979, a study of library instruction programs in forty high schools was done by Joyce Merriam, Reference Librarian at the University of Massachusetts, Amherst.[10] The study found that school librarians attempted to provide at least minimal amounts of library orientation and instruction to students and that the typical high school program was almost identical to that presented to freshmen at the University. Teacher apathy toward integrating library skills into classroom instruction, fragmented library instruction given on a one-to-one basis, and lack of a formal, planned bibliographic instruction program were identified as problems.

As a result of the study, Ms. Merriam recommended many changes in library instruction at both levels. Among these recommendations were: librarians should teach students that the same skills can be used in various types of libraries; teachers should be encouraged to integrate library exercises into their curricula; Schools of Education should prepare prospective teachers for integrating library skills into their classrooms; school and academic librarians should work together to help students make the transition from high school to academic libraries. Another result of the study was a Library Instruction Colloquium held in Amherst in June, 1979. School and academic librarians met to discuss problems, exchange ideas and samples of instructional materials, and share knowledge.

The University of Tennessee, Knoxville

The University of Tennessee has initiated an active program of cooperation with fifteen high schools in Knoxville city and county.[11] A videotape introduction to the library is shown to students by the school librarian prior to their visit to the library. Students may come to the library individually, and class groups with the accompanying teacher are encouraged to take advantage of the regular bibliographic instruction program. High school teachers and advanced placement students are entitled to free library cards. The service is heavily used and library staff are pleased to see that the books in demand by high school students do not necessarily parallel those needed by university students.

In order to alleviate the problem of books not being returned promptly and reduce the traffic into the library, a demonstration project is being developed which will allow librarians from two high schools to dial directly into and search the university library's database. Items requested would be sent out to the library via a delivery system. In addition, a conference is planned which would bring the librarian, a teacher of the librarian's choice, and the curriculum specialist from each of the fifteen high schools together with the university librarians.

State University of New York, Albany

In New York there is statewide interest in cooperation among high school and university libraries. At SUNY, Albany, the university library has established policies which encourage visitations from high school classes.[12] Teachers must arrange in advance for the class visits, and each student must have an assignment to complete. Upon arrival, a slide tape is shown which orients the students to the library; the bibliographic instruction coordinator then explains how to access library holdings. Librarians, including those from Technical Services, provide small-group tours of the building before the teacher and students begin work on assignments. Because of the enthusiastic response to this program, a half-day conference was held at SUNY, Albany, in 1984. Speakers shared their knowledge gained through several years of teaching college-bound seniors. In addition, local high school librarians and teachers discussed the preparation of students for college work via assignments and field trips.

THE FUTURE

Although many library-related articulation projects currently exist, there is relatively little information about them in the library or education literature. Academic and school librarians, working together as colleagues, need to continue developing programs and to publicize them. As an investment in the future, academic librarians should also be working with students and faculty in teacher training programs to promote the importance of information gathering skills and attitudes conducive to lifelong learning.

The future of articulation between high school and college libraries is bright. In the pursuit of educational excellence there will be increasing demand to provide better information-gathering skills and eliminate the need for remedial instruction. Academic librarians have a responsibility to work with secondary schools to ensure that students are adequately prepared for the transition to college level research. We should carefully consider our role in the articulation process and continue to explore the many possibilities open to us.

REFERENCES

1. Gene I. Maeroff, _School and College: Partnerships in Education_ (Princeton, N.J.: The Carnegie Foundation for the Advancement of Teaching, 1983), p.2.

2. American Association for Higher Education, "High School/College Partnerships", _Current Issues in Higher Education Annual Series_ 1(1981).

3. _Alliance for Excellence: Librarians Respond to A Nation at Risk_ (Washington, D.C.: U.S. Dept. of Education, 1984).

4. Julius Menacker, _From School to College: Articulation and Transfer_ (Washington, D.C.: American Council on Education, 1975), p. 9.

5. Maeroff, p. viii.

6. Ibid., p. 3-5.

7. Barbara E. Kemp and Alice M. Spitzer, "Let's Connect: High School/University Cooperation in Bibliographic Instruction", _Medium: Journal of the Washington Library Media Association_ 9 (Winter, 1985): 4-7.

8. Charles R. McClure, _Chickasha Cooperative Bibliographic Instruction Project: Final Evaluation_ (Stanford, California: ERIC Document Reproduction Service, 1981), ED 203 360.

9. Telephone conversation with Susan Hollifield, University of South Carolina, Aiken, Library, June 13, 1985.

10. Joyce A. Merriam, "Helping Students Make the Transition: A Study", in Carolyn A. Kirkendall, ed., _Teaching Library Use Competence: Bridging the Gap from High School to College_. Papers presented at the Eleventh Annual Library Instruction Conference held at Eastern Michigan University, May 7-8, 1981 (Ann Arbor, Michigan: Pierian Press, 1982), pp. 1-12.

11. Telephone conversation with Angie LeClercq, University of Tennessee, Knoxville, Library, June 12, 1985.

12. Telephone conversation with Jacquelyn Gavryck, Bibliographic Instruction Coordinator at State University of New York, Albany, Library, June 12, 1985.

END-USER INSTRUCTION - WHAT ARE YOU DOING?

Sharmon H. Kenyon
Humboldt State University
Arcata, California

Abstract. The purpose of this idea brief is to discuss with other librarians how they are dealing with the issue of end-user instruction. What, if any, kinds of programs do they have for faculty, staff, students, or community users? Is it part of the regular library instruction program? What are the staffing and equipment requirements? Do you think libraries should be doing this kind of instruction? I will start the discussion by describing what we are doing at Humboldt State University.

Keywords and Phrases. End-user, instruction, faculty, microcomputer, Pro-Search.

As more people are becoming acquainted with microcomputers and realizing the potential for gaining access quickly and efficiently to certain kinds of information, it seems as if there will be greater demand for this new kind of "reference tool." Many of the popular microcomputing magazines carry ads for BRS AFTER DARK, and DIALOG's KNOWLEDGE INDEX as well as for the various kinds of networks like CompuServe, Easynet or BCN. All of these ads say how easy it is to use these services and gain the information needed easily and quickly. Recent issues of PC World[1] have also had articles geared to nonlibrarians which describe how to perform an online search.

What are academic librarians doing about this potentially large market of microcomputer users who want to utilize these sources as efficiently as possible? It is my belief that we need to be in the forefront of developing end-user instruction, or we may be left out in the cold wondering what happened.

At Humboldt State we have been interested in trying to do some kind of end-user project; but with the usual problems of decreasing budget and staff, we had a difficult time selecting a starting point. After hearing a paper done by Susan Swords Steffen[2] at the 1984 Online meeting, where she described her program for teaching faculty at St. Xavier College in Chicago how to do their own searching, several of us at Humboldt State decided to do a similar project for Fall 1985.

We are beginning with the faculty because they are a smaller group and less equipment and staff time will be required (we hope). Also, requests for on-campus faculty workstations have been made and access to microcomputers is becoming easier. We regard this faculty end-user program as the jumping-off point for an end-user instruction program which will eventually (and I stress eventually, at this point) include all of our users.

Presently we are in the planning stages. Four of us will be team-teaching this workshop. The format is to be a one-day, six-hour workshop, followed by one hour of practice time scheduled at a later time with one of the four librarians involved in the workshop. For this first time we have received a small grant from the university to underwrite the computer and class materials cost. The first class will be offered free; and it is a one unit, faculty development class.

We plan on setting up four locations to do some searching the day of the workshop. We will be using one IBM-PC loaded with Menlo Corporation's Pro-Search, plus three terminals in various locations in the library.

Now that I have briefly described our program, I'd like to ask for questions and throw open the discussion to hear what other colleges and universities are doing in this area.

REFERENCES

1. Barbara Newlin, "On-Line Search Strategies," PC World 3, no. 5 (May 1985): pp. 226-233.

2. Susan Swords Steffen, "College Faculty Goes Online: Training Faculty to Search in a Liberal Arts College," in Online '84 Conference Proceedings (Weston, CT: Publications and Conferences for the Information Industry, 1984), pp. 232-238.

TEACHING MICROCOMPUTER LITERACY: NEW ROLES FOR ACADEMIC LIBRARIANS

Linda J. Piele, Judith Pryor, and Harold W. Tuckett
University of Wisconsin-Parkside
Kenosha, Wisconsin

Abstract. While microcomputer labs and software collections are increasingly a part of college and university libraries, most librarians are not instructing users in microcomputer literacy, despite the clear need of many users for such instruction. In many cases, librarians do not believe that it is their role to provide such instruction. This paper will contend that it is indeed their role, and that if one views microcomputers as important tools for information retrieval and management, librarians' role in teaching users about them is vital. By examining the experience of one academic library in assuming a central role in the admininistration of a microcomputer lab and in campus-wide microcomputer literacy instruction, changes in librarians' professional roles are suggested, and the implications of such a role are examined.

Keywords and Phrases. Microcomputers; bibliographic instruction; professional roles; computer literacy; information literacy; microcomputer labs.

Microcomputers and software collections for the use of patrons have become a feature of many college and university libraries over the past few years. In 1981, libraries adding such services were rare enough to be reported individually in the library press. By 1984, according to a survey reported in Library Journal, 45.7 percent of the college and university libraries responding make microcomputers available to the public and 43.4 percent do so with software.[1] In a survey of ARL libraries taken in January 1984, 24 of 85 respondents reported having microcomputer facilities for users.[2]

Colleges and universities looking for locations to place microcomputers for the use of students and faculty have tended to view any library with available space as a suitable location largely due to such factors as central location, long hours, ability to provide access and control for software, and service orientation. For their part, libraries have accepted, welcomed, or actively sought responsibility for these additional services. For most, support for the curriculum by providing access to instructional and application software has probably been the primary rationale. Other possible purposes included collection of data available on floppy disk and support for general computer literacy, end-user online searching, word processing, continuing education, and faculty development.[3]

Additionally, a few libraries have had special library educational missions in mind, such as the use of computer-assisted-instruction software for library instruction. Few, however, have considered the specialized teaching skills that instruction librarians possess and the implications of these skills for microcomputer labs. (A notable exception, as reported in the periodical Small Computers in Libraries, is the Mann Library Microcomputer Center at Cornell University.)[4]

A major problem faced by libraries adding microcomputers is the necessity of coping with the lack on the part of many users of microcomputer training and their overwhelming need for assistance. Methods adopted to deal with this problem range from posting signs advising patrons to go to the computer center for assistance to hiring and training student assistants to staff the area. Many patrons are not comfortable learning on their own; many don't even realize that they don't need to know how to program to use a microcomputer; and even if assistance is available, many are reluctant or uncomfortable in seeking it out. Thus, there is a strong need for various types of group training and instruction.

Even with this obvious need on the part of users, however, academic librarians--including instruction librarians--are not generally providing such instruction. Possible reasons for this situation may include a lack of clarity on many campuses as to the unit responsible for providing such assistance, lack of microcomputer skills and/or confidence on the part of librarians, and the fact that many librarians simply don't think it is their role to teach microcomputer skills--it sounds too much like teaching computer science.

This paper will take exception to these assumptions, particularly the last one. It will be argued that the microcomputer--far from being seen as a programmer's instrument--should be seen, at least as far as the needs of many faculty, staff, and students are concerned, as an information retrieval and management tool, and, as such, something with which librarians should be vitally involved. Furthermore, the implications of this point of view and developments in technology and telecommunications will have profound implications for the professional roles of academic librarians in the future. By examining the experience of one academic library in assuming a central role in the administration of a microcomputer lab and campus-wide microcomputer literacy instruction, one such appropriate role will be suggested, and the implications of such a professional role examined.

In the fall of 1982, a microcomputer lab was made available to the users of the Library/Learning Center at the University of Wisconsin-Parkside. This unit was chosen by the University administration as the most suitable to house and administer a campus microcomputer facility because of its service orientation and open and non-intimidating atmosphere.[5] Although it has grown considerably since that time, this site remains the sole microcomputer facility for this campus of approximately 5000 students. Two of the major goals of the lab were to support the curriculum and to provide a facility to promote general computer literacy for the entire campus community. For the reasons cited above, librarians soon realized that there was a strong need to offer general microcomputer instruction.

To respond to these needs, two librarians from the Public Services staff began regularly offering a hands-on general orientation workshop to introduce students, faculty, and staff to the use of microcomputers. After the need for follow-up workshops on several applications--word processing, file management, and electronic spreadsheets --became apparent, workshops on each of these applications were taught the following semester. All workshops were two-hours in length and taught in two-person teams, with librarians serving alternately as "presenter" and "trouble-shooter."

After approximately one year, the seven reference/instruction librarians in the Public Services Division reached the collective decision that they should all participate in this program. All librarians had attended in-house hands-on workshops similar to the orientation workshops, and many had trained themselves further in the use of microcomputers by learning to use a particular application program to accomplish a library or professional task. The team-teaching method allowed those who had not taught workshops before to work initially with one of the more experienced workshop leaders. Although most librarians found that teaching the workshops initially required extensive preparation and was stressful, all were reasonably comfortable in this role within a few months. As a result of the participation of a total of seven librarians as instructors, the library was able to offer a workshop approximately every two weeks without creating an unreasonable work load for any staff member and to expand its workshop offerings to include one on the use of bibliography management software.

Over the course of the preceding year and one-half, as librarians had increased their level of computer literacy and awareness, they had become aware that the objectives of the microcomputer instruction program should be expanded. The potential applications of microcomputers to library research tasks became more apparent with new information becoming available--in some cases exclusively---in machine readable format, whether on floppy or optical disks or via telecommunications. An online catalog was also in the foreseeable future. Librarians became convinced that instruction in information literacy--regardless of the format of the information in question--was an important goal of the bibliographic instruction program and that microcomputer literacy was an important sub-goal.

Librarians therefore developed a series of seminars directed at faculty on the use of microcomputers as a tool to enhance library-related research and teaching tasks. Included in the series were presentations on end-user searching, management of bibliographies and research notes, and presentation graphics. Unlike the workshop series, these seminars are more conceptual in nature. Relevant software is demonstrated, but no hands-on experience is offered. Plans call for inviting faculty and staff members from other campus units who have had specialized microcomputer expertise to participate as instructors in future seminars. Librarians also experimented on a pilot basis with incorporating instruction on these topics into the ongoing bibliographic instruction program.

The workshops and seminars have been both well-attended and well-received; formal evaluations, informal feedback, and librarians' perceptions have all been generally very positive. In terms of the specifics of designing and offering workshops, the hands-on instruction method turns out to be effective, particularly for novice computer users, whose most basic need is to use a microcomputer successfully. The hands-on approach was used in order to meet this need by minimizing theory and emphasizing a "learning by doing" approach. Assigning two students to each microcomputer works well for hands-on instruction; not only do they get sufficient hands-on experience, but they are often able to assist each other, reducing the amount of classroom time that must be devoted to trouble-shooting.

Hands-on workshops are, however, time-consuming for both students and instructors. Teams of at least two persons are essential for teaching introductory hands-on workshops of more than five persons. Trained student assistants serving as trouble-shooters can be used effectively in many cases as the second member of the team. The time-consuming nature of hands-on microcomputer instruction will require that strategies and methods for integrating it into the existing bibliographic instruction curriculum be carefully developed. Although researchers using a library can profit from use of a number of microcomputer applications, it takes a considerable amount of time to teach each of these skills thoroughly. It has proven to be unwise to attempt to have students incorporate more than one of these skills into the research process initially. A first step for many bibliographic instruction programs may be simply to incorporate information on library-owned software programs appropriate to library research-related tasks into classroom presentations for upper-division and graduate students.

Unlike the hands-on workshops, the seminars have assumed a basic level of familiarity with the use of microcomputers on the part of those attending. This format has turned out to be well-suited to meeting the need simply to make patrons aware of software suitable for particular purposes and how it might best be used. In general, teaching skills and experience gained previously by librarians active in bibliographic instruction programs have been helpful and relevant to the task of developing and teaching microcomputer workshops and seminars.

There have been a number of specific benefits at UW-Parkside resulting from the new role of academic librarians as instructors in microcomputer literacy. Many patrons who might otherwise never have utilized microcomputers have become enthusiastic beneficiaries of the productivity potential inherent in microcomputer applications. Faculty, in particular, have been prepared to introduce their students to discipline-specific applications of microcomputers which otherwise might have been ignored. Further, the emerging role of librarians as technologically adept professionals with expertise in the latest technology has enhanced the image of librarians with a number of faculty and administrators. Finally, the expertise gained by librarians in microcomputer applications has paid off in gains in operational efficiency, as the library staff has increasingly utilized micros for a variety of in-house applications.

Librarians have traditionally been the interface between patrons and information, possessing an understanding of the way information is organized while at the same time being able to work well with people. This fundamental role remains even with the new technology, but the skills needed by librarians, researchers, and students will change. As more sources of information become available via computer, librarians must assume leadership roles in working with users to insure their ability to access and manage this information.[6]

Librarians can play a key role in promoting general computer literacy on their campuses. The microcomputer is an important information retrieval and management tool, and librarians have an obligation to help users utilize it for research and information purposes. Further, as patrons increasingly use microcomputers to access information from remote locations, librarians' roles will be more concerned with consulting with and teaching users about the new technology. Librarians, more than perhaps any other group on campus, are attuned to working with people to access and manage information. Faculty are facing up to the necessity of integrating microcomputers into the curriculum. The assumption of a proactive and dynamic role by librarians will help them to play central roles in the technological future of the university.

REFERENCES

1. John Berry, "Library Use of Microcomputers: Massive and Growing," Library Journal 110:48-49 (Feb. 1, 1985).

2. Microcomputers in ARL Libraries (Washington, D.C.: Association of Research Libraries, Office of Management Studies, 1984), p. 6.

3. Linda J. Piele, "Summary of Survey Results," Newsletter of the ACRL Microcomputer Services in Academic Libraries Discussion Group (June 1985).

4. Howard Curtis, "The Mann Library Microcomputer Center," Small Computers in Libraries 4:8-9 (Dec. 1984).

5. Alan E. Guskin, Carla J. Stoffle and Barbara E. Baruth, "Library Future Shock: The Microcomputer Revolution and the New Role of the Library," College and Research Libraries 45:180-182 (May 1984).

6. Richard M. Dougherty and Wendy P. Lougee, "What Will Survive?" Library Journal 110:43-44 (Feb. 1, 1985).

THE EFFECT OF AN ENDUSER TRAINING PROGRAM ON AN ONLINE SEARCH SERVICE

Judith G. Robinson and Julia R. Shaw
University Library Services
Tompkins-McCaw Library
Virginia Commonwealth University

Keywords and Phrases. Enduser, Online Search Service, Evaluation.

University Library Services of Virginia Commonwealth University began an enduser training program in February of 1985 at Tompkins-McCaw Library on the Medical College of Virginia Campus. After reading numerous articles in the library journals concerning the possible impact of enduser searching, the librarians at Tompkins-McCaw Library became interested in the effect the training program would have on the library's Online Search Service.

A scan of the literature reveals how the library profession views the possible impact of enduser training. Hewison and Meadow express the idea that people involved in automation and who feel most comfortable with computers will become enduser searchers while those who are less computer literate will continue to use intermediaries. Haines, Janke, and Baker foresee that intermediaries will only be involved in more complex searches. Another trend predicted by Griffith is the evolution of the "non-professional" intermediaries who, while having no formal training, will become experts for their organizations. Janke also proposes that cost is a factor in the enduser versus intermediary executed search debate.

In order to determine any changes in the number or type of searches submitted to Tompkins-McCaw Library's Online Search Service due to the Enduser Training Program, the use of the search service by each trainee is being studied. Any computer searches requested by the enduser trainees during the past two fiscal years have been reviewed. All searches submitted by the trainees to the Library's Online Search Service during the next year will also be reviewed. Each search request is studied to establish the department and school of the requestor/trainee, the method of payment (grant, department budget code, or cash), the charges incurred by the patron, the number and dates of each search requested, and the level of difficulty of the search. Three levels of difficulty were established, basic, average, and sophisticated. A basic search consists of a one-term or author search. The average request includes combining two to three search concepts or thesarus terms, and the sophisticated search may involve coordination of numerous search items, free-text searching, registry number and cross-file execution.

Of the 48 endusers trained thus far, 24 have used the Library's Online Search Service within the last two years. Of those 24, 11 have used the service 1 time, 8 have used the service 3 to 4 times, and 4 have used the service 6 to 8 times. One participant is a research assistant for the Department of Surgery and has submitted 125 searches for the faculty and staff of the department during the past two years.

No decrease in the use of the Library's Online Search Service has been determined thus far. During the next year it is anticipated that as the endusers become more familiar with system commands and the mechanics of preparing a search strategy, their use of the Library's service may diminish or stop completely. The infrequency of search requests demonstrated by 11 of the trainees (1 request during the review period) may not encourage the kind of repetition needed to be comfortable with system commands. University Library Services is presently reviewing the charging system and may decide to raise the current charge of five dollars per file searched. If higher charges are implemented the Library's Online Search Service may no longer be less expensive than enduser searching. During the year, the progress of the enduser trainee from the Department of Surgery will be of particular interest due to the high number of searches received from that department.

As Griffith has predicted, the professional searcher may be replaced by the "non-professional".

Now that enduser training is a reality in libraries, speculation as to its effect can and should be replaced by efforts to obtain concrete figures. Models and means for obtaining these results are now open for discussion.

REFERENCES

1. Baker, Carole A. "Colleague: A Comprehensive Online Medical Library for End User." Medical Reference Quarterly 3 (Winter 1984): 13-27.

2. Griffith, Jeffery C. The Impact of the Enduser on the Online Profession. In Online '84 Conference Proceedings. Weston, Conn.: Publications & Conferences for the Information Industry, 1984.

3. Haines, Judith S. "Experiences in Training End-User Searchers." Online 6 (November 1982) 14-23.

4. Hewison, Nancy S. "Whatever Shall We Do About User-Friendly Online." Medical Reference Quarterly 2 (Winter 1983): 67-70.

5. Janke, Richard V. Just What is an Enduser? In Online '84 Conference Proceedings. Weston, Conn.: Publications & Conferences for the Information Industry, 1984.

6. Meadow, Charles F. Individualized Instruction for Data Access. In 1st International Online Information Meeting. Oxford: Learned Information, 1977.

COLLECTION MANAGEMENT

BREAKING ROLE AND SPATIAL BARRIERS:
THE SYLLABUS EXCHANGE IN BIOETHICS FOSTERS COLLABORATION BETWEEN
A RESEARCH LIBRARY, INTERDISCIPLINARY SCHOLARS AND CLINICAL PRACTITIONERS

Judith A. Adams
Oklahoma State University

and

Mary Carrington Coutts
Kennedy Institute of Ethics
Georgetown University

Abstract. The National Reference Center for Bioethics Literature at the Kennedy Institute of Ethics has responded to the pressing need for new teaching programs in the interdisciplinary field of medical ethics by establishing a Clearinghouse for Curriculum Development and a Syllabus Exchange. Syllabi are solicited from academic, medical school, and high school faculty worldwide. A database is created utilizing the M300 microcomputer and dBase III software. The Syllabus Exchange and the Clearinghouse allow the research library to assume a new role as communications facilitator for a network of scholars and clinical practitioners traditionally separated by disciplines and professional activities.

Keywords and Phrases. Curriculum Clearinghouse, Syllabus Exchange, Special Libraries, Medical Ethics, Interdisciplinary Research.

The Joseph and Rose Kennedy Institute of Ethics was established at Georgetown University in 1971, with incentive grants from the Joseph P. Kennedy, Jr. Foundation, to stimulate scholarly dialog and assist policy analysis of issues surrounding medical care and biomedical research. The accelerating pace of technological advances in medicine during the last two decades, the concomitant revolution in treatment modes, and the emerging ability of medicine and genetic research to alter the lives of individuals have incited widespread concern, regulatory and legal action, as well as constant dialog among medical professionals, policy makers, academic scholars, and the general public. Everyone is aware of the media attention and ethical deliberation surrounding such issues as the artificial heart, Baby Jane Doe, Baby Fae, resuscitation decisions in hospitals, living wills, abortion, the allocation of economic resources in health care, gene therapy, reproductive technologies such as in vitro fertilization and embryo freezing, and the rights of animals in research.

THE DEMAND FOR HUMANISTIC MEDICAL EDUCATION

The academic discipline of Bioethics, that is, the analysis of ethical, moral, and values issues arising in medicine and biomedical research, is obviously a highly interdisciplinary field which has emerged only in the last decade and has firmly established itself in colleges, universities, and professional schools. In the 1981 compendium, Human Values Teaching Programs for Health Professionals, Edmund Pellegrino reports on the burgeoning of formal teaching programs devoted to human values issues in medicine. While eleven programs were in existence in 1972, sixty-five universities and medical schools had established such programs by 1981.[1] Outside the professional schools, there has also been an explosion of interest in bioethics along with ethics in other professions, such as engineering, business, and law. The Teaching of Ethics in Higher Education, a report published in 1980 by the Hastings Center, states that there are bioethics courses "by the hundreds" at the undergraduate level.[2]

The need for assistance in course development in the area of the humanistic aspects of medicine has been accentuated in recent months by the publication of the findings of the Panel on the General Professional Education of the Physician and College Preparation for Medicine of the Association of American Medical Colleges. Their 1984 report, Physicians for the Twenty-First Century,[3] finds an urgent need for extensive integration of the humanities and social sciences in the professional education of physicians. In coming to a conclusion similar to that voiced in A Nation At Risk: The Imperative for Educational Reform,[4] the Panel perceived a "continuing erosion of general education . . . an erosion that has not been arrested but is instead accelerating." The present education system devoted almost totally to the acquisition of clinical, technical, and scientific "knowledge" is seen to be insufficient for the development of a good physician. The report asserts that "all physicians, regardless of specialty, require a common foundation of knowledge, skills, values, and attitudes . . . . Ethical sensitivity and moral integrity, combined with equanimity, humanity, and self-knowledge, are quintessential qualities of all physicians." The acquisition of these attributes can be fostered, the Panel believes, by some shifting of emphasis from memorization of facts to studies in the social sciences and humanities on both the baccalaureate and professional school levels.[5]

Additional impetus for new course development has come from recommendations for a basic curriculum for the teaching of ethics in medical schools developed and published in 1985 in the New England Journal of Medicine by a distinguished group of physicians and ethicists. Having surveyed the current status of the teaching of medical ethics, the group finds "the need for the application of ethical knowledge and skills in medicine sufficiently compelling to justify a recommendation that all medical schools require basic instruction in the subject." Such a curriculum should "provide practicing physicians with the conceptual moral reasoning, and interactional abilities to deal successfully with most of the moral issues they confront in their daily practice."[6]

THE NATIONAL REFERENCE CENTER FOR BIOETHICS LITERATURE

The Kennedy Institute's National Reference Center for Bioethics Literature is the only library in the world devoted to the acquisition, organization, and dissemination of materials in the interdisciplinary field of Bioethics.[7] The Institute and the National Library of Medicine also support the Bioethics Information Retrieval Project which produces the computer database, BIOETHICSLINE, and its annual print equivalent, the highly regarded Bibliography of Bioethics.[8] For twelve years, the library and the Information Retrieval Project have collaborated to assemble a comprehensive collection of the bioethics literature, and to provide a sophisticated, efficient system for bibliographic control and access. The activities, publications, and collections of the National Reference Center and Information Retrieval System, including publication of the major research tools in the discipline, have supported scholarship, government policy making, and course development throughout the emergence and establishment of this field, not only in the United States but also by assisting professors and practitioners from around the world, notably, Great Britain, Australia, France, Germany, Spain, Canada, Belgium, and Japan.

In early 1985, the Kennedy Institute of Ethics applied for a grant from the National Library of Medicine to expand its Library staff, facilities, and services in order to establish the National Reference Center for Bioethics Literature.[9] One of the new roles supported by this grant is a Clearinghouse for Curriculum Development in Bioethics. The library staff has recognized needs for both centralized collection of curriculum materials, and the development of a mechanism for contact among professionals teaching in this field. The establishment of the Clearinghouse is the first structured means for those teaching bioethics in universities, medical and nursing schools, as well as high schools to exchange information with their colleagues regarding course design, content, and materials. The project expands the role of the research library from collection and dissemination to enhancement and structuring of the "invisible college" of scholars and practitioners in the emergent field of bioethics. Since those developing courses in this area come from diverse disciplines including philosophy, psychology, sociology, clinical medicine, humanities, policy studies, law, and biology, they do not have the advantage of established disciplinary channels, such as associations, journals or newsletters, to address curriculum needs. We feel the Clearinghouse for Curriculum Development, with its Syllabus Exchange and its publications activities, is filling this gap and providing several vehicles for increased communication resulting in the enhancement of course design and content. Allen B. Veaner, in his recent assessment of the next decade in academic librarianship, calls for the implementation of mechanisms to gain exposure for the "invisible" activities and the "abstract constructs" which constitute academic librarianship. The Clearinghouse successfully provides the staff with one of the mechanisms suggested by Veaner, namely, "collaboration with faculty as expert intermediaries in the research process."[10]

THE SYLLABUS EXCHANGE

The Clearinghouse for Curriculum Development solicits and acquires syllabi, course descriptions, reading lists, study and examination questions from faculty who have developed courses in the field. Staff decided that course materials from the high school to professional school levels would be acquired since requests for assistance received in the library over the years reflect significant course activity from primary education to medical schools and continuing education for professionals.

Dissemination of syllabi and course materials is achieved by a Syllabus Exchange. A computer database has been developed to assist organization of and access to syllabi and other course materials. Utilizing the M300 microcomputer and dBase III software for database construction, information retrieval, and report generation, staff may access syllabi and other course materials by several fields: name of course instructor, course title, subject, level of course, and institution. Boolean logic and textword searching capabilities are also possible.

Visibility for the Syllabus Exchange and dissemination of its materials are fostered by the production of two recurring curriculum development publications. A listing of syllabi received by the Clearinghouse is published quarterly as an appendix to the National Reference Center's monthly publication, New Titles in Bioethics, a subject classified listing of new books and other substantial publications acquired by the National Reference Center. Each entry provides course title, name of professor, institution, an indication of course level or student audience, and subject keywords assigned by the National Reference Center staff. Following are examples of entries from the first quarterly listing.

SE0004 PRINCIPLES AND METAPHORS IN BIOMEDICAL ETHICS. James F. Childress. Kennedy Institute of Ethics, Georgetown University. Fall, 1985. Graduate. 14p. (Physician Patient Relationship, Euthanasia, Withholding Treatment, Public Policy, Resource Allocation, Organ Transplantation, Bioethics.)

SE0008 TAKING HUMAN LIFE: CASES AND PRINCIPLES. J. Bryan Hehir. Kennedy Institute of Ethics, Georgetown University. Fall, 1984. Undergraduate. 4p. (War, Abortion, Euthanasia, Value of Life.)

SE0011 MEDICINE IN THE COMMUNITY: ETHICS TUTORIAL. Neville Hicks. Department of Community Medicine, University of Adelaide (Australia). 1985. Graduate Medical Education. 4p. (Ethics, Bioethics.)

SE0016 LEGAL AND BIOETHICAL ISSUES IN HEALTH CARE MANAGEMENT. Cynthia Northrup and Gladys White. School of Nursing, Georgetown University. Fall, 1984. Graduate. 4p. (Nursing Ethics, Law and Medicine, Allowing to Die, Withholding Treatment.)

SE0019 ETHICAL ISSUES IN HEALTH CARE. LeRoy Walters. Kennedy Institute of Ethics, Georgetown University. Fall, 1985. Graduate. 4p. (Resource Allocation, In Vitro Fertilization, Gene Therapy, Bioethics.)

SE0025 COST-BENEFIT ANALYSIS IN HEALTH CARE. Alain C. Enthoven. Graduate School of Business, Stanford University. Spring, 1986. Graduate. 6p. (Economics, Costs and Benefits, Technology Assessment.)

SE0027 STUDY GUIDE IN MEDICAL ETHICS (independent study program). Richard C. Mc Millan. Department of Psychiatry and Behavioral Science, School of Medicine, Mercer University. 1985. Graduate Medical Education. 17p. (Bioethics.)

SE0029 THEOLOGY AND ETHICS OF BEHAVIOR CONTROL. Clyde J. Steckel. United Theological Seminary. Spring, 1985. Graduate. 7p. (Behavior Control, Psychosurgery, Electroconvulsive Therapy, Psychopharmacology.)

Furthermore, the full text of a selected outstanding syllabus is published as a regular feature of the Kennedy Institute of Ethics Newsletter. Syllabi chosen for publication in this manner are accompanied by a brief discussion of course rationale and objectives prepared by the course instructor, reading lists, and occasionally examination questions.

Faculty designing courses can contact the National Reference Center and Clearinghouse via a toll-free telephone number (800-MED-ETHX). Many requestors wish to receive specific syllabi listed in the quarterly lists published by the Clearinghouse; others need unspecified syllabi geared toward certain audience levels or subjects, such as health care policy, reproductive technologies, death and dying issues, patient's rights, resource allocation and justice in health care delivery. Appropriate syllabi are quickly and accurately identified by searching the Syllabus Exchange database. For requests that must be mailed, a $2.00 per syllabus charge is assessed to cover photocopying, staff, and distribution costs. Charges are payable via check or major credit card through the National Reference Center's document delivery service.

The National Reference Center and the Kennedy Institute of Ethics had several means already in place for initially publicizing the establishment of the Syllabus Exchange. Information on projected services and requests for submission of syllabi and other course materials have been printed in New Titles in Bioethics. In publication since 1977, New Titles has approximately 250 subscribers who represent a worldwide core group of bioethicists. In addition, a special mailing, geared to provide focused visibility, was routed to all members of the Kennedy Institute of Ethics. Similar information is also appended to issues of the National Reference Center's Scope Notes publications. Scope Notes are 10-20 page issue briefs on topics of current interest in bioethics, such as Baby Fae, Living Wills, and Ethics Committees in Hospitals. Scope Notes receive wide distribution assisted by publicity for specific issues in such publications as Library Journal and the Hastings Center Report, the "gatekeeper" journal for the field of bioethics.

Publicity releases have also been submitted for publication in the major journals in bioethics as well as important publications in the wider field of Science, Technology, Society (STS) Studies, namely: Hastings Center Report, Journal of Medical Ethics (England), Bioethics News (Australia), Science, Technology and Human Values (Harvard-MIT), STS: Curriculum Newsletter of the Lehigh University Science, Technology and Society Program, the Newsletter of the Teachers' Clearinghouse for Science and Society Education in New York City, and the SSTS Reporter of the Science Through Science, Technology and Society program at Pennsylvania State University.

The Clearinghouse for Curriculum Development and its Syllabus Exchange are new and their success cannot yet be accurately assessed. Depending on response to the services, the National Reference Center and the Institute will consider publication of a paperback volume of the full texts of selected syllabi.[11] Another activity which may gather support is the offering of a curriculum development workshop for faculty in the field of bioethics. End user access to the Syllabus Exchange database, electronic mail, distribution of the entire database or subsets on diskettes are options that will be appraised in the future, depending on the usage and utility of the database and services.

The National Reference Center for Bioethics Literature and previously the Bioethics Library have always played active roles in supporting research and teaching in the field of bioethics. An international community of researchers, students, and professional practitioners depend on its comprehensive collections, as well as its organization and dissemination efforts. With the Clearinghouse for Curriculum Development and the Syllabus Exchange, a research library and database producer assumes a new role as a communications facilitator of a network of scholars and clinical practitioners traditionally separated by a diversity of disciplines and professional activities. At the present time, when the need for the fostering of humanistic values and ethical sensitivity in professional as well as general education has been recognized and curriculum modification is being demanded by eloquent and prestigious spokespersons, the research/special library can emerge as a major force for the implementation of innovative cross-disciplinary teaching programs.

REFERENCES

1. Edmund D. Pellegrino, "Introduction," Human Values Teaching Programs for Health Professionals, edited by Thomas K. McElhinney, (Ardmore, Pa.: Whitmore Publishing Co., 1981), p. v.

2. The Teaching of Ethics in Higher Education; A Report By the Hastings Center (Hastings-on-Hudson, N.Y.: Hastings Center, 1980), pp. v, 5. This assertion is also supported by the listing of specific courses in the EVIST Resource Directory: A Directory of Programs and Courses in the Field of Ethics and Values in Science and Technology (Washington, D.C.: American Association for the Advancement of Science, 1978). Pages 116-160 cite 337 undergraduate and graduate courses dealing with social/philosophical perspectives on health care, the life sciences, and the behavioral sciences.

3. Physicians for the Twenty-First Century; Report of the Panel on the General Professional Education of the Physician and College Preparation for Medicine (Washington, D.C.: Association of American Medical Colleges, 1984).

4. U.S. National Commission on Excellence in Education, A Nation At Risk: The Imperative for Educational Reform (Washington, D.C.: Government Printing Office, 1983).

5. Physicians for the Twenty-First Century, pp. xi, xii, 1-4.

6. Charles M. Culver, et al., "Basic Curricular Goals in Medical Ethics," New England Journal of Medicine 312: 253-256 (24 January 1985).

7. The National Reference Center for Bioethics Literature presently holds over 10,000 books; a twelve-year collection of over 150 journals in bioethics and supporting disciplines, a subject-classified collection of over 40,000 article-length documents including court decisions, bills, laws, newspaper articles, articles from scholarly journals, and pamphlets.

8. Bibliography of Bioethics, Vols. 1-9 edited by LeRoy Walters, Vols. 10- edited by LeRoy Walters and Tamar Joy Kahn (Vols. 1-6: Detroit: Gale Research, 1975-1980; Vols. 7-9: New York: Free Press, 1981-1983; Vols.10- : Washington, D.C.: Kennedy Institute of Ethics, 1984-). The BIOETHICSLINE database is available in the MEDLARS system of the National Library of Medicine.

9. Program Announcement REA-NIH-NLM-EP-85-1.

10. Allen B. Veaner, "1985 to 1995: The Next Decade in Academic Librarianship, Part I," College and Research Libraries 46: 209-229 (May 1985), see esp. p. 216.

11. A published collection of syllabi for another interdisciplinary field, History of Technology Studies, has proven to be highly successful. See The Machine in the University: Sample Course Syllabi for the History of Technology and Technology Studies, comp. and ed. by Stephen H. Cutcliffe and the Technology Studies and Education Committee for the Society for the History of Technology (Bethlehem, Pa.: Lehigh University Science, Technology and Society Program, 1983).

COMPUTER ACCESSIBLE MATERIAL IN THE
ACADEMIC LIBRARY: AVOIDING THE KLUDGE

Katherine S. Chiang
Albert R. Mann Library
Cornell University
Ithaca, NY 14853-4301

Abstract. Computer accessible material should be an integral part of an academic library collection. This paper discusses the issues to be considered when constructing a program for the collection and service of these new formats.

Keywords and Phrases. Microcomputer software, Collection development, Microcomputers, Academic libraries.

KLUDGE

In computer jargon a makeshift solution to a programming problem, usually introduced to solve a last minute bug, is called a 'kludge'. It is the lazy, or desperate, programmer's alternative to redesigning a program. Some software programs are kludges from beginning to end -- jury-rigged constructions that work, but require band-aid patches at every turn.

As libraries add computers and computer readable material to their collections a kludge can result. It is all too easy to purchase a program, then consider how to catalog it, and when a patron requests it on loan, create a circulation policy. That kludge is compounded when, ten minutes later, the patron returns with a question about the program, and an on-the-spot decision is made on how much reference help will be offered.

After a year of this system a library may have a set of policies on computer readable materials. But it will be a kludge of the highest order, a poorly constructed, hot-spot approach to library collections and services that is inconsistent, inefficient, and unprofessional.

Many things can suffer from this failure to plan. Mistakes are expensive because the learning curve is high for these new technologies and much staff time can be lost on false starts. Also, the chances of obtaining adequate funding from the parent institution may be jeopardized by an unsystematic approach.

THE MANN LIBRARY PROGRAM

A library must have a plan; that fact was recognized several years ago by the administration of the Mann Library at Cornell. They decided to create a comprehensive program to integrate computer accessible material into the collection and services of the library. The skeleton of that program is now in place. Clear definitions of the philosophies and policies which govern computer accessed material at Mann have been established.

Two events were pivotal to the completion of this initial phase; the library was designated as one of three sites for a College funded microcomputer facility with two full time staff lines, and a librarian specifically responsible for computer accessed material was hired. With those facilities and staff in place the creation of the program proceeded smoothly.

The field of computer readable materials has crawled out of infancy into adolescence. And, like a teenager, it is completely uncontrollable, growing unpredictably, at an alarming rate, and shifting constantly. This inherent unpredictability required we work simultaneously on the general and specific aspects of the program, deciding on its overall scheme as we filled in the details.

First we addressed several philosophical problems which center around an a priori premise: there will be no discrimination against information based on its format, with the corollary: computer accessed material should be integrated into the collection. Thus our existing philosophies of library collections development and services apply to this new area.

However, the application of the basic philosophies to the computer formats requires careful thought. Obviously different policies on physical access are necessary due to hardware constraints, the licensing conventions of the microcomputer software industry, and the levels of expertise needed to extract data from mainframe tapes and online systems.

But another, more subtle, difference exists. Software can exploit the 'intelligent' nature of the microcomputer to produce a new kind of information that has no print equivalent. We strove for a balance between the extremes of abandoning our established policies because the format is new and presents physical problems, and ignoring the differences the 'intelligence' of the computer brings to information, since that would be to ignore the potential of the medium.

Our ultimate goal is an elegant program: well designed, flexible enough to grow into new technological developments, able to absorb errors, and with a logical, efficient flow of work and services. We want a program patrons will immediately perceive as credible and professional.

COLLECTION DEVELOPMENT AND SERVICES

We divided the design of the program into two sections: collection development, and services. We wrote a new program for computer readable information, but the mission behind the collection did not change; we collect to meet the teaching and research needs of the Cornell community. Therefore the focus remained primary over secondary sources (i.e. research results over textbooks), and sources of academic information over personal computing needs (i.e. Census data rather than a tax computation package.)

We presently collect data (accessed either by microcomputers or mainframes), non-bibliographic databases available online, and microcomputer applications software -- subject programs and generic office productivity programs that either can be used to access and control information or are heavily used on campus. (Online bibliographic databases are already integrated into our system.) As information in mass storage systems like laser or CD-ROM disks are published they too will be added to the collection.

We collect anything accessible through our hardware. This is not seen as a limitation on our collection scope because if necessary we would obtain the hardware required to access any material essential to our mission.

Microcomputer software

Microcomputer applications software can be subdivided into subject and generic programs. To refine our collection scope, subject programs were further divided into computer assisted instruction (CAI), decision, and analysis programs.

CAI programs are written to teach the user. These programs parallel the programmed learning texts which the library does not purchase, and we are not collecting CAI packages.

Analysis packages contain programs or formulae to process data input by the user, their closest print parallels are books of formulae or papers on methodology and techniques. Minitab, for example, performs statistical operations on data input by the user. We purchase relevant packages, but will rarely collect more than one package using the same formulae.

Decision aid programs integrate programs or formulae and resident data with data input by the user into the final results. The nutrition, or diet analysis programs fall into this category. The user can enter the food consumed in a meal, and the program calculates calorie, vitamin and mineral consumption based on the user data and the food composition tables resident in the program. This sequence parallels the process patrons follow in the library as they gather data and analytical techniques from the literature and combine that information with data they have gathered. We purchase relevant packages, but as with analytical programs, we do not duplicate programs that use the same base data and analysis.

By far the majority of programs produced are what can be called generic productivity programs. Hundreds of these programs exist for equally as many applications. We listed the applications that might be of interest to academics and refined that list using the premise that our primary responsibility is to assist patrons in the control of published information, especially bibliographic information. Any generic packages that directly, or indirectly, assist patrons in this mission are appropriate to our collection.

The core categories in this area are:
- bibliographic file management programs that can process external (downloaded) and manually entered files, search them, and formulate output to user specifications.
- expert systems that apply analytical programs to a knowledge base constructed by the user.
- online search aids or gateway systems that provide an interface between the online searcher and the database. We are comprehensively collecting either working or demonstration versions of programs in the above categories.

Programs of secondary importance include:
- communications programs that establish protocols for data transfer between computers, allowing remote access to databases.
- indexing programs that aid in the creation of book or article indexes.
- database management programs that can be used to organize and retrieve information, and are often used to access numeric data on disk. We are collecting representative packages in these categories.

We acquire representative examples of word processing programs because they can be used to reformat downloaded files for import into bibliographic file managers, and we acquire spreadsheet and statistical programs that can be used to access numeric data on floppy disks.

Other programs of academic interest, such as authoring and graphics programs, are not being collected at this time.

Data

We collect both microcomputer and mainframe accessible data, including textual/numeric, full text, calculative, and directory or reference information. We duplicate print sources if the machine readable format provides additional analytical flexibility. We do not collect undocumented data, considering it the computerized equivalent of unpublished research notes.

We obtain access to any online databases containing information within our collection scope. We will evaluate those systems requiring subscription fees much as we do serial subscriptions.

SERVICES

Service for such a collection could range from technical support of the hardware, programming, and assistance in running a program to handing the patron a disk and a manual.

We divided our services into three levels, to be defined for each area of our collection. Our most basic level is reference; we have minimal knowledge of a program, are aware of what is available, where packages are indexed, and the individuals on campus willing to consult.

Our second service level is formal group instruction, either in the concepts and/or the use of categories of programs, or of individual packages, this requires we maintain a working knowledge of the programs involved.

Our highest service level is consulting. In certain areas we give individual instruction and advice on the concepts or use of categories of programs and individual packages. An in-depth knowledge of a program is required at this level.

We are committed to the consulting level for bibliographic file management programs, expert systems for the microcomputer and online search aids/gateway programs. For most of the other applications software and data we collect we provide instructional or reference level assistance, although, as always, that is subject to change.

CONCLUSIONS

The development of a computer accessible material program is challenging and exciting. Such a collection can provide library patrons with an unprecedented level of information. We are the experts in the organization of information and its retrieval and we can dispel the stereotype of our profession as hidebound Keepers-of-the-Books if we coolly and competently assume control of information in whatever form it appears.

A MODEL INTERACTIVE AUTOMATED ACQUISITIONS SYSTEM

Colleen Cook
Texas A&M University Library
College Station, Texas

Keywords and Phrases. Acquisitions systems, automated library systems, interactive library systems, interfaced library systems, direct transmission, linking systems

Over the past decade the bibliographic utilities, as well as publishers and book vendors, have designed and marketed acquisitions systems. Some libraries have developed local systems, while others have acquired an acquisitions package as one among several functions in a multipurpose, integrated turnkey system. Each of these acquisitions systems has inherent strengths and weaknesses concomitant with the originator's major purpose in system design. For many systems the acquisitions function was merely a by-product of a system largely designed for other purposes. The acquisitions process presents needs that must be specifically addressed in a system tailor-made to satisfy acquisitions requirements. As yet no system designed has fully met the diverse needs of academic libraries in 1986.

An ideal acquisitions system for an academic library would be locally-based, integrated into a multi-purpose automated system, and interfaced with databases nationally to address the following considerations presented by the acquisitions process. An acquisitions system should be designed:

1. to verify in-print status
2. to verify local processing status, e.g., owned, on-order, claimed, received, in-process, tickler, etc.
3. to verify bibliographic data
4. to transfer bibliographic information automatically
5. to minimize turnaround time from point of order to receipt of book.

To satisfy these requirements, the components and interfaces of a model acquisitions system might be described as follows:

1) the Local System

Many acquisitions routines are condusive to local system applications -- e.g. fund accounting, in-house tracking of orders, printing of orders, etc. Ideally, acquisitions in-process information should be available in an in-house database so that library users might know whether a book is on-order when inquiring the local online catalog. The on-order/in-process database should also be searched for duplication of outstanding orders during the ordering process. Bibliographic data should be transferred to a local system from a vendor, publisher or bibliographic utility database if at all possible.

2) Bowker Databases

The online equivalent of Books in Print and similar tools should be searched to determine in-print status and cost.

3) Dealer and Publisher Databases

Once in-print status is verified, librarians decide whether to order a title from a vendor or directly from a publisher. This decision involves a classic time vs. money trade-off. Ordering directly from a publisher is the fastest and surest route, but vendors oftentimes supply warehoused materials at substantial discounts. As a result online verifiability of stock availability in vendor and publisher warehouses would be of substantial benefit to librarians and would alleviate the guesswork involved in supplier selection.

Once the decision is made from whom to order a book, a substantial savings in time could be realized if orders were transmitted directly to suppliers online through direct transmission links.

4) OCLC or Other Bibliographic Databases

Bibliographic databases would be accessed to transfer orders not found in Bowker databases, but which a library wanted to order anyway--e.g., foreign publications, ephemeral publications, out-of-print publications. This automatic transmission of data would reduce the requisite number of keystrokes needed to order, and would trap information in a standardized format alleviating the need to tag acquisitions/ordering information when merging into a local bibliographic database.

The following questions are posed by the scenario described above:
1) Does the model described adequately meet the needs of academic libraries in an acquisitions system?

2) Is the model acquisitions system as described feasible and practical?

3) What is the priority ranking of the various interfaces outlined above?

4) What is the trade-off threshold for cost vs. convenience in interfacing the various systems described?

5) How can a discussion of an interlocking system as described be initiated among the interested parties? What body should initiate the discussion? How?

ACKNOWLEDGMENTS

The author gratefully acknowledges the assistance of Tim Saito, Systems Programmer, Texas A&M University Library, in the preparation of the illustrations to this manuscript.

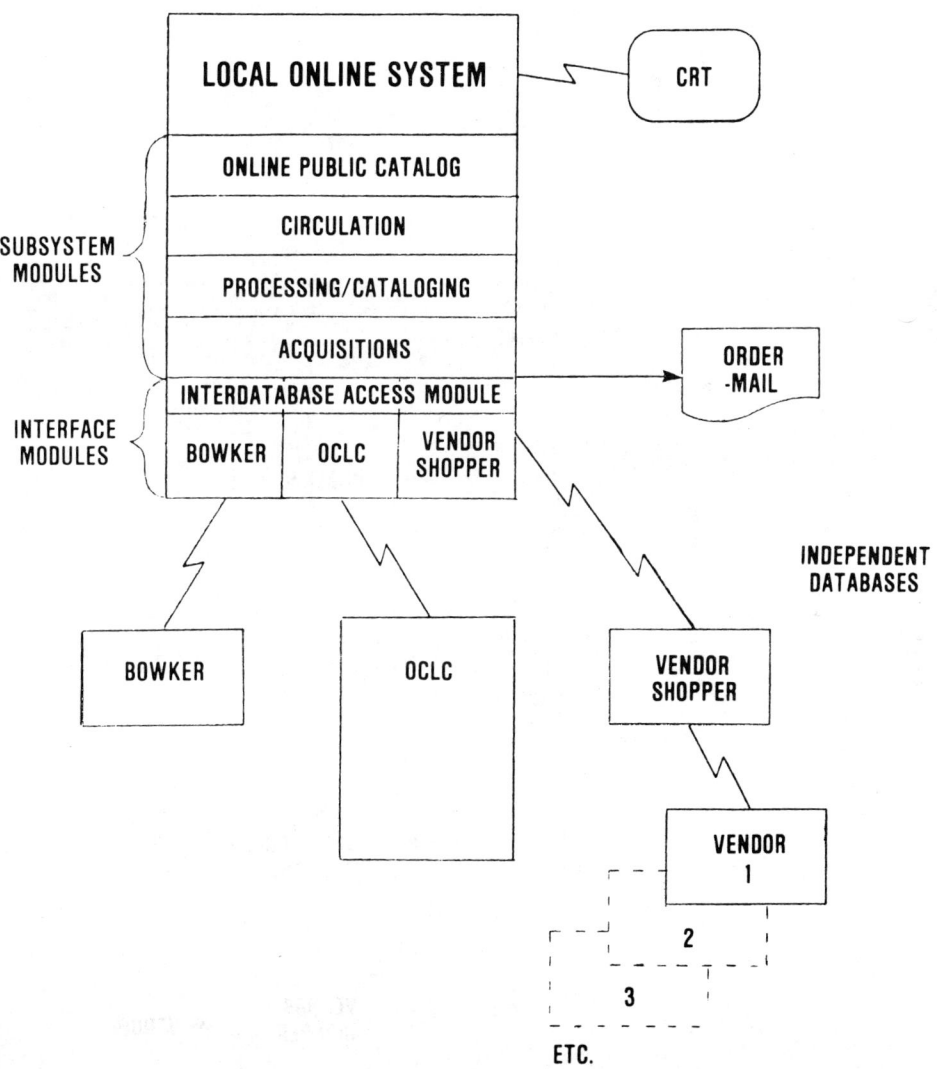

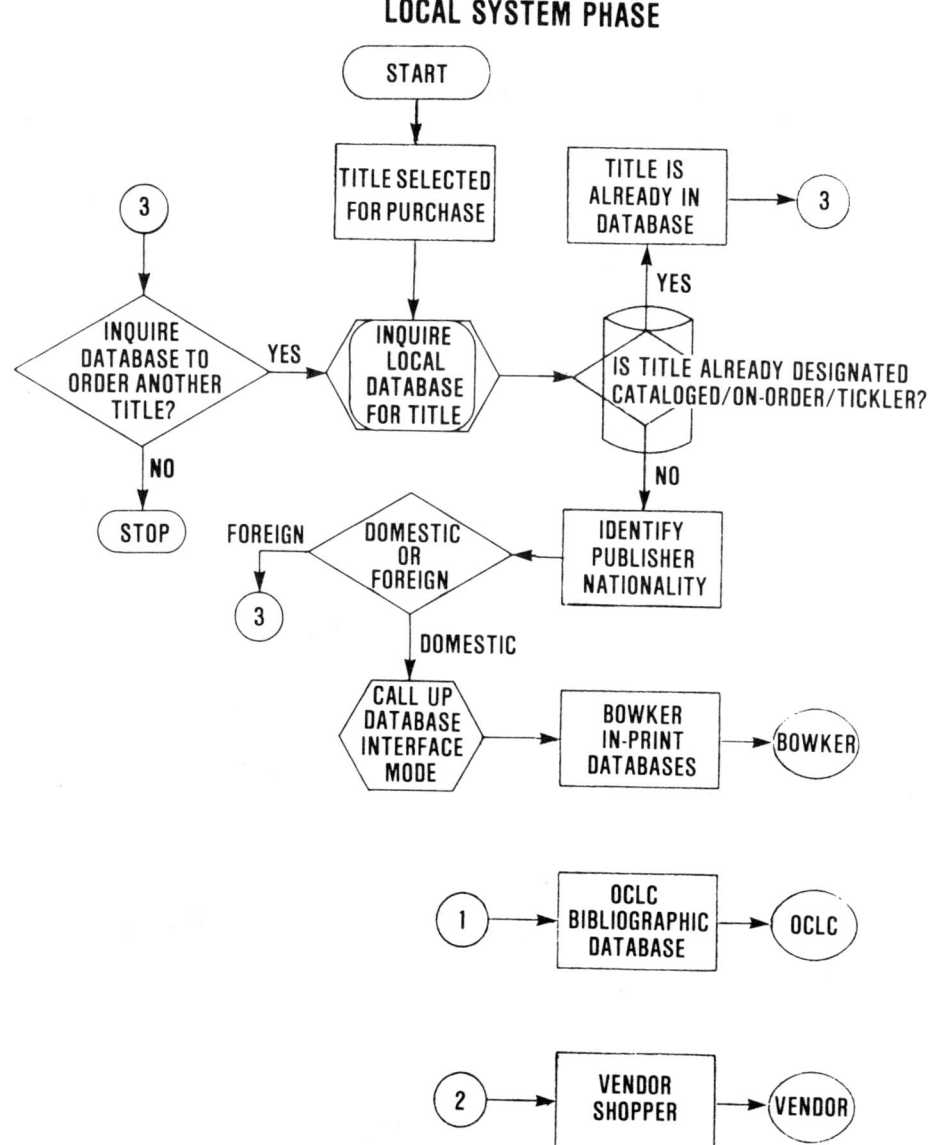

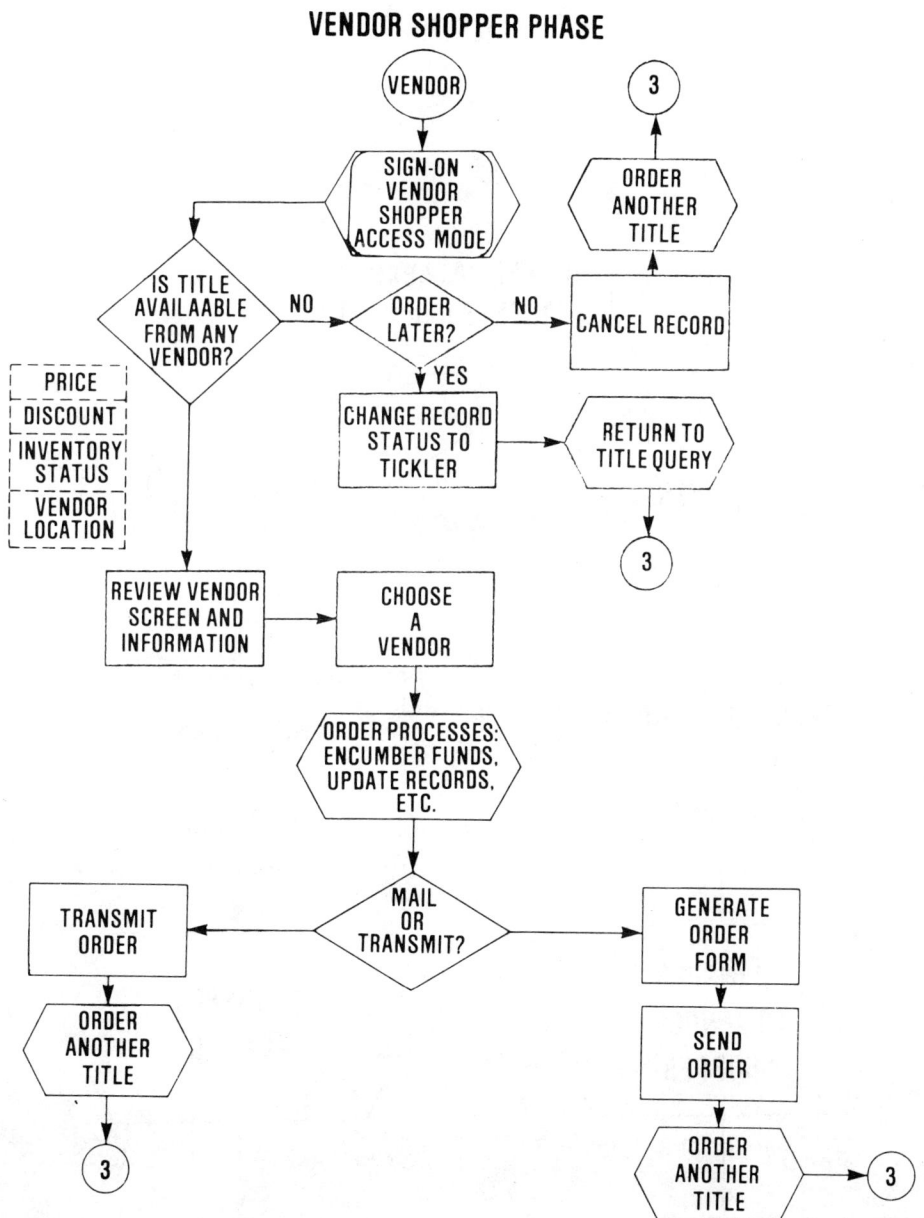

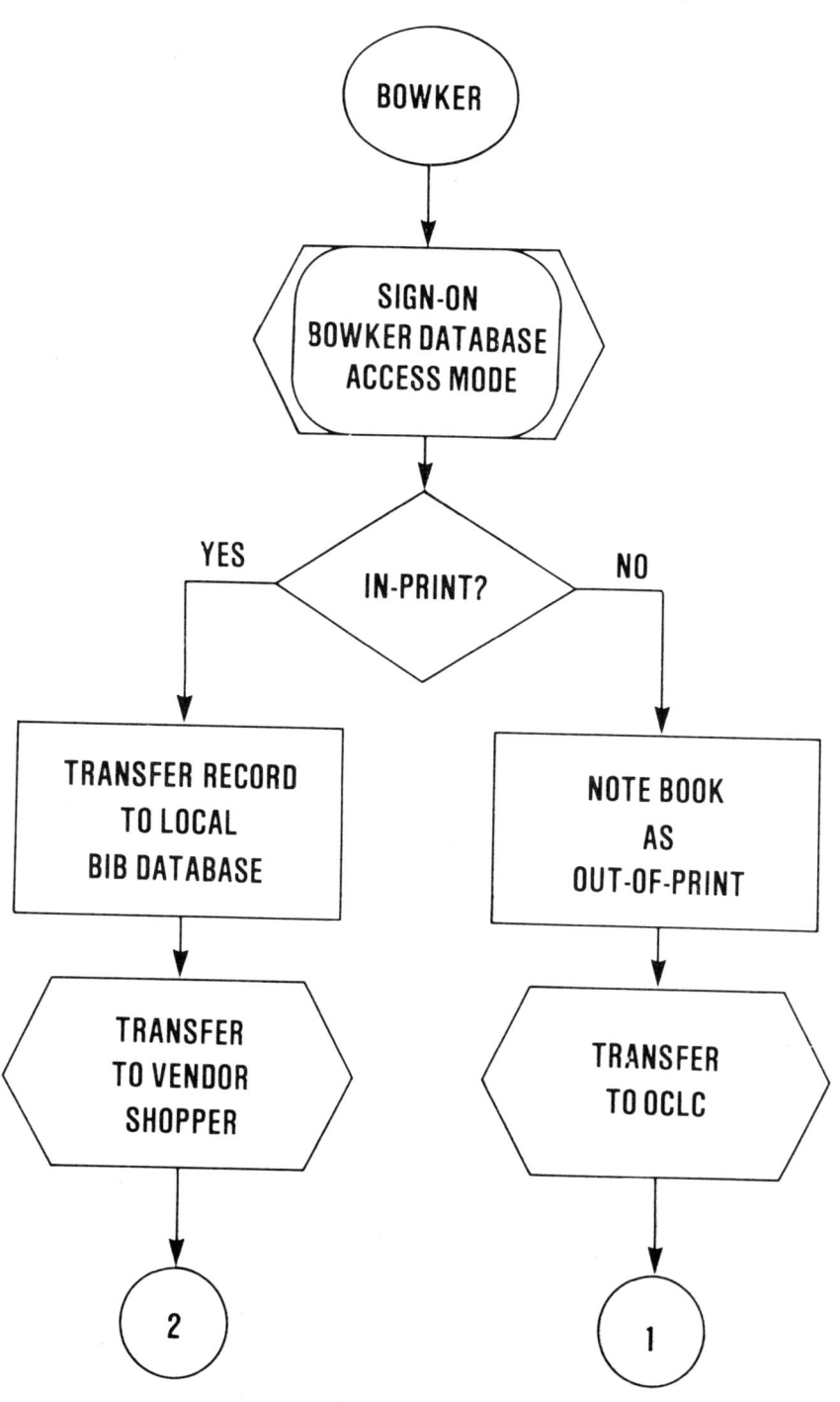

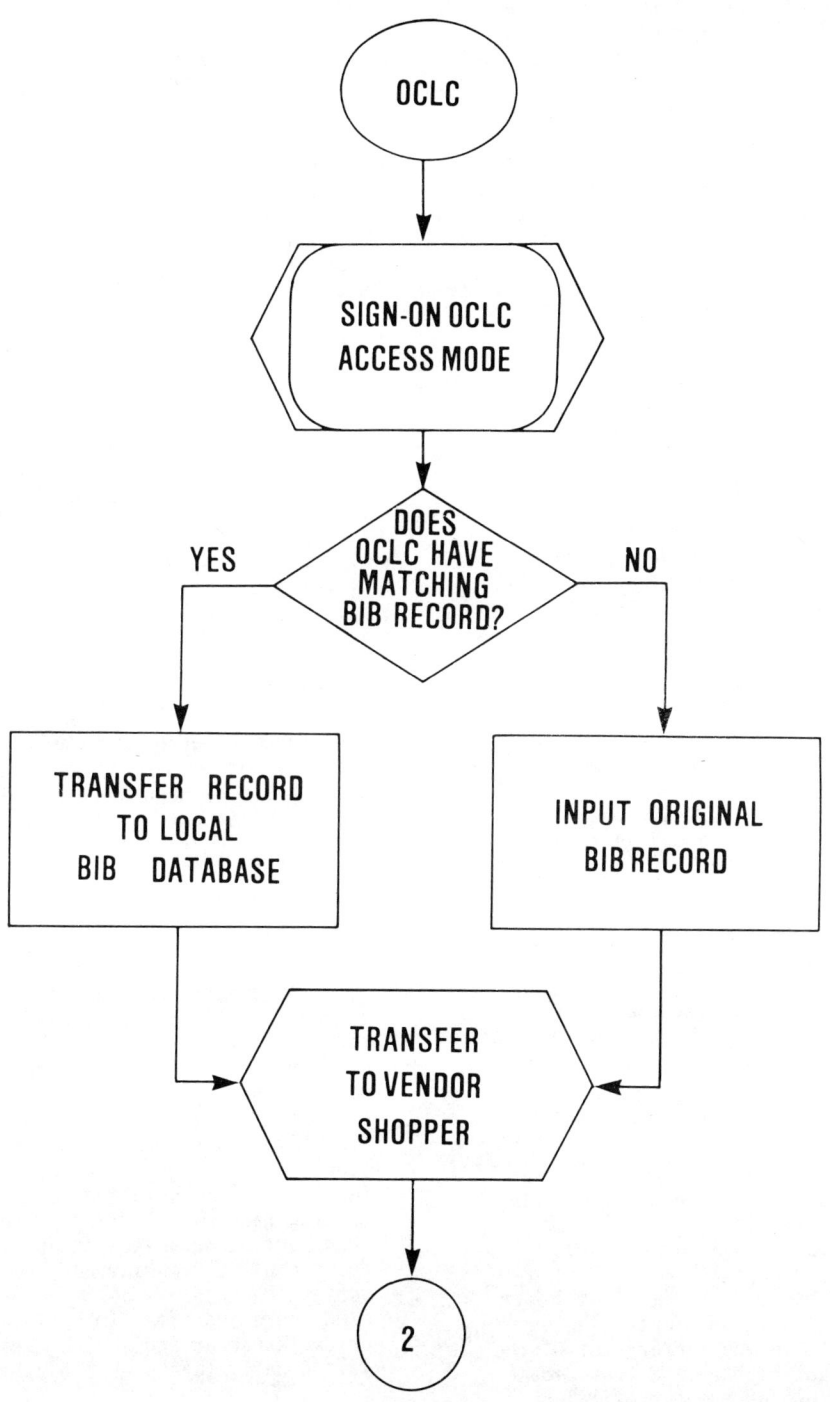

HARDCOPY IN TRANSITION: THE PLAN FOR A PROTOTYPE AUTOMATED
STORAGE AND RETRIEVAL FACILITY FOR LOW USE LIBRARY MATERIALS AT
CALIFORNIA STATE UNIVERSITY, NORTHRIDGE

Norma S. Creaghe and Douglas A. Davis
California State University, Northridge
Northridge, California

Abstract. California State University, Northridge (CSUN) has submitted a building program for a new phase of its main library that includes a prototype of a large automated storage/retrieval system (AS/RS) capable of housing 950,000 volumes. It will be closely integrated with an advanced online catalog and circulation system. It is estimated the AS/RS storage will save $13,000,000 in comparison with a new building with conventional shelving and equal capacity.

Our position is that an AS/RS is a practical, economical and innovative solution to the problems of constantly growing collections and escalating library construction costs. It will solve crowding problems while Librarians assess and compare the many formats in which information will be available in the year 2000 and give them time to decide which ones to use and how to use them. We believe this large scale library test of a current technology, the AS/RS, would provide a wealth of important technical and functional knowledge regarding storage and use of low-use materials in academic libraries.

Keywords and Phrases. Automated access facilities; Automation of library processes--book storage; Browsing; College and University Libraries--space problems; Obsolescence of books, periodicals, etc.

INTRODUCTION

Academic libraries are facing a dilemma: Their space consuming collections of books and periodicals continue to multiply. They are outgrowing buildings built during the library construction boom of the 1960's and 1970's. Construction costs for new library space have escalated. CSUN's Oviatt Library, completed in 1973, cost $28.75 per gross square foot.[1] The comparable 1985 cost would be $98.03.[2] Governing boards are becoming more and more reluctant to fund construction of library buildings or additions, buildings that will once again become inadequate within the next five to ten years and thus start the cycle over again.

California State University System (CSU), with an undergraduate and masters degree enrollment of 300,000, is seeking ways to solve the critical library space shortage on its nineteen campuses. A 1984 space survey of nine of its campuses showed a combined space shortage of 313,960 assignable square feet.[3] A system-wide acquisition of 450,000 volumes each year creates an annual need for an additional 45,000 square feet.[4]

The 28,000 student California State University, Northridge, is a typical large CSU campus. It has one of the system's most serious space problems. The library houses its 850,000 volumes in two separate buildings. By 1990, it will have a space deficit of 72,935 square feet. The campus master plan is to move the library out of the older 70,499 square-foot Library and consolidate services in one building for greater efficiency. The combined space deficit in 1990 would total 143,434 square feet.[5] As a result of the Chancellor's Office survey and CSUN's critical need for library space, the two combined forces to assess the alternatives and the feasibility of those alternatives.

STORAGE ALTERNATIVES

Open Book Stacks

Classified open book stacks have become by far the most popular mode of book storage for academic libraries in the United States. Patrons prefer the convenience and the opportunity to browse. Open stacks would probably become almost universal were it not for high facility construction costs, currently $13.50 per volume in the CSU system. This high cost is difficult to justify in a medium size academic library where studies show that about 30% of the collection is used once a year or more and 40% of the collection may not be used in five years.[6] Maintenance costs are also high and open stacks do not provide an ideal environment for book preservation. Therefore, numerous alternate methods of book storage have been employed in academic libraries despite the popularity of the open book stacks.

Regional Depositories

The use of an inexpensive site and low-cost compact shelving schemes has long made depositories an affordable solution to the overcrowding of libraries with seldom used materials. The current construction cost of such a facility is estimated at $4.20 per volume for the University of California's regional depository.[7] This is a substantial saving. However, the cost of transferring materials to the depository, changing catalog records, staffing another facility and transporting requested materials noticeably reduces construction savings. Browsing is inconvenient because of the remote location or limited hours and often impossible due to compact or unclassed arrangements. Requests for materials usually take 1 or 2 days to fill.

Compact Shelving

Numerous ingenious compact book stack designs have been available to librarians for some time, as the extensive review by Keyes Metcalf in

1965 shows.[3] Compact stationary shelving that significantly increases capacity makes browsing impractical if not impossible. Movable aisle shelving has been used with considerable success in certain cases. An outstanding recent example is the new 2.2 million volume University of Illinois facility which permits patron browsing.[9] It houses the entire humanities collection which is large and has a low use per volume ratio.

Automated Storage/Retrieval Systems

Another high density storage option is a mini load Automated Storage/Retrieval System (AS/RS). Similar facilities, known as Randtrievers, were installed in four libraries in the mid-seventies; one, at the Ohio State Health Sciences Library, is still in use. Since being widely adopted by industry during the past decade, AS/RS's have undergone major improvements and have proven to be highly reliable. CSUN proposes to use AS/RS technology interfaced with an online catalog and circulation system to create an on-site Automated Access Facility (AAF) to house 950,000 volumes in 8000 square feet at the estimated cost of $4.28 per volume.[10]

AUTOMATED ACCESS FACILITY

Adapted to library use, an Automated Access Facility will store the books or library materials in bins placed mechanically on mini-load industrial rack assemblies arranged along aisles up to one hundred feet long and rising as high as forty feet. The mechanical retriever, an electrically driven, forklift-like mechanism on a mast, will run on floor-mounted and overhead rails in aisles between the two racks it serves. Activated by the patron from the online public catalog, the retriever will remove the bin containing the book from the rack and deliver it to the work station. An operator, guided by a video display, will take the book from the bin, check it out and deliver it to the patron. Then the operator will, using a light pen entry, assign any returned book awaiting storage into the bin. The retriever will return the bin to its permanent location in the rack. Though each bin will have a permanent location, most books will be assigned to bins in random order.

An AAF can be incorporated into a building as it is being constructed or built as an addition to an existing structure. At CSUN, the 8000 square foot, 950,000 volume capacity AAF will be part of a 90,123 assignable square foot addition to the main library. It will provide storage for up to 119 volumes per square foot (in a forty foot high area) as compared to the ten volumes per square foot in conventional open stack shelving.[11]

With an anticipated completion date of 1990, CSUN's AAF will be located adjacent to and be served by the Circulation Department. It will contain six aisles and six work stations and will usually be operated by one to three attendants. The 12,396 bins will be 24" deep, 48" wide and of three heights, 4.5", 12" and 15", to accommodate the different sizes of materials to be stored--books, periodicals, pamphlets, phonorecords, microforms, curriculum and other non-book materials.[12]

Selection of Materials to be Stored

Initially, approximately 50 percent of the library's anticipated 1990 volume count of 1,070,000 will be stored in the AAF and 520,000 volumes will remain in the open stacks. Selection of books and periodicals to be placed in the AAF will be done in consultation with the faculty, based on listings of volumes having little or no circulation since 1981. Circulation statistics for books will be derived from online circulation data and for periodicals from annual periodical use surveys.

Selection of other materials will be determined by the nature, use and format of the material and whether there are bibliographic records for them in the online public catalog. If materials in the AAF experience significant circulation, they will be transferred to the open stacks. In order to keep the open stack collection size constant, additional books and periodicals will have to be identified, reviewed and transferred to the AAF on an annual cycle.

Costs and Savings

The architect's estimate of the cost of the 90,123 assignable square feet (ASF) addition is $15,202,000, with the AS/RS unit costing $1,918,400. This is $12,870,000 less than the estimated cost of $28,072,000 for an addition of equal book capacity with conventional storage. The AAF will offer custodial cost savings of $258,253 annually.[13] This savings will be partially offset by the cost of the full time technician and the maintenance contract required to maintain the facility at optimum performance and prevent downtimes.

Service to Patrons

A patron at an online catalog terminal will be able to discern if a book is in the AAF and initiate a request for it. Interfaced with the online catalog, the AAF computer will activate the AAF retrieval mechanism and make the book available to the patron within five to ten minutes. Actual mechanical retrieval time is estimated to be two minutes, with three to eight minutes allowed for the operator to remove the material from the bin and for queuing.[14]

The increased security the AAF offers will save patrons time that would be spent looking for books on the open shelves that may be in use in the library, on the waiting shelves, misplaced, or missing. All library materials stored in the AAF will be secure from pilferage, and book deterioration will be slowed because the facility can be maintained at optimum temperature, humidity, and light levels.

Browsing

An obvious disadvantage will be a patron's

inability to browse the AAF collection. However, the online catalog will offer abundant possibilities for browsing. By using the online catalog's key word and subject indexing, a patron will be able to find all the library's monographic holdings on the subject no matter where they are stored, including those not ordinarily shelved in the same classification. Further, the Library's 520,000 volume open stack collection of actively used materials should fulfill most browsing needs.

Down Times and Losses

Everyone who uses computer systems knows the possibilities of technological failure. However, current industrial facility managers report that with a proper AAF maintenance program, it is realistic to expect the system to be up 95-98% of the time.

There is the possibility that books will become misplaced. However, this should be rare because access will be limited to trained operators, who will conduct a running inventory during slack periods.

Generation of Records

Automated circulation systems now store specific information as to which books are circulated, but more books are used inhouse without the use being recorded. Once low circulation items are transferred to the AAF, all uses will be recorded automatically. This information will be used, when the AAF is filled, to determine which items should be retained, sent to remote storage or discarded.

THE LONG TERM ROLE OF THE AAF

An AAF will long remain a valuable asset to an academic library in any probable future library environment. It will be fully justified as an economical and useful form of storage, if book acquisitions continue at near the present rate. More likely, its exact usage records will permit an effective deselection process which will greatly reduce the net rate of collection growth. Combined with the probable slow transition from books to electronic media, an AAF may postpone the need for future library construction indefinitely. If the transition to electronic media becomes almost universal in the distant future, the AAF will offer an ideal repository for preservation of present day books.

CONCLUSION

The desirability of building a major AAF in an academic library is clear. Indefinite continued growth of traditional libraries is not an option in the CSU, and probably elsewhere, due to cost. No major trend exists to indicate the demise of the book in the useful life of the AAF, even though electronic media will revolutionize the way research is done and libraries do business. Favorable experiences in industry and comparison with other low cost storage alternatives suggest an AAF may be the most desirable solution to reducing the cost of storage of low use library materials while enabling their utilization by patrons. A full scale prototype AAF test at a suitable university is called for to see if this very promising concept offers a solution to storage problems that are a major concern of all large academic libraries.

ACKNOWLEDGEMENTS

The authors wish to recognize John Kountz, Associate Director of the CSU Division of Library Affairs, for his initial work on the concept of using an AS/RS as a solution to library space shortages; Thomas Harris, Director of the CSU Division of Library Affairs, for recognizing the abilities of the CSUN Libraries' Director and his staff to adapt such a system to their particular needs; and Norman E. Tanis, Director of CSUN Libraries, for being able to envision the possibilities of an AAF at CSUN and for his successful efforts in procuring funding for the feasibility study.

REFERENCES

1. Jerrold Orne, "Academic Library Building in 1973. "Bowker Annual of Library and Book Trade Information, 1974 (New York: Bowker), p.282.

2. "Library, Phase II with Automated Access Facility: Program Justification, 1986-87," California State University, Northridge, 1985, p.31. Photocopy.

3. "California State University Library Space Study: Chancellor's Office Commentary." Systemwide Library Space for Period 1984-2004, Office of the Chancellor, the California State University, Long Beach, CA 1984, p.1. Photocopy.

4. "Long Range Planning for Library Space Needs in the CSU: An Innovative Approach," Division of Library Affairs, Office of the Chancellor, California State University, 1984, p.3. Photocopy.

5. "Library, Phase II," p.3.

6. Douglas Davis, "Maintenance of Circulating Books in an Academic Library," California Librarian, 38(2):27 (April 1977).

7. "Cost Contrast of CSU Proposed High Density Storage Versus UC Remote Storage," Systemwide Library Space Study for Period 1984-2004, Office of the Chancellor, the California State University, Long Beach, CA, 1984, p.3. Photocopy.

8. Keyes D. Metcalf, Planning Academic and Research Library Buildings (New York, McGraw-Hill, 1965), pp.157-65.

9. Martin H. Collier, "Sixth Stack Addition," Library Journal, 107:2235-37 (Dec. 1, 1982).

10. "Cost Contrast," p.3.

11. "Library Phase II," p.2.

12. Leo A. Daly, "Oviatt Library Automatic Storage/Retrieval System and Phase II Building Addition Study," California State University, Northridge, 1984, pt.2, p.3. Photocopy.

13. "Library Phase II," p.31.

14. "Cost Contrast," p.3.

DEVELOPING-WORLD IMPRINTS IN ACADEMIC LIBRARY COLLECTIONS

David L. Easterbrook
University of Illinois at Chicago Library
Chicago, Illinois

Keywords and Phrases. Collection development, Developing world, Area studies.

This brief will emphasize the tremendous growth both in quality and quantity of scholarship in the developing world in the social sciences and will highlight the need to focus expanded collection development energies on such publications in North American libraries. Despite the well-known technical problems faced in building collections including such imprints, the brief argues that the internationalization of social sciences research and the development and expansion of national universities, research institutes, and publishers in the developing world calls for sensible responsive action or else our collections will become increasingly parochial during a period in which publications from the developing world containing the results of important social science research become increasingly important to a broader constituency of users. [1]

The essence of the concern raised in this brief was articulated by Kenneth Prewitt, President of the Social Science Research Council, in an address to a recent Association of Research Libraries meeting. Prewitt particularly stressed the growing internationalization of social science scholarship outside of the western world noting its importance to social science scholarship in North America. He explained that we no longer were in a situation where the best from abroad came to North America for exposure and expressed his concern that our libraries may not be acquiring that growing portion of the world's social science literature being published outside the western world. [2] Prewitt's assertion is admirably demonstrated for East Africa in an article by the compilers of a supplement to a well-respected bibliography and in the introduction to the supplement itself. [3] It was found that between the 1963-74 and 1974-80 volumes that the total number of entries had nearly doubled. A significant growth as well in the proportion of entries published within East Africa is also notable. Statistics documenting the growth of publications in the developing world are not difficult to locate, even if they may be somewhat out of date. They show the East African case is not out of line with what is happening elsewhere. [4]

Recognizing that a considerable portion of this social science literature is in English is important, for that can help remove it, perhaps, from some of the "stigmas" attached by many to area studies materials--hard to acquire, hard to process, rarely used, etc. Recognizing that this literature will be increasingly important to both undergraduate and graduate readers as well as faculty in North American academic libraries, the following questions, among others, need to be addressed:

1. Are there increasing requests in academic libraries for such materials?
2. How important might such materials be to various reader populations in academic libraries?
3. How should information about significant developing-world imprints be brought to the attention of selectors? Should Choice change its editorial policy and include titles that are not readily available for purchase in North America? Should the editors of Books for College Libraries III make a conscious attempt to include such titles?
4. How might ACRL's Asian and African Section or the several specialized area studies librarians' associations and committees assist academic libraries without established area studies expertise in assessing their needs in this area?

REFERENCES

1. Recent works looking at the growing internationalization of social science research include: James S. Coleman, "The Internationality of Science and the Nationality of Scientists" in Dimensions of Higher International Education, ed. by William H. Allaway (Boulder: Westview Press, 1985), pp. 44-47, David Court, The Idea of Social Science in East Africa: An Account of the Development of Higher Education (Nairobi: University of Nairobi, Institute of Development Studies, 1981), Ethics, Politics, and International Social Science Research, ed. by Michael P. Hamnett (Honolulu: Institute of Culture and Communication, 1984), Introduction to Intercultural Studies (Paris: UNESCO, 1983), Social Research in Developing Countries, ed. by Martin Bulmer (Chichester: John Wiley, 1983), and Social Sciences and Public Policy in the Developing World, ed. by Laurence D. Stifel (Lexington: Lexington Books, 1982). Recent works looking at the academic setting this brief is concerned with include: Philip G. Altbach, Research on Foreign Students and International Study (New York: Praeger, 1985), Bridges to Knowledge: Foreign Students in Comparative Perspective, ed. by

Elinor G. Barber (Chicago: University of Chicago Press, 1984), *International Role of the University in the Eighties: Proceedings of the Michigan State University International Year Conference...1982* (East Lansing: International Studies and Programs, Michigan State University, 1982), Scott Jaschik, "Seeking to Compete in World Economy, States Back International Education," *Chronicle of Higher Education* 31:14(4 December 1985):1, 18-19, Richard D. Lambert, *Beyond Growth: The Next Stage in Language and Area Studies* (Washington: Association of American Universities, 1984), Robert A. McCaughey, *International Studies and Academic Enterprise: A Chapter in the Enclosure of American Learning* (New York: Columbia University Press, 1984), and Frank Newman, *Higher Education and the American Resurgence* (Princeton: Carnegie Foundation for the Advancement of Teaching, 1985), pp. 99-108.

2. Kenneth Prewitt, "The Challenge from the Social Sciences," in Association of Research Libraries, *Minutes of the 101st Meeting...1982* (Washington: Association of Research Libraries, 1982), pp. 47-50. See also Kenneth Prewitt, "The Impact of the Developing World on U.S. Social Science Theory and Methodology" in *Social Sciences and Public Policy in the Developing World*, pp. 3-19. Of related interest is Peter A. Gourevitch, "Research Trends in Western Europe: The Collapse of Boundaries" in *The State of Western European Studies: Implications for Collection Development* (New York: Haworth Press, 1984), pp. 13-25.

3. Brenden Finucane, "The Economic Literature for Kenya, Tanzania, Uganda, 1974-1980: An Analysis," *African Research and Documentation* 33(1983):12-22. The initial bibliography and its supplement are: Tony Killick, *The Economies of East Africa* (Boston: G. K. Hall, 1976) and Tony Killick, Lawrence Rupley, and Brenden Finucane, *The Economies of East Africa, 1974-1980* (Boston: G. K. Hall, 1984).

4. Statistics can be found in the UNESCO *Statistical Yearbook*. Statistics and analysis can be found in a number of titles including Philip G. Altbach, *Publishing in the Third World: Knowledge and Development* (London: Heinemann, 1985), Philip G. Altbach, *Publishing in the Third World: Trend Report and Bibliography* (New York: Praeger, 1980), S. I. A. Kotei, *The Book Today in Africa* (Paris: UNESCO, 1981), Datus C. Smith, Jr., *The Economics of Book Publishing in Developing Countries* (Paris: UNESCO, 1977), and Hans M. Zell, *Publishing and Book Development in Africa: A Bibliography* (Paris: UNESCO, 1984).

ASSESSING COLLECTION DEVELOPMENT ORGANIZATION IN A SMALL ACADEMIC LIBRARY

Lynne Gamble
California Polytechnic State University Library
San Luis Obispo, CA 93407

Abstract. Assessing the collection development organization in a library is a task done more often than is generally realized. A planned study approach is available as part of the CAP program from the Association of Research Libraries and has been used by many large academic libraries. Another approach, outlined in this article, advises a review of existing structures, acknowledging and correcting problems, making specific job descriptions and assessing the degree of interest in participating. The structure is then designed around the job to be done and the personnel available. This type of study is especially applicable to small academic libraries.

Keywords and Phrases. Collection development. Organization. Bibliographers. Selectors. Assessment. Academic library.

INTRODUCTION

All too often small academic libraries still have collection development organizations that have evolved around existing personnel. A library with a strong acquisitions librarian combines acquisitions and collection development: a library with a strong reference or public services head combines reference and collection development. Sometimes a librarian has been designated as the collection development librarian and a structure has simply grown up around this person. These home-grown systems often work well, despite their Darwinian origins, until there is a change in the staffing or the system has grown stale. Then, an assessment of the collection development structure is needed.

MODELS OF THE COLLECTION DEVELOPER: SUPERBIBLIOGRAPHER AND COLLECTION MANAGER

According to William E. Hannaford, Jr. in "Collection Development in College Libraries":

> There are, at the present moment, at least two widespread models of the collection developer in practice. One is that of the superbibliographer, a Renaissance person supposedly so well-versed in all of the literatures and languages of the world, or at least the publishing practices, that he or she can mold and shape a collection almost singlehandedly. The second model is that of the collection manager. In this model, the collection developer has the primary function of overseeing the building of the collection; the molding and shaping of the collection--its very design--must come from or through the hands of this person.[1]

Hannaford further argues that the superbibliographer model is now outdated and seldom used, that the collection manager model is the one most libraries have adopted, and the one seen most often in modern libraries. Part of the collection manager's job is to motivate others to do selection and other collection development work, or as he phrases it, "to continually cajole and hustle" to get things done.

Although the collection manager model is a widely accepted one, problems do exist. Often, the person suffers from real lack of authority to evaluate and possibly dismiss volunteer selectors who are not doing a good job. Because he is not the line supervisor, he cannot always demand more time from selectors to do collection development projects. It is important that this person has the complete support of the library director to achieve collection development goals. Moreover, it can be tiresome after a number of years "to continually cajole and hustle" to get things accomplished.

Other models which are currently being used in collection development activities are derivatives of Hannaford's superbibliographer. The full-time bibliographer model is one in which the individual is an expert in his subject area. Besides doing material selection, he would be called upon by the faculty for participating in curriculum review, class presentation and workshops. There is no doubt that many bibliographers may fit this role and that is commendable. However, complaints have reigned from the beginning that the full-time bibliographers tend to be isolated from the rest of the library and from the students and faculty. They are not seen by the public and are not sought out for consultation by the faculty. Instead, they must set up their own faculty contacts which brings charges of nonproductive work.

The reference/bibliographer model is another "superbibliographer" derivative. This individual works with the public and is familiar with their wants and needs. Accordingly, this person is the most knowledgeable about the type of collection development needed and will make the best selection in his special subject area. Unfortunately, what often happens is that reference librarians are not given time to do collection development, have no clerical support for these activities, or may not have the interest required for this type of work. When this happens, collection development clearly becomes a secondary function of their job.

ORGANIZATIONAL PATTERNS

In "Collection Development and Selection: Who Should Do It?," John Ryland identified three organizational patterns:[2]
- (a) Reference bibliographers in a variety of subject areas.
- (b) Twenty or more librarians from throughout the library dealing with one or more academic departments.
- (c) Full-time bibliographers.

These patterns have been combined in many ways; full-time bibliographers and volunteer selectors, branch librarians, bibliographers, etc. The current "catchword" for a library selector pattern where librarians have dual job assignments is "matrix" pattern.

ARL libraries often follow a pattern of an assistant director for collection development, some full-time bibliographers, and a bevy of part-time bibliographers, selectors, liaisons, subject specialists or whatever they may be called. The larger the library, the more full-time bibliographers they are likely to have.

Small academic libraries, on the other hand, do not usually have an assistant director for collection development. They still have the traditional divisions with an assistant director for technical services and an assistant director for public services. In the California State University system (of which Cal Poly is one school), an informal survey revealed that on the other eighteen campuses, a myriad of organizational structures exist, and many are in the process of being changed.

OTHER ASSESSMENT STUDIES

For large academic libraries, the current popular method of dealing with the assessment of the collection development structure is through part of a self-study program designed by ARL's Office of Management Studies called CAP (Collection Analysis Project). Typically, CAP activities are carried out by a library staff study team and several task forces. The task forces investigate individual matters, and the study team is responsible for developing a course of action out of the separate reports.[3]

In a CAP study at Notre Dame, they were able to identify problems in their collection development structure and make recommendations for solving or easing these problems such as adding another full-time bibliographer and further defining time parameters and job responsibilities for liaison/selectors.[4]

CAL POLY STUDY

Our library was no exception in regard to the need for an organizational assessment. The collection development structure, which once worked, was no longer functioning well. Only seven out of seventeen library selectors were seen as active in selecting materials. Sixty-six out of approximately 800 faculty were active selectors and these faculty represented only twelve of twenty-nine instructional departments.

The CAP study, used at larger libraries, was more involved and more time consuming than we thought necessary for our needs. Instead, a collection development assessment committee was formed to review the present collection development structure and propose improvements. The structure consisted of a volunteer library selector system with a collection development librarian at the head. A corresponding faculty contact existed for subject areas aligned with departments. However, the collection development librarian reported to the head of the acquisitions/collection development department. An assistant director for collection analysis operated separately with no staff. The committee was charged to:
- Review other collection development organizations' models and determine the collection development organization structure for this library.
- Determine if the library selector system should be continued.
- Clarify the role of the library selector if the system was continued.

The committee examined the various models, patterns, and structures used at both large and small academic libraries. It did not take long to determine that the volunteer selector system with a collection manager was firmly entrenched in the traditions of the library. Although the library selector/departmental contact system had been instituted during the late 1960's when rapid growth and large book budgets overwhelmed the one-person superbibliographer system, it had had enough success even in lean times to attract many devotees in the library even though many were not presently active in collection development work. Some librarians had developed subject expertise and good faculty relations which they felt were advantageous to the library; others liked the prestige of the job. Unfortunately, the loose volunteer system did not adequately encourage serious participation for all subject areas.

The strengths of a library selector system were seen as five-fold in that it provides these benefits:
- (1) The manpower to cover a diverse curriculum.
- (2) Utilization of subject expertise among the librarians.
- (3) An avenue for faculty contact.
- (4) Professional growth for librarians.
- (5) Selectors who do public service work and are aware of current demand for materials.

The weaknesses of a library selector system were examined as well:

- (1) No support services for selectors.

(2) Confusion over responsibilities.
(3) Inconsistent collection development.
(4) Little or no training for library selectors.
(5) Two supervisors.
(6) Lack of communication between selectors and collection development staff.

The committee felt that many of the shortcomings of a selector system could be modified to make the system workable again. The results of committee discussions on the library selector system led to these conclusions:

(1) The collection development selector coordinator or head needs to have the support and authority to provide leadership for the library selectors.
(2) Specific job descriptions are required for both the coordinator and the selector so that responsibilities are clear.
(3) A built-in evaluation system for the selector is needed.
(4) The coordinator needs to communicate well and be able to motivate the selectors.
(5) Training is needed for library selectors.
(6) The amount of time a library selector should spend on his collection development duties should be spelled out either by number of hours per week or on a percentage basis.
(7) The collection development organization needs to be able to furnish clerical support to the selectors so they will not have to depend on their own staff or do the clerical work themselves.

JOB DESCRIPTIONS

At this point the committee began work on two new documents, the collection development coordinator or head job description and the library selector job description. Moreover, the job description for the assistant director for collection analysis was examined for clarification of duties.

Once the library selector job description was completed, the committee surveyed the librarians to see who would be interested in participating in collection development once they saw the extended responsibilities of the selector position. The committee also wanted to see what kind of time commitment each person and his supervisor would be willing to give. In the questionnaire, librarians were asked to choose the subject areas they wanted and give a specific number of hours per week that they could devote to collection development. Supervisors were asked to approve the assignment of hours. In only one case did the supervisor object to the amount of time the librarian wished to use.

Surprisingly to the committee, sixteen out of the twenty-four librarians wanted to serve as library selectors even with the increased responsibilities of the job and subsequent evaluation. Because of the interest shown, the committee decided to continue the volunteer selector system in its revised form. The committee recommended that a collection development department be organized so that all collection development activities could be centralized. The assistant director for collection analysis would become the assistant director for collection development, and the collection development librarian would be named head of the department. They would work together with the collection development head becoming the selector coordinator and concentrating on current selection; and the assistant director overseeing the total development of the collection, preservation, deacquisitions, and budgeting.

Generalizing from this committee's experience, one way for a small academic library to proceed with an organizational assessment is by:

(1) Reviewing collection development organizational structures currently in use.
(2) Reviewing the strengths and the weaknesses of the present system.
(3) Seeing if the present collection development organization can be salvaged, or if a new organization should be substituted.
(4) Making job descriptions for the tasks to be done.
(5) Soliciting volunteers and making assignments to fit job descriptions.

CONCLUSION

The assessment of the collection development structure can be a healthy process for a library. Problems are ferreted out and resolved. Staffing can be changed and modified to reflect changing needs and interests of the librarians. While the CAP studies are standard for ARL libraries, the assessment method advocated here is a practical approach for small academic libraries.

REFERENCES

1. William E. Hannaford, Jr., "Collection Development in College Libraries" *Library Resources for College Scholars* (Lexington, Virginia: Washington and Lee University, 1980) 14.

2. John Ryland. "Collection Development and Selection: Who Should Do It? *Library Acquisitions: Practice and Theory* 6 (1982) 13-17.

3. Association of Research Libraries, Office of University Library Management Studies. <u>Collection Analysis in Research Libraries</u>. (Washington, D.C.: Author, 1977).

4. University of Notre Dame. University Libraries. <u>Collection Analysis Project Task Force On Operating Practices in Collection Development. Final Report.</u> (Notre Dame, Indiana, June 1981).

INTEGRATING MICROFORMS WITH GOVERNMENT DOCUMENTS: A THIRD ALTERNATIVE

Edward Herman
State University at Buffalo
Buffalo, NY

Abstract. Two advantages of combining all government documents, regardless of format, and all microforms into one Documents and Microforms Department are discussed. 1) This approach enables librarians to more easily coordinate solutions to the difficulties users of each format face. 2) This approach enables librarians to provide services that emphasize "information," not "document retrieval." Also, librarians are urged to consider how well their existing collections are integrated into general library services before expanding into new services.

Keywords and Phrases. Government information; Microforms; Lockwood Library, State University at Buffalo.

The literature advising document librarians how to organize collections to handle Government Printing Office microfiche most effectively has generally considered two alternatives. One is to store the microfiche in the documents department with other government publications and the other is to house the fiche in the micrographics area with other microformats. A third alternative has received only limited attention in recent literature. Lockwood Library of the State University at Buffalo has recently adopted this third alternative, the combining of all government documents, regardless of their format, and all microformats into a Documents and Microforms Department.[1]

The advantages of doing so are considerable because library patrons often face similar problems when attempting to use either type of material. Equally important, it is hoped that maintaining both formats in one department will tend to focus library service upon "information retrieval," rather than document retrieval. Before going into the details of this, a brief history of documents and microforms in Lockwood Library will be presented to place the subject within context.

OVERVIEW OF DOCUMENTS AND MICROFORMS IN LOCKWOOD LIBRARY

Government publications and microforms were housed in one department until Lockwood Library was moved to a new suburban campus in June 1978. At that time, two departments under separate administrators were established, the Government Documents Department and the Current Periodicals/Microforms Department. The Director of Libraries decided to recombine the two areas in January 1983 after the Head of the Current Periodicals/Microforms Department requested to be transferred into another position. The Head of the Documents area was given responsibility for the new Government Documents and Microforms Department, while the Circulation Department accepted responsibility for current periodicals.

I was originally opposed to the idea because I was looking forward to the Documents Department becoming a Documents and Numeric Database Center, reasoning that many of the numeric databases currently available are generated by the Federal government. I wanted to see the Documents Department inundated with computer terminals and library users who would seek information from these terminals, not microform cabinets. I was hoping to spend my time assisting people with computer terminals, not microforms.

However, I have since begun to realize that combining the two departments would increase the effectiveness of services provided to library clientele. The advantages of doing so in Lockwood Library have similar implications in other libraries.

ADVANTAGES OF RECOMBINING THE TWO DEPARTMENTS

The similarities between problems library patrons face when using documents and microforms are considerable. Selected ones include:

Bibliographic control: Though the bibliographic control over both types of materials are better than ever before, it is still very much inadequate when compared to books and journals. In most libraries neither government publications nor microforms are completely listed in card catalogs. It has been said that both types of materials suffer from the malady of the "bibliographic blues."[2]

Moore's Law: According to Moore, people will use information resources that are most easily accessible, even if more authoritative sources are available. When this principle is applied to documents and microforms, library users conceivably avoid using them because it is not cost effective or convenient to do so in terms of the amount of effort and time expended to locate information. Consequently, both materials are underutilized, while people often fail to recognize the wealth of information available in them.

Staff: Library staff often discourage use of documents and microforms through their negative attitudes regarding the formats. What was once said about the librarian--government publication relationship by a leading library educator holds true almost as well for microforms: "The huge world of documents is so imposing, varied and complex that one is not surprised to find a host of librarians who wish devoutly to dissociate themselves from the wretched materials."[3] Additionally, library users need specially trained staff when using either type of material, staff who can locate and retrieve, both formats, as well as staff who can fix paper jams in reader/printers quickly and efficiently.

These similar problems need similar types of solutions. Related problems facing the identical organization can be resolved more effectively if they are dealt with together, rather than separately. Maintaining one combined department offers greater problem solving potential, since possibilities of separate departments each going their own way in uncoordinated fashions are eliminated.

For instance, attempts to improve access to materials not under bibliographic control might best be accomplished when dealing with the sources in a consistent fashion. Separate, uncoordinated endeavors can confuse, rather than assist, library users.

Turning to bibliographic instruction, three elements of a successful microform instruction program at the University of Pittsburg could be incorporated into a program for both documents, as well as microforms. Participants were given information about the medium to remove fears concerning its use, information about available resources and methods used to access them, and instruction in operating readers.[4] Coordinated programs such as these should result in increased utilization of both sources.

RECOMBINING THE TWO DEPARTMENTS CAN CREATE AN ATMOSPHERE OF INFORMATION RETRIEVAL RATHER THAN DOCUMENT RETRIEVAL

Library patrons will benefit from the recombination of documents and microforms because this will enable library staff to work within an atmosphere that emphasizes "information retrieval," rather than "document" retrieval.

For example, consider the individual who is seeking current information pertaining to tax reform. A wide range of sources are available in both documents and microforms. I believe that it is far more likely library personnel would encourage our researcher to use the Congressional Information Service Index and the American Statistics Index in conjunction with the indexes to and microfilm copies of the New York Times and the Wall Street Journal if all information were available in the same part of the library.

Data in a recent study can be interpreted to indicate that a combined documents and microforms area has the possibility of becoming a center for public affairs-type information described immediately above. Paula Watson and Kathleen Heim studied document circulation statistics in Federal Documents Use In The Research Library Setting.[5] They discovered that the majority of respondents to their questionnaire were undergraduate students who most often borrowed materials classified according to the Superintendent of Documents scheme in the Y4's. Congressional hearings and committee prints, materials which are most often newsworthy and of public importance, are classified in the Y4's. Considering that the documents covered in the study were current ones published since 1980, library staff could have assisted researchers in locating additional information in newspapers and/or microformated journals.

Moreover, two studies, the first by McCaghy and Purcell, and the second by Hernon, indicate that social science faculty who are document users do not use the Documents Departments of their home institutions. They acquire their documents directly from the issuing agencies or use the materials in other libraries. According to McCaghy and Purcell, most use documents that are not more than five years old,[6] and according to Hernon, most use documents that are not more than three years old.[7]

Based upon this information, I submit that a faculty member who uses government publications is more likely to have in his personal library a document that is three years old than a newspaper that is three years old. The same faculty member would most likely consult a microformated version of the newspaper in his institution's library to obtain his data, rather than a personal copy of the original newspaper. Once that professor consults his newspaper in a documents and microforms department, he might begin to understand that his library could possibly satisfy some, if not all, of his document information needs.

Documents and microforms can be used together not only when locating information about current topics, but when locating data about historical ones as well. For example, the library patron seeking information on the American Revolution can use many different sources in a combined documents and microforms department, without having to be referred elsewhere. These might include: The Letters of the Continental Congress

British Parliamentary Debates

Journals of Parliament

Early American Newspapers

Library of American Civilization

The American Culture Series

This type of service enables library staff to place premium emphasis upon information, rather than document, retrieval.

CONCLUSION

It is hoped that combining documents and microforms departments will result in benefits, all of which will affect service to library users positively. It will foster greater cooperation between the two areas. Reference librarians will have more of a need to refer patrons to a documents and microforms department that houses two types of materials instead of one. When library users ask for information from the New York Times, document and microform librarians always have the possibility of convincing the researchers to use documents as well as newspapers. The reverse holds true when people use the Department to obtain information from documents.

Perhaps, initiative among library administrators, and documents and microforms personnel to combine their respective services might result in the departments obtaining greater autonomy to try new solutions for solving old problems. This will undoubtedly result in new mistakes. However, much can be learned from these mistakes.

I have begun to realize that the reorganization in Lockwood Library would not detract from the possibilities of providing services to numeric database users, but has the potential of adding to it. One of the most significant challenges facing librarians today is the need to integrate all information sources into library services. We must begin doing better jobs integrating into general library services the various types of information formats that have been around for years before attempting to deal with the newer ones. If the Documents and Microforms Department proves itself able to better integrate both mediums into general library services than had been the case before, the Department will have earned the right to become a Documents, Microforms and Numeric Database center in the future.

I expended significant energies learning much from this transitional experience. First, librarians can not remain static in times of change. We must be flexible enough to understand viewpoints other than our own, even if we do not agree with them at first or ever at all. This will help us develop better ideas that lead to improved services to library users.

Today it is very easy to become excited about the new technologies the literature tells us ought to be available in libraries. Numeric databases are of particular significance to document librarians due to recent activities of the Congressional Joint Committee on Printing.[8] I do not wish to play down the significance of these technologies, nor do I imply that libraries ought to ignore them. However, it is important for document librarians to ask a question prior to delving into these advances: how well are we integrating document services (or document/microform services, as the case might be,) into general library services? In other words, borrowing from Charles McClure's example, do our library users have the same probability of locating information in government publications, regardless of format, and microforms, as they do in other sources?[9]

Perhaps those libraries that can answer affirmatively are prepared to assume services for numeric databases. However, those which answer negatively ought to think more about how they might integrate traditional resources, such as books, journals, government publications and microforms, into general library services before undertaking additional ones. Numeric databases in libraries where the more traditional sources have not been integrated adequately into general operations will probably become just another medium that is not integrated adequately.

Energies need to be devoted not only towards making the most effective uses of new types of information sources, but also towards improving access to information sources that have been around for years.

REFERENCES

1. This alternative has been discussed by Steven Zink.("The GPO Reduced To Size: Microforms and Government Publications," in Nancy Jean Melin, Serials and Microforms: Patron-Oriented Management. (Westport, CT.: Meckler Publishing, 1983), 92-93.) He mentions that several universities have recently combined documents and microforms into one department or have moved them adjacent to each other. These include Louisianna State University, University of California at Davis, University of California at San Diego and Rice University. Moreover, Deborah A. Raikes stated that documents and microforms were combined under one department head at Princeton University in 1980, even though both areas are on

separate floors. ("Microforms at Princeton," Microform Review 11, No. 2 (Spring 1982): 105.) Diane Harvey in, "Documents and Document Librarianship in RLG Libraries," also mentions the subject. (Nancy Jean Melin, ed., Serials and Microforms, 128.)

2. Charles McClure, "Administrative Integration of Microformated Government Publications: A Framework For Analysis," Microform Review 6, No. 5 (September 1977), 261.

3. Joe Morehead, "U.S. Government Documents-- A Mazeway of Miscellany," RQ 7, No. 3 (Spring 1968), 132.

4. Marilyn P. Whitmore, "An Innovative Approach to User Acceptance of Microforms," Journal of Academic Librarianship 9, No. 1 (May 1983), 76.

5. (Washington, D.C.: Council on Library Resources, 1984.) ED 245 689.

6. Dawn McCaghy and Gary R. Purcell, "Faculty Use of Government Publications," College and Research Libraries 33, No. 1 (January 1972, 11.

7. Peter Hernon, Use of Government Publications By Social Scientists. (Norwood, N.J.: Ablex Publishing Corporation, 1979), 112.

8. The Committee's recent publication, Provision of Federal Government Publications In Electronic Format To Depository Libraries is a significant study of the issues. (Washington, D.C.: G.P.O., 1984).

9. McClure, "Administrative Integration of Microformated Government Publications," pp. 267-9.

BEYOND THE BOOK: COLLECTION DEVELOPMENT AND THE SPECIAL COLLECTIONS LIBRARIAN

Gretchen Lagana

University of Illinois at Chicago

Abstract. The purpose of this idea brief is to examine energies for transition as they relate to special collections librarianship with attention focused on collection development. The role of "papers" collections and non-print materials is presented as an important component of special collections. The field of popular culture is cited as an example of the need for primary research materials in non-traditional fields.

Keywords and Phrases. Rare books, special collections, manuscripts, collection development, popular culture, non-print materials.

In A Canticle for Leibowitz, Walter M. Miller's extraordinary novel of a small, southwestern monastery and its efforts over more than twelve centuries to save the "Memorabilia", the bits of knowledge that survived a hydrogen holocaust in the 1960s, a priest reflects on his fear of the future. It is the third millennium and he understands that now, after so many hundreds of years, a remaissance is imminent. He says to his friend, Benjamin, the hermit:

> "Do you realize how much things have changed in the past two centuries?...Since the death of the last civilization, the Memorabilia has been our special province, Benjamin. And we've kept it. But now? I sense the predicament of the shoemaker who tries to sell shoes in the village of shoemakers."
>
> The hermit smiled. "It could be done, if he manufactures a special and superior type of shoe."
>
> "I'm afraid the secular scholars are already beginning to lay claim to such a method."
>
> "Then go out of the shoemaking business, before you are ruined."[1]

As with the priest, change is no stranger to the special collections librarian. Forty years ago the term special coll-ctions was infrequently used, and keepers of rare books and manuscripts, "operated quite outside the pattern of organized libraries. Each group, the rare book curators and the general librarians, tended to be suspicious of the other and thus there was little opportunity for fruitful conversation or cooperative effort."[2] With the organization of the Rare Book and Manuscript (RBMS) Section of the Association of College and Research Libraries (ACRL) in 1958, one of the most important of many developments for special collections librarians during the 1950s and 1960s, much of that suspicion disappeared. Today, special collections librarians find themselves integrated in the mainstream of librarianship. Their contributions in areas such as library security and conservation/preservation are highly valued by the profession at large. Their work in computer-assisted systems for cataloging books and related materials, and the role they play in national as well as international bibliographic projects (such as the ESTC, the Eighteenth Century Short-Title Catalogue, a computer-assisted retrospective bibliographical project) is accomplished with the cooperation and support of the general librarian. RBMS continues to play an increasing role in these and other projects, through its committees, conferences, and publications. However, if special collections librarianship is to avoid the predicament of the shoemaker in a village of shoemakers, attention must be directed to an area especially crucial to the special collections librarian--collection development.

For many librarians the very term "special collections" conjures up images of the rare book and manuscript collections described with such eloquence by distinguished librarian-scholars of an earlier period: William Warner Bishop, William Jackson, Robert Vosper and Louis B. Wright, to name only a few. These collections, dominated by holdings in classical literature, history, theology, jurisprudence, philosophy, science and mathematics, reflected pre-World War II university curricula. Yet in the past quarter of a century, subtle and important changes in both the subject matter and format of collections organized for special collections departments have taken place.

In addition to the printed book, many special collections departments now contain significant printed "papers" and manuscript collections of research quality. These may vary from neighborhood and local records, corporate archives, underground materials to the wide range of materials produced by issue-oriented groups. The list is extensive. They offer the librarian what is initially an inexpensive way to mount an active special collections program, one which can be as relevant to the community as it is to the research and instruction programs of the university. But there are other reasons, too, why special collections librarians are collecting these materials. For many smaller institutions, the contraction of the rare book market, coupled with steep price increases makes the acquisition of rare books prohibitive. Private collections of research quality are becoming as scarce as the institutional funds to purchase them. And the gradual disappearance (concomitant with the rise of the modern academic research library with its extensive system of networks and interlibrary loan systems) of that staple of the special collections department, the faculty member's personal research library, closes still another door.

Papers collections, indeed, most non-book materials housed in special collections departments must receive more attention from RBMS members as well as the general librarian. They remain an important component of many special collections departments and they have their own set of problems in the areas of acquisitions, accessioning and cataloging, storage, accessing, preservation, and security, all of which need to be addressed. If the special collections department is to play an active role in the intellectual life of the university, special collections librarians must begin to learn how papers and other non-book collections support instruction and research in fields that often bypass the library. Certainly there are many. Urban history, social welfare, women's studies, mass communication, the performing arts, industrial, graphic, and communication design are a few of the new fields that are often represented in the library by secondary, rather than primary research materials. Many faculty in these areas, and some librarians, cry out to deaf ears for library support.

One such example is the field of popular culture. In 1973 an article appeared in College & Research Libraries calling for academic libraries to support this generally ignored area.[3] Four years after the publication of that article, studies concerned with popular culture and the library began to appear with increasing frequency. In 1978 the University of Kentucky in Lexington published the proceedings of a symposium it held on popular culture and the library.[4] The Drexel Library Quarterly devoted an entire issue to popular culture in 1980. A recent (1985) book is entirely concerned with the subject of popular culture and in 1985 College & Research Libraries published a major article on the subject.[5] The three topics most often treated in this extensive literature are 1) descriptions of existing popular culture collections, 2) rationales for including popular culture holdings in academic libraries, and 3) the need to introduce the field of popular culture to library science education.[6] A number of articles contain stinging rebukes to the librarian. Writes one author: "A cursory survey of the list of topics discussed at any annual meeting of the PCA (Popular Culture Association) makes it quite clear that what librarians have traditionally identified as "trash", "entertainment", and "escape literature" are the basic resources of popular culture research."[7]

Popular culture is a field especially suited to special collections, where many of the materials of the field may already lay buried in existing collections. And any consideration of popular culture necessarily raises another issue of importance to special collections librarians: the collection of non-print materials. Many of the newer fields rely on a wide range of materials, including non-print, to understand and interpret the meaning and background of the subject or period under study. When American-Lithuanians mounted a "Ban the Soviets" campaign against Soviet participation at the 1984 Olympics held in Los Angeles, they generated a whole body of printed and manuscript material: letters, reports, broadsides, newspaper articles to list just a few. They also mounted a series of local television interviews, which were video-taped, and which convey information no student or scholar of this issue can afford to be without.

Information comes in many forms today. Nina Matheson writes: "We know that there is a total restructuring in progress of who, what, and how information is created, owned, and shared. We librarians, no less that steelworkers, will be out of work unless we, like them, reexamine our basic assumptions and develop new strategies for staying in business."[8] One stragegy for the special collections librarian is to be alert to fields like popular culture which are neglected by other areas of the library. Another is to comb existing special collections to identify materials of research value in these fields that already exist. A third strategy is to work with the faculty and library administration to acquire appropriate collections regardless of the former.

In a world where the book no longer serves as the central mode of communication, the librarian will need to consider the full range of materials available. The disinclination to collect anything but the book will quickly turn the special collections librarian into a caretaker rather than a broker of information. Should that occur, then like the shoemaker, the librarian might as well as go out of business.

REFERENCES

1. Walter M. Miller, Jr., A Canticle for Leibowitz (New York: Bantam Books, 1968), p.143-44.

2. Robert Vosper from a report quoted in "ACRL at Midwinter," College & Research Libraries 19 (March 1958), p. 151.

3. Jack Clarke, "Popular Culture in Libraries," College & Research Libraries 34 (May 1973), p. 215-18.

4. Wayne Wiegand,ed., Current Issues Symposium II: Popular Culture and the Library (Lexington: Office of Continuing Education, College of Library Science, University of Kentucky, 1978).

5. Robert G. Sewell, "Trash or Treasure? Pop Fiction in Academic and Research Libraries," College & Research Libraries 45 (Nov. 1984), p. 450-61; Frank W. Hoffman, Popular Culture and Libraries (Hamdon: Library Professional Publications, 1985).

6. Major popular culture collections include the Popular Culture Library at Bowling Green University, the Nye Popular Culture Collection at Michigan STate University, the Hess Collection at the University of Minnesota, as well as collections housed in the Library of Congress, the Special Collections Division at the University of Kansas Library, Kent State University, the University of Illinois at Urbana-Champaign, and the Wisconsin State Historical Society Library.

7. Gordon Stevenson, "The Wayward Scholar: Resources and Research in Popular Culture," Library Trends, 25 (April 1977), p. 779-818.

8. Nina Matheson, "The Academic Library Nexus," College & Research Libraries 45 (May 1984), p. 208.

CAPTURING THE MAINSTREAM: AN EXAMINATION OF PUBLISHER-BASED AND
SUBJECT-BASED APPROVAL PLANS IN ACADEMIC LIBRARIES

Karen A. Schmidt
University of Illinois at Urbana-Champaign Library
Urbana, Illinois

Abstract. Approval plans in large academic research libraries have had mixed acceptance and success. Much of the negative reaction may be caused by not designing a plan suitable for the book market and the needs of research libraries. The author compares the viability of subject- and publisher-based plans for academic libraries in both domestic and international markets, and presents the case for the over-riding success of the publisher-based plan for domestic publications, and subject-based plan for international markets. The intrinsic differences between the two types of plans are discussed, and the publishing industries of North America and Europe are reviewed for their impact on approval plans covering various countries. The experience of the University of Illinois-Urbana Library is presented as a specific case for the relative success of both types of plans. The collection, the library organization, and the vagaries of the publishing industries of many countries form the basis for selecting the proper plan which is most economical.

The consensus of the research on approval plans appears to be that approval plans are effective and efficient, but only when certain objective realities are present. These practicalities include having a clearly-defined collection development statement; library selectors who understand the collection development policy, agree with it, and are prepared to work together for the mutual benefit of the collection; an approval plan profile which reflects this collection development policy; an adequate acquisitions staff to evaluate properly the plan in view of changing curricula, the plan's return rate, and the collection's needs; and, a vendor who can appreciate the idiosyncrasies of each library and can perform according to the library's expectations. The research, unfortunately, in the main part revolves around the question of having or not having an approval plan, and around the mechanics of slips and streamers and stamping. The question of types of plans has not been examined in detail, yet there are several factors affecting types of plans which bear examination, and are, in fact, of primary importance.

The profile of an approval plan is a coded representation of areas in which the library wishes to collect. It usually consists of key terms and vendor-specific numbering schemes of an intricate nature. The profile is the key to translating a library's approval plan needs to the vendor. It also is the major source of trouble, is time-consuming for both the vendor and library to create, and is, almost invariably, in a constant state of flux. All the other factors which are commonly thought of as being points of difficulty with approval plans - problems such as uneven shipments, or inadequate selection - are factors internal to the library or the vendor, and thus, within their individual power to correct. The profile is the only way in which the vendor and library interact, and is, therefore, the heart of the subject-based approval plan.

Because of the importance of, and potential for, problems which the subject profile presents, it is useful to look at various types of approval plans in academic libraries, in order to see if some simplification of the subject plan can be made. It is common for academic libraries which accept the notion of approval plans to have at least two different types of plans: a subject-based plan and a university press plan. The latter is, of course, a specialized publisher-based plan. With the subject-based plan, the library's collection development statement (or some subset thereof) in key-term or coded form is matched with the vendor's subject profile. Readership levels are negotiated, as are costs and the subjects to be included with the vendor. The books which are sent are chosen on the basis of these arrangements, the selectors come to agreements on where titles belong, and the acquisitions department monitors in a continuing manner the results of the agreements reached. No matter how detailed the arrangements are, subject-based plans have inherently a measure of subjectivity in matching subject concepts to individual titles. Conversely, in a university press plan, a list of accepted university presses are agreed upon at the beginning, and the books from these presses are sent. The agreement approaches that of a standing order or blanket order, although it is uncommon for a vendor to reject any returns of non-selected books. Providing the vendor is reliable, and since the basis for selection is utterly objective, little or no monitoring is necessary.

It is illuminating to review what happens to each title under the two types of plan. In a subject-based plan, selection occurs on many levels. The vendor acts as the selector at the first instance, and may profile books from publisher's blurbs, and re-examine the book once it is in hand. The book is matched to the library's profile, the vendor makes appropriate purchasing agreements with the publisher and the book is sent to the library. Once in the library, the selection process begins again, with selectors reviewing the book and making selections and negotiations with other librarians. The subject-based plan becomes, in effect, a bookstore, in which books are examined and selected or rejected. The subject plan also poses the question of whether a particular title will be sent: "profiling" is a kind of classification process, and the vendor's classification may not match that of the subject selector. If the profiling is at all detailed, the book may be described differently from the way the selector might expect, and, thus, may not be sent. Many vendors supply the library with various types of lists of titles expected on approval. Such lists can be checked, although this is a time-consuming process. Anyway, the lists may not match titles sent. The obvious answer is to send all firm orders to the approval vendor, although this is not usually a wise use of resources, since libraries should use different vendors for different materials, depending upon the vendor's individual strengths.

In university press plans, true selection as an intellectual process occurs only once, when it is agreed that a press will be included in the plan. Selectors are familiar with the products of the university presses, and accept that a title published by, say, the University of Chicago Press will be scholarly and necessary to the academic library collection. Selectors may review the books as they arrive, but rarely do they select (or, more accurately, reject) titles. The vendor is not required to pre-select and describe the book, although there are many who do. This type of plan has the added benefit of assuring what will be received, without reviewing vendor lists or selecting vendors on the basis of approval plan agreements.

The nature of the domestic market is such that many publishers seek out what might be perceived as "territories" of publishing, which are well known to informed librarians. As an example, it is accepted that Wiley Scientific will produce scholarly scientific titles which will be of interest to academic libraries. It is likely that such libraries will have standing orders for Wiley's various series publications. Similarly, we recognize that Harper & Row will publish worthwhile literary authors, and good books of general interest. Because of this generalized knowledge, librarians as selectors feel comfortable with the works of the domestic trade market. It is likely that these books will become part of the library's collection, but a subject-based plan cannot, by its nature, reflect this knowledge. Libraries construct elaborate profiles, ask vendors to determine if each title fits, then begin the selection process again by re-assessing each title in light of their collections.

It is a common configuration within the academic research library to have subject specialists, who may be independent subject librarians or bibliographers, or may be part of an acquisitions department or other technical service area. These persons usually are well-trained in their particular area of expertise to identify and select items from a wide array of material. It is, therefore, a very inefficient use of personnel resources to ask these librarians to become involved in the selection of easily identified and acquired material. Just as it is not good economic or professional sense to ask original cataloguers to handle OCLC cataloguing, neither is it practical or cost-efficient to request that trained bibliographers identify Harper & Row books. Their knowledge of their subject area is far better spent in identifying fugitive and difficult materials than in dealing with what can easily and reasonably be expected to be an automatic acquisition for an academic library collection.

Conversely, a publisher-based plan provides economies in a number of different ways. First, the books expected are known quantities. Like the university press plans, once a publisher is selected, the selection process is virtually over. There is, therefore, a savings in both selectors' and acquisitions staff time. There also may be materials budget advantages, if vendors are willing to increase discounts for more easily managed approval plans with a high rate of acceptance. Money tied up in continuations budgets for publishers' series may be "freed" to purchase series titles as they appear in monographic form; this may well enable fund managers to handle yearly expenditures more easily.

Publisher-based plans do not ignore subjects, but subordinate them to the overall concept. One may request that books on, say, theology be exempted from coverage, or be provided as details on "exclusion forms" instead. Of more importance are the readership level and format of the books. One may exclude popular level titles, and reprints or expensive editions. The fewer the exclusions, though, the more effective and understandable is the plan.

As described later, the University of Illinois-Urbana Library made the shift from subject- to publisher-based approval plans, following a very simple experiment which is believed to be beneficial to every large academic research library having a subject-based approval plan. Recent annual publisher's catalogues from a few well-known publishers were chosen and checked against our holdings. It was found that the holdings of these titles were well over ninety percent. In checking to see if these titles had come as a result of our subject-based plan, or because of individual firm orders, the results were less cheering: a significant portion (and in some subject areas, a majority) of titles came as a result of firm orders. The approval vendor supplied a list of publishers issuing a significant number of titles received as a result of our subject-based approval plans, which was modified somewhat to reflect the specific interests of our library collection. Because of the findings of the study, a change from an unsatisfactory (in terms of titles received and titles rejected) subject-based to publisher-based approval plan was implemented.

The results in terms of the return rate for books, the ability to predict which titles are expected, and the savings in personnel time and energy for both professionals and support staff have been significant, as has been the currency of acquisition of mainstream domestic titles.

Do the same considerations apply when dealing with non-domestic titles? Foreign publishing has a different structure from that of America. The same objectives of the collection development policy, and the same factors concerning approval plans, exist. What is different is the publishing houses, their physical distance from North America, and our own knowledge of the publishing industry in Europe and elsewhere. To develop successful collections representative of these foreign countries, it is extremely important to have current and accurate access to information concerning new publications. While Publishers' Weekly and like publications keep selectors informed about North American publishing, there are few European publications which reach us in a timely fashion and allow us to make selections immediately. Additionally, foreign print runs are usually smaller than American, which increases the necessity to purchase quickly. Our knowledge of the publishing houses, too, is lessened not only because of simple geography, but also because the business of publishing in Europe and Asia frequently is carried out in a manner which sometimes mystifies us. For example, it is a common misconception that European publishers and vendors can give North American libraries discounts, but for some inexplicable reason refuse to do so (Anti-Americanism, perhaps?). In fact, there are no discount schedules to pass along to customers in North America, due to the economics of publishing in many of these countries. Likewise, copyright agreements between European and United States and Canadian publishers are ill-understood. It is not uncommon to find selectors 'playing the market' by trying to second-guess which Springer or Oxford University Press edition will cost less or be published first. Such misconceptions about the European publishing industry reveal the extent to which we need to rely upon our European and other foreign vendors for their understanding of their own economic and scholarly communities and their ability to translate our needs into their business language. A factor of great importance is the homogeneity of the publishing industry in Europe, Western Europe particularly. Publishers tend to deal in one subject area to an even greater extent than is done in the United States. The effect upon the development of a traditional subject-based approval plan is significant.

With all these considerations, the argument against approval plan subject profiles makes less sense than it does with domestic publishers. While all the inherent problems with the subject profiles still obtain, regardless of the geographical region, the less information known about a group of publications, the more meaningful the role of the vendor in the collection development process. Thus, it is likely that an academic research library will depend on a European vendor's subject profile to obtain books quickly, unless that library has a subject specialist so familiar with the publishing market of the country in question that a subject profile for that country is redundant. However, it is important to reiterate that publishing houses in many parts of Europe are focussed upon relatively narrow subject ranges and have more homogeneity of readership level than their American counterparts. A subject-based plan for foreign countries, therefore, is not unlike a publisher-based plan for this country.

As a case in point, the University of Illinois-Urbana Library has a number of approval plans, both subject- and publisher-based. As described above, the domestic subject-based profiles were replaced by publisher-based profiles, because the subject profiles were imperfect representations of the collection development needs of the Library, and because the selectors did not have sufficient faith in the profile to provide the books they thought appropriate for the collection. The subject-based profile caused very high return (rejection) rates, some of which approached sixty percent, an economically intolerable situation. Now, the publisher-based plan[3] has return rates of less than ten percent. Additionally, the Library has subject-based profiles with several European vendors, who are able to interpret the Library's needs into specific book selections. In the case of area studies, the Library relies on blanket orders which are not primarily based on subject consideration, but, like publisher-based plans, limit what is sent by broad subject and format categories. Over the past few years, following the simple maxim that subject-based profiles are more likely to succeed when less is known about an area's publications has proven to be a successful formula for acquiring the easy-to-identify titles.

It is important for academic libraries to ask not only the "why" of approval plans, but also the "what." It is the less obvious management question concerning approval plans, and is the more important. Once committed to an approval plan - which should be an accepted and useful component of collection development for academic libraries - it is far more interesting and useful to review exactly what the plan is and can do. Does it duplicate the work and knowledge of the selectors? If the library's selectors are professionals trained in the subject area, it is unlikely a subject plan is needed for domestic publications. What kind of staff will maintain the mechanical points of the plan? If the approval plans take more than 1.0 to 1.5 FTE to maintain, then the plans are too cumbersome. If there is adequate knowledge about the publishers of any one country, then there is little need for a subject-based plan. The approval plan is an adjunct to good selection and economic management of the academic library. It does not replace the need for a collection development statement, nor is it a replacement for the subject specialist, but a useful tool which provides for the greatest use of the professional potential within academic libraries, by freeing selectors from mundane activities and, thus, enabling them to concentrate on the truly professional aspects of their work.

LIBRARY ADMINISTRATION

THE DEVELOPMENT TEAM

Dwight F. Burlingame
Bowling Green State University
Bowling Green, Ohio

Abstract. The need for additional resource development for academic libraries is recognized. One way to proceed is by developing a team approach with the development office on campus. Principles of team play in the development context are received as well as other approaches librarians can utilize to enhance their fund-raising efforts.

Virtually all libraries--public, school, academic, and special--face financial problems. Why is this the case today? If one examines the current mission and goals of libraries, and tomorrow's expected results, we begin to realize the depth of our problem.

The academic library continues to support the teaching, research, and service needs of its many and varied clientele. Additionally, it is faced with the complex problems of the rapid growth rate of information, its cost, and delivery. Further, quality library service is expensive. New technologies are also expensive and sources of funding are increasingly difficult to obtain. Traditional funding for library programs are being overburdened at the local, campus and state levels at a time when federal support is being reduced.

Declines in enrollment of traditional students for many private and state supported colleges and universities coupled with legislators unwillingness to provide tax dollars for education spells trouble. With expansive missions, increased costs and reduced financial resources, libraries are forced to examine alternatives----one such alternative is to seek alternative funding sources. Breivik and Gibson noted in 1979 that; "The overall financial situation for libraries is such that the profession must be ready, actively and openly, to seek all possible funding sources." (Breivik, pp. 8-9) They go on to state that "Most libraries seem reluctant to engage in major fund-raising efforts." (Breivik, pp. 8-9).

Today we are witnessing more and more librarians expressing the desire to become actively involved. There is a vast amount of material available in the professional literature of fund raising with encouraging signs of more application in librarianship. How can we maximize our efforts for the best results? I argue that the route we need to take is in cooperation with the campus development office. Of course, this argument presupposes a climate that can make this possible.

Many of us in librarianship unfortunately think of development as the Madison Avenue slick of the local united fund drive. This attitude is often a combination of cynicism, ignorance, and skepticism. We can no longer afford to maintain such snobbery. Development, fund raising, and institutional advancement require a well-defined management team with the best talent available, including librarians.

One avenue for many academic librarians to begin to give and receive information is by serving on the college or university development advisory committee or council. Such bodies are usually charged to provide information to the development office regarding institutional priorities for fund-raising efforts. Active participation on liaison committees can be an important element in connecting the library needs to the overall campus or community development strategies and programs. Competition among colleagues for priority within the development goals of the parent institution or body is often evident. Recognizing the existence of such competition and illustrating the library's unique contributions to almost all areas will help ensure a successful library development program.

We must take a broad view of development activities. Not only is involvement of directors, board members, and others important; but our <u>attitude</u> toward development is also critical to success. It is important to understand that institutional advancement, alumni relations, public affairs, government relations and the like are not <u>just</u> fund raising. It is time and, in fact, is necessary, that we appreciate the vital component which fund raising represents in our organizations and that we provide appropriate support for such activity.

Money is needed for quality library programs. The success of raising money for a library fund-raising campaign is certainly going to be directly related to an exciting and vital program which will entice patrons, legislators, and donors to support. No one likes a loser, and certainly no one bets on him twice. Donors want to become part of an exciting and significant program. The cue for librarians is clear in this regard. It is crucial that the development officer inspires contributions by the ability to converse intelligently about an exciting and lively library. The team approach becomes even more critical in developing such an understanding.

Over the course of several years, I have listened to many librarians and to several development officers talk about their respective roles in fund raising. Librarians, in particular, have often said, 'That's their job.' or 'his job--not mine.' Librarians who persist in this kind of attitude need to stop and take a second look.

The establishment of what is commonly referred to by development professionals as a constituent-based program is a desirable framework in which to apply the development team approach. To maximize this approach it is appropriate to review essential principles of team play. The following are suggested as major guidelines for the librarian and the development office to follow:

1. Listen to the team member--A concerted effort to listen to the other is crucial. Recognition of valuable contributions of a team member can be most important. Do not be afraid to suggest an idea which may appear extreme.

2. Communicate often with your team members--Every development officer will have at least one vivid recollection of the time that he/she called on a foundation or private donor who didn't know of the library's program and need. And had he/she been aware of it last Thursday, it would have been the perfect project to raise with donor X. Clear communication and joint planning of needs prevent, or at least lessen, the frequency of this kind of horror story.

There is little substitution for the knowledge gained by the development officer in the mutual formation and revision of a list of needs. Periodically reviewing the list will facilitate a familiarity with the library needs by the development officer and thereby improve his ability to be conversant with your needs. This process also allows one to update priorities.

3. Praise your team member's progress and try not to play one-up-manship. Does it really make a difference who received the grant? More important is that the library has been successful in meeting a need by an alternative source of funding.

4. Correct errors of your team member in private and provide for a climate which encourages open and frank criticism. Recognize that he/she will look at things differently and often approach common problems differently.

5. Develop a climate which is informal and relaxed. Certainly, having lunch or dinner with the development officer and building relationships that encourage openness will facilitate your success.

6. Maintain enthusiasm--Even if you do not like development work, enthusiasm for your cause must be evident. A maxim often heard in the fund-raising field is "The response of the prospective donor will be in direct proportion to the commitment and enthusiasm of the solicitor."

7. Maintain a clear understanding of goals--In order for any partnership to survive, there must be clear understanding of/or agreements between the two parties. Many librarians and development officers suffer from what some describe as the "eighties blues" because of the tremendous pressure to obtain scarce resources. A beginning point must be built upon a clear mutual understanding of what kind of library one is striving to build. If common goals are not present, the partnership will soon find itself split and attempting to reach goals by driving through a fog with no fog lights.

8. Develop mutual respect--Along with a clear understanding of goals must go mutual respect for each other's competence and expertise. How often have librarians portrayed the typical development man as a smooth, good looking athletic type; a somewhat shallow intellectual? Development work requires competent individuals. Professional respect for fund-raisers should dictate our action just as we expect such respect for librarians.

Applying the above guidelines should assist in looking forward and in broadening our base of support. Continuing to make friends, cultivating internal and external friends, and developing an influential base is imperative. We simply cannot let internal problems prevent us from directing valuable attention to support groups. It is not surprising that during the last few years, numerous new "Friends" groups for libraries have been established. There are few more important matters for our attention at this juncture than the generation of additional resources. If such activity is taken for granted, levels of support will in fact, deteriorate and some sources may well disappear.

Working with grants officers and development officers in your college or university can lead to additional support for the library. Including a section for library materials in grant requests to meet the needs of special projects can lead to additional collection development money. One of the best ways to integrate this activity is by having developed a clear understanding and awareness on the part of the development staff of the library's needs.

Librarians who recognize that fund raising is a team effort which requires a willingness to work together and a clear understanding of common goals will be well on their way to successful development efforts. A leadership role played by the librarian in seeking funds certainly will increase the chance for success. Administrators, trustees, and potential donors often prefer to hear about the library's needs and opportunities from the librarian. Finally, the personal satisfaction gained in working for an important cause cannot be over emphasized.

FINANCING ACADEMIC LIBRARIES: MAKING THE TRANSITION FROM ENROLLMENT
GROWTH TO QUALITY ENHANCEMENT

John M. Cooper
Harvard University
Cambridge, Massachusetts

Abstract. Recent studies addressing virtually every aspect of the quality of higher education have raised expectations for improving colleges and universities. Translating expectations into actions requires resources, and providing adequate funds for maintaining and improving the quality of academic libraries will require changes in the structure and use of funding formulas. Many library formulas are enrollment-driven making library funding vulnerable to stable or declining enrollment. Some states have used cost studies and ACRL library standards to design formulas that rely less on enrollment. Redesigning funding methods to recognize fixed costs changes the underlying premise from one that funds should flow from enrollment growth to one linking funding with programmatic changes. The next challenge is to add factors that reward successful management and enhance the quality of libraries.

Keywords and Phrases. Funding, enrollment, quality, ACRL standards, costs.

INTRODUCTION

Recent studies addressing virtually every component of a college education have raised expectations for improving the quality of higher education. Translating expectations into action requires resources, and providing adequate funds for maintaining and improving the quality of academic libraries will require changes in the structure and use of funding formulas. Most formulas currently used by state-level coordinating and governing boards to calculate library funding requirements are enrollment-driven. Those formulas were developed fifteen to twenty years ago in response to expectations of rapid enrollment growth, and as long as enrollment increased more funds were recommended for libraries. Projections of stable or declining enrollments and the focus on quality bring into question the assumption that enrollment should be the primary determinant of library funding. Whether academic libraries will have the resources to respond to expectations for higher quality will depend in large part on redesigning funding formulas.

Approximately half of the state coordinating or governing boards use a formula approach to developing appropriation recommendations presented to governors and state legislatures.[1] Although formulas are also used by some university systems in allocating funds among constituent campuses, this paper examines state-level formulas which are used in developing requests to governors and legislatures for state funding. While state formulas do not govern campus-level budget allocations to libraries, they can exert a strong influence as an expression of state priorities. Furthermore, the structure and logic of formulas can affect how state decision-makers perceive the funding needs of colleges and universities. Clearly, university administrators, including library directors, have an important stake in understanding and influencing funding formulas.

Although one frequently hears of "the formula", a formula budgeting process consists of several different formulas. To the casual observer these funding formulas appear to be objective, quantitative methods for predicting the funds necessary for operating costs of colleges and universities. Actually, formulas express policy judgements about the mission, quality, governance and organization of higher education.[2] The twin policy questions examined in this paper are what alternative approaches can be used to replace enrollment as the dominant formula variable and how can formulas be redesigned to reward quality improvements in libraries.

ENROLLMENT-DRIVEN FORMULAS

Although concern is being expressed about the strong relationship between enrollment and funding which is built into virtually all formulas, change is occurring slowly. A 1982 survey found that thirty-one state higher education finance officers perceived a breaking down in the relationship between enrollment and state funding.[3] However, two years later the NIE Study Group on Conditions of Excellence concluded that approximately 75 percent of the education and general revenues in all public institutions were still dependent on enrollments.[4]

A survey of library formulas used for fiscal year 1985-86 conducted in preparation of this paper found that the enrollment/funding relationship is still built into many library formulas in one of two ways. Library funding is calculated either using a cost rate per student or as a percentage of funding calculated for instruction. The library formula used by the Alabama Commission on Higher Education is an example of the cost rate per student method. Developed in 1973 and modeled after the Texas formula, student semester credit hours are multiplied by the following cost factors:

Undergraduate	$ 5.46
Grad. I (Masters)	$10.97
Grad. II (Doctoral)	$46.97
Law	$28.98

An example of the second method is the South Carolina Commission on Higher Education's formula which calculates library funding as 10 percent of instructional costs. Since instructional formulas are driven by enrollment, library funding is vulnerable to enrollment declines in both methods. Table 1 classifies several states according to the type of enrollment-driven library formula used for fiscal year 1985-86. Formula states that have moved away from enrollment as the dominant variable are not shown in Table 1 and are discussed in a later section on redesigning formulas.

TABLE 1. CLASSIFICATION OF LIBRARY FORMULA METHODS

Rate Per Student		Percentage of Instruction
Alabama	Kentucky	Louisiana
Connecticut	Texas	South Carolina
Tennessee		Georgia
Missouri		West Virginia
Ohio		Mississippi

During the 1960's and early 1970's, when most formulas were developed, libraries benefited from the assumption that operating costs varied according to enrollment. The assumption incorporated into Alabama's formula, and others like it, is that the cost of providing library services to each additional student is the same for an institution with 2,000 students and one with 20,000 students. In addition, the underlying assumptions are that library costs increase or decrease proportionately to increases or decreases in enrollment, and, at the margin, the cost of serving one more or less student is equal to the average cost of delivering library services to all students. Table 2 shows the results of simulating the impact of a five percent enrollment decline for a doctoral institution having a total enrollment of 15,000 full-time students. Variations in total funding recommendations (column 1) illustrate the diversity of assumptions and costing methods used in developing cost rates. Another important difference is the marginal impact (column 4) on funding of a decline in enrollment.

when a substantial portion of library costs are fixed or are not influenced by enrollment changes. Case studies of budget reallocations or reductions found that while support areas are often first targets for reductions, a short-term solution to funding reductions often becomes a long-term problem.[5] Reductions in a library's collection, hours of operations, and range of services have an adverse ripple effect on instruction, research and an institution's ability to attract and retain faculty and students. Changing library formulas to more accurately reflect cost behavior is one of several approaches for redesigning formulas.

REDESIGNING LIBRARY FORMULAS

Studies on the major influences on library costs have found a substantial portion of library costs to be fixed or influenced by factors other than enrollment. Any producer of goods and service, whether public or private, incurs certain fixed costs regardless of size. Enrollment is just one of several variables reflected in standards developed by the Association of College and Research Libraries (ACRL). The formula for calculating the number of volumes is influenced much more by the number and type of academic offerings than by enrollment. It takes a change of 400 full-time students to have the same impact as adding a single masters field (when no higher degree is offered).[6] Consequently, funding formulas utilizing ACRL standards as a basis for calculating cost would be less sensitive to enrollment declines.

Fixed costs associated with many academic functions are extremely hard to quantify, but ACRL standards can provide a basis for redesigning funding formulas to reflect fixed costs. In 1979 the University of Wisconsin System initiated a study of fixed and variable costs because of a concern that the state funding formula did not adequately reflect actual cost behavior.[7] One purpose was to better understand the resources required for academic libraries if they were to

TABLE 2. SIMULATION OF 5% ENROLLMENT REDUCTION ON LIBRARY FORMULAS

State	15,000 Enrollment	Avg. Funds Per Student	5% Enrollment Decline	Funds Loss Per Student
Alabama	$3,028,134	$202	($151,408)	$202
Connecticut	$3,615,802	$241	($181,050)	$241
Texas	$2,947,701	$196	($147,385)	$196
Kentucky	$4,288,427	$286	($205,883)	$275
Arkansas	$3,333,873	$222	($103,500)	$138

Comparing the average library funding provided per student (column 2) for 15,000 students with the reduction in funding per student shows that some states (Kentucky and Arkansas) have developed formulas which moderate the impact of enrollment declines on funding calculations.

While some reduction in overall institutional funding may be appropriate if a declining enrollment trend is occurring, unintentional and severe consequences occur to libraries when a formula subtracts the average cost per student

continue providing adequate support during a period of declining enrollment. The Wisconsin study found that fixed costs represented 67.1% of total library costs for four nondoctoral institutions.

ACRL standards provides the basis of a "core funding" formula developed in 1982 by the Arkansas Department of Higher Education. A fixed amount of funding is recommended for a core library program supporting existing academic programs and a base enrollment level. Fixed core amounts vary for four types of institutions and base enrollment levels as shown in Table 3.

TABLE 3. ARKANSAS CORE FUNDING FORMULA 1985-86

Inst Institutional Group	Enrollment Base	Fixed Cost Base	Marginal Rate Per Student Above Base
Doctoral	10,000	$2,643,873	$138
Masters	5,000	$1,141,414	$138
Other 4-Year	2,000	$ 468,636	$138
Two-Year	500	$ 105,627	$138

The average funds per student in the core program ranges from a high of $264 for doctoral to a low of $211 for two-year, considerably higher than the marginal rate of $138. The lower marginal rate is derived from ACRL standards allowing 15 volumes per FTE student.

Other states have also successfully incorporated the use of ACRL or other appropriate standard into library formulas. A special task force revised the library formula used by the Maryland State Board for Higher Education. Changes came in response to concerns of university librarians that funding guidelines based solely on enrollment were too simplistic and unrepresentative of the scope and nature of library services. The revised library guideline consists of five parts: a fixed cost component; a component for normal book purchases based on five percent of the American Library Association standards for each library; a component to reflect faculty needs; a component for research needs; and a component for enrollment.[8] The Virginia Council of Higher Education has added a basic staffing requirement regardless of enrollment with the use of Association of Research Libraries or other appropriate standard in calculating expenditure requirements for maintenance of current collections.[9] The revisions made by these states rest on the assumption that a library must support a relatively fixed array of academic courses, mix of faculty, and research programs.

Redesigning funding methods to recognize fixed costs changes the underlying premise from one that funding should flow from enrollment growth to one linking funding with programmatic decisions. If significant enrollment decline is forecast or is occurring, decisions to cut back library funding should result from a review of the scope of academic programs and desired library services. For example, cancellation of health care periodical subscriptions should come from a decision to phase out a graduate program in public health rather than from a forced reduction caused by an enrollment-driven formula.

Incorporating into funding formulas an analysis of library volumes required by ACRL or other appropriate standard draws attention to the gap between existing and required volumes. Several states have recommended funding, in addition to formula amounts, to allow institutions to progress toward meeting library standards. During the last three biennia $6.4 million has been appropriated from capital improvement funds to Arkansas colleges and universities to address arrearages in library collections. Capital funding has been in addition to regular state operating funds. Funding for each institution was recommended to either close the gap between existing volumes and ACRL standards by ten percent or add two percent to total volumes required by ACRL standards, whichever was greater.[10] The North Dakota State Board of Higher Education approved a task force plan to attain, over the next three biennia, library collections and services comparable with other academic libraries in the region.[11] A total of $317,155 was recommended for the 1985-87 biennium. A final example of over formula funding is contained in the Virginia formula described earlier. Institutions showing a major deficiency in library holdings may request additional funds for reducing the deficiency.

State action to address library deficiencies is certainly laudable, but is it sufficient? What if institutions choose not to spend additional funds for library volumes? Extra funds to reduce deficiencies could supplant funds normally budgeted for collection replacement without increasing the total library budget. If additional funds are provided in proportion to the deficiency, what incentive or reward is provided for institutions which have struggled to improve library collections? Why should institutions that starve library budgets be rewarded with larger funding recommendations? An important task in redesigning formulas is to encourage effective library management and planning by rewarding performance. However, efforts to redesign library formulas have not responded to the challenge of creating formulas which reward successful results.

THE NEXT CHALLENGE--ENHANCING QUALITY

Many of those responsible for making state funding decisions are seeking ways to link quality with funding. Funding formulas that strive to treat similar institutions alike can have a "leveling" effect on institutional quality.[12] For example, using a statewide average cost rate for a group of similar libraries benefits the ones below average and inadequately supports more diverse or specialized libraries. None of the library formulas reviewed for this paper attempt to hinge a portion of funding to excellence in the delivery of library services. Some formulas may even retard improvements by yielding larger funding recommendations for those libraries with the weakest collections compared with ACRL standards. If an institution embarks on a program to improve its library collection and services by raising private funds, by budget reallocations, or other strategy, the institution assumes all the risk and anxieties. The addition of selective funding incentives could encourage institutions to take risks that could enhance quality.

Every formula has a reward or incentive system, and since 1979 Tennessee has been experimenting with performance-related funding. The Tennessee policy allows an institution to earn an additional amount, up to two percent of its budget, determined by performance on five variables.[13] The variables assess overall performance such as the number of programs accredited or the performance of graduates on tests in their major fields. A recent study by the Education Commission of the States found that innovations various states have undertaken in the last several years encourage quality improvement.[14] The most common approaches provide special funds for quality improvement for specific programs or general areas, deemphasize enrollment as a basis for appropriations, and provide special endowments or matching grants to attract top faculty.

Much of this paper discusses redesigning formulas to deemphasize enrollment as the driving force for funding. Going beyond that step to innovations which enhance quality is desirable but not without problems. Where quality determines a portion of funding, there will be winners and losers. Were a portion of funding linked to attainment of ACRL standards, tremendous pressure probably would mount to dilute the standards so more institutions could qualify. Developing new measures of performance could be costly and might result in giving attention to the most easily measured efforts rather than the most important aspects of library services. It might be that after a few years of trying, states will abandon efforts to design funding strategies which enhance quailty. However, if states persist in their efforts, those library administrators willing to contribute to the process may be among the winners. Given the contributions that technological advances can make toward improved library services and the critical importance of libraries to an institution's instructional programs, funding innovations which address quality could very likely result in improved funding for library services.

REFERENCES

1. Francis M. Gross, "Formula Budgeting and the Financing of Public Higher Education: Panacea or Nemesis for the 1980's," The Association for Institutional Research Professional File, 3 (Fall 1979).

2. William H. Pickens, "Statewide Formulas to Support Higher Education" (Paper prepared for the National Conference of State Legislatures, June 1980).

3. Larry L. Leslie, "Recent Financing Developments in the 50 States" in Survival in the 1980's: Quality, Mission and Financing Options, ed. R. A. Wilson. (Tucson, Ariz.: Center for the Study of Higher Education, 1983).

4. National Institute of Education, Involvement in Learning: Realizing the Potential of American Higher Education. Final report of the Study Group on the Conditions of Excellence in American Higher Education. (Washington, D.C.: NIE, 1984).

5. James A. Hyatt, C. H. Shulman, and A. A. Santiago, Reallocations: Strategies for Effective Resource Management (Washington, D.C.: National Association of College and University Business Officers, 1984).

6. The Association of College and Research Libraries, Standards for College Libraries. (Chicago, Ill.: ACRL, 1975).

7. National Association of College and University Business Officers, Costing for Policy Analysis (Washington, D.C.: NACUBO, 1980).

8. Maryland State Board for Higher Education, Operating Budget Guideline Development. (Annapolis: State Board for Higher Education, 1984).

9. Virginia Council for Higher Education, Operating Budget Guidelines and Special Requirements for 1984-86 Biennium (Richmond: CHE, December 1982).

10. Arkansas Department of Higher Education, General Revenue Recommendations for Arkansas Higher Education (Little Rock: ADHE, October, 1984).

11. North Dakota State Board of Higher Education, Funding North Dakota Higher Education. (North Dakota State Board for Higher Education, November 1984).

12. Paul T. Brinkman, "Formula Budgeting: The Fourth Decade" in Responding to New Realities in Funding, ed. L. L. Leslie, New Directions for Institutional Research, no. 43 (San Francisco: Jossey Bass, 1984).

13. E. Grady Bogue and Wayne Brown, "Performance Incentives for State Colleges," Harvard Business Review (Nov.-Dec. 1982).

14. Education Commission of the States, Catalog of Changes: Incentives for Quality and Management Flexibility in Higher Education (Boulder: ECS, 1984).

MANAGING VALUES IN AN ACADEMIC LIBRARY

Mary Ann Griffin

Villanova University Library

Villanova, PA

Abstract. Developments in technology, in organizational structure, and in higher education are placing increasing demands on library managers. The library director, once primarily concerned with finances, and the management of collection, staff, and facilities, must increasingly be concerned with the articulation of values. The author recommends that the formulation and promulgation of a value system is essential to organizational success.

Keywords and Phrases. Values, Management, Values Articulation, Organizational Values

Books such as In Search of Excellence, Making America Work, Change Masters and others seek to convince their readers of the importance of an accepted value system to effective organizational performance. They repeatedly stress the necessity of values management within an organization. While values management is not a new concept in the literature of management generally, it is not one which has received much attention in library literature. What do we know about the management of values in academic libraries?

As organizations, libraries seek to fulfill certain purposes and goals. Because academic libraries are departments of a larger organizational unit, the college or university, and not entities unto themselves, the academic library functions within that larger setting. Higher education is a value-laden process. The tradition of academic life is the "search for truth." Fairness, intellectual inquiry, tolerance of ideas, respect for the facts, dissemination of knowledge are all values that are readily associated with the higher education community. However, higher education is not reputed to be an area exhibiting great management expertise. In the opening pages of their book on the American College President entitled Leadership and Ambiguity, Michael Cohen and James March describe colleges and universities as having problematic goals, unclear technology and fluid participation.[1] A brief explanation of these terms is useful for the consideration of values management. An organization suffers from problematic goals when it bases its operation on a variety of ill-defined and often inconsistent preferences. Unclear technology implies that the organization often uses procedures resulting from accidents of past experience or from imitation of what other institutions are doing. Fluid participation describes the situation where the amount of time and effort that individuals give to the organization is not consistent. (An example is the faculty member who works within the context of a profession more than within the context of a specific institution.) Cohen and March summarize the higher education realm with the phrase "organized anarchy." Being more generous, some researchers of management consciously use the term "environment" rather than "organization" when describing colleges and universities. Whatever the shortcomings or benefits, higher education is the setting in which academic libraries operate. As a component of this larger functioning unit, the academic library should work toward fulfilling specific educational goals and institutional purposes, and in so doing reflect organizational values.

Librarians seek to organize and make available for use thousands or even millions of items. They purchase items that they feel have potential for use, they categorize them and add them to the collection, they help users find what they need among the vast stores of information and they try to retrieve items that have not been returned after they have been borrowed from the premises. How do these activities reflect organizational values? If fundamental objectives are the selection, acquisition, cataloging, lending and retrieval of items, how is the library really different from Joe's local rent-a-tool operation?

The purposes of most academic libraries are similar. They might be described in the following way:
-building a collection of information for present and future use
-providing access to information
-serving as consultant in the use of information resources
-instructing in the process of information retrieval.

These purposes could be summarized with the phrase "facilitating the information to knowledge process." This summary statement reflects the instructional mode of higher education.

In his recent book, The Management of Values,[2] Charles McCoy states that an organization reflects its values through the goals it sets for itself. This rather simplistic sounding statement contains the implication that a value system drives the formulation of policies, goals, and practices. Most people would readily agree with the advisability of such a situation. The reality is that all too often the formulation of policy results from reaction to immediate pressures. Referring again to the higher education environment, one sometimes senses that institutional policy formulation could more accurately be described as aiming at an erratically moving target. While the academic realm is replete with values, institutions have often not used their values to effectively guide their practices. It's been my experience that libraries are frequently acknowledged to be among the best managed operations on campuses. Given the managerial reputation of academe perhaps this is not a significant feat. Although the profit and not-for-profit sectors are driven by different motivations, it is not surprising that library administrators look to the realm of business to extract practices that might have successful application in their own setting.

The popular book, In Search of Excellence, discusses the values of excellent companies.[3] The authors tell us that: 1) the values are usually stated in qualitative rather than quantitative terms; 2) financial or strategic objectives are never an end in themselves, but are related to whatever else the company expects to do well; 3) the values are meant to inspire everyone in the firm; 4) values are often identified through the juxtaposition of certain factors; e.g. cost versus service, operation versus innovation, formality versus informality, control orientation versus people orientation. Peters and Waterman also list values that are dominant in excellent companies:
  -belief in being the best
  -belief in the importance of the individual
  -belief in superior quality and service
  -belief in the importance of informality to enhance communication
  -belief in the importance of details in doing a job well
  -belief that most members of the organization should be innovators
  -recognition of the importance of growth and profit.

Again and again, one reads in management literature that managing the values of an organization is at the core of effective leadership. Tom Watson, Jr. of IBM, one of the "excellent companies," stated almost thirty years ago:

I firmly believe that any organization, in order to survive and achieve success, must have a sound set of beliefs on which it premises all its policies and actions. Next, I believe that the most important single factor in corporate success is faithful adherence to those beliefs, And finally, I believe that if an organization is to meet the challenges of a changing world, it must be prepared to change everything about itself except those beliefs as it moves through corporate life.[4]

What can be said about the values or beliefs of academic libraries? In particular, what are the organizational values in your library? It is likely that many of us cannot readily answer that question. If that is the case, it indicates that explicit values are not pervasive in the library organization. Some would say that's not important since most librarians have a sense of what library values would be. But that response is subject to the same problems as the following statement: Don't ask me to define real art, I know it when I see it.

Each person who works in an organization brings an individual set of values to the workplace. Values provide guidelines to interpret the significance to an individual of certain happenings. Everything a person does is based on values, that are either consciously or unconsciously held. Unless organizational values are promulgated and accepted by employees as worthy, values held by individuals become the ones that are exhibited in the workplace. This may mean tha lack of consistent application of values within the organization. It may mean a department or division orientation rather than a library orientation. It may mean organizational drift, whereby decisions are made in response to pressures rather than by taking commonly held beliefs into account. It may mean excessive agonizing in decisionmaking at all levels, or frequent questioning of decisions.

Prevalent values of excellent companies have been noted. What might be some examples of values of an academic library? Undoubtedly, these would vary somewhat from one library to another. Some values might be:
  -equal access to information
  -providing a balanced collection
  -superior assistance to users
  -the importance of each staff member to the organization
  -the importance of scholarly endeavors.
Most of us could readily accept these values. Other more controversial ones might include:
  -information without charge
  -the importance of access to information rather than collection building
  -the importance of the librarian rather than the collection as the source of information
  -the librarian as teacher rather than information provider
  -the importance of an informal atmosphere to library effectiveness.

When values of an organization are not readily evident, the logical question that follows is: How can the values of a library organization best be determined? One response to this question might be that those in top levels of management know the important values. That may well be true. However, unless these values are then successfully transmitted to all employees of the organization, the values are not organizational values. The values may be informing policy at top levels, but what is happening with the translation of policy into action further down the line?

Managing values within an organization presupposes that a manager can identify and promote the criteria (or values) by which policy will be formulated. If the exact nature of the values is not known, values clarification techniques exist that can be used to identify most strongly held values. The values clarification process involves a logical analysis whose results specify values that are freely chosen after carefully considering alternative values. The values must become positively accepted, publicly affirmed and acted upon repeatedly to have validity as a values system.[5] Sociologist Philip Selznick tells us:

Truly accepted values must infuse the organization at many levels, affecting the perspectives and attitudes of personnel, the relative importance of staff activities, the distribution of authority, relations with outside groups, and many other matters.6

"Structured Chaos" is a phrase used by Peters and Waterman to describe one of the hallmarks of excellent companies. While it may seem that "chaos" might better describe the situation in some academic libraries, "structured chaos" is the aim of those striving for excellence. In this kind of environment, a sense of individual responsibility, an action orientation and the ability to deal with ambiguity are important characteristics along with genine acceptance of specified organizational values.

Let's consider what might be some specific outcomes of values management:
  (1) staff members become more conscious of the values that they and the organization have in common (or at odds)
  (2) motivation is greater when employees are aware of value priorities of the organization
  (3) common organizational values allow an effective work environment even when cultural values may be in conflict
  (4) interpersonal conflicts can be made more objective when there are expected value norms for the organization
  (5) encouragement of innovation has less problematic results when there are commonly held values
  (6) managers can become more aware of the degree of correspondence between organizational values and the values of the constituency served.

It is becoming increasingly crucial for library managers to set priorities and make choices. They are being faced with a variety of pressures: technological developments and accompanying technical problems, an expanding range of organizational activities, employees who seek involvement and participation but who also bring more specialized skills and thus more autonomy to their work environment, increasingly decentralized decisionmaking, greater complexities in relationships such as those arising from library cooperatives or funding agencies.

The real difference between organizational success and failure is no doubt determined by the degree to which the library utilizes the energies and talents of its people. But, as much as we need them, good people are not enough in this time of transition. Library management must help staff members find common cause with each other. This is done by nurturing an overall perspective rather than by just maintaining organizational equilibrium, and by deepening the consensus about beliefs and commitments. This means that staff members are well aware that they are part of one organization and contribute to shared goals. The inner cohesion produces a coordination of activity that can surpass in significance that which can be achieved through organizational hierarchies or policies and regulations.

Human resource management, financial management, collection management, and facilities management have all received substantial and ongoing treatment in the library realm. It is time that values management also receives due recognition and is consciously practiced.

REFERENCES

1. Michael D. Cohen and James G. March, *Leadership and Ambiguity: the American College President* (New York: McGraw-Hill, 1974), p.2-3.

2. Charles S. McCoy, *Management of Values: the Ethical Difference in Corporate Policy and Performance* (Boston: Pitman, 1985).

3. Thomas J. Peters and Robert H. Waterman, Jr., *In Search of Excellence: Lessons from America's Best-Run Companies* (New York: Warner, 1984), p.284-285.

4. Thomas J. Watson, Jr., *A Business and Its Beliefs* (New York: McGraw-Hill, 1963), p.5.

5. Dale D. Simmons, *Personal Valuing* (Chicago: Nelson Hall, 1982), p.18.

6. Philip Selznick, *Leadership in Administration* (New York: Harper & Row, 1957), p.26-27.

STRATEGIES FOR CHANGE

Carol A. Johnson and Michael D. Kathman
Alcuin Library, St. John's University
Collegeville, Minnesota

Abstract. Change is an inescapable part of the automation process, and any change has the potential for a constructive or destructive effect on the library organization. Change is accompanied by fear, both realistic and unrealistic, which must be dealt with during all stages of the automation process. As a result, any library considering an online system needs to be aware of the effects of change and consider the human factors in its planning process. This paper details the Joint Library's experience with anticipated and unanticipated changes occurring during the planning stages for automation.

Keywords and Phrases. Online Catalog; automation; change; Microcomputers; PERT; Myers-Briggs.

The Joint Library of the College of Saint Benedict and St. John's University has been in serious pursuit of an online catalog since 1981. The further we progressed, the more apparent it became that the human factors relating to change were as important, or perhaps more important, than hardware and software considerations. The future online catalog raised concerns, doubts and fears on the part of all staff and became a catalyst for the restructuring of the library organization. This paper deals with the strategies that evolved as we prepared the staff for what would become a major change in their library careers.

Until the decision to begin preparation for an online catalog was made in 1981, we, as a staff, had been relatively safe from dramatic change. We were not adequately prepared for the wide-ranging effects of this undertaking, even though the literature on the topic of automation is replete with warnings concerning automation's possible effects upon the mental health of an organization involved in this, seemingly endless, process.

Rosabeth Moss Kanter, in an article entitled "Managing the Human Side of Change", wrote that even the routine changes that occur every day in the business world could "...be accompanied by tension, stress, squabbling, sabotage, turnover, subtle undermining, behind-the-scenes footdragging, work slowdowns, needless political battles, and a drain on money and time - in short, symptoms of that ever-present bugaboo, resistance to change."[1] As a staff, we had experienced our share of routine, everyday changes, and so were aware of the truth of Ms. Kanter's observations. If even small changes could provoke the above reactions, it would have been naive to assume that a major innovation such as the online catalog would not cause adjustment problems for all concerned.

While reactions to the automation project were not as drastic among the library staff as some listed above, specific fears were recognizable to some degree in everyone. Among the fears described by Kanter, which were observed to some degree in all staff, were the following: fears concerning job security, job change and possible future competence, the uncertainty of the future with accompanying loss of control the questioning of familiar routines and habits, and the extra work automating would likely require[2]. To the extent that the existence of these fears was predictable they were also manageable.

To promote communication and team-building among the professional staff and to find an antidote for possible future misinformation and misunderstanding, a one day retreat for the professional staff was held. This retreat was facilitated by a psychologist experienced in group dynamics. Prior to the meeting, all participants voluntarily took the Myers-Briggs Type Indicator Test, a measure of personality dispositions and interests. The workshop's focus was entirely positive, and the test helped each of us to recognize the particular strengths we possessed. The complementary nature of personalities, skills and talents, and the necessary balance they provided to the organization became very clear. Since the primary purpose of the retreat was to enhance communication skills, role-playing of various simulated interactive situations was also used; these practiced skills were then taken back to the library, to be used by a more aware, and more effective staff.

The same fears professionals experienced concerning automation were just as real for support staff, and with good reason. Historically, one of the practical advantages of computers was the elimination of many of the tedious clerical functions likely to be found in libraries. All systems must be paid for, and early theory promoted cuts in support staff as a method of obtaining the necessary funds. To counter this fear, a decision was made that no currently employed individual would be laid off due to the implementation of the system. Attrition would be used if it was necessary and desirable to recover funds from the personnel budget.

In the early stages of planning, it became evident that the current organizational structure had to be modified in order to produce a Request for a Proposal (hereafter referred to as RFP) for vendors that met our needs, a document which we understood, and was not just "lifted" from other libraries. In February, 1983, the director appointed a systems librarian to be responsible for moving the process from an idea to a document to a system. Since there was no provision in the budget for a new position to meet this need, the appointment required the re-allocation of responsibilities formerly assigned to this librarian, to permit her to assume the new position. In September, the key players on the staff, representing all library departments, were identified and brought together in an Automation Committee. The committee's mandate included: the evaluation of sample RFPs; the study of current library processes to identify possible future problems with the automated system; the establishment of time lines for system implementation; and the determination of the order of decision making.

The Automation Committee sought early on to involve the entire staff in the planning process. The committee was concerned that everyone would need to feel ownership in the selected system to avoid problems in future implementation. This total staff involvement, through the mechanism of the automation committee, included: the re-evaluation of the library's goals and objectives; review and critique of sample RFPs; preparation of a Program Evaluation and Review Technique chart (hereafter referred to as the PERT chart); staff and departmental meetings; solicitation of questions and ideas; attendance at workshops; production of the Request for Information (hereafter referred to as RFI); attendance at vendor demonstrations; visits to other libraries with operating systems; the preparation of the final RFP; the establishment of mandatory requirements; and much informal consulting over a period of three years. The method used to produce the actual RFI and RFP was time consuming. Each department reviewed pertinent specifications from available RPFs, and the resulting comments, corrections and additions were used to produce the Joint Library's document.

The intense involvement of staff during the early stages of planning lessened after the RFI was issued, but informal consulting with concerned departments and individuals continued throughout the entire process. As vendor responses to the RFI were received, any interested individual could participate in the decision process. Over time, confidence in the process and the individuals working on the project grew, and fears that individual departmental needs would be overlooked, lessened. In retrospect, this process was invaluable. Each pertinent section of the RFP for the system was developed and is understood by the individuals who will have to implement it.

In an attempt to identify possible future problems automation might pose, the committee reviewed all current processes, policies and procedures by tracking all materials through the current system from selection through acquisitions, cataloging, and finally circulation. This process raised a number of issues. It became apparent that the tendency of library departments to function automonously, which to some extent was current library policy,

would not be possible once an integrated system was in operation. In addition, the Automation Committee decided that the organizational structure of the library would have to change from a format to a functional structure to better coordinate professional responsibilities within the library. (This decision was affected to some extent, by the need to re-allocate the systems librarian's former responsibilities.) As a result, there has been a shift toward broadening Collection Development's responsibility for all material selection, regardless of format, and a movement toward the integrating of all technical services areas into one centrally coordinated department. The integration of the technical services area is not complete, but we are confident that the change will make the implementation of the new online catalog an easier task. The uncertainty and disturbance caused by this integration was much greater than anticipated. Merging departments, creating new divisions and reporting structures, re-allocating responsibilities from professional to professional, and from professional to para-professional, are changes that must be accomplished gradually and carefully. Even now the full effects of these changes have yet to be realized.

However, it was clear that these changes had to occur before system implementation for two reasons: first, if there were to be problems with the organizational change, we wanted to insure that those problems were not perceived to be the result of the automation project; and second, we felt that the automation project would progress in a smoother fashion if the weaknesses in the current manual system were first eliminated.

An unanticipated result of the shifting of responsibilities, from professional to para-professional, was the speeding up of a basic change that has been occurring in most libraries for the last fifteen years - the more efficient utilization of a highly qualified para-professional staff. The responsibilities of professional librarians now include long-range planning and budgeting, aspects of collection development, such as selection, de-selection, policy-making, and aspects of patron instruction and assistance. The para-professionals maintain and operate the library's daily functions and special collections. There is a delicate balance of contributions by and from all library staff, professional and para-professional. Neither group can perform well, or function at all, without the input of the other group.

To counter natural fears concerning computers, personal computers were introduced into the library operations long before the formal automation project began. First uses occurred in bookkeeping and accounting. Staff with an interest in microcomputer applications were encouraged to pursue this interest and, over time, microcomputers became essential tools for all. Microcomputers are used currently for budget preparation, academic departmental accounting for collection development, reference and library instruction bibliographies, collection guides, overdues, the federal depository item number file, equipment inventory files, correspondence, and much more. The computers have proven themselves indispensable to all who use them, and over the past few years, have served to educate our staff not only to the capabilities of computers, but also to the often seemingly obtuse whims of computer logic and software. The experience of using even a packaged software program has been invaluable in helping to prepare the staff for future computer applications in the library.

Generally, staff attitudes towards computers, over the past three years, evolved in three stages. These stages generally came in concert with whatever stage of the automation planning process we were in at the time.

Stage One - Initially, staff were slow to use microcomputers for a variety of reasons. These included the fear of appearing inept in learning new skills, lack of interest, an inability to adapt the computer to their job or function, or a perceived lack of time to learn the new skills. In connection with the future online system, there were real concerns for departmental prerogatives and needs, and fear of job changes and/or job loss.

Stage Two - Microcomputers were becoming desirable tools which various staff began to use in new and imaginative ways to help them in their responsibilities. Interest in the automation committee's progress was considerable; and interest in the planned online catalog was coupled with doubts that a system would ever be purchased.

Stage Three - As the automation committee disbanded and primary responsibility for the automation project shifted to the Director and Systems Librarian, the intensity of staff interest on behalf of departmental needs declined, microcomputers became a necessity instead of a luxury, and staff expectations concerning the online system became more knowledgeable and realistic.

Once a vendor was selected and implementation began, the PERT chart served as a valuable communication tool for all staff, and enabled us to monitor progress over the two year implementation period. (This type of planning chart permits the project manager to break the project down into manageable parts showing the interdependence of all the project activities, identify problem areas and estimate time schedules.)[3] Regular meetings were held with the staff divided into Public Services, Cataloging and Acquisitions groups. Each group was provided with a list of pertinent activities and due dates. The meetings centered on the progress made to date, what needed to be done, and how best to do it.

Results

Many of the changes effected through the planning process for the future online system, such as increased computer literacy, increased staff confidence, and a tailor-made RFP, were of a predictable and welcome nature. The most dramatic and difficult aspects of automation change were those that were not anticipated. The effects of these unanticipated changes on the organizational structure, including the restucturing of professional and para-professional roles, and the complicated human relationships operating within the organization, will be with us long after our first online system has been replaced.

In summary, organizational changes directly resulting from the anticipated online system include:

1. The appointment of a systems librarian;

2. Changes in professional responsibility from form to function;

3. The beginning of an evolutionary movement toward the integration of all technical services into one department;

4. The continuing evolution of the para-professional's role in the library.

The last three years of the automation process, hapily, have resulted in greatly increased computer literacy among library staff, and have produced an optimistic, more venturesome staff, less intimidated by technology and the changes that may lie ahead. In addition, an unanticipated benefit of this process has been the improved relationship and better cohesiveness between various staff and departments. We can now appreciate the complementary nature of the contribution each of us makes to the library organization.

REFERENCES

1. Rosabeth Moss Kanter, "Managing the Human Side of Change," *Management Review* 74:52 (April 1985).

2. Ibid., p. 52-54.

3. James A. Senn, *Analysis and Design of Information Systems* (New York, N.Y.: McGraw-Hill Book Company, 1984), p. 567-568.

SELECTED BIBLIOGRAPHY

Barbara Conroy. "The Human Element: Staff Development in the Electronic Library." *Drexel Library Quarterly* 17 (Fall 1981): 91-106.

James W. Driscoll. "People and the Automated Office." *Datamation* 25 (November 1979): 107-112.

Rosabeth Moss Kanter. "Managing the Human Side of Change." Management Review 74 (April 1985): 52-56.

Henry C. Lucas Jr. Coping with Computers: a Manager's Guide to Controlling Information Processing. New York: The Free Press, 1982.

John N. Olsgaard. "Automation as a Socio-Organizational Agent of Change: an Evaluative Literature Review." Information Technology and Libraries 4 n. 1 (March 1985): 19-28.

Daniel Robey and Dana Forrow. "User Involvement in Information System Development: a Conflict Model and Empirical Test." Management Science 28 (January 1982): 73-85.

Mary L. Schramel. "The Psychological Impact of Automation on Library and Office Workers." Special Libraries 72 (April 1982): 149-156.

James A. Senn. Analysis and Design of Information Systems. New York: McGraw-Hill Book Company, 1984.

Victor A. Vyssotsky. "Computer Systems: More Evolution than Revolution." Journal of Systems Management 31 (February 1980): 21-27.

Robert W. Zmud and James F. Cox. "The Implementation Process: a Change Approach." Management Information Systems Quarterly 3 (June 1979): 35-43.

TECHNICAL SERVICES: PUBLIC SERVICES BEHIND CLOSED DOORS

Georgene A. Timko
Northeastern State University
Tahlequah, Oklahoma

Abstract. The theme "Energies for Transition" reflects the new atmosphere in technical services. Technical services has reached a transition point. Library literature indicates that it is not going to be replaced, integrated or phased out but that a stronger service orientation will be its new focus. This service philosophy will require us to work closely with our colleagues in public services. Communication, cooperation, and coordination must replace the traditional rivalry between technical services and public services for personnel, resources and the director's attention.

My paper will propose that technical services need to conduct their own public relations program. Three suggestions will be offered to help accomplish this program. First we must explain what we do and why we do it. Second, we should foster a "service to the public" attitude among the staff. Third, we must improve communication and coordination with public service departments.

The conference theme, "Energies for Transition," reflects the new atmosphere in technical services. For several years now, articles in library literature have predicted the demise of our department. David Peele requests that we take our professionals out of the inner sanctum and send them to the reference desk.[1] Michael Gorman suggests doing away with technical services departments.[2] But as Mark Twain said, "the reports of my death are greatly exaggerated." Technical Services has not been phased out or replaced but dramatic changes have invaded the "back room."

One of the most dramatic changes that needs to be advertised, fostered and increased, is a stronger service orientation in technical services. The title of my program, "Technical Services: Public Services Behind Closed Doors," is not a spur-of-the-moment creation for an eye-catching title, nor is it a sequel to a country western song. It is a philosophy that permeates a lot of back rooms.

The motto first came into being several years ago. While conducting a tour of the library, our Head of Public Services brought the group into the technical services room. I welcomed them, adding with a mischievous gleam in my eye, "we are also known as Public Services Behind Closed Doors," I paused for a moment to see what dramatic effect my pronouncement would have on my listeners. The ceiling didn't fall in, the floor didn't crack, and no one understood the inside joke. However, I liked the sound of it and adopted it as our slogan.

The effort to make "service" in technical services meaningful will require us to work closely with our colleagues in the public area. Cooperation requires mutual understanding of each other's role in providing service to the library patron. Communication, cooperation, and coordination must replace the traditional rivalry between the departments for personnel, resources and the director's attention. My paper will propose that technical services departments need to conduct their own public relations programs and will offer three suggestions to get their programs started.

The first suggestion is that we should explain to others what we do and why we do it. At some libraries, it may be valuable to start by explaining our roles to each other in the technical services room as well as to the public area staff. It gives us an opportunity to re-evalute some procedures, streamline some, and possibly discontinue others.

At one large institution where I worked, we had a tour of technical services for the entire library staff. The individual staff members took pride in explaining each part and how it fit into the whole process. Subject bibliographers found out how important it was to fill in all the information on a book purchase request form. Catalogers realized some of the things that could go wrong when vendors send the wrong materials. Reference staff found out from where those subject headings come. The end result was that everyone had a greater understanding and respect for each other's duties.

Technical services is a team effort. Its people function best as a team. There are really no separate departments within technical services. It is one flowing process. Processing is the first step in preparing information for the patron, whether in book, serial, microform, or audiovisual format.

Webster's New Collegiate Dictionary defines "process" as "1) something going on; 2) a natural phenomenon marked by gradual changes that lead toward a particular result; and 3) a series of actions or operations conducing to an end." Many people will agree that there is always "something going on" in the back room. Technical services is a "natural phenomenon marked by gradual changes" when each process flows naturally in the next. Acquisition people must be aware of what the catalogers will require. Catalogers should be aware of details that make life easier for the people who prepare the books for the shelves. Technical services is a "series of actions or operations." Materials must be ordered quickly and carefully. Items must be cataloged with speed and accuracy. Producing catalog cards or an online catalog requires understanding of how the patron might approach the subject. Even the art of labelling is crucial. If a book has an incorrect call number on the spine, it is effectively lost to the user. It all requires team effort to make the "process" work.

The second step in our public relations program is fostering a "service to the public" attitude among the technical services staff. Sometimes the staff must work in very crowded quarters or in extremes of temperature. Working conditions do affect performance and tempers. We have the same tensions and pressures that our colleagues in the public area face. In fact, we have double trouble. We serve two publics - the library patrons and the other librarians.

Through the years the name of our department has been changing from technical "processing" to technical "services." Referring again to Webster's dictionary, "service" has twenty-four definitions. Fortunately, only three are applicable.

The first definition is "conduct contributing to the advantage of another or others." Our function in technical services is certainly for the advantage of others. Cheney and Williams in their book, Fundamental Reference Sources, suggest that indirect reference services involve the preparation and development of cataloging, bibliographies and other reference aids. These aids help in providing access to the library's collection. The preparation and development of these aids recognize the significant role of the processing services of the library as indispensable to their reference function.[3] The art of acquisitions, cataloging and classifying is to aid the user in finding the materials he needs quickly and easily. We supply the access to the material.

The second definition of "service" is "an act or means of supplying some general demand, especially of conducting some public utility." The card catalog or an online catalog is a perfect example of a technical services utility. It is our responsibility to insure the creation and maintainance of the main index to the book collection. Printouts of serial holdings, order lists, and new accession bibliographies are a few of the services we supply.

The third applicable definition of "service" is "any result of useful labor which does not produce a tangible commodity." In the industrial era, traditional technical service librarians conceptualized their function as only manufacturing products such as the public utilities mentioned above. They did not worry if it took six months to a year for materials to be ordered, cataloged and processed. In the new age of service industries, modern librarians perceive their role as providing services which are intangible commodities. Our intangible commodities are the processes of acquiring, cataloging, and physically processing of materials as quickly and efficiently as possible.

In the three ways listed above, technical services contributes to the ultimate institutional and professional goals of the library. If the public area people maintain that their department is the sole reason the library exists and that they are the only ones who provide service, they deny the fact that they use any resources to serve the patron. Library service is a totally cooperative venture. The achievement of service goals requires constant cooperation rather than competition with the public area.

This statement brings me to the third stage of our public relations campaign, which is better communication and coordination with our other half, public services. The more we understand about each other's work, the better interstaff relations will exist. A formal declaration to be read at staff meetings is not required, but an attitude of understanding and cooperation is necessary.

Technical services has at times been accused of fostering outdated rules and procedures. Who has not heard, when asking the question, "why are we doing this?" the answer, "because we've always done it that way!" That answer is no longer valid and we are hearing it less and less. Instead of the bastion of status quo, technical services has become the leader in change. It was the cataloging function that brought the first winking green-eyed monster (sometimes known as a CRT) into libraries and revolutionized library work forever. Even the smallest library has felt the impact of technology that began in technical services. Automation has been creeping into other aspects of library work, such as acquisitions, interlibrary loan, serials, and circulation. This announcement may be news to some public service people, but your integrated online system starts here. Planning without input from both technical and public services will not serve the patron adequately.

To cultivate a better working relationship, some important duties can be shared. Subject bibliographers or reference staff can do a preliminary check of materials to see if the items are already owned by the library. One of the most helpful duties we found, is having reference people assist with filing in the public catalog. There is no quicker way to convince librarians of the need for an online catalog then to have them spend a couple of hours filing.

On the other hand, technical services people like to get involved with tracking down a problem citation. OCLC can be made to give up its secrets if you have the right touch and the latest search strategy. Technical services also contains some hidden treasure troves of information. For example, publishers' catalogs can provide a subject approach for collection development. The name/address directory on OCLC provides telephone numbers and addresses of most major publishers and libraries.

Some libraries have staff members who spend part of their time doing reference work and part of their time cataloging or rotate jobs every six months. This method certainly gives one an understanding of the problems each face daily. Cross-training and staff exchange are a direct approach to achieving service goals.

We recently conducted an OCLC workshop for the entire library staff. Even the audiovisual people attended. Searching basics and enhancements and the four major subsystems were covered. Everyone came away with a greater appreciation of the technical expertise we must have to work with OCLC.

Last, but certainly not least, we must hear an occasional "thank you." Public service people receive their morale boost from patrons who smile their gratitude or who become enthusiastic about a new lead in their research. Sometimes they even hear a "thank you." Technical services people usually see public area people only when they have a complaint. Mistakes made by reference people walk out the door. Mistakes made by technical services people come back to haunt us.

In closing, no meaningful change can even begin to occur until we change the very important characteristic called attitude. It is up to each individual to start a public relations campaign. Now is the age of transition. Specialists and people with narrow expertise need to be replaced by librarians who comprehend the importance of patron service, the potential of automation and the contribution of technical services.

REFERENCES

1. David Peele, "Staffing the Reference Desk," _Library Journal_ 105 (Sept. 1, 1980): 1078.

2. Michael Gorman, "On Doing Away With Technical Services Departments," _American Libraries_ 10, no. 7 (July/August 1979): 435.

3. Frances Neel Cheney and Wily J. Williams, _Fundamental Reference Sources_. 2d ed. (Chicago: American Library Association, 1980), p. 2.

PERSONNEL

THE PLATEAUED LIBRARIAN
SOLUTIONS FOR IMPROVING PERFORMANCE LEVELS

James F. Comes
Ball State University Library
Muncie, Indiana

Abstract. The subject of this paper is career development for the plateaued librarian who cannot reasonably expect a promotion for an extended period of time. Several career definitions are presented and characteristics of selected career paths described. Regardless of the individual's age and reason for reaching a plateau in their career, effectiveness can be maintained. The manager can initiate one or more intervention strategies to recognize and support the effectively plateaued librarian through positive attitudes, interpersonal skills, and awareness of the librarian's work history.

Key Words and Phrases. Career Development, Plateauing, Career and Performance, Managerial Interventions.

There is an extensive body of empirical data accumulated by psychologists, social psychologists, and sociologists concerning movement into and through careers. The basic premise of this presentation is that the career development literature can offer support to librarians in their professional and personal endeavors. The purposes of this paper are: 1) To selectively review the career development literature related to plateauing; 2) To describe and examine the career of the plateaued librarian; 3) To explore the manager's role for counseling and intervention; 4) To discuss the implications for librarians.

For this presentation plateauing is defined as occurring when an individual is no longer promoted in an organization or cannot reasonably expect a promotion for an extended period of time. For many people the concept of career plateauing may indicate failure, shelf-sitters, defeat, stagnation, cessation of movement, obsolescence, or boxing-in. The book, The Peter Principle, supported this negative stereotype of plateauing, depicting the career path terminating at the individual's level of incompetence.[1]

Before discussing the plateauing of careers, some attention must be given to the concept of career. The term "career" carries a surplus of meanings which make it extremely difficult to treat the topic in a precise and unambiguous manner. Hall, for example, has identified five distinct meanings of the word "career."[2]

* Career as advancement related to vertical mobility, moving upward in organizational and professional hierarchies.
* Career as a profession. Certain occupations constitute a career.
* Career as a life-long sequence of jobs. All employed people have job histories.
* Career as a sequence of role-related experiences encompassing the movement into, through, and out of any social role.
* Career as a life-long sequence of work attitudes and behaviors which combine the third and fourth definitions.

A somewhat different frame of reference describing the concept of career is offered by Driver, who examines the concept of career in terms of timing, permanence, and direction.[3] He has characterized careers in four ways.

* Steady State People choose their career field early and stay with it for life, with no grand plans for advancement.
* Linear People choose their career fields early, develop plans for upward movements in their field and carry them out.
* Spiral Career People work in several related fields which may or may not be related for intervals of five to seven years.
* Transitory People job hop, moving from one job field to another.

There is no direct relationship between these patterns and specific skills or areas of work. However, there are fields which may be characterized as "linear," e.g., the corporate management arena, from regional to national sales to vice president of marketing, or as "steady state," e.g., educators, lawyers, or doctors.

Regardless of how we see ourselves, the structure of the organization assures us of a career plateau. A small percentage of jobs are available at the executive level, but most professional and technical people achieve their highest job level a number of years before retirement. Schein illustrates movement through and upward in the organization utilizing a three-dimensional cone-shaped model (see Fig. 1).[4] Movement within the organization occurs along three conceptually distinguishable dimensions.

* Movement by function or department along the perimeter. There is limited involvement in library operations.
* Movement toward the center or centrality where decision making occurs. There are opportunities for participation in projects, committee work, or formulation of policies, all of which may support promotion or merit awards.
* Movement vertically, increasing or decreasing the individual's rank in the organization.

As employees move from the perimeter to the center, and then vertically, there are fewer positions above. Upward mobility is perceived as offering status, power, achievement, and higher salaries, whereas plateauing is not always viewed positively or productively.

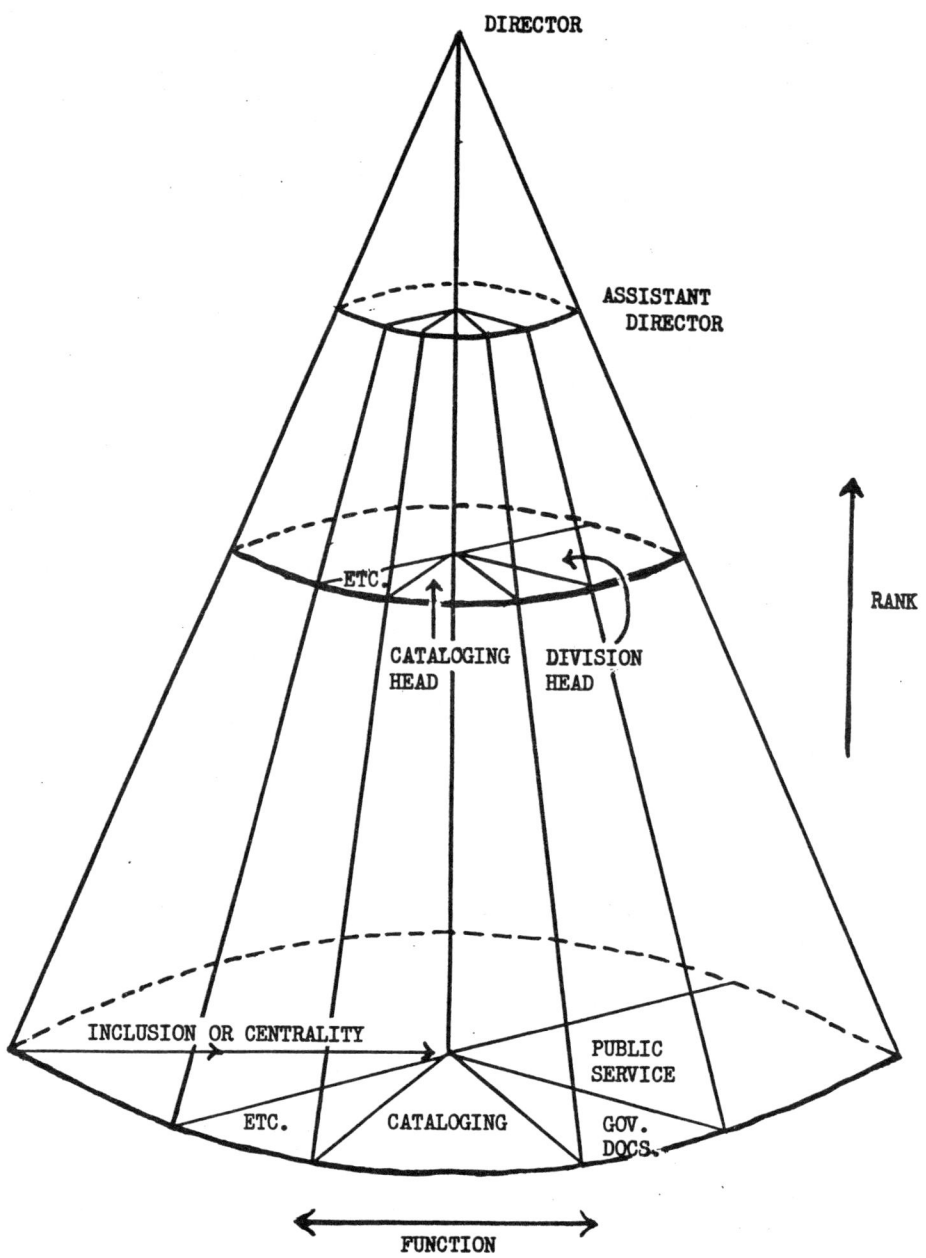

Figure 1. A three-dimensional model of an organization.

A positive and instructive model of plateauing has been proposed by Ference, classifying career states and utilizing two criteria: current performance and the likelihood of future promotion (see Fig. 2).[5] The model delineates principle career stages of the plateauing process. In cells II and IV are the Stars and Learners.

* Stars - employees are performing beyond expectations and are seen as having potential for further advancement.
* Learners - individuals are performing below their potential but have high potential for advancement.

Cells I and III represent plateaued employees and are identified as Solid Citizens or Deadwood.

* Solid Citizens - are performing satisfactorily but have little chance for advancement for organizational or personal reasons.
* Deadwood - are performing below expected levels and have limited opportunities for advancement.

Plateauing may be caused by organizational or personal decisions. Organizational factors resulting in plateauing may include economic factors, qualified individuals exceeding the number of jobs available, the value of the individual in his/her present position, or discrimination. Some employees are plateaued because they have failed to acquire new technical skills, lack desire/ambition, or have given priority to personal goals versus career goals. Much attention is given to the "stars" in organizations through visibility, recognition, and autonomy; and to the "deadwood" with corrective, control, or remedial measures. I am proposing that "solid citizens" need attention as well since they may make a recognizable contribution to the services offered by the institution. They may have five to fifteen years or more before retirement, and without support and recognition, they, too, may become "deadwood."

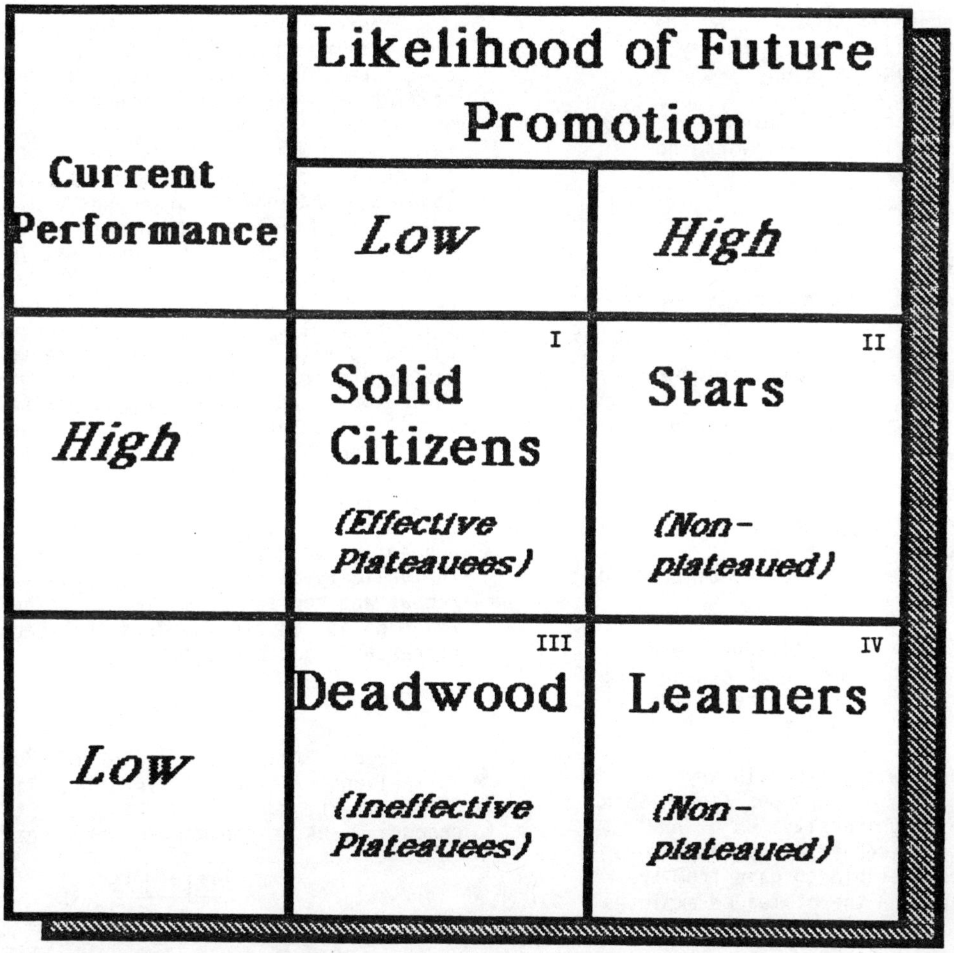

Current Performance	Likelihood of Future Promotion	
	Low	High
High	I Solid Citizens *(Effective Plateauees)*	II Stars *(Non-plateaued)*
Low	III Deadwood *(Ineffective Plateauees)*	IV Learners *(Non-plateaued)*

Figure 2. A model of careers.

Assuming the organization intends to provide an environment in which employees can expect support for their career development efforts, what steps can the manager take to maintain an effective performance level of the plateaued employee? First, the manager will need to go beyond the formal duties of assessing ongoing performance and potential, and manage the plateaued librarian more effectively through feedback, recognition, and exposure. Second, however awesome the job of being a career counselor is, the manager with plateaued librarians can develop the proper attitude, refine his/her interpersonal skills, and seek the knowledge necessary to improve performance levels.

The manager's attitudes should:[6]

* Be positive and reinforcing.
* Acknowledge the importance of matching the organizational needs and individual's needs.
* Recognize that career success can be achieved without relying on upward mobility.
* Actively support effective performance through "solid citizens."

The manager's _skills_ should encourage personal growth, facilitate self-inquiry, and personal problem solving through:

* Questioning - open and closed.
* Listening - active, passive, and non-evaluative.
* Silence.
* Reflection.
* Participation - active and passive.

The _knowledge_ and _awareness_ needed by the manager includes:

* Knowledge of the subordinate's work history.
* Systematic perspective of career development involving self, family, and the community.
* Strengths and needs of the subordinate.
* Dynamics of the organization and leadership styles.
* Awareness of the employee's feelings and values.

Utilizing these skills, attitudes, and knowledge, some interventions which can be used to sustain the effective performance of the plateauee are:

* Lateral change within the library, to another library, or to a position within the college or university.
* Mentoring to a younger or new employee. Both parties are able to gain from the relationship, and the plateaued employee is able to redirect his/her career in a more effective manner.
* Job enrichment which may include expanding the breadth of duties, accepting new responsibilities, or being relieved from or delegating some routine tasks.
* Engaging in educational opportunities such as formal degree programs, workshops, seminars, training programs, or assessment centers.
* Job rotation or special assignments to change the environment, provide new duties, or skill demands.
* Acquiring new job skills to enhance the chances of career advancement, i.e., developing skills and/or expertise critical to the unit, department, or university/college.
* Networking to develop a system or network of contacts inside and outside the organization, thus providing relevant career information and support for the individual.
* Professional counseling to identify strengths, weaknesses, career planning skills, work-self conflicts on job performance, etc.
* Changing jobs--a subtle way to leave a plateau.
* Early retirement incentives offered by the institution.
* Moonlighting to promote personal interests, teaching, developing one's own business, consulting, etc.

There are several reasons for attending to the plateaued librarian. As the post-war baby boom takes effect, employees will be plateauing earlier and in greater numbers as many public and private institutions expand at a slower rate.[7] How will the librarian react to nonexistent or limited upward mobility and to the knowledge that their career has plateaued ten to twenty years before retirement? This problem was reported in the study by Berstein and Leach for the ALA Office for Library Personnel Resources.[8] The authors reported that almost fifty percent of the librarians surveyed were not happy with their career progress; most librarians are motivated by challenging and varied work; and performance appraisal and performance feedback systems are in need of improvement. Career development, if allowed to happen randomly, or to stagnate, could result in frustration, burn-out, loss of talent, and ineffective service. "The challenge to top management is to develop climates that acknowledge the validity of plateaued librarians and to accept and confirm committments to quality work which do not involve desires or expectations of hierarchial advancement."[9]

ACKNOWLEDGEMENTS

Special thanks is due to Stan Hodge, collections development librarian at Ball State University Libraries, for his comments and encouragement in the manuscript preparation.

REFERENCES

1. Lawrence Peter and Raymond Hull, _The Peter Principle_ (New York: Morrow, 1972).

2. Douglas T. Hall, _Careers in Organizations_ (Santa Monica, CA: Goodyears Publishing Co., 1976).

3. Michael J. Driver, "Career Concepts - A New Approach to Career Research," in *Career Issues in Human Resource Management*, ed. Ralph Katz (Englewood Cliffs, New Jersey: Prentice-Hall, 1982), p. 23-32.

4. Edgar H. Schein, "The Individual, The Organization, and the Career: A Conceptual Scheme," *Journal of Applied Behavioral Science*, 7:401-426, (April 1971).

5. Thomas P. Ference, James A. F. Stoner, and E. Kirby Warren, "Managing the Career Plateau," *Academy of Management Review*, 2:602-612, (October 1977).

6. Andrew H. Souerwine, "The Managers as Career Counselor: Some Issues and Approaches," in *Career Development in the 1980s: Theory and Practice*, eds. David H. Montross and Christopher J. Shinkman (Springfield, Illinois: Charles C. Thomas, 1981), p. 363-378.

7. James F. Wolf, "Career Plateauing in the Public Service: Baby Boom and Employment Bust," *Public Administration Review*, 43:160-165, (March/April 1983).

8. Ellen Berstein and John Leach, "Plateau," *American Libraries*, 79:178-180, (March 1985).

9. Ference, "Managing the Career," p. 611.

PAY FOR PERFORMANCE: THE TE*MS EXPERIMENT

Constance Corey and Virginia Steel
Arizona State University Libraries
Tempe, Arizona

Abstract. Decisions concerning the award of merit money are often painfully difficult to make, especially when peer review is included in the process. This paper describes the implementation of an innovative merit evaluation system, TE*MS, in the Arizona State University Libraries. TE*MS (Team Evaluation and Management System) combines anonymous peer review of job-related behavioral characteristics (TE) with a management system (MS) in which supervisors evaluate the progress made by each librarian toward individual performance objectives. The paper includes a brief analysis of the positive and negative features of TE*MS as applied in an academic library.

Keywords and Phrases. Performance evaluation, peer review, TE*MS (Team Evaluation and Management System), merit evaluation.

Performance evaluation to determine how to award merit money has long been a problem for many institutions. This paper describes the trials and tribulations of one academic library which implemented a new merit appraisal system during the past year. A description of the methodology used as well as the results of the first attempt at implementation are included.

In July 1984, the Board of Regents of the State of Arizona mandated a change in the salary structure of the state universities, de-emphasizing across-the-board increases and placing increased emphasis on pay for performance. In the fall of 1984, the Arizona State University Libraries implemented an existing merit evaluation system, which was ultimately deemed a failure for the following reasons:
- The criteria used to distinguish levels of merit were too vague.
- Evaluators were inconsistent in their application of the criteria.
- There were only two levels of merit, which proved to be too few.
- The committee approach to peer review was inadequate due to lack of firsthand knowledge of performance and insufficient documentation on which to base decisions.
- The preparation of narrative statements in support of merit recommendations required an inordinate amount of time.

After reviewing the problems associated with the award of merit for 1983-84, the ASU Librarians' Council voted to experiment with TE*MS (Team Evaluation and Management System), an innovative performance review methodology developed by Dr. Mark Edwards, an ASU faculty member with expertise in the area of performance evaluation. The anticipated benefits of the use of TE*MS included the following:
- More explicit criteria.
- Integrated, anonymous peer review.
- Enhanced accuracy and validity of the performance review system.
- Incorporation of performance goals into the review process.
- Less time required to complete the evaluations.
- Feedback to peer reviewers.

TE*MS METHODOLOGY

TE*MS is a two-part evaluation system that combines peer review with the principles of management-by-objectives to arrive at a numerical score for each individual. The two parts of TE*MS are team evaluation (TE) and management system (MS). Dr. Edwards' research has shown that TE*MS results in a fairer and more accurate evaluation of performance than does either peer review or supervisory evaluation alone (Edwards 1985). An explanation follows of how each of the two parts of TE*MS is implemented and the final score calculated.

TE (Team Evaluation)

This section of TE*MS is based on the tenet that peer evaluation is as reliable and valid as supervisory evaluation (Mumford 1983). In order to assure reliability and validity, the mechanism for peer review must be structured so that each reviewer has a clear understanding of the criteria on which to evaluate peers, and each person must be evaluated by associates who work closely with that person and thus have considerable knowledge of the person's day-to-day performance. To achieve the most accurate peer review possible, TE*MS incorporates the following steps:

1. The individuals to be evaluated establish and define the criteria on which their performance will be rated (exhibit 1).
2. Individuals then weight the evaluation criteria to reflect the relative importance of each criterion to their specific jobs (exhibit 1) and select five peers who are familiar with their performance. These five people constitute the evaluation team (TE) (exhibit 2).
3. Team members separately and anonymously evaluate the individual's performance, rating each criterion on a scale of 1 to 5 (exhibit 3).
4. The TE*MS administrator uses software developed by Dr. Edwards to tabulate the scores for each individual, criterion by criterion. Next, the administrator applies a safeguard program called "intelligent consensus." This program identifies those criteria on which there is significant lack of agreement among raters. If any raters are shown to be consistently lenient or harsh, their scores are normalized. The TE*MS administrator then multiplies the

consensus scores by the criteria weightings, adds those scores, and reaches a final TE score ranging between 1 and 100.

MS (Management System)

In keeping with the fundamentals of management-by-objectives, individuals are asked to list their annual performance goals and to weight those goals by dividing 100 points among them. This is done at the beginning of the evaluation year. At the end of the year, the supervisor evaluates the progress made by individuals toward their goals, assigns points to reflect that progress, adds the results, and arrives at a total MS score ranging between 1 and 100.

TE*MS (Team Evaluation and Management System)

To calculate the final score for each individual, the TE and MS scores are combined (exhibit 3). The two scores are weighted equally unless the intelligent consensus has revealed totally invalid peer ratings in the TE section. In these cases, the MS score is weighted more heavily than the TE score.

The results of the entire TE*MS evaluations for individuals are given to the individuals and their supervisors. The individuals may then see how their peers have rated them on each criterion and how their supervisors have rated them on performance goals. In addition, persons serving on rating teams receive rater feedback reports which tell them whether they agreed with the consensus or not and whether they were lenient or harsh in their ratings (exhibit 4). This feedback provides information on how individual raters compare with other raters, a feature of TE*MS that is not often included in other evaluation systems.

IMPLEMENTATION AT ASU

When the ASU Libraries voted to experiment with TE*MS this year, the plan was to test the system first with selected departments. Final merit decisions were not expected to be made until fall, and a pilot test would allow us to develop and modify the system before full implementation.

In mid-March, however, we were notified that merit evaluations were to be completed in the spring. The question then was whether to go ahead and use TE*MS without the pilot test--and with very little time for development--or to discard the idea and find an alternative. In spite of some reservations, we decided to continue the TE*MS experiment on an accelerated basis.

Fortunately, TE*MS developer Mark Edwards agreed to help us with implementation. Within days, forms had been prepared and the evaluation criteria established, using input solicited from librarians. Instructions were given on how to assign criteria weightings and select TE members. An open meeting was called to give librarians the opportunity to discuss the criteria and to notify them that, if they wanted to be considered for merit, they should submit their criteria weightings and team member names by a given date.

Evaluation forms were then sent to TE members and another meeting was held to explain the peer review process. During the next few days, team members, working individually and anonymously, completed the evaluations and turned them in for processing.

While the TE scores were being processed, work began on the MS portion of the system. Librarians were asked to weight the annual objectives which they had established the year before during the regular performance evaluations. Administrators were given the option of completing the MS section at this time, but most elected to wait for the TE results before proceeding.

TE scores were distributed in early May, with one week allowed for completion of the Management System evaluations. By late May, the MS scores had been processed and the complete TE*MS rating sheets distributed along with a handout showing the array of scores for all participants (exhibit 5).

In September rater feedback reports were distributed to TE members, and a meeting was held to discuss the entire TE*MS process.

ASSESSMENT

The foregoing only hints at the human side of implementing a radically new evaluation system. Not surprisingly, the exercise engendered a great deal of fear and pain as well as some pleasant revelations. Some typical comments: "It doesn't make any sense." "I know it won't work." "Peer evaluations are invalid." "The criteria don't reflect what I do." "We should never have done this in such a hurry." "Hey! The team evaluations took only ten minutes apiece!" "This was easier than I thought it was going to be."

Did we realize the benefits we had hoped to achieve with TE*MS? Yes and no.

More explicit criteria. Compared to previous years, the criteria used were far more explicit in describing specific job-related behavioral traits. Despite the fact that librarians had developed the criteria, however, their final consensus was that they did not like them. Before TE*MS is used again, the criteria will be further modified.

Integrated, anonymous peer review. This was achieved, with somewhat unexpected results. The commonly held belief had been that hand-picked teams would result in artificially high scores on the TE portion of the evaluation. In fact, the opposite occurred--proving, perhaps, that the system works, but not without shattering some egos in the process.

Enhanced accuracy and validity of the performance review system. Dr. Edwards claims that we achieved this, but the majority of our colleagues do not believe that it is so.

Incorporation of performance goals into the review process. Because TE*MS was adopted at the end of the evaluation year, performance goals were incorporated late in the process. Although it would have been preferable to weight the goals at the beginning of the performance year, this generated less controversy than one might expect.

Less time required to complete the evaluations. This turned out to be one of the most popular aspects of the TE*MS experiment, with many evaluators reporting that team evaluations had been completed in less than twenty minutes each and MS evaluations in less than thirty.

Feedback to peer reviewers. The problem of providing rater feedback without revealing TE consensus scores for each ratee proved to be a major source of confusion and disappointment. This, combined with the delay in distribution of the report, resulted in frustration and lack of interest.

CONCLUSION

At ASU, the collegial form of governance provides librarians a forum in which they may both develop their own personnel policies and critique those with which they are dissatisfied. It would be an understatement to say that the TE*MS post-mortem was lively, with our colleagues expressing the following concerns about TE*MS:
- The evaluation criteria were slanted too heavily toward job behaviors as opposed to specific accomplishments.
- The formulas used for calculating TE*MS scores were not well explained nor universally understood.

All of their other concerns focused on performance evaluation, regardless of the methodology used. These reactions to evaluation are all quite typical, as borne out by the literature (Cederblom 1980). Inevitably, some people do not like being evaluated at all; some question the value and validity of peer review; and others simply do not believe in pay for performance. Nevertheless, evaluations, peer review, and pay for performance have all been mandated at ASU, and the authors believe that TE*MS has merit as an evaluation alternative.

REFERENCES

1. Mark R. Edwards and J. Ruth Sproull, "Safeguarding Your Employee Rating System," Business 35 (April-June 1985): 17-27.

2. Michael D. Mumford, "Social Comparison Theory and the Evaluation of Peer Evaluations: A Review and Some Applied Implications," Personnel Psychology 36 (Winter 1983): 867-81.

3. Douglas Cederblom and John W. Lounsbury, "An Investigation of User Acceptance of Peer Evaluations," Personnel Psychology 33 (Autumn 1980): 567-79.

TE*MS CRITERIA WEIGHTING FORM

Please distribute 100 points, in multiples of 5, among the following criteria.

Job-Related Performance Criteria

_____ **Interpersonal Skills**
Develops and maintains smooth and effective working relationships with superiors, peers, subordinates; interacts effectively with library patrons; maintains good relationships with campus units outside the library; supports, encourages and fosters cooperation among subordinates; is approachable.

_____ **Professional/Technical Knowledge**
Keeps up-to-date in knowledge of the library profession in general and, if appropriate, subject area; possesses sufficient job knowledge to perform effectively in assigned responsibilities.

_____ **Professional/Technical Competence**
Applies professional knowledge in all areas of responsibility; provides professional/technical advice to others within the libraries and to library patrons.

_____ **Communication Skills**
Communicates clearly orally and in writing; keeps subordinates, peers and superiors informed; uses both formal and informal communication channels appropriately.

_____ **Initiative and Reliability**
Persists with extra effort to attain objectives; overcomes obstacles to get the job done; takes initiative in identifying and completing work that needs to be done.

_____ **Planning and Organizing**
Formulates short- and long-range goals and objectives; forecasts possible problems for the unit/organization and develops strategies for addressing these problems; organizes work in order to accomplish the most important assignments first; handles problems before they escalate into crises; completes assignments in a timely manner.

_____ **Decision-Making/Problem-Solving**
Makes sound and timely decisions, taking into account all relevant information; develops effective and creative solutions to organizational problems; recognizes and responds effectively to unexpected situations.

_____ **Teamwork**
Cooperates with peers, subordinates and superiors; shares equally in departmental responsibilities and activities; participates in accomplishing library projects and objectives.

EXHIBIT 1

TE*MS: TEAM EVALUATION RATER SELECTION FORM

Please list five individuals with whom you interact in your job and who are in a position to make valid observations of your job performance. If fewer raters are available, list fewer, but five are strongly recommended.

Name	Frequency of Contact	Internal/ External	Rater Relationship
1. _____	_____	_____	_____
2. _____	_____	_____	_____
3. _____	_____	_____	_____
4. _____	_____	_____	_____
5. _____	_____	_____	_____

Frequency of Contact

1 = Once a month; 2-8 = times per month; 9 = 9 or more times per month

Internal/External

Internal = Someone from within the department
External = Someone from outside the department

Rater Relationship

Example of a team selected by a Reference Librarian:

Title	Relationship
Head, Reference Department	+1
Reference Librarian Colleague	0
Reference Department Paraprofessional	-1
Catalog Librarian	0
Head, Library Instruction	+1

EXHIBIT 2

TE*MS EVALUATION FORM

TEAM EVALUATION ("TE")

Please circle the performance level that best applies to each criterion.

<u>**Job-Related Performance Criteria**</u>

N	1	2	3	4	5	Interpersonal skills
N	1	2	3	4	5	Professional/technical knowledge
N	1	2	3	4	5	Professional/technical competence
N	1	2	3	4	5	Communication skills
N	1	2	3	4	5	Initiative and reliability
N	1	2	3	4	5	Planning and organizing
N	1	2	3	4	5	Decision-making/problem-solving
N	1	2	3	4	5	Teamwork

TE SCORE _____

MANAGEMENT SYSTEM ("MS")

List, weight and evaluate the primary objectives of each librarian as established at the beginning of the evaluation year.

<u>**Objectives**</u>   <u>**Weight**</u>   <u>**Score**</u>

1.

2.

3.

4.

5.

MS SCORE _____

AVERAGE SCORE _____

EXHIBIT 3

RATER FEEDBACK REPORT

CRITERIA	1	2	3	4	5	6	7	8	HALO
RATEES	CONSISTENCY WITH THE TEAM CONSENSUS								
ANN	*	*	H	*	*	*	H	*	GOOD
CARLA	L	*	*	L	L	*	*	L	GOOD
PAUL	*	*	*	*	*	*	*	*	GOOD
ROB	*	-	-	L	L	*	*	*	GOOD

CONSISTENCY

- * = Within 20% of the Team Consensus
- H = More than 20% higher than the Team Consensus
- L = More than 20% lower than the Team Consensus
- - = Criterion not rated

HALO INDEX

- GOOD = More than 20% variation among criteria
- POOR = Less than 20% variation among criteria

EXHIBIT 4

ASU TE*MS SCORE ARRAYS
(ALL LIBRARIANS)

SCALE	TE SCORES
96-100	X
91-95	XXXXX
86-90	XXXXXXXXXXXX
81-85	XXXXXXXXX
76-80	XXXXXXXXXXXX
71-75	XXXX
66-70	XXX

SCALE	MS SCORES
96-100	XXXXXXXXXXX
91-95	XXXXXXXXXXXXXXXXXX
86-90	XXXXXXXXXXX
81-85	XXXXXXXXXXX
76-80	XX
71-75	
66-70	

SCALE	TE+MS SCORES
96-100	
91-95	XXXXXXXXXXXX
86-90	XXXXXXXXXXXXXXXXX
81-85	XXXXXXXXXXXX
76-80	XXXXXX
71-75	
66-70	

EXHIBIT 5

JOB DESIGN FOR THE
AUTOMATED TECHNICAL SERVICES ENVIRONMENT

Kathleen M. Hays
Milton S. Eisenhower Library
The Johns Hopkins University
Baltimore, Maryland

Abstract. Automation has an impact on the work which we perform in the academic library technical services operation. Much research has been devoted to the effects of automation on industry, but technology is also changing the library workplace. The VDT, the primary medium of change, has been implicated as a factor in job-related stress.

The scientific priciples of job design first suggested by Charles Babbage and Frederick Taylor should be re-evaluated in light of more recent research. One way to relieve job stress is to redesign technical services jobs based on the sociotechnical model of job design, which attempts to balance social factors with technical considerations.

Keywords and Phrases. Job design, Sociotechnical model of job design, VDT, Stress, Job enlargement, Job enrichment.

INTRODUCTION

As production systems become more and more mechanised and automated, the nature of human work is increasingly either what is "left over," or whatever is required in terms of operation, maintenance, or monitoring of automatic equipment. Thus a new nature of work--and a new QWL [quality of work life] for workers concerned--may be said to have been emerging during the introduction of automation in recent decades.[1]

That automation is changing our world, and within it the work that we do and how we do it, is a self-evident truth for academic librarians. Most of the research of the past twenty years on technological change in the workplace has focused on the industrial organization, which exists for the production of goods; but some of the results of this research are applicable to the academic library's business of processing information and particularly to library technical services.

THE AUTOMATION OF TECHNICAL SERVICES

The academic library technical services operation has traditionally revolved around a plethora of paper files. Our professional visionaries now look forward to the day when all files will be online, accessible and manipulable through a VDT (visual display terminal) which can be physically located anywhere in the system. A typical scenario in which all the standard tasks are automated is as follows: a searcher locates the appropriate record in the resource database, downloads it to the local online system, and creates a purchase order. Any correspondence concerning the order is handled via the online electronic mail system. When the item is received, it is checked in and invoiced online. The item is sent to a cataloger, who upgrades the online acquisitions data to a full bibliographic record if necessary. The local system automatically checks headings and notifies the cataloger if a heading is either new or in conflict with an existing heading in the system. Lists of new headings are searched online in the authority file of the resource database and the authority record downloaded to the local system.

The projected impact of this scenario on technical services staffing has been described on several occasions. A recent example can be cited from Allen B. Veaner's paper on the future of academic librarianship:

> In the 1985-95 decade we may expect to see:
> - Fewer catalogers; possibly none in junior, community, and small colleges, as out-of-the-ordinary cataloging will be done by contract ... Even the bulk of a university library's cataloging may be bought from a contractor or consortium, such as the Research Libraries Group.
> - Fewer clerks, as more academic library routines, e.g. circulation and acquisitions, under continuing fiscal pressures, fall into a few well-defined nationwide standard systems implemented with vendors' standard software packages, i.e. turnkey systems.[2]

Those staff who remain in technical services may be redistributed in a pattern described as the "polarisation hypothesis," which pictures automation producing a small number of highly skilled jobs and a larger number of unskilled jobs. If one assumes that the highly skilled positions will be filled by professionals--managers and supervisors, and the increasingly rare professional cataloger--our concern here is with people who will perform the monotonous tasks which remain. Many of these tasks will be carried out by clerks seated in front of a bank of VDT's.

JOB STRESS AND THE VDT

The VDT as the essential tool of library automation has come under scrutiny as a source of various health problems ranging from eye strain to risks associated with high levels of radiation. These problems have been discussed in the literature[3] to the extent that at least one state (New Mexico) has mandated VDT health and safety measures for state employees.[4] Among the health problems attributed to the VDT is stress.

In terms of physics, stress is an applied force or system of forces that tends to strain or deform a body. Human beings under physical, mental, or emotional pressure are also considered to be under stress, which can result in measurable changes to the human body.

New Mexico's Executive Order No. 85 is especially interesting because it addresses the issue of job stress related to VDT use as well as health and ergonomic considerations, and requires that jobs be diversified to alleviate stress. Recent research on stress has reported a significant positive correlation between prolonged VDT use and high levels of stress. Robert M. Mason in his Library Journal column "Mason on Micros" writes

> One Swedish researcher points out that a VDT operator experiences the same stress (as measured by excretions of adrenaline and rising blood pressure) as a bus driver at rush hour ... [Other Swedish researchers] found significantly higher stress reactions and complaints of stress in workers who used a VDT over 50 percent of the time compared with a control group who used a VDT less than 10 percent of the time ... For workers who used a VDT between 10 percent and 50 percent of the time, the VDT was viewed as simply another tool for their work. There was no difference in stress reactions between this group and the control group.[5]

The National Institute of Occupational Safety and Health (NIOSH) found higher levels of stress among VDT operators in clerical jobs than any other occupational group.[6] Mason, in his brief consideration of the problem as it relates to libraries, concludes that some concern is justified.

OTHER SOURCES OF STRESS

The use of VDT's is not the only source of job stress related to job design. Other factors which are applicable to technical services jobs are 1) constant sitting; 2) repetitive, monotonous tasks which require constant attention; 3) underutilization of skills; 4) unreliable or unpredictable system response; 5) lack of control. These characteristics, in combination with other sources of stress such as environmental conditions and socio-economic factors, have a cumulative effect on the stress level of the worker, his or her satisfaction with the job, and ultimately the productivity of the unit or department.

THE SOCIOTECHNICAL MODEL OF JOB DESIGN

Some of the basic assumptions which shape our thinking about the organization of work derive from the theories of two men: Charles Babbage (1792-1871) and Frederick Winslow Taylor (1856-1915.) Babbage formulated the principle of separating the intellectual component of work from the manual component, the former to be paid at a higher rate; Taylor broke work down into measurable units and analyzed it based on time and motion studies. Juxtaposed with Taylor's job rationalization methodology inherent in the "machine theory" of scientific management is the current sociotechnical systems model, which analyzes work as a system neither exclusively technical nor exclusively social. The sociotechnical model recognizes the interaction between technical requirements and social factors and attempts to optimize the balance between the two.

Job design is the process of defining the contents of the job, the procedures and equipment to be used, and the interrelationships between jobs. Research by Eric Trist, F.E. Emery, K.W. Bamforth and others on the application of sociotechnical systems theory to job design has been summarized by Thomas W. Shaughnessy in his article "Technology and Job Design in Libraries: a Sociotechnical Systems Approach."[8] Some of the psychological requirements important to job design which have been derived from this research include an optimum variety of tasks within the job; a meaningful pattern of tasks which relate to the completion of a whole, identifiable piece of work; optimum length of work cycles; autonomy, discretion in setting standards, and development of a sense of responsibility for the work; tasks which require skill and are deserving of respect; inclusion of auxiliary and preparatory tasks; and tasks that make a contribution to society at large, that have a perceivable impact on others. These principles should be kept in mind when considering the appropriate approach to designing jobs for the technical services operation.

Job enlargement and job enrichment, singly or in tandem, are the approaches selected most often in the sociotechnical systems model. Five implementation concepts have been defined by J. Richard Hackman and others: 1) combining tasks (job enlargement); 2) creating natural work units; 3) establishing client relationships; 4) vertical loading (job enrichment); 5) opening feedback channels.[9] We can examine each of these concepts briefly and look for applications in technical services.

1) Combining tasks, or job enlargement, can help avoid the highly specialized (and monotonous) tasks which workers find stressful. Job enlargement is sometimes called "horizontal loading." An example from library technical services might be to assign pre-order searching, keying, vending, etc., to the same person rather than breaking the tasks down into separate, specialized jobs.

2) Creating natural work units, similar to job enlargement in that it may involve adding tasks, enhances the intelligibility of the work and gives the worker a sense of responsibility for and involvement in the "product" by grouping tasks together to form logical sets. An example might be to assign one or more workers total responsibility for processing materials received on blanket order: searching, creating acquisi-

tions records, invoicing, and cataloging those items with adequate bibliographic data in the resource database.

3) Establishing client relationships is a technique used in business whereby an employee has total responsibility for certain clients or accounts. A valid technical services example might be to assign individual catalogers responsibility for liaison with subject area librarians or faculty members.

4) Vertical loading, adding to a job the control and authority for decision-making usually reserved to a higher level, is also referred to as job enrichment. An example might be to assign copy catalogers responsibility for establishing productivity standards as individuals or as a group.

5) Opening feedback channels is another technique used in business with less obvious applications to academic library technical services, but an example might be to assign catalogers responsibility for quality control of the database rather than reserving that function for the supervisors or for another unit entirely.

SUMMARY

There are job design choices for us to make, both aside from and inherent in the technological changes which we face in this period of transition. We as managers need to be aware of stress factors related to VDT use and plan accordingly, creating jobs which maintain VDT assignments at or below the 50 percent level and which offer as much diversity as possible. Jobs can be expanded horizontally to include related tasks, so that the worker develops a sense of the wholeness of his or her work; or vertically to incorporate some of the control and decision-making responsibility traditionally exercised by supervisors or professionals.

The long term challenge in implementing automation in the academic library technical services environment is not just the improvement of productivity and efficiency of the operation, but to bring about that improvement as a result of designing jobs which motivate and satisfy the needs of our employees.

REFERENCES

1. _Automation and Work Design: a Study Prepared by the International Labour Office_, Ed. by Federico Butera and Joseph E. Thurman (Amsterdam: North-Holland, 1984), p. 26.

2. Allen B. Veaner, "1985-1995: the Next Decade in Academic Librarianship, Part I," _College & Research Libraries_ 46:209-229 (May 1985), p. 222-223.

3. For a concise summary see Tobi Bergman, _Health Protection for Operators of VDTs/CRTs_ (New York: New York Committee for Occupational Safety and Health, 1980). Another recent article is R. Bruce Miller, "Radiation, Ergonomics, Ion Depletion, and VDTs: Healthful Use of Visual Display Terminals," _Information Technology and Libraries_ 2:151-158 (June 1983.)

4. _Chicago Tribune_, 17 June 1985, p. C18.

5. Robert M. Mason, "Human Resources and the Micro System," _Library Journal_ 110:44-45 (March 15, 1985), p. 45.

6. _An Investigation of Health Complaints and Job Stress in Video Viewing_, Department of Health and Human Services, National Institute of Occupational Safety and Health (Cincinnati, 1981.)

7. Mason, "Human Resources and the Micro System," p. 45.

8. Thomas W. Shaughnessy, "Technology and Job Design in Libraries: a Sociotechnical Systems Approach," _Journal of Academic Librarianship_ 3:269-272 (Nov. 1977.)

9. Conveniently summarized in J. Richard Hackman et al., "A New Strategy for Job Enrichment," in _Personnel: a Book of Readings_ (Dallas: Business Publications, 1979), p. 53-74.

ACADEMIC LIBRARIANS' WORKLOAD

Eileen E. Hitchingham
Oakland University Library
Rochester, Michigan 48063

Abstract: As new responsibilities are added to traditional ones performed by academic librarians, knowledge of how we expend our time becomes important. Time analysis is one way to get a better handle on library priorities in regard to staff resources. This paper gives "snapshot" results of a 7-day period in an academic library. A brief comparison is made with faculty in other disciplines.

Keywords and Phrases. Workload, academic librarians, time analysis, research time, service time.

NOT ENOUGH TIME

A few years ago William Miller wrote a provocative article outlining a problem that he identified as a malaise abroad in reference departments everywhere.[1] Paradoxically, the problem as he articulated it stemmed from success. Libraries have been quite successful in mounting new (additional) programs such as bibliographic instruction and intermediary-provided on-line searching of databases. More recently we have advanced into the realm of end-user training for database searching. However, libraries have been less than successful in pruning or reassessing the priorities of already established and functioning services, given that overall staff resources have remained steady or, more likely, declined. Miller predicts burnout, deterioration in the quality of services, and inter-staff flareups as camps form in alignment with innovation or preservation regarding services.

Reference services are not the only functions that suffer from more being piled on top of what is already a difficult to manage mix of responsibilities. Automation is taking its own new bite of available librarian resources for systems assessment, staff training, software review, and sometimes just tinkering to make it go. Shrinking collection funds lead to a climate where approval plans, with their own attendant development and monitoring systems to be put in place, are being reviewed by collection development librarians in smaller and medium-sized institutions. This same shrinkage increases the need for more outreach efforts and dialogue between collection development librarians and faculty in the subject disciplines regarding student curriculum needs, and faculty research needs. Interlibrary loan is growing into Document Delivery. This means that any librarians involved in this function must not look only to the library down the road that might be able to supply the needed item in a timely manner, but must also consider and incorporate procedures for obtaining needed materials from the commercial organizations that are proliferating.

Forecasting needs in academic librarianship for the next decade, Veaner calls for library schools to recruit only the "best and the brightest" and to develop in these "best" students analytic, financial, interpersonal, promotional, supervisory, leadership, and labor expertise skills.[2] Many of us currently in the academic library world can project at least another 10 to 30 years in harness before being put out to pasture, so it seems that this catalog of skills, if not already acquired, presents yet another agenda for action for each of us, as well as for the students in the educational pipestream.

As Miller indicated, assessment of priorities is one of the steps we need to take before we can begin to cope with the changes we have already put in place, and the changes that will challenge us in the near future. One measure of our current priorities is the time (staff resources) that we expend on particular library functions or activities. This paper examines the method and the "snapshot" results from a time analysis over a seven-day period in an academic library. Time analysis is suggested as a way of taking stock of our priorities as expressed by what we do.

THE SETTING

The Library is part of a medium-sized state university with 9,200 FYES students, primarily commuters. In addition to the College of Liberal Arts, it has five professional schools, and offers a number of master's level programs and three doctoral programs.

Most of the Library's collections and services are housed in one building. The Instructional Technology Center, which manages AV equipment and film rental, television production, and a small performing arts collection, is housed in a separate building.

At the time of this analysis the staff consisted of 13 librarians and the Dean of the Library; 6 Administrative Professionals (Assistant to the Dean, Business Manager, Serials Manager, and 3 instructional technology professionals); and 21 clerical staff members.

The librarians have had faculty rank and status since 1972, and are organized as part of the AAUP collective bargaining group. Like the rest of the faculty there is no explicitly stated "workload" of a specific number of hours per week for work; prior to 1972 the librarians had a 37.5 hours per week explicit responsibility, with compensatory time for hours in excess. Annual salary reviews, and reappointment, tenure and promotion reviews stress tripartite responsibilities for librarians in the areas of job, scholarship, and service. Both types of reviews place a heavy emphasis (70 to 80 percent) on the importance of meeting job responsibilities. Except for cataloging, most assignments have been fluid for the last several years. All librarians have participated in the bibliographic instruction program, most librarians have scheduled reference desk time (some less busy reference desk hours are covered by paraprofessionals and students), and a number of librarians have shared in or coordinated functions such as archives, online database searching, collection development, circulation, and interlibrary loan.

Flexibility has been needed to provide backup coverage for sabbaticals, and spring/summer sessions. Librarians are scheduled for 10 months instead of the more common academic library practice of 11 months (i.e., 20 to 24 vacation days). In actual practice, some librarians find that responsibilities cannot be neatly tied up in a 10-month segment, so even if they are "off" spring or summer, some things still have to be carried through to completion.

THE METHOD

The study was carried out for a one-week period (seven days) in March 1984. Only librarians (exclusive of the Dean) were included in this study. One librarian chose not to participate in the process.

Librarians maintained a timelog of library, university, and professional activity. Each librarian had a timesheet for each day in the study. Weekends were included. The timsheets were divided into 15-minute segments, and covered a time period from 7 a.m. to midnight. Participants were asked to write a brief phrase indicating the activity that occurred in the 15-minute period. At the same time, or later in the day, they coded their notation for function (listed on the timesheet) and type of activity (also listed on the timesheet).

The Library functional activities included:

    Archives
    Acquisitions
    Bibliographic Instruction
    Cataloging
    Collection Development
    Circulation
    Committees, Library, not directed to a functional area
    Committees, University, not directed to a functional area
    Committees, External, not directed to a functional area
    Computer Searching
    Documents Service
    Hotline (Reference) Service to public libraries
    Interlibrary Loan
    Reference
    Research and Analysis
    Scholarship
    Other

"Committees, Library, not directed to a functional area" covers those things which relate to library operations but do not fit into one of the normal functional areas, for example, a special group set up for space utilization decisions, an automation task force, or a serarch committee. On the other hand, if the librarians involved with collection development form any special sub-group for a project, this is still considered to be in the collection development category. The Hotline service, funded by a county grant, is a special reference and interloan service provided to public libraries in the county. Research and analysis includes studies which occur on a regular basis throughout the year and special studies to meet one-time needs. Scholarship can include work toward an additional master's or other advanced degree, as well as a conference presentation or development of a publication.

The type of activity that could be coded with each functional aspect listed included:

    BI-class prep, class, grading
    Book truck reviewing
    Committee for a functional area
    Computer searching with the user
    Document development (reports, memos, etc.)
    Filing
    Friday folder reviewing
    Going or coming from places
    Number manipulation
    OCLC use
    Phone call from outside
    Phone call by librarian
    Reference at desk
    Respond to another person's request- request from Library
    Respond to another persons's request- request from University
    Respond to another person's request- request from external source
    Supervision
    Typing
    Word processing
    Mail
    Other

The activity list was not meant to be inclusive of all possible activities, but rather, to reflect a number of activities that several or all librarians might encounter. The other category was designated for any specific activities not mentioned, for example, giving a tour to a visiting member of an accrediting team, dealing with a user who has a complaint, or trouble-shooting a printer malfunction. Each librarian scheduled for reference desk responsibilities has a regular turn at reviewing new acquisitions for additions to the reference collection (book truck reviewing), and all librarians have the opportunity to make comments regarding potential reference additions, by reviewing publisher blurbs and reviews for publications which are routed each week (Friday folders). Word processing should probably be considered as both document development and actual production of the paper document, since most people using this route compose as they are going along and then print the document.

Timesheets were collected at the end of the day and tabulated after the seven days were completed.

THE RESULTS

Summary results for functions and activities are given in Table 1 and Table 2. Table 3 gives a composite look at the division of effort among job or library functions, service (committee work or similar meetings related to the University or external agencies), and scholarship.

Table 1
SUMMARY RESULTS - FUNCTIONS

	TOTAL HOURS	PERCENT
ARCHIVES	12.8	2.4
ACQUISITIONS	6.0	1.1
BIB INSTRUC	24.3	4.5
CATALOG	20.3	3.8
COLL DEV	54.5	10.2
CIRC	11.8	2.2
COMMIT, LIB, NF	40.3	7.5
COMMIT, UNIV, NF	36.8	6.9
COMMIT, EXTERN, NF	37.5	7.0
COMPUTER SEARCH	29.0	5.4
DOCUMENTS	15.5	2.9
HOTLINE	27.5	5.2
ILL	11.3	2.1
REFERENCE	76.5	14.3
RES & ANAL	22.3	4.2
SCHOLARSHIP	71.8	13.5
OTHER	35.5	6.7
TOTAL HOURS	533.3	

A total of 533 hours were noted for the one-week period. Reference, collection development, and scholarship each accounted for 10 percent or more of all functional time expended. With other excluded, the biggest activity areas include reference at the desk at 10 percent, and document development at 9 percent. Other accounts for 43 percent of all activities, indicating that each of the functions calls for a number of specific activities not categorized in the main list. A cross tabulation of function with activity (not given here) showed that less than 3 percent of time fell in the other/other category.

Table 2
SUMMARY RESULTS - ACTIVITIES

	TOTAL HOURS	PERCENT
BI CLASS	18.8	3.5
BK TRK REVIEW	6.0	1.1
COMMIT, FUNC AREA	16.8	3.1
COMPUT SEARCH W USER	13.5	2.5
DOC DEVELOP	47.8	9.0
FILING	4.8	0.9
FRI FOLDER	6.8	1.3
GOING & COMING	12.5	2.3
NUMBER MANIPULATION	17.0	3.2
OCLC USE	8.5	1.6
PHONE FROM OUTSIDE	5.8	1.1
YOU PHONE OUT	8.5	1.6
REF AT DESK	52.3	9.8
RESPOND, LIB	18.3	3.4
RESPOND, UNIV	12.3	2.3
RESPOND, EXTERN	15.0	2.8
SUPERVISE	13.0	2.4
TYPING	1.5	0.3
WORD PROC	6.5	1.2
MAIL	19.5	3.7
OTHER	228.5	42.9
TOTAL HOURS	533.3	

Crossing function with activity also reveals that for a number of areas which we might consider as focused on direct user contact, for example reference, computer searching, and bibliographic instruction, there is a considerable amount of time expended which does not relate to traditional time with the user at the reference desk, or doing a computer search, or revolving around a particular BI class. For example, reference had 76 hours total, but reference at the desk accounted for 2/3 of this time. Cross comparisons show that at least part of this other time comes from reference or information type requests which come to the librarian from other members of the library, the university, or an external agency. If people know you they will call you!

The situation is similar with computer searching and bibliographic instruction. The actual time spent in preparation and doing any one particular search is about half of the effort expended for computer searching. Billing, notifying the searching group of changes, developing promotional materials, or talking to potential users about what a computer search can or cannot do, eats up an appreciable amount of time. Preparation for a specific BI class, meeting the class, and grading worksheets for the class took 3/4 of the BI time; however, additional joint or singular efforts are needed for revisions of handouts used by all instructors, contacting faculty, and assigning BI classes. A closer analysis showed that if all library--related functions were considered (excluding service and scholarship) there was almost 2 to 3 hours of other library activity needed for every 1 hour of direct user contact involvement.

On a percentage basis (Table 3) the balance between library responsibilities, service and scholarship commitments approximates the weight assigned in annual and reappointment reviews. Individually, however, the key characterization was variation. Total hours ranged from 32 to 56 hours for the librarians participating. Library function ranged from 18 to 46 hours; service from 0 to 20.5 hours; and scholarship from 0 to 20.5 hours.

WHAT'S NORMAL?

The Sunday magazine section in the newspaper I read has a syndicated column called The Average American. It highlights all sorts of interesting trivia for self comparison, e.g., 90 percent of Americans are asleep by midnight. The appeal of this column is a good indication of the widespread desire to know how we "measure up." Unfortunately, there is no standard yardstick for time allocation for functional activities in libraries. Time allocation for specific functions is likely to depend upon local political and environmental needs, the capabilities of the staff, the size of the staff, and the particular library governance structure--hierarchical, collegial, or a mixture.

Without debating whether librarians should be compared to other faculty, it is interesting to make some comparisons with earlier workload examinations of the academic environment. Most of the reported studies depend upon a survey in which the individual gives an estimate of the number of hours per week, or per year, spent in teaching, research, and service.

Estimates

Wyant and Morrison give results estimated by some library school faculty at six schools.[3] They report a weekly total hours average of 55.4 hours. The average time for teaching was 32.3 hours (58.3 percent).

For four Nebraska state colleges and Iowa State University, Wendel found that faculty total weekly averages by school ranged from 50.4 hours to 52.9 hours.[4] The amount of time spent on teaching and advising was similar for the state colleges (34.4 hours to 37.6 hours) and somewhat lower for Iowa State (28.5 hours). Iowa State faculty estimated considerably more research time (12.6 hours or 24.6 percent of total time) than the faculty at the state colleges (2.6 to 4 hours of research). Wendell also lists a number of earlier studies which report faculty workload activities ranging from 40.9 to 84.1 hours a week.

For faculty members at the University of Queensland, Fry reports an estimated average of 1,200 hours per year out of 2,119, or 56.6 percent of faculty time, is spent on teaching, if teaching is defined to include class contact hours, associated work, and thesis supervision.[5] Research efforts account for 578 hours or 27.2 percent of workload. The remaining hours are involved with administrative or other work (not defined).

Table 3
SUMMARY RESULTS
JOB, SERVICE, SCHOLARSHIP

	TOTAL HOURS	%	AVERAGE HOURS DAY*	AVERAGE HOURS WEEK
LIBRARY FUNCTION	387.3	(72.6)	6.5	32.3
COMMITTEE (U & E)	74.3	(13.9)	1.2	6.2
SCHOLARSHIP	71.8	(13.5)	1.2	6.0
TOTAL	533.3		8.9	44.5

*If based on five-day week

TABLE 4
HOURS PER WEEK IN PROFESSIONAL ACTIVITIES

	Job/Teaching	%	Research	%	Service	%	Total
Librarians	32.3	(72.6)	6.0	(13.5)	6.2	(13.9)	44.5
NSF Colleges	21.6	(54.7)	10.5	(26.6)	7.4	(18.7)	39.5
NSF Universities	14.9	(33.8)	19.7	(44.7)	9.5	(21.5)	44.1

Time Logs

Studies which involve actual detailed time reporting in regard to workload seem to note somewhat fewer hours per week of total activity. Fairchild, chairperson of a Guidance and Counseling Department, outlines a method for time analysis.[6] His report of his activities over a period of a year show 1,773.5 hours. This includes 40.2 percent of time for teaching, and 35.8 percent for research. Based on a 40-hour week, the hours reported would account for 44.3 weeks of activity.

Campbell, a professor of Business Administration, uses a method similar to that noted by Fairchild and reports self-study data for a period of six years.[7] Based on a 48-week year, Campbell shows work hours per week of 42.7, 50.4, 42.5, 44.4, and 40.8. Teaching time for these years ranged from 24 to 39 percent of the week's time; research responsibilities filled from 38 to 68 percent of a work week's hours.

The current examination of librarians' log of activities most closely parallels the method used in an NSF study of science and engineering faculty in universities and four-year colleges.[8] Science/engineering faculty as defined in that study included faculty in engineering, environmental sciences, life sciences, mathematical/computer sciences, physical sciences, psychology and social sciences. Each participant completed a worksheet for each day of a one-week period. In the NSF study contact of participants occurred over a one-year period, so variations in work intensity caused by periods of non-work related activity, for example, vacations, are refelcted in the data. Table 4 compares the distribution of activity for the librarians in this study with the science/engineering faculty in colleges and universities. In this comparison data from the NSF study regarding income producing time expenditure was deleted since it was not included for librarians. The NSF category professional enrichment was added to research hours, because the definition parallels some things that would be considered as research/scholarship for the librarians, for example, coursework.

The librarians showed workloads comparable to those reported for science and engineering faculty in universities, and greater than those indicated by these categories of faculty in colleges. The most striking difference is the division of effort in the three areas. Librarians are devoting most of their work time to the primary responsibilities of the job. Measured by hours, the service loads are somewhat similar to those shown by other faculty, so the emphasis on job is at the expense of research-related work.

SOME REFLECTIONS

From smallest to largest academic library, there are some similar functions that we are all addressing by "spending" some allocation of librarian time. In addition, we "spend" time on our own special library situational needs. While there is no national norm for an academic workload, it seems that the concept of a 40 to 50 hour week for all responsibilities fits a pattern that has developed in a number of other disciplines.

However, because many academic librarians support the concept of a tripartite responsibility for job, research, and service activities for themselves, the "job" part of the responsibility cannot be expanded indefinitely. It is likely to stabilize at a point somewhat less than a 40-hour week. Introduction of something new in regard to library functions means a paring away or replacement of something old that was done before. This can occur after a planned decision, or as the result of individual time management decisions. The results from a library-wide timelog study can provide a basis for better understanding our current time emphases, and making planned decisions for keeping, paring, or replacing services.

REFERENCES

1. William Miller, "What's Wrong with Reference: Coping with Success and Failure at the Reference Desk," American Libraries 15:303-322 (May 1984).

2. Allen B. Veaner, "1985 to 1995: The Next Decade in Academic Librarianship, Part II," College & Research Libraries 46:295-308 (July 1985). See pp. 301-303.

3. June Wyant and Perry Morrison, "A Faculty Workload Survey," Journal of Education for Librarianship 12:155-161 (Winter 1972).

4. Frederick C. Wendell, "The Faculty Member's Workload," Improving College and University Teaching 25:82,84 (Spring 1977).

5. Neville H. Fry, "Academic Staff Workloads in a University," The Journal of Educational Administration 19:95-105 (Winter 1981).

6. Thomas N. Fairchild, "Development and Utilization of a Faculty Time Analysis System—An Aid to Accountability in Higher Education," Assessment and Evaluation in Higher Education 6:218-229 (December 1981).

7. Colin Campbell, "An Empirical Model for Faculty Time Analysis," Assessment and Evaluation in Higher Education 7(2):181-185, 1982.

8. National Science Foundation, Activities of Science and Engineering Faculty in Universities and 4-Year Colleges 1978/79. National Science Foundation, Division of Science Resource Studies (Washington, DC: U.S. Government Printing Office, 1981), p. 1. NS 1.22:Sci 2/9 1978-79.

THE FLOW OF HUMAN RESOURCES:
A TURNOVER AGENDA FOR ACADEMIC LIBRARIANSHIP

James G. Neal
The Pennsylvania State University
University Park, PA

The academic library is a service organization heavily dependent upon its employees, with personnel costs representing a major portion of operating budgets. Skillful management of valuable human resources, especially as pressures for cost containment and accountability increase, is a key determinant of library effectiveness.

Employee turnover, that is the termination of employees and the hiring of other staff to replace them, is a complex phenomenon demanding a systematic view and an awareness of many variables within both the organization and the environment. Academic library managers must improve their understanding of the turnover process and its impact on the employee, the work group, and library, and the larger academic and library communities.

Individual academic libraries and the academic library profession must consider and begin to implement the following elements of an action and research agenda on employee turnover.

At the library level, a four-step program should be implemented: begin to collect and analyze data on turnover patterns, encourage university and college administrators to promote institution-wide turnover monitoring procedures, identify those factors which are contributing to turnover problems in the library through the carrying out of exit interviews, and organize remedial actions which address the main causes of turnover.

The Association of College and Research Libraries must play a leadership role in the promotion of turnover management in academic libraries. Guidelines for the collection, measurement and reporting of turnover data are needed. This would encourage the establishment of benchmark statistics for types of employees, for different sizes of libraries, and for geographic areas. Conference programs and workshops, and assignments to appropriate ACRL committees to generate information about turnover in academic libraries, would encourage understanding and sensitivity to the importance of turnover.

Research on turnover-related topics must be promoted and the results broadly disseminated. The literature of organizational behavior and industrial psychology contains well over 1,000 studies dealing with the causes and impact of turnover. The analysis of turnover trends in individual libraries for different employee groups and the study of various variables related to turnover are needed.

There are two key variables involved in turnover activity. The first is job satisfaction - the extent to which employees have a positive and affective attitude toward their jobs. Important elements are: employee selection, work assignment, pay and benefits, promotion opportunities, nature of supervision, work environment, and employee development. The second variable is opportunity, the extent to which alternative occupational roles are available. Factors include: the overall condition of the economy in a region, the type of occupation and average level of earnings, the status of the labor market, the concentration of employers, the existence of a secondary labor market, and the availability of alternate income sources.

Research has demonstrated that three employee groups are characterized by high rates of turnover: employees whose spouses are members of "temporary systems," such as educational institutions; employees who work as secondary wage earners; and young, talented, managerial employees. In addition, studies indicate that employees with low lengths of service, new employees, usually have higher rates of turnover than those with high lengths of service, senior employees. The extent to which these trends exist in academic libraries demands our attention.

The impact of turnover is a complex of costs and benefits, although the negative consequences tend to be more visible and to have clearer implications for organizational effectiveness. There are the costs of recruitment, selection, and training. There is the negative effect on employee morale, productivity and conflict. On the other hand, turnover helps keep salary costs down, creates opportunities for upward mobility, encourages staffing flexibility and organizational restructuring, brings new employees with new ideas and experiences into the organization, and reduces the frustration created by dead-end jobs.

Academic libraries can contribute significant data to the research on employee turnover. Numerous desirable and related studies in an essentially virgin field can be cited: the professional versus organization commitments of academic librarians; the development of secondary job markets for librarians; other forms of withdrawal as a substitute for turnover; student employee turnover; vacancy management in academic libraries; internal movement of employees through transfer and promotion; sources of innovation in the academic library; turnover rates and the achievement of affirmative action goals; the impact of technological change on turnover; the itinerant workforce in the university community; tenure for academic librarians and the maintenance of organizational vitality; compensation in academic libraries as compared with regional trends; manpower supplies and needs in librarianship.

The flow of human resources within, between and out of academic libraries is a critical management concern. More careful analysis of the turnover process and broader discussion of its characteristics in the academic library are required.

Questions for discussion:

1. Is employee turnover a problem in academic libraries?

2. What factors are contributing to high rates of turnover among certain employee groups?

3. What factors are contributing to low rates of turnover among other staff groups?

4. What has been the negative and positive impact of turnover on academic libraries?

5. How can academic library administrators more effectively manage employee turnover?

A LIBRARY MIDDLE MANAGER LOOKS AT PERFORMANCE APPRAISAL

Barbara P. Pinzelik
Purdue University Libraries
West Lafayette, IN 47907

Abstract. A basic role of the library middle manager is to insure that the library support staff perform effectively. In carrying out the performance appraisal procedures required by most libraries, the inexperienced manager assumes that proper application of the process will solve the organization's personnel problems. More experienced managers have doubts about the effectiveness of performance appraisal, which they may attribute to their lack of skill. A search of the management literature reveals the depth and complexity of decades of research into the process. Some of the many variables which affect the validity and effectiveness of performance appraisal are incorporated into a model for the middle manager.

Keywords and Phrases. Performance appraisal. Personnel evaluation. Middle management.

A LIBRARY MIDDLE MANAGER LOOKS AT PERFORMANCE APPRAISAL

Libraries are labor-intensive organizations in which it is essential that all staff members perform effectively. Public services staff may be in contact with the public for hundreds of hours each week, often with minimal supervision. For the health of the organization, these contacts should be successful. Technical services staff are creating public records which are written evidence that the library knows (or does not know) what it is doing.

To create order out of possible chaos, supervisors must do the best possible job of hiring, training, and managing support staff. In libraries, librarians often become managers without supervisory training or experience. It is not at all unusual for a new librarian to be given the responsibility for supervising experienced support staff.

A supervisor confronted by an organization's performance appraisal requirements instinctively grasps the reasons for the procedures and the benefits to be gained. However, after brief experience conducting staff appraisals, the middle manager begins to realize that a very complex process is taking place. It is then that questions begin to arise:

1. Is my assessment fair?
2. How do my ratings compare with those of other managers?
3. Who will have access to this information?
4. How will others use and interpret my comments?
5. How effective can I be in improving performance of my staff by this means?

An informal survey taken by Evans indicates that although librarians believe that performance appraisal is important, they have little or no confidence in the ultimate value of the process.[1] When appraisal interviews seem unsatisfactory or ineffectual, the supervisor may feel the need to learn more about performance appraisal in order that he or she can either conduct them more effectively, or expend the energy required on something more productive. Unfortunately, an attempt to research this topic reveals that the literature is overwhelming. Researchers have been studying the process for decades, and current research flourishes. *Business Periodicals Index* for August 1983/July 1984 alone lists over 60 articles on "job performance." *Psychological Abstracts* in 1983 lists over 200 articles on "job performance" and "performance evaluation."

DEFINITION

For the purpose of this paper performance appraisal will be defined as the formal means by which an organization documents a worker's value. A typical appraisal is a discussion between the supervisor and the staff member during which the supervisor formally documents the employee's performance on a scale of "poor" to "outstanding" in categories such as: (1) Knowledge of job, (2) Quality of work, (3) Ability to learn, (4) Initiative, (5) Cooperation, (6) Judgment. Written comments can be added to illuminate the ratings. The procedure is then summarized with an overall evaluation and recommendations involving goals for future improvement in performance, plans for further training, or some general action plan for the future. Examples of appraisal instruments used in libraries are in ARL Spec Kit #53.[2]

Although most people, workers and managers alike, will say they think the idea of performance appraisal is good, Mayer notes that in practice few will actually carry out the process unless strong operating controls are present.[3]

HOW PERFORMANCE APPRAISALS ARE USED

Management has found a great variety of uses for performance appraisal. It is used to determine compensation, to coach the employee and improve performance, for feedback, for promotion, for documentation, training, manpower planning, discharge, layoff, and research. Evans and Rugass list 16 functions expected of the appraisal process.[4]

To the employee, the appraisal is an occasion to find out what the supervisor thinks about his or her performance and some indication of the rewards system as it relates to that performance. To the supervisor, the opportunity for a periodic, formal discussion with the worker is an important one. To the organization as a whole, system wide documentation of employee ratings provides at least the illusion that their reward system is fair.

VALIDATION STUDIES

Considerable research on validity of performance appraisal has taken place, and many problems of validity have been documented. Steers identifies some of the most common errors.[5] Ratings can be affected by overly strict or overly lenient managers. Many raters make a central tendency error which puts all their employees within a narrow range. A halo effect exists where a rater assigns the same level for each factor being evaluated. Recency error, where the most recent behavior influences the evaluation, or critical incidents (usually unfavorable) influencing the rater's perceptions may be a problem.

A review article by Landy and Farr summarizes the influences in the performance appraisal process.[6] They present the model shown in Figure 1 and define the components.

Roles. Roles include rater characteristics, ratee characteristics, job-related variables, and interaction of these characteristics. Hundreds of research studies on differences in characteristics of the rater such as sex, age, educational level, and a variety of psychological variables provided few general conclusions. Cognitive complexity and rater experience were identified as the two variables meriting further study.

Personal characteristics of the ratee seem to have some influence on rater judgments. While research shows that there is no interaction effect of sex on judgment, both male and female raters may have common sex role stereotypes.

Context. Context is defined as factors not explicitly related to the ratee, rater, or instrument--such as the intended use of the ratings. Research has shown that those used for administrative purposes are more lenient than those used for research.

Vehicle. Vehicle (rating instrument) studies have been exhaustive, with the result that little progress has been made in developing an alternative to the graphic rating scale. Organizations often attempt to change their performance appraisal documentation, hoping it will improve the accuracy of the process. Studies show there is little one can do to improve accuracy in this way.

Rating Process. Rating process variables include rater training, rater anonymity, and sequence of ratings. Rater training has been shown to be effective. Anonymity appears to make no difference in rater decisions. No general pattern has emerged from research concerning effect of serial position on ratings.

Results. Results of the combinations of these variables still require research before it is known whether what has been measured is the behavior pattern of ratees or the cognative constructs of raters.

Component model (Landy and Farr)

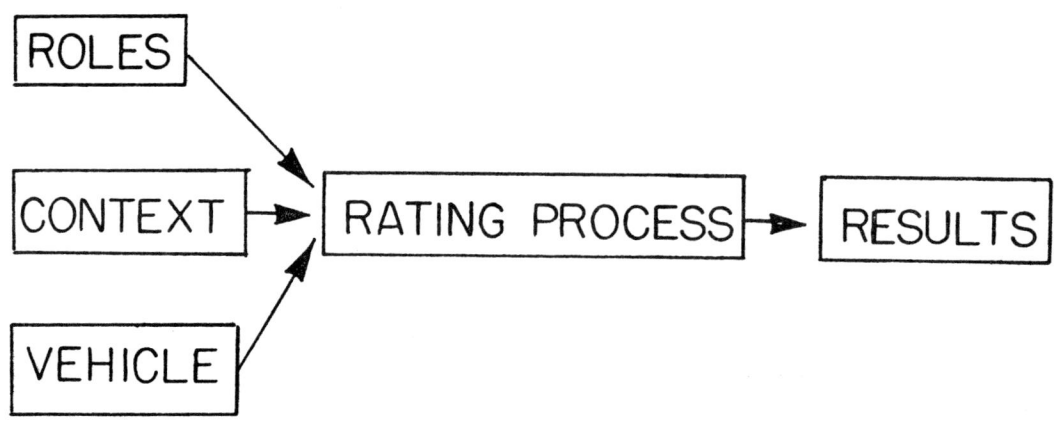

Figure 1

Another review of the literature, published in 1979 by Kane and Lawler reports that the effectiveness being demanded of appraisal systems has outstripped what the present state of knowledge can supply. They present the epigrammatic model shown in Figure 2.

Epigrammatic Model (Kane and Lawler)

$$E = f(M, O, M \times M, O \times O, M \times O)$$

Figure 2

Where E = Appraisal effectiveness.
M = Appraisal methodology.
O = Organizational environment.
M x M = Interactions among aspects of appraisal methodology.
O x O = Interactions among aspects of the organizational environment.
M x O = Interactions between appraisal methodology and organizational environment.

Kane and Lawler cite many studies which point to their conclusions that "observers differ considerably in their ability to do an effective job," "the personal characteristics of the rater interact with the personal charactistics of the object to affect the quality of the appraisal data, " and "effective managers tend to value initiative, persistance, broad knowledge and planning ability. Less effective managers tend to value cooperation, company loyalty, good teamwork, tact, and consideration."

These two review articles identify many of the elements in performance appraisal. They show some of the many variables influencing the process. The enormous amount of research into how these variables relate to and influence each other offers a vision of infinite possibilities for the final outcome. To clarify these relationships, constructing one's own model can provide a more comprehensive overview.

A MODEL FOR THE MIDDLE MANAGER

A supervicial impression of the process can be described as the circle shown in Figure 3. The worker (ratee) is responsible for the job performance. The performance is filtered through the rater's perceptions, and is documented on the appraisal form. The information documented is used by the organization to support various decisions, resulting in promotion, higher compensation, etc. These results influence the ratee to perform as desired by management, and the cycle continues through the next appraisal.

Circular Model

Figure 3

After the model is committed to paper, it is obvious that each element is influenced by many variables. Adding some appropriate variables creates the more complex model shown in Figure 4.

Some of the more obvious characteristics of the ratee include personality (whether abrasive, assertive, compliant), health, dexterity, intelligence, motivation, and experience. These tend to be "givens" and are little changed by the organization.

Job related characteristics include suitability and adequacy of training, provision of proper equipment and space, dependence on others to complete tasks, accuracy of the job description, and general design of the job.

Characteristics of the rater include personality, health, intelligence, experience, training, and biases. The rater's supervisory style is important to the outcome. Frequency of contact, opportunity to observe, relationship with ratee, recall of observations, influence of other employees, influence of other raters, relationship to management, and orientation are all factors that make a difference.

Filtering the perception of the performance through all these variables, one comes to the appraisal instrument, which is the means by which we take a "snapshot" of the results. The format of the instrument, determined by management, has some effect on the process. The form, complexity, frequency, appropriateness to the job being rated, interactivity, and timing are some of the influences.

A MODEL FOR THE MIDDLE MANAGER

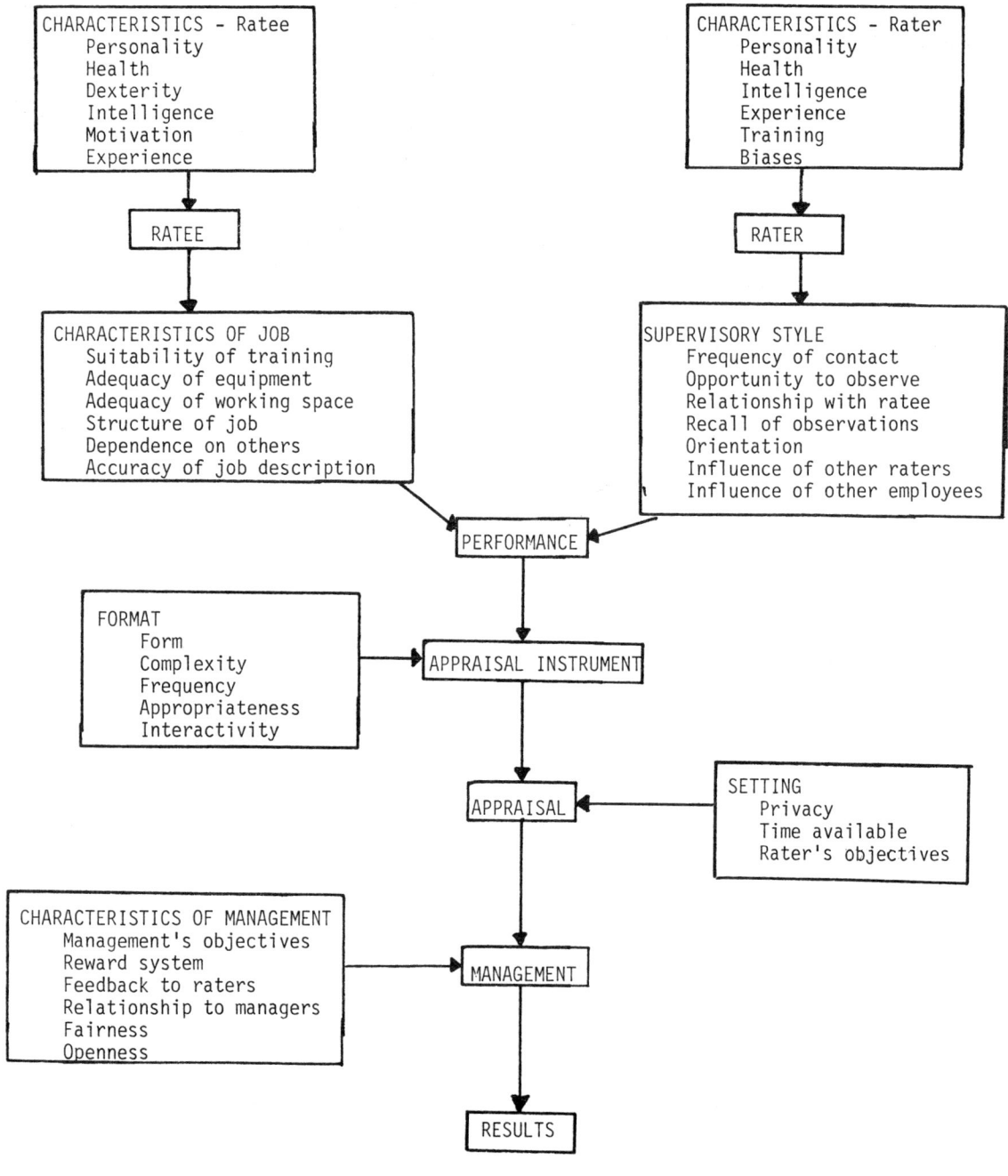

FIGURE 4

The appraisal interview itself is influenced by the setting--the amount of privacy available, the time available for the actual interview, the time invested by the rater in preparation, and the objectives of the rater.

Results are influenced by the management style. Management's objectives, the reward system, feedback to raters, and relationship to managers are influences. If there is openness and trust, documentation will differ from that produced by an atmosphere of secrecy and possibility of punishment. If there is a perception of fairness at the top level, appraisal hyperbole will be minimized.

Feedback must exist or the effort expended by the participants will gradually decrease. It should be obvious to the rater and ratee that their efforts have been observed, negatives noted and positives rewarded.

CONCLUSION

Faced with this large number of variables, any one of which could damage the validity of the process or destroy its effectiveness, it is no wonder that the library middle manager questions the ultimate value of the appraisal process. To achieve better control, managers need to understand their own goals and set some priorities. The manager's purpose can be to establish rewards, to make the employee feel good, to give top administration the impression that the manager is doing a good job, or to improve staff performance. Many managers hope (probably in vain) to achieve all of the above.

It is also important to know the goals of library management. The middle manager needs to know how the ratings will be used, if the organization's goals for the appraisal are the same as the manager's, or if something more is expected.

Once the manager's purpose is clear, he or she must decide which factors can be controlled and focus on those. Changing the characteristics of an employee is not as easy as changing the characteristics of a job. Controlling the setting of the appraisal interview is easier than changing the format of the appraisal instrument. Improving one's supervisory style is more rewarding than trying to change the characteristics of management.

By focusing on controllable factors, the manager can reduce some of the uncertainty. For the assessment to be fair and to be effective in improving performance the manager needs all the control possible. A better understanding of the appraisal process makes these goals more achievable.

REFERENCES

1. G.E. Evans and B. Rugass, "Another Look at Performance Appraisal in Libraries," Journal of Library Administration 3, no.2 (Summer 1982): 61-69.

2. Association of Research Libraries Office of Management Studies. SPEC Kit #53-- Performance Appraisal in ARL Libraries (Washington, DC: ARL, 1979).

3. Herbert H. Meyer, "Split Roles in Performance Appraisal," Harvard Business Review 43, no.1 (Jan. - Feb. 1965): 123-9.

4. Evans and Rugass

5. Richard M. Steers, Introduction to Organizational Behavior (Santa Monica, Good Year Publishing Company), 1981, pp. 400-413.

6. Frank J. Landy and James L. Farr, "Performance Rating," Psychological Bulletin 87, no.1 (Jan. 1980): 72-107.

7. Keffrey Kane and Edward E. Lawler III, "Performance Appraisal Effectiveness: Its Assessment and Determinants," Research in Organizational Behavior 1 (1979): 425-78.

STAFF UTILIZATION IN BRANCH LIBRARIES: A RESEARCH REPORT

Carolyn A. Snyder and Stella Bentley
Indiana University Libraries
Bloomington, IN

Abstract. The study reports the findings of a comparison of the perceptions of public services staff of utilization of their time and the actual recorded time utilization. There are significant differences between the estimated time and actual time spent on public services, collection development, and administrative activities by professional staff, and between technical services and administrative activities by support staff. Research was funded by the Council on Library Resources and done in the Indiana University-Bloomington Libraries.

Keywords and Phrases. staff utilization, branch libraries, public services staffing

INTRODUCTION

During 1984-85, we conducted a study, funded by the Council on Library Resources, of the costs of public services in an academic research library. The study was developed because public services personnel are feeling increasing pressure to provide new and expanded services (e.g., online searching, instruction and orientation, collection development activities) while maintaining or increasing the levels of traditional services and responsibilities (reference, liaison with users, management and supervision). As several current efforts demonstrate, there is considerable interest among public services personnel and research library administrators to determine the problems and needs, assign priorities, assess current approaches, and plan for changes in public services. Our study provides an added dimension to the current efforts to assess and evaluate public services.

The study was built on work which had already begun in the Indiana University-Bloomington Libraries to examine public services issues. A two-day workshop was held in February, 1983, to provide an opportunity for librarians to explore public services issues and to discuss program priorities in order to improve the library's performance and the quality of service provided to users. Personnel in the public service departments and branch libraries have subsequently looked at their utilization of time and developed working drafts of priorities for their units. There is a great concern with the amount of resources seemingly necessary for some activities, and the multiple demands placed on limited resources.

Consequently, we determined that the first part of our study would be an investigation of staff utilization within public services units. This report examines staff utilization in four branch libraries. The research questions which guided the study were:

1. How much staff time is devoted to various activities?

2. Is there a difference between estimated and actual time devoted to various activities? The null hypothesis is that there is no difference between estimated and actual time devoted to the various activities.

THE STUDY

Four branch libraries were selected for the study, two of the larger (Fine Arts and Biology) and two of the smaller branch units (Journalism and School of Library and Information Science) in the Indiana University Libraries. Studying these four branch libraries allowed us to analyze staff utilization in pairs of very similar branches, and to compare and contrast the use of staff in different situations. The size considerations included number of staff, volumes, and circulation. The Journalism and School of Library and Information Science (SLIS) Libraries each have one full-time library faculty member and one full-time support staff member. The Biology and Fine Arts Libraries each have two full-time faculty members. In addition, Biology has three support staff, and Fine Arts has five support staff.

Preliminary information which we gathered from each of the public services units included an estimate of the percent of time spent on the following activities: technical services, public services, collection development, and administration. Estimates of the overall percentages for professionals, support staff, and student hourly employees were included. The four branches provided the following estimates:

	Professional	Support Staff	Student Assistants
Public Services	34%	41%	71.2%
Technical Services	5%	43%	27.9%
Collection Development	31%	3%	0.9%
Administration	30%	12%	-

For the study of actual time utilization, time spent on various activities in the branch libraries was recorded for a typical two-week period by each staff member--library faculty, support staff, and student assistants. Specific activities were recorded for each fifteen minute segment of time on a form devised for this purpose by the researchers and branch library heads. Personnel in the four branches helped design the form to represent most effectively the activities of their units. The form identified three categories: public services, technical services, and administrative activities. Collection development was included as a subcategory of administrative activities. Public services was subdivided into fifteen categories including bibliographic instruction, reference, circulation, searching for materials, preparing bibliographies, and computer assisted reference services. Technical services had twelve categories including processing materials, filing, card catalog maintenance, checking in serials, and preservation activities. Administrative activities included fourteen categories such as collection development, preparing payrolls, hiring and supervision, participating in committees and task forces, preparing reports and budgets, and planning.

STUDY RESULTS

Table 1 presents the total percent of time spent on each activity within the branches during the two-week period. Most interesting is the range of the total percent of time spent on the broad categories among the four branch libraries. For public services, Journalism had 55.4%, SLIS 51.9%, Biology 80.0%, and Fine Arts 66.2%. The libraries with larger staffs had more staff time devoted to public services than did the two smaller libraries. The Biology Library, with the largest percent of time on public services, has a reference librarian. For technical services, Journalism had 11.1%, SLIS 21.4%, Biology 19.9%, and Fine Arts 11.9%. Different situations among the four probably account for the varying percentages for technical services (for example, SLIS does in-house cataloging of some materials, and Biology has extensive serials subscriptions requiring checking and record keeping). For administrative activities, Journalism had 33.5%, SLIS 26.6%, Biology 16.5%, and Fine Arts 21.9%. It should be noted that a greater proportion of time is spent on administration in the two smaller branches.

The results show very similar public services time utilization in the Journalism and SLIS Libraries which are comparable in staff size and in collection size. Biology and Fine Arts, the larger branch libraries, have more varied staff utilization when compared to each other. Considerably more time was spent on public services in the Biology Library which may have been due to some staff vacancies at the time of the study (a reference librarian in Fine Arts and a technical services assistant in Biology).

Table 2 gives the percent of time per activity for the head librarians of each of the branches. There were similar results for three of the four librarians. Most important to note is how little time each of the head librarians spent on public services. In Fine Arts the branch head spent 4.9% of time on public services, in Biology 4.7%, in Journalism 17.2%, and in SLIS 6.9%; in all cases, this is considerably less time than they estimated. The four averaged 8.4% of time on public services, while their average estimate was over 33%. There was a much greater difference for the time spent by branch heads on technical services activities, ranging from no time to 28.2%. With the exception of the Biology Head, the actual time spent is close to the perceived time spent on technical services activities. The average estimate was 5% while average actual time was 8.7%. The branch heads spent most of their time in administrative activities with a high of 94.8% for Fine Arts, 82.8% for Journalism, 86.9% for SLIS, and a low of 67.1% for Biology (the Biology Head utilized much more time for technical services activities). Even after collection development is removed from the administrative category, a significantly greater amount of time is spent on administrative activities (70.8%) than they estimated (30%). In the collection development subcategory, branch heads reported spending from 7.2% to 19.9% of their time, with an average of 12.1%. It is interesting to note that the time devoted to collection development is much less than the head librarians had indicated when they estimated their activity time. The average estimated time on collection development was 31%. Since the IU Libraries have been engaged in an inventory and evaluation of the collections and the writing of a formal collection development policy, it is understandable that the librarians' perceptions were that they spent much more time on collection development than they actually did. Table 3 shows the estimated and actual percent of time spent on each activity by the head librarians. The hypothesis test for sample proportion versus hypothesized value was used to determine if there is a significant difference. The difference is significant at the .01 level for all activities but technical services. In summary, technical services was the only category where estimate matched actual time utilization of the head librarians of the four branches.

Since the branch heads spend relatively low percentages of time on public services activities, the public services of branch libraries is provided primarily by support staff and student assistants. While we knew that most evenings and weekends are staffed only by hourly student employees, it was the perception of unit heads that librarians and support staff spent more time on public services than they actually do. Table 4 shows that the support staff employed as circulation supervisors in the two larger branch libraries, Biology and Fine Arts, spent respectively 87% and 48.2% of their time on public services activities, while the Fine Arts reference assistant and circulation assistant averaged 72% of their time on public services activities. The Biology and Fine Arts Libraries each have a support staff employee for technical services, and these employees spent over 85% of their time on technical services. In the Journalism and SLIS Libraries, however, each with one full-time support staff, even the support staff member did not spend as much time on public services as had been anticipated (Table 5). In Journalism the percentage of time was 30.9% and in SLIS 33.4%. These two individuals devote 10% of their time to technical services and 56 to 59% to administrative activities. Overall, the support staff employees in the four branches averaged 40% of time on public services (compared to an estimate of 41%), 23% on technical services (the estimate was 42.5%) and 36.6% on administrative activities (the estimate was 12%). The major functions in the administrative category were supervising and planning. The estimates were accurate for public services but not for technical services and administrative activities. Table 6 shows the estimated and actual time spent on the four general categories of activities by support staff employees. The hypothesis test for sample proportion versus hypothesized value shows a significant difference at the .01 level for the percent of time spent on technical services and administrative activities.

We also examined the utilization of student hourly employees (Table 7). From 76 to 98% of their time was spent on public services activities, with most of this time spent on circulation, reshelving, and processing reserves. The most interesting finding, however, is that the two smaller branches, Journalism and SLIS, used student employees for a much broader range of tasks than did the two larger libraries. Technical services activities--especially serials checking, processing books and card sets, searching and typing orders, and card catalog maintenance--required 15% of the time of student employees in Journalism and 30% in SLIS. The Biology Library also used some student time (8.6%) for technical services, primarily for its extensive serials collections.

An interesting finding is the extent to which comparable units in terms of size and staff utilized staff in very similar ways. While a more extensive study would be required to verify our findings, it is clear that the utilization of student employees in a branch library is dependent on the number of full-time staff within the library.

SUMMARY

The estimates of staff utilization in the four branch libraries was very different from the reality. The head librarians who thought that they spent a third of their time on public services, a third on collection development, and a third on administration, actually spent most of their time on administration. They averaged only 8% on public services and 12% on collection development. Certainly the general impression that public services librarians are being pressured to do more all the time, and that they do not have enough time to spend on public services, is verified. The average amount of time spent by all personnel in the four branches on public services activities is 63%. This time, however, is primarily accounted for by student assistants who staff circulation desks and reshelve materials and by support staff who supervise the circulation activities. Support staff too spent much more time on administration and less on public services than estimated.

This study shows that there is a need to examine further and assess the functions being performed by various staffing levels within branch library units. It is important to determine what functions are appropriate to each staffing level, and to insure that proper training is provided for all employees. The key public service role of student employees requires that they be trained and prepared for such work. Support staff must be given adequate training to develop the necessary skills for the variety of tasks and responsibilities needed in a public services unit. Finally, this study strongly indicates the necessity for librarians to have administrative abilities. Clearly, both preservice and inservice education must provide the background and skills required for individuals who are so heavily involved in administrative functions.

TABLE 1

TOTAL TIME BY ACTIVITY FOR ALL EMPLOYEES

	Biology %	Fine Arts %	Journalism %	SLIS %
Public Services	80.0	66.2	55.4	51.9
Technical Services	19.9	11.9	11.1	21.4
Collection Development	2.1	1.1	3.8	1.3
Administrative	16.5	21.9	33.5	26.6

TABLE 2

BRANCH HEADS - PERCENTAGE OF TIME PER ACTIVITY

	Biology %	Fine Arts %	Journalism %	SLIS %
Public Services	4.7	4.9	17.2	6.9
Technical Services	28.2	0.3	0	6.3
Collection Development	13.4	7.9	19.9	7.2
Administrative	67.1	94.8	82.8	86.9

TABLE 3

ESTIMATED VS ACTUAL TIME - BRANCH HEAD LIBRARIANS

	Estimated	Actual
Public Services	33.75%	8.43%*
Technical Services	5.0 %	8.7 %
Collection Development	31.25%	12.7 %*
Administrative	30.0 %	70.8 %*

*Significant difference at the .01 level

TABLE 4

SUPPORT STAFF - PERCENTAGE OF TIME FOR BIOLOGY AND FINE ARTS BRANCHES

	Biol Circ Mgr.	Biol CLO3	FA Circ Sup.	FA Circ Asst	FA Ref Asst	FA Assc & Ref	FA CLO3 T.S.
Public Services	87.0	5.5	48.2	71.8	73.5	57.7	5.0
Technical Services	0	88.2	0.8	9.4	26.4	19.5	83.2
Administration	13.0	6.3	51.4	19.7	0	23.0	11.9

TABLE 5

SUPPORT STAFF - PERCENTAGE OF TIME FOR SLIS AND JOURNALISM

	Journalism	SLIS
Public Services	30.9	33.4
Technical Services	10	10.3
Administrative	59.1	56.3

TABLE 6

ESTIMATED VS ACTUAL TIME - SUPPORT STAFF

	Estimated	Actual
Public Services	40.75%	40.33%
Technical Services	42.5 %	23.08%*
Collection Development	2.5 %	0
Administration	11.75%	36.6 %*

*Significant difference at the .01 level

TABLE 7

HOURLY - PERCENT OF TIME PER ACTIVITY

	Biology %	Fine Arts %	Journalism %	SLIS %
Public Services	91.4	98.4	76.1	77.5
Technical Services	8.6	1.5	15.0	30.3
Administrative	0	0.2	8.8	1.1

SUGGESTED GUIDELINES FOR SALARY DETERMINATION IN AN ACADEMIC LIBRARY

Jeanie M. Welch
Lamar University
Beaumont, TX

Abstract. For use in hiring and equity adjustments, the Library Faculty at Lamar University has constructed a suggested formula for professional salaries. The Salary Schedule Review Committee devised a suggested salary formula which included guidelines for determining the following salary criteria:
1. Base salaries (according to rank) based on other academic salaries at the parent institution, within the state, and nationally
2. Percentage increments according to the following criteria:
   a. Education beyond the MLS
   b. Previous professional academic library experience
   c. Areas of responsibility
   d. Skill requirements
   e. Unique expertise (discretionary)
   f. Market considerations (discretionary)

The Salary Schedule Review Committee also devised a worksheet to determine suggested salaries for every professional position.

Keywords and Phrases. College and university librarians, Salaries, Classification and pay plans, Personnel.

INTRODUCTION

In previous years at Lamar University the limited number of professional staff and the relative equality of positions and education of that staff precluded any necessity for formal, written salary guidelines. As the staff grew and hiring qualifications increased, it became obvious that the "rabbit out of the hat" method of salary determination would no longer suffice. Therefore a Salary Schedule Review Committee was appointed to study this problem and present suggested guidelines to the library faculty. This report summarizes the results of the committee's work and presents suggested guidelines for the formulation of salaries for academic librarians.

Lamar University is a state-supported institution of approximately 13,000 students and is classified as a IIA institution by the American Association of University Professors. The library has over 700,000 volume equivalents and purchases approximately 4,000 serial titles. There are currently fifteen library faculty members, eligible for tenure and holding faculty status and faculty ranks from instructor to associate professor.

In preparing for the formulation of suggested salary guidelines the Salary Schedule Review Committee surveyed the literature on academic library compensation and received information on library compensation policies from twenty-seven other Texas public universities. A salary formula subcommittee was established to devise criteria for constructing a suggested formula for salary determination. The subcommittee found that compensation policies fell into the following categories:[1]
1. Free form--salaries set on an ad hoc or individually negotiated basis
2. Professional ranking--salaries set according to professional development and achievements, similar to practices in other academic departments
3. Positions--salaries set according to job requirements, similar to criteria used in private industry
4. Mixed--a combination of the aforementioned categories

Other considerations included policies mandated by the parent institution or by the state legislature. Some institutions also used prevailing national and/or state library compensation statistics to determine beginning, mid-range, and upper level salaries.

In determining criteria for suggested salary guidelines, the formula subcommittee decided to use a mixed system and to consider four areas:
1. Determination of suggested base salary schedule according to academic rank
2. Individual qualifications based on education and professional experience
3. Components of each professional position by functions, skill requirements, and responsibilities
4. Determination of the value to be assigned to each component

Such considerations as committee assignments, special projects, peer evaluations, meritorious service, and publications were not included in the suggested salary formula as their recognition and inclusion at Lamar University are encompassed by merit increases and incentive awards.

DETERMINATION OF BASE SALARIES

Because Lamar University library faculty have faculty status and faculty rank the formula subcommittee decided to use overall faculty salaries, not academic library salaries, when determining suggested base salaries. The subcommittee reviewed the mean salaries by rank at the parent institution (Lamar University), the mean faculty salaries of other Texas IIA public institutions with similar ranks (as reported by the American Association of University Professors),[2] and the means of a sampling of faculty salaries advertised by rank in the October 5, 1983, issue of the Chronicle of Higher Education. For an example of the procedure used to determine the base salary for librarians with the rank of instructor see Appendix I.

Institutions which do not give faculty status or rank to librarians may wish to substitute national and regional academic library salaries in determining the base salary. A sampling of advertised salaries could be taken from the "Positions Available" section of the Chronicle of Higher Education or from such library publications as College and Research Libraries News.

Taking the mean salaries from local, state, and national academic ranks into consideration, as well as the constraints of the library budget, the formula subcommittee set suggested base salaries at the following levels for 1983/84:
1. Instructor (b_1)--$18,000
2. Assistant Professor (b_2)--$20,000
3. Associate Professor (b_3)--$22,000

Suggested base salaries were determined with the knowledge that they should be reviewed and revised periodically to reflect overall changes in faculty salaries at the parent institution, as well as regionally and nationally.

COMPONENTS OF INDIVIDUAL QUALIFICATIONS

The second step in determining suggested salary guidelines for professional librarians was to conduct an analysis of individual qualifications. Many academic libraries grant increments for additional education, usually computed as a predeterminied percentage of the base salary. The determinant fields for individual qualifications are listed in the suggested formula in Appendix II and are summarized below:
1. Completed post-graduate studies (other than the MLS)
2. Previous professional academic library experience

COMPONENTS OF PROFESSIONAL POSITIONS

The third step in determining suggested salary guidelines for professional librarians was a thorough analysis of all professional library positions. Other academic libraries have conducted such classification projects over the years, either using their own criteria or using established personnel classification systems utilized in the private and public sectors. The formula subcommittee used internally-determined criteria, based on areas of responsibility and skill requirements for each professional position below that of library director. A simplified and flexible set of determinant fields was constructed by dividing library functions into areas of responsibility and skill requirements. These determinant fields were "cross-disciplinary," i.e., found in more than one position but not in all.

The determinant fields for professional library positions fell into the following categories:
1. Areas of responsibility (supervisory, fiscal, public contact, planning and development, and collection development)
2. Special skills (automated and administrative)

Two discretionary determinant fields were added for use when deemed appropriate by the library administration. Skill requirements needed in only one particular department or position (e.g., serials cataloging or media production) were addressed under market considerations, one of the discretionary fields listed below:
1. Unique expertise (non-required but performance-enhancing skills and/or knowledge)
2. Market considerations (the competitiveness of certain job skills and/or positions in the job market)

A detailed schedule of determinant fields is included in Appendix II.

DETERMINATION OF COMPONENT VALUE

The last step in compilation of the suggested salary formula was assigning percentage values (or multiples) within each determinant field. Assignment of values was based on the assumption that the functions of each library department below the administrative level (e.g., cataloging or reference) were of equal value in library operations. Different values were assigned to reflect only differing levels of skill requirements and/or responsibilities within a particular department. These values are included in Appendix II. Each value was multiplied by the base salary to determine the dollar increment to be added to the suggested base salary for each rank.

The suggested salary formula (S) was expressed as $S = b + b \cdot \Sigma x$ (salary equals the base salary plus the sum of the component values of each appropriate determinant field (x) multiplied by the base salary). The formula was applied by taking the suggested base salary and adding to it the dollar values of the determinant fields applicable to each library faculty member and position. For example, a librarian with a second master's degree received a value of 2% (or a multiple of .02). If the librarian were an instructor, the value would be multiplied by the base salary of $18,000 ($b_1$). The amount equalled $360 (18000 x .02) and when added to the base salary equalled $18,360. If the librarian also had limited patron contact, with a value of 1% (or a multiple of .01), an additional $180 (18000 x .01) was added, increasing the salary to $18 540. A sample worksheet for determining the salary of a reference librarian with the rank of instructor is included in Appendix III.

APPLICATION OF THE FORMULA

The formula was constructed in order to be applied for two purposes--hiring and equity adjustments. When creating new positions, filling vacancies, or granting in-house promotions, the suggested formula may be utilized when setting a salary range for vacancy announcements or when making an offer to a candidate. The formula could also be applied to correct past inequities or to make salaries commensurate with revised skill requirements and/or responsibilities in existing positions.

ADAPTABILITY OF THE FORMULA

The suggested formula was devised to be flexible enough for use in a classification system instead of a faculty ranking system (such as Librarian I through Librarian IV) and to allow for the inclusion of additional skill requirements, such as foreign language or computer programming capabilities. Values (percentages or multiples) could also be changed to reflect changes in library procedures (e.g., increased automation) or in position requirements (e.g., a change in the number of people supervised).

CONCLUSIONS

In designing suggested guidelines for salaries it is important to try to construct a formula that is simple to understand and implement and as unbiased, inclusive, and flexible as possible. However, it should be kept in mind that no set of suggested guidelines will please everyone, and some positions will defy "fitting the mold." There will be the need for compromise at all levels of discussion and compilation. It is beneficial to circulate suggested guidelines and revisions with sample worksheets to the entire library staff before it is presented for discussion. It also may be useful to construct a chart to illustrate any changes in salary position for present staff members.

Above all, suggested guidelines should be done on an objective and impersonal basis. A thorough analysis of all library positions, procedures, and responsibilities should be done either before or during the compilation of salary guidelines. Construction and implementation of salary guidelines done as methodically as possible should produce a realistic and equitable salary schedule that conforms with market conditions, budgetary constraints, and institutional, state, and national legal requirements.

ACKNOWLEDGEMENTS

I wish to express my gratitude to Miss Maxine Johnston, Director of the Mary and John Gray Library, Lamar University, for her support of this project, and to Miss Linda Dugger, Chairperson of the Salary Schedule Review Committee, for her invaluable contributions and leadership on this project.

REFERENCES

1. William C. Jones, Salary Compensation Systems for Librarians: A Study of Ten Members of the Association of Research Libraries. (Washington: Association of Research Libraries, 1981). Also available from ERIC, ED 214 542.

2. "The Annual Report on the Economic Status of the Profession, 1982-83," Academe 69, no. 2 (July-August 1983):64-68.

APPENDIX I

Determining a Base Salary

1. Determine average salaries by rank at the parent institution
2. Determine average salaries by rank at similar institutions within the state or region
3. Determine average salaries by rank nationally

Add the three averages salaries together, then divide the sum by three. Lower the divided sum to the nearest thousand.

Example

Determining a suggested base salary for a librarian with the rank of instructor at Lamar University for the academic year 1983-84:

1. Average salary for an instructor at Lamar University, academic year 1983-1984 $18,245
2. Average salary for instructors at other Texas state universities classed as IIA by the American Association of University Professors and using similar ranks[1] $18,768
3. Average salary for instructors listed in 31 advertisements in the October 5, 1983, issue of the Chronicle of Higher Education $17,967

TOTAL $54,980

DIVIDED BY 3 $18,326

LOWEST TO NEAREST THOUSAND=SUGGESTED BASE SALARY $18,000

APPENDIX II

Schedule of Determinant Fields

Determinant Field	Application and Increment
I. Completed Post-Graduate Studies	Hiring & equity
A. Certificate of advanced studies	1%
B. Additional master's degree	2%
C. Earned doctorate	3%
II. Professional Academic Library Experience (after receipt of first professional degree)	Hiring & equity
A. Lamar University library experience	1% (per year – equity)
B. Other professional academic library experience (recognition of other professional library experience at discretion of library administration)	.5% (per year – hiring)
III. Areas of Responsibility	Hiring & equity
A. Supervisory responsibility	
1. Other professionals	.5% (per person FTE)
2. Library and media technical assistants	.75% (per person FTE)
3. Clerks	1% (per person FTE)
4. Student assistants	.25% (per person)
B. Fiscal responsibility	
1. Cash management	1%
2. Fiscal records and vendor contact	2%
3. Budgetary allocation and control	3%
C. Public responsibility	
1. Limited--some patron contact and/or handling of patron problems	1%
2. Routine--regular patron contact and/or handling of patron problems	2%
3. Substantial--regular patron contact and/or handling of patron problems plus formal instruction	3%
D. Planning and developmental responsibility	
1. Departmental	1%
2. Interdepartmental coordination	2%
E. Collection development	
1. _Choice_ cards	.5%
2. Substantial--responsible for liaison with faculty and for entire subject area, including _Choice_ cards	2%
3. Overall--responsible for coordination of collection development in all areas, leadership in collection development, and all areas not covered by liaison librarians	3%
IV. Special Skills	Hiring & equity
A. Automated functions	
1. Circulation	3%
2. OCLC	
a. Transactions within subsystems	2%
b. Creation of original permanent records	3%
3. Database searching	3%
B. Administrative responsibility	5%
V. Unique Expertise (discretionary)	Equity 1 – 5 %
VI. Market Considerations (discretionary)	Hiring ±1 – 10% (applied to sum of base salary + increments, should never be less than the base salary)

APPENDIX III

Sample Worksheet

Name Jane Doe   Rank Instructor

Position Reference Librarian   Year 1983/84

    Base Salary $ 18,000

    Post-Graduate Studies   2%

    Professional Experience
        Lamar (Years ____ x 1%)   ____%
        Other (Years 4 x .5%)   2%   360

    Areas of Responsibility
        Supervisory   ____%
        Fiscal   1%   180
        Public Contact   3%   540
        Planning   ____%
        Collection Development   2%   360

    Special Skills
        Automation   3%   540
        Administrative   ____%

    Unique Expertise   ____%

    Market Value   ± ____%   ± _____

    Total Formula Salary $ 20,340

    Actual Salary $ _____

    Differential in Dollars   ± $ _____

    Differential Percentage   ±   _____ %

This sample worksheet is for a reference librarian with a second master's degree in a subject field and four years professional experience at other universities. This position requires cash management, formal library instruction, liaison with faculty for collection development, and database searching. This worksheet is for hiring purposes, but does not include any discretionary determinant fields.

READER SERVICES

INTEGRATION OF AN ONLINE SEARCH SERVICE INTO THE REFERENCE DEPARTMENT

Sandra E. Belanger and Rosemary Thorne
Clark Library, San Jose State University
San Jose, CA

Abstract. In academic libraries, online searching services and reference departments often have to compete for a share of the same resources, *i.e.* budgets and personnel. This paper examines how San Jose State University Library solved the problems of shrinking budgets, space crunch and loss of trained searchers by integrating the online search service into the reference department. The article describes the planning stages and interim organization necessary to effect the required changes. The paper also delineates how to simultaneously provide patron services and train online searchers, and includes discussions of recommended policy and procedure adjustments, and problems encountered. The conclusions analyze the use of this method in establishing a new online search service as well as its effect on academic reference service.

During the 1983-84 academic year, San Jose State University Library was faced with impending budget cuts which could have meant the loss of 11.3 serialized librarian positions. In this uncertain climate, five tenure-track librarians left for employment elsewhere, including the Program Head for Online Reference Services in the Library and four experienced searchers. In less than six months, the Library had lost most of its experienced searchers, including important coverage in the physical sciences, and was unable to replace the Program Head for Online Search Services.

With budget cuts and the loss of trained staff, several problems had to be faced: how to administer the program without a separate program head; how to increase the searching expertise of remaining librarians; and how to handle the growing demand for searches from students and faculty. In addition, we wanted to decrease the search turn-around time (speeding up administrative processes and decreasing the time between request and printed results), get better fiscal control over the online budget, review policies and procedures, plan for future expansion, and better control equipment and supplies. These tasks had to be accomplished simultaneously while continuing to provide service to patrons.

METHODS

Reorganization Committee

A reorganization committee was created to look at possible solutions. The "streamlining committee" consisted of one experienced searcher, a library assistant experienced in reorganizational concerns of reference, and the student assistant who had been working with the online program for some time. The committee examined recordkeeping procedures and forms in order to streamline the operation. Where possible, functions were consolidated, recordkeeping simplified, and decisions made on what records were needed and in what form for budgetary concerns. Under existing conditions, the online budget has to be expended during the fiscal year or funds are lost.

Searcher Questionaire

A brief questionaire was sent to all librarians trained in online searching. They were asked where the online lab should be placed (first or fifth floors), whether to retain the existing subject file to previous searches, and what adjustments were necessary in how cash payments should be handled. Searchers were also queried as to how competent they felt they were, how much searching they could handle, subject areas of expertise, whether a refresher in searching techniques was needed, subject areas where training was needed, and lastly, any comments or suggestions they had as to how online reference should be restructured. This was their chance to indicate pet peeves, ideas, and dreams.

Literature Review

A review of published literature on computer literature searching and reference was conducted. Most of the articles discovered were concerned with the recognition and establishment of online searching as a function of reference services. How could searching be used at the reference desk? What relationship did it have and should it have to traditional reference work? The article by Connie Lamb in 1981 summarized current practice when she said: "In response to the question on organization, most institutions indicate that their online search services are a part of or an extension of Reference and several more designate their position as part of Public Services in general."[1]

While no articles discussed how to modify an existing service, some articles did identify several suggestions on areas to change. Most notable were:
(1) Searching can be a consulting experience, with sharing of expertise.[2]
(2) Some checklist or packet of information for patrons should be prepared.[3]
(3) All reference librarians should search all online sources.[4]
(4) Librarians with search appointments liked them. Search sessions varied with as much as one hour appointments.[5,6,7]
(5) Orientation programs should be included to change staff attitudes.[8]
(6) Search interviews are very important, longer

than reference interviews, and should be held with the person doing the search.[9,10]
(7) Librarians need more training to handle searching effectively.[11,12,13,14]
(8) A fully integrated or centralized system should be used for distributing and record-keeping on searches.[15]
(9) Librarians should be able to point out alternative sources to search questions where appropriate.[16,17]
(10) Handing out searches causes delays in completion of searches, and can bypass a searcher's special expertise.[18]
(11) Efficient operation in search turn-around time is needed.[19]

All of these suggestions were discussed and considered for inclusion in reorganization of search services at San Jose State University.

REORGANIZATION

A two-step reorganization process was chosen. Step one would involve an interim organization to be used during the spring 1984 semester. Step two would be the trial run during the fall 1984 semester of the new organization.

Previous Organization

Online searching was first offered to students and faculty at San Jose State University in 1981. The Online Search Services Coordinator, who reported to the Public Services Division Head, was assigned student assistant help to handle the clerical functions. The Coordinator handled emergencies, training, organization, problems and excess searches. In a later reorganization, the Coordinator was designated a Program Head, with 60% administrative time, similar to other administrative positions in the Library. Reference librarians completed searches as assigned or volunteered for searches. Some searchers completed considerably more searches than others. More difficult or esoteric searches suffered delays as no one wanted to complete them. Additional delays were encountered in contacting the patrons, some of whom were only available at odd hours. Prints were distributed from the reference desk, but cash payments had to be handled from the online office.

Interim Organization

During the spring 1984 semester, one librarian was designated as program chair who distributed searches as equally as possible among the remaining searchers, based on expertise level, subject interests, and time allocated to online reference. In practice, simple ERIC searches were distributed to inexperienced searchers, and engineering, business and science searches were handled by the more experienced searchers. Searchers still had to contact patrons and run the search at their convenience. The most experienced searchers handled emergencies, problems, and demand for special services such as online demonstrations.

At the same time, the reorganization committee reviewed and streamlined functions handled by the online reference program. For example, a subject card file had been kept on searches in the theory that searchers could look at past searches for strategy and/or valuable prints. In practice, this time-consuming file was seldom consulted. The practice of photocopying search results to accompany this file was also discontinued.

In the past, the Hewlett-Packard 2621p terminals and manuals were in two separate rooms, the online lab and the online office. With the exception of a terminal for the reference desk, these were consolidated into the online lab for the convenience of the searchers. An inventory of database manuals was begun to discover the extent of the collection and to update the collection where necessary. With only some of the manuals cataloged into the Library's main collection, no complete record of the collection existed. Since many less-experienced searchers found the terminals somewhat complicated to use, extensive refresher training was conducted.

We have run quick searches at the reference desk since the online service began in 1981. When a ready reference search was run, the printout was photocopied for the student so that the printout could be used for logging-in. The time-consuming procedure resulted in the reference librarians being away from the desk for longer than desired. We revised these procedures, creating a form to record necessary information: time on, time off, costs, databases used, kind of questions, etc. The printout could be given directly to the patron. In this way we continued through the semester while developing the new organizational system to be tried during the fall semester.

Trial Run

Discussion of the trial run period during the fall 1984 semester can be divided into five sections: administrative organization, reference desk, handling of searches, handling of emergencies, and modifications made during the spring 1985 semester.

Administration. The new administrative organization placed control of the online program under the reference department head as an integral part of the reference department rather than as a separate service. An advisory committee was formed, the Online Steering Committee. The reference department head served as a member of the committee along with three searchers and the online student assistant. The committee's charge was to serve as a planning and policy making group. As such, the committee pinpointed training areas, provided training to two beginners, held an open house to acquaint all Library staff with the facilities, investigated and made recommendations on policy, procedures and the purchase of new equipment.

The new administrative organization required clerical assistance on a permanent basis rather than student assistant help. The committee recommended hiring a half-time clerical assistant to handle duties previously handled by the student assistant, such as logging in and invoice preparation plus new responsibilities including all record keeping, equipment and supply maintenance, vendor contacts, and special projects. The clerical assistant also served as secretary of the Online Steering Committee. In the past, the Program Head had completed some of the necessary record keeping, but now the clerical assistant handled day-to-day operations including keeping a running account of current budget figures.

The program changes meant a revision of several policies and the documents supporting these policies. Searches were limited to students, staff and faculty. Community patrons were referred to other search services in the area. For eligible patrons, searches were offered on a "search on demand" basis. Reference staff no longer had to weed patrons as to suitability of the search topic or require patrons to do some preliminary research in the indexes first. These tasks were handled during the search interview appointment. A records policy was created. In the past all full and ready reference searches were kept on the theory that the older searches might help on the creation of a new search. Now records are kept for a year: the current semester plus the previous semester.

Reference Desk. Patrons asking at the reference desk for a search, or referred to the search service, were given a packet containing an appointment form, a description of what a search is and what is received, a detailed breakdown of the charging policy, and the search request form. Questions about the process were answered by reference librarians. Patrons were requested to make an appointment during scheduled online lab hours (one hour in the morning and one hour in the afternoon) and the appointments were entered into the online calendar (a three-ring notebook at the reference desk). Completed search request forms turned in to the reference desk were placed in a basket to be taken to the lab. Patrons unable to make scheduled appointment times were referred to the reference department head or scheduled at other times at the discretion of the reference librarian/searcher who takes the search. Ready reference searches were performed at the reference desk at the discretion of the librarian from a reference question. These patrons could be referred to a full search if appropriate. Some problems were experienced with reference staff who continued to grill patrons as to the advisability of the search, or refused to set up appointments, and with non-reference staff unfamiliar with searching, but working occasional hours at the reference desk.

Handling of Searches. Searches were completed during half hour appointments in the lab. The searcher would discuss strategy with the patron and proceed to run the search. A ready reference search could be run or the patron could be referred to printed sources if these were more suitable to the search topic. The lab was staffed with two reference librarians, one experienced and one less-experienced searcher. As part of their reference assignment, librarians were scheduled in the online lab for 18 staff hours per week (1-4 hours per person), with experienced searchers putting in more hours than the less-experienced ones. The two librarians worked as a team at first to prepare searches. The less-experienced searcher could observe, learn from the experienced searcher, and pick up tips. Then the non-experienced searcher tried simple ERIC searches under the guidance and assistance of the experienced searcher. Someone was always available to help with equipment and searching problems. Every searcher was to search every subject. Where possible, searchers were notified of difficult topics ahead of time. Patrons were requested to be present for the search. No-shows were asked to reschedule. At patron request, the search could be run in his/her absence. When no appointments were scheduled, the time was to be used for training and practicing on free databases to increase expertise.

Emergencies. The most important emergencies that arise when using an appointment approach are staff absences. Absences known in advance were handled by crossing off appointment blocks. For example, our scheduled department meetings were on Tuesday afternoons. Since non-reference librarians were used to staff the reference desk during these times, this period of online appointments was permanently crossed off the calendar. In the case of illnesses, blocks were crossed off or replacements found where necessary. When these options were unavailable, such as large segments of the staff down with the flu, patrons were called and asked to reschedule the appointments. Patrons unhappy with search results were handled in one of two ways. If possible, the searcher who ran the search was notified to discuss and possibly rerun the search. Otherwise an experienced searcher would soothe the patron and rerun the search at no cost to the patron. Errors were charged to training.

RESULTS

Searching Activity. The changes made to the online searching program at San Jose State University Library resulted in increased searching activity, increased searcher expertise and more patron satisfaction. As seen in Table I (see page 5), the online searching program experienced a 15% growth change between 1982-83 and 1983-84 and a 33% growth change in 1984-85. We handled more searches with less staff. The reduction in the number of training searches in 1984-85 reflects a moritorium placed on these funds because allocated searching funds had been spent during the fall 1984 semester. More funds were requested for regular and ready reference searching for spring 1985, but training and live demonstrations to classes were discontinued to conserve funds. The large number of ready reference searches shown for July-Dec. 1984 (283) reflected satisfaction with the new Texas Instruments Silent 700 series terminal purchased for use at the reference desk, replacing a terminal that was more difficult to use. Searchers responded to the new terminal so well that the ready reference search policy had to be rewritten with more restrictions as to databases used.

Lab Appointments. Between the two semesters, the lab appointment times were discussed. To further discussion of use of the different time blocks, a short study was run on lab hour usage. The average number of searches run per time slot varied from 1.8 to 2.3, with Wednesday and Friday morning labs receiving the smallest number of searches, and Monday and Thursday morning labs receiving the most search appointments. No significant differences were shown, at least not enough to discontinue a particular lab time or significantly increase another lab appointment time. Lab appointments were retained for the spring 1985 semester and lengthened to allow more searcher preparation at the request of searchers. Lab hours were expanded by a half hour to allow searchers more time to prepare in advance of a search, and three temporary librarians were added to the online lab schedule. Online lab hours were increased to 37 staff hours per week, with 1.5 to 3 hours per person.

Searcher Expertise. From statistics collected, we measured searcher expertise in terms of the average cost of a search and the number of databases used. We expected the average cost to drop slowly. The average cost of a search dropped from $17.96 in 1982-83 to $16.50 in 1983-84 and $13.98 in 1984-85. At the same time the average number of databases used rose from 3.1 in 1982-83 to 3.4 in 1983-84 and dropped to 2.5 in 1984-85. Searchers showed more willingness to experiment in different and/or unfamiliar databases in 1983-84 and showed more confidence in choosing databases to search in 1984-85. Searchers were able to handle a variety of subject areas and reflected a more participative attitude. In the lab, searchers were supportive of each other, asked more questions than in group sessions, and demonstrated willingness to learn more about searching in general and searching of specific databases. Several training sessions were held during the spring 1985 semester, including sessions on advanced searching tips, Dialog2 and Wilsonline. Several more are planned on searching specific subject areas such as engineering, business, etc.

The most frequently used databases were tabulated. These are shown in Table II (see page 5). The 1983-84 list reflects the changing expertise of our searchers. Several searchers who left in 1983-84 had extensive science backgrounds and the engineering librarian was on maternity leave. The most experienced searchers had backgrounds in business and the social sciences, which are clearly reflected in these results. The 1984-85 list of databases more accurately shows databases searched in all subject areas during lab hours. The heavy use of Medline, ABI/Inform, and the engineering databases indicates patron demand in these areas. No advertisement or promotion of the service has been attempted so databases reflect areas where faculty recommend student searches, word of mouth referrals, and librarian referrals from the reference desk.

Patron Responses. Patron responses to the online lab hours can be seen in several ways. Out of 403 regular searches scheduled in 1984-85 only 23 (or 6%) were no-shows that did not reschedule for another time. The search evaluation form was changed to measure more accurately patron satisfaction. We were concerned with whether results of searches were on target and whether results were achieved on time. This would indicate a quicker response time with more hits. During 1983-84, 21% of the evaluation forms were returned and 13% during 1984-85. No comparison of the data between years could be made because of alterations made in the evaluation form.

Evaluation forms for 1984-85 were examined for comments from patrons about the search service to identify recommended changes from the users' point of view. Patrons made the following comments and/or suggestions:
(1) Recommended the service be promoted more extensively.
(2) Found the appointment system very helpful.
(3) Found librarians very friendly and very helpful.
(4) Gained a better idea of what material was being found.
(5) Gained insights into the research process; from the need to narrow the topic and know precisely what was wanted to why articles located manually don't always turn up during a computer search.

CONCLUSIONS

An online reference service clearly can be included as part of the Reference Department, using the administrative structure of the reference department, with the addition of sufficient clerical support and a policy-making committee. It is clear that academic libraries, libraries faced with budget reversals, and libraries planning to add online search services should consider this arrangement. This is one method for maximizing the resources at hand while planning for development and growth. It allows for more controlled growth and searcher training. We have been able to help each other progress, satisfy users, and plan for careful growth at the same time. We anticipate that as we advertise the service to campus departments, the service will grow. We must seek more resources or plan to contain growth in the future. The appointment system encourages all searchers to retain their skills while usage of the service can be constricted as necessary.

TABLE I

TOTAL SEARCHING ACTIVITY BY TYPE ON DIALOG AND BRS

Type of Search	Fiscal Year 1982-1983 Total	Fiscal Year 1983-1984 Total	Fiscal Year 1984-1985 J-D	J-J	Total
Regular Search	197	333	215	188	403
Ready Reference Search	153	199	283	190	473
Training Search	87	99	53	14	67
Total	537	631	551	392	943
Percent Growth	---	+15%			+33%

TABLE II

MOST FREQUENTLY USED DATABASES

1982-1983		1983-1984		1984-1985	
Database	Connect Hours	Database	Connect Hours	Database	Connect Hours
ERIC	38.86	ERIC	38.86	ERIC	35.26
Psych-info	16.39	Psych-info	17.86	Medline	16.88
Medline	8.38	Biosis	6.25	Psych-info	13.22
Biosis	8.13	ABI/Inform	6.20	ABI/Inform	9.01
Inspec	3.06	CA Search	2.15	Inspec	6.87
Compendex	2.31	Magazine Index	1.35	Compendex	5.68
Sociological Abstracts	1.89	Management Contents	1.35	America, History and Life	3.57

REFERENCES

1. Connie Lamb, "Searching in Academia. Nearly 50 Libraries Tell What They're Doing," Online 5: 80 (April 1981).

2. Russ Chenoweth, "The Integration of Online Searching in Reference Service," The Reference Librarian 5/6: 120 (Fall/Winter 1982).

3. Ibid., p. 121, 123-124.

4. Ibid., p. 120.

5. Ibid., p. 126.

6. Pauline Atherton, "On-Line Bibliographic Services in Academic Libraries: Some Observations," in Online Bibliographic Services. Where We Are Where We're Going, ed. Peter G. Watson (Chicago, Illinois: American Library Association, 1977), p. 26.

7. Ryan E. Hoover, "Computer Aided Reference Services in the Academic Library," Online 3: 36 (October 1979).

8. Ibid., p. 34.

9. Simone Klugman, "Online Information Retrieval Interface with Traditional Reference Services," Online Review 4: 266 (September 1980).

10. Sara D. Knapp, "The Reference Interview in the Computer-Based Setting," RQ 17: 320-324 (Summer 1978).

11. Ryan E. Hoover, "Computer Aided Reference Services in the Academic Library," Online 3: 33-34 (October 1979).

12. Cerise Oberman, "Management of Online Computer Services in the Academic Reference Department," The Reference Librarian 5/6: 140-141 (Fall/Winter 1982).

13. David Rouse, "Is This Search Necessary," in Proceedings, Online '84 Conference, October 29-31, 1984 (Weston, Connecticut: Online Inc., 1984), p. 210.

14. Glenn R. Lowry, "Improving the Initial Performance of Novice Online Search Intermediaries," Vol. 19 of Proceedings of the ASIS Annual Meeting, (White Plains, New York: Knowledge Industry Pub., 1982), p. 174.

15. James M. Kusack, "Integration of On-Line Reference Service," RQ 19: 64-65 (Fall 1979).

16. Ibid., p. 65.

17. David Rouse, "Is This Search Necessary," in Proceedings, Online '84 Conference, October 29-31, 1984 (Weston, Connecticut: Online Inc., 1984), p. 210-211.

18. Russ Chenoweth, "The Integration of Online Searching in Reference Service," The Reference Librarian 5/6: 125 (Fall/Winter 1982).

19. Janis Jordan Larson, "A System for Management of an Online Search Service," in Proceedings, National Online Meeting, April 10-12, 1984, (New York: National Online Meeting, 1984), p. 171.

EARS--THE PHOTOCOPY SOLUTION

Marilyn Borgendale
University of Maryland Health Sciences Library
Baltimore, Maryland

Abstract. At the Health Sciences Library, EARS (Electronic Access to Reference Service) was developed in order to serve library patrons at remote sites. EARS is based on the library's electronic mail system with links to the online public catalog. It is menu-driven allowing users to request a computerized literature search; reference information; or a photocopy of a journal article.

The paper discusses the impact the EARS photocopy service has had on the library staff and services. The existing staff has been able to undertake the added tasks of EARS. Response to the system has been positive from both patrons and library staff.

Keywords and Phrases. Electronic access to reference service; Photocopy service; Document delivery; Staff allocation; Off-site access; Automation of library processes.

In October 1962 the first photocopy machine was installed at the Health Sciences Library of the University of Maryland. One staff member was assigned exclusive responsibility for all phases of its operation. All orders for copying had to be approved by the director or associate director. The official policy to the library staff also stated:
"The Xerox is purposely in a non-public area of the library and is not available for general 'sightseeing' by the public. Please do not indicate its location more than 'in a locked area, or non-public area.' Beyond that, send insistent patrons to the librarian's office."

A lot has changed in the past 23 years. Nearly two million copies are made each year on the library's twelve photocopiers. Now the library is grappling with the challenges of new computer and communications technology which are enabling libraries to provide new levels of service. Although we are not there yet, eventually new technology will take information transfer beyond photocopiers.

Libraries need to explore means to provide library services, including photocopies, to patrons at remote sites with the existing staff and resources. People's information needs can and should be satisfied at their workstations, in accordance with the concept of a library without walls.

The Health Sciences Library is creating an electronic library to meet this challenge. The Integrated Library System (ILS) was implemented in 1981, and currently the library is utilizing the Circulation Control, Cataloging, Serials Check-In, and Online Public Catalog modules of the ILS. The word processing, accounting, and electronic mail functions have been implemented on the same minicomputer system.

Within this environment, the Electronic Access to Reference Service (EARS) system was developed. Information requests are transmitted between off-site users and the library through a program based on the electronic mail module. EARS can be accessed by patrons from their office or home with either a terminal or a microcomputer with the same mechanisms they have been using to access the online catalog. Funding support has been provided by a Medical Library Resource Project Grant from the National Library of Medicine.

This paper discusses the impact of EARS-- specifically the photocopy service component-- on the library staff and services.

SERVICE AND DESIGN

EARS can be accessed from remote sites 24 hours a day. Once connected to the Library's Information Network, users are presented with a menu which offers the following choices:
1. To search the online catalog
2. To request reference service (EARS)
3. To read mail
4. To log off
5. Library News

When EARS is selected, the menu with the services is presented. The services include:
1. Computerized literature search
2. Photocopy of a journal article (which becomes an interlibrary loan request if the library does not own the journal, and the patron has chosen that option)
3. Reference query
4. Order a book not owned by HSL (which may be a recommendation for purchase, an interlibrary loan request, or both)
5. Return to main menu

EARS was envisioned as a tool to enable library users to access services easily and conveniently, while ensuring that the library staff is provided with all the information they need to fill the requests. Users worked with library staff to design the screens and menus to make them as "friendly" as possible.

When one of the EARS services is selected, users are prompted to supply all necessary information. Each prompt requires a response, but any response to a question is acceptable to the computer. For photocopies, the copyright notice is displayed and must be acknowledged once during each EARS session, regardless of the number of photocopy requests actually made. Services which require fund and budget numbers are indicated on the menu. The charge for EARS photocopy service is 10 cents per page plus 50 cents service charge per article. Self-service photocopying costs 5 cents per page with a debit card. No additional service charges have been added for computer searches or interlibrary loans requested through EARS.

Patrons are notified of the status of their requests by telephone, or may register to be contacted via electronic mail. Completed EARS requests are sent through campus mail or may be picked up at the Reference Desk.

USER RESPONSE

EARS has been favorably received by library patrons--enthusiastically by some. It has enhanced the image of the library on campus.

Data from the system logs shows the proportional use of the available services:
  Book Request   2.5%
  Literature Search 2.6
  Photocopy   91.1
  Reference Query   3.8
The log also indicates that the average input time per request is less than a minute and a half.

The photocopy option is overwhelmingly the most requested because it is a service which has not previously been offered via the telephone. The library's experience with EARS has shown that people are more apt to use new technology if it really eliminates work on their part and is not simply an alternative method of obtaining service.

WORKFLOW AND STAFFING

Providing photocopies of journal articles without the patron appearing in person to fill out a request form and to locate the item is a new type of service for the Health Sciences Library. The initial plan for EARS development did not include the photocopy service because of the potential impact it could have on staffing. The library planned a $1 service charge anticipating the need to hire extra staff to perform these additional tasks. However, during the six month pilot project it became clear that the staff time needed for journal retrieval and problem solving is much less than expected. On the average an article can be processed in less than five minutes. The library decided that a $.50 service charge would cover costs.

With EARS, the photocopy requests are automatically routed to the Circulation Department. Circulation staff have the computer print the requests on the system printer; they verify the citations, resolve any problems, and copy the documents. If a journal is not owned by the library, the request is referred on to the ILL-Borrowing operation. In fact, many patrons send photocopy requests through EARS knowing they will be directed to ILL. Nearly 15 percent of the requests received become an interlibrary loan.

The EARS mailbox is checked at least twice each day the library is open. Primary responsibility for the photocopying service has been assigned to the evening staff. Although a minimum number of employees are necessary evenings and weekends to keep the building open and cover one another for meals and breaks, their time is not fully utilized by these activities. When the circulation assistants are not scheduled at the desk, they have time for other duties. Also, during these hours there is no competition for access to the three staff copiers! Almost 90 percent of the copying is done by the evening staff. The library guarantees a 48 hour turnaround time, but has been able to provide copies within 24 hours.

Much of the retrieval of journals is done by the shelvers. They know where the titles are and can find them efficiently. This way they are also performing quality control on their own work for timely and accurate shelving.

The time involved in checking holdings and verifying incorrect and incomplete citations has been much less than expected. Spelling errors, abbreviations, missing authors and titles, and mismatched volumes and years are taken in stride as staff become "detectives" to solve the problem. Some requests require the assistance of the reference librarian, and the staff must occasionally go online to verify citations. Very few requests have been returned to patrons unfilled because the staff could not decipher them.

EFFECT ON LIBRARY OPERATIONS

Filling EARS photocopy requests has given the staff much more empathy for the needs and frustrations of library patrons. As a result, greater efforts are being made to ensure that the library's bibliographic tools are accurate and that the staff is more sophisticated in using them.

EARS also requires the staff to take greater responsibility for better communication and coordination. Processing photocopy requests may involve staff from many areas: circulation, reference, interlibrary loan, or serials. Nevertheless, the library's internal functions are invisible to the patron who has one access point and one pick-up point.

EFFECT ON PHOTOCOPY SERVICE

Once it was realized that the existing staff could take on the added responsibility of retrieving journals, the nonelectronic service was expanded. A patron may complete a paper form, send or deliver it to the library, and the request will receive the same treatment as if sent through EARS. Many patrons prefer this "full-service" option either because they lack the computer hardware necessary to utilize EARS or prefer not to use the computer. Sometimes patrons use it for items they cannot find on the shelf when they are retrieving materials themselves. One patron simply cuts up his

MEDLINE searches and tapes the pieces onto the form.

Use of the library's photocopy service has increased with the implementation of EARS, reversing the trend over the previous few years for use to decrease. During fiscal year 1984/85 the staff completed 3,116 photocopy requests which is a 16 percent increase over the previous year. EARS and the full-service option accounted for 57 percent of the requests and the latter was implemented in the middle of the year. Patrons are willingly paying the service charge for the additional service. Yet, self-service copying remains popular because of its convenience and low cost with a debit card.

Currently the photocopy service is available only to those patrons with valid campus fund and budget numbers. The library is exploring ways to make the service available to others without being overwhelmed by small cash transactions. In the School of Social Work, for instance, requests are being routed through the school's Learning Resources Center librarian who maintains the accounting records.

CONCLUSION

Overall, the impact of the EARS system on the staff has been positive. The circulation staff perceive their role as being part of something special. The enthusiasm for new electronic development has been shared with the staff from the beginning, and they have responded favorably. The added tasks have actually increased the challenge and variety of their jobs.

Library services and job responsibilities are continually changing as technological advances allow, or demand, that libraries provide new levels of service. EARS is only a first step. Soon we may be laughing at our fancy new electronics in the same way we now laugh at the installation of our first Xerox machine.

LIBRARIAN SATISFACTION WITH COMPUTER BIBLIOGRAPHIC SEARCHING

Kevin Carey
University of Illinois at Chicago
Chicago, Illinois

Abstract. Computer searching is a reference service in academic libraries where good communication is essential. Successful computer searches are the result of an active exchange of information that combines subject expertise by the patron and search experience by the searcher. This paper examines the comments from interviews with twelve reference librarian searchers. It identifies their criteria for successful searching as a dynamic process between the searcher and the patron. The value of recognizing this process has implications for training programs and end-user instruction.

Keywords and Phrases. Computer Bibliographic Searching; Computer End-User Training; On-line Searching; Reference Interview Process; Reference Services.

Computer searching is an area whose focus in the library literature has usually been on patron satisfaction with the service. Articles that typify this approach look at the usefulness of search results in terms of recall and precision and how valuable the citations are to the patron. Good examples of such articles are Richard Blood's "Evaluation of Online Searches,"[1] Doris Marshall's "To Improve Searching, Check Search Results,"[2] and Arleen Somerville's "The Pre-Search Reference Interview - A Step by Step Guide."[3]

In this paper I look at librarian satisfaction with the search process. I see the search process as having three parts: a pre-search interview, an online session, and a review of the resulting bibliography. Other articles have often looked at review of the bibliography as the quantifiable measure of successful searching. I am interested in the quality of criteria that are present in successful searches from the searcher's perspective. To do this, I interviewed twelve online searchers in several reference departments of a major urban university library. The searchers work in a general reference department, a science library, and a health science library. They have a range of searching experience from one to nine years and represent subject coverage of medicine, education, the social sciences, engineering, business, and the physical sciences. Although twelve interviews may seem a small number for analysis, the searchers have trained at a large number of academic settings, as well as in special, medical, and public libraries. So, they reflect a large background of experience.

I asked the searchers twelve open-ended questions that allowed them to draw from their experience. (A list of the interview questions appears at the end of this paper.) The questions covered topics in the search process, such as patron preparation, the pre-search interview, searcher preparation, and the online session. The questions were prompted by my own experience and expectations as a searcher. I wanted to analyze comments about the search process as a dynamic interaction between the searcher and a patron. My objective was to answer three questions:

1. What criteria did searchers use to define a successful search?

2. What did they expect from the patrons to search satisfactorily?

3. What recommendations could they make for improving the searcher-patron relationship in the search process?

The point of the study is to show that successful searching requires active participation by both the searcher and the patron throughout the search process. The process is a negotiation of expectations, subject expertise, and search experience. The searcher has to trust in the patron's knowledge of the topic; the patron has to trust in the searcher's ability to find appropriate information online. The human component is critical to the study's premise that successful searching is not measured solely by patron satisfaction with the search process. The study is intended to add to a more well-rounded view of computer searching in the library literature.

Searchers want patrons to be interested in the search process and expect them to provide subject expertise in the preparation of the search strategy. Searchers appreciate patrons who will work with them, but who do not challenge their authority. Individual searchers spoke of their wish to be respected for their expertise in searching as a reference skill. Two searchers mentioned that they dislike intrusive patrons who tell the searchers how to perform the mechanics of a given search. This was a point echoed by the librarians who search without patrons present and prefer it that way. They, however, go through the pre-search interview in considerable detail with their patrons. The image that comes to mind is one of the patron playing Dr. Watson to the searcher's Sherlock Holmes in a common investigation of information.

More than anything else the interviews revealed that successful searching and librarian satisfaction mean matching the patron's expectations with the librarian's expectations. For the librarian, these expectations are: that the patron will know something about the topic, that the patron will be articulate and able to explain the topic in simple statements, that the patron will be flexible with regard to the fee, within a given range, that the patron will not be narrow-minded about the results and will accept some interpretation of the topic, and that the patron will accept the searcher's familiarity with the computer system and advice on an appropriate database, appropriate search strategy, and the amount of retrievable information available.

The searchers feel that the patron's expectations of them are: that the searcher will understand the topic statement and not misinterpret it, that the searcher will know how to use the system and have technical expertise, that the searcher will do the search as efficiently and inexpensively as possible, that the searcher will explain the search results and any reasons for a small bibliography, that the searcher will follow through with suggestions and advice on other appropriate reference sources, such as indexes, bibliographies, and referrals to collections.

A successful search is defined as matching the expectations already mentioned. It is crucial that there be some verbal exchange between the searcher and the patron in the search's preliminary stages so that they agree on the major points. After that communication the patron's presence becomes an option for some searchers. It is important to have the patron around before and after the search for preparation and feedback, but is not always necessary during the search. Some searchers like to have the patron present during the online session so that the patron can see any problems or limitations that may develop. If the patron is not present, the searchers emphasized the importance of discussing the topic in detail in a pre-search interview.

The searchers stressed a commitment to providing a high-quality service to the patrons. A search is not simply a mechanical manipulation of data but a creative process involving expertise and innovative thinking. In one case, a searcher is involved in information retrieval for patient care by the medical staff. The program, called LATCH for Literature Attached to Chart, requires the searcher to conduct searches in a very short time period and to be responsible for document delivery. The searcher takes the work very seriously and checks with the medical staff after each search to evaluate the information, its usefulness, and relevancy. This process clearly takes the searcher-patron contact beyond the traditional reference setting and shows the critical importance of having a common understanding of teamwork in the search process.

The librarians voiced a strong interest in knowing that their searches provide information that is useful and used by the patron. Post-search feedback is not common and is a source of frustration for the searchers. They appreciate both negative and positive comments: if negative, the searchers could redo the search and correct the problems in its strategy; if positive, the comments would bring confidence and a reinforcement of their ability.

It was considered important to deal directly with the patron, not a second party such as a friend or secretary. Other people do not know in sufficient detail what the patron wants. Dealing with people besides the patron wastes the searcher's time and may mean duplication of effort.

Individual searchers had different approaches to the amount of information that they would give the patrons during the pre-search interview and while online. The searchers would usually explain the mechanics of searching and give information on vendor programs for individual use if the patron was interested, but this varied by librarian. Some searchers never explain technical information unless there is a problem with the system or the search strategy. The searchers at the medical center who usually work without the patron present have a formal end-user training program to handle interest by the medical staff. Librarians who regularly search with the patron present will explain the online process if its helps in the formation of the search strategy. These searchers almost always go over the thesauri and rotated-term indexes with the patron in a team effort; they explain the technical details as needed in each search.

I asked the searchers to describe their ideal search environment and to describe a particularly good search and a particularly bad search based on their experience. They could comment on any aspect of the search process for the first question. They could draw from any search or a combination of searches in their experience for the second question.

For the ideal environment, the searchers mentioned the type of room (that it be well-lit, private, quiet), type of equipment (that there be a highspeed printer of good quality), time allowed for the search (one hour or longer with gaps between searches to accommodate lengthy online sessions), cost (partial or complete subsidy by the library for all searches), and type of patron. Searchers like patrons to be open-minded about the limits of searching, to be attentive during the online session, and willing to work within a given price range.

In the actual search environment searchers distinguish between undergraduates and graduate students but not between lower and upper division undergraduate students. Generally, graduate students are thought to have more realistic expectations of how the search can help them. They are more sophisticated library users who know how to integrate search information with other research techniques. They are genuinely interested in their topics, often doing research for a thesis or dissertation. They understand what vocabulary terms the searcher needs to do the search and come prepared to explain their topics, subject terms, and the names of authorities writing in that area. They have usually gone through the appropriate printed indexes prior to the search. After the search they request occasional follow-up searches that build on some aspect of the original search.

The searchers cited patron contact as a major reason for good and bad searches. For the most part, librarians did not mention bad results but disappointment by the patron as the source of a bad search. There were occasional glitches with the computer system, but mishaps usually occurred when there was a misunderstanding by patrons about cost, the anticipated size of the bibliography, and the availability of the material. Some patrons thought that the search would provide the full text of articles or that it was possible to search several databases simultaneously. Sometimes patrons did not understand the end product. Searchers pointed out the lack of understanding by patrons about the searcher's information needs; topics were either too broad, too narrow, or too vague. Some patrons were unhappy with a low recall and blamed the searcher if there was not much information on their topic in the computer system. Bad searches often happened when there were unrealistic expectations by the patrons that could not be matched by the system. Other contributing factors were patrons who did not understand the dynamics of the search as an interactive process, did not get involved in the online session, or did not show any interest in the results.

Good searches were when the searcher was able to bring something extra to the search and surpassed the patron's expectations. There was good human interaction and the searcher felt challenged by the topic and its access points in the system. Searchers enjoyed trying new databases and creating search strategies that were not routine concept combinations. In a good search, the patron showed enthusiasm and knowledge of the topic, participated actively in the online session, and reported on the usefulness and quality of the bibliography after the search. The searcher was able to bring more to the search than the patron had anticipated or thought possible, and the patron appreciated the extra effort.

The point of this paper has been to demonstrate that computer searching is an interactive human process as well as a system process. The comments that the searchers made during the interviews can be transformed into recommendations for improving the searcher-patron relationship. Searchers want patrons to participate in the search process and to work with the searcher as a team. Good searching means linking the patron's expectations with the searcher's experience. The satisfaction of both depends on a common understanding of the elements that have been mentioned. Understanding and building on the human value of the search process is critical to providing a computer search service as valuable to the patron as any other area of reference work. It makes sense that a good search that meets a searcher's criteria for excellence will also meet a patron's criteria since they are worked out during the course of the search. The satisfaction of the searcher and the patron are interdependent. A responsible librarian will not feel good about a search if the patron does not; likewise, a searcher will feel pleased when the search yields more than the patron expected. The psychological benefits affect both people. The searcher is able to recognize how the quality of the search helped the patron in a way not possible through the printed sources. This advantage is one of the justifications for offering a computer search service in a reference setting.

It would be useful in future studies to ask both searchers and patrons parallel questions about the quality of a given search. This study shows the validity of considering the search process, not just the search results, when evaluating a computer search service. It also highlights the need to consider searcher satisfaction, as well as patron satisfaction, with that process.

Sample Interview with Online Searchers

Searcher's Name:

Number of Years of Search Experience:

Range of Databases Used:

Subject Areas Usually Searched:

Questions:

1. How important is previous research by the patron on the topic to be searched?

2. Does the patron talk about the extent of his/her familiarity with the topic to be searched? How much and in what detail?

3. Do you ever look at written drafts of a patron's proposal or report before searching? If so, do they help?

4. How important is the pre-search interview with the patron? Why? Is it more important to do with the person than over the telephone? Why? What information do you cover in the pre-search interview?

5. Do you prefer searching with or without the patron? Why? Which do you usually do in your searches?

6. What constitutes a good search in your experience? What are the components of a good search? What information do you need from the patron to perform a search properly?

7. When do you discuss money in the search process?

8. Can you describe the search process once you are online, i.e. - what steps you do, what steps the patron does, etc.?

9. What amount of preparation do you do before a search? Is this for database review, topic strategy, or both?

10. Do you notice any difference in the contact that you have with undergraduates and graduate students? With lower-division and upper-division students? Can you describe the difference?

11. What would be your ideal search environment? What components would it have?

12. Can you think of a particularly good search and a particularly bad search that you have done in your experience as a searcher? What factors determined both? For the bad search, how could it have been better? For the good search, what made it better than the average search? Please be specific and consider all possible factors.

Ask if the searcher has any general comments at the end of the interview. Allow time for observations after each open-ended question and after all questions have been asked.

ACKNOWLEDGEMENTS

Special thanks to Patricia Tegler, Systems Librarian, Kirkland & Ellis Library, for her help in shaping the paper for its final form.

REFERENCES

1. Richard W. Blood, "Evaluation of Online Searches," RQ 22, no. 3 (Spring 1983): 266-277.

2. Doris B. Marshall, "To Improve Searching, Check Search Results," Online 4, no. 3 (July 1980): 32-47.

3. Arleen N. Somerville, "The Pre-Search Reference Interview - A Step by Step Guide," Database 5, no. 1 (February 1982): 32-38.

PSYCHOLOGICAL NEEDS AND SOURCE LINKAGES IN
UNDERGRADUATE INFORMATION-SEEKING BEHAVIOR

Kathleen Dunn
Loma Linda University
Riverside, CA

Abstract. Psychological motivations for information search is an important area of research that has received relatively little attention. This study addresses those motivations in an academic environment. Psychological needs motivating undergraduates to seek information in the context of continuing motivation are identified. In addition, the study identifies categories of sources used to satisfy their need for information, and empirically establishes significant relationships between the motivating needs and categories of sources used.

Keywords and Phrases. Information-seeking behavior; needs; psychological motivation; continuing motivation; sources; undergraduates; need-source linkages.

INTRODUCTION

Information-seeking is a behavior, a human activity like writing a memo, driving a car, or talking on the phone. Since it is a behavior, it is logical to propose that it stems from sources common to all behavior. Psychologists have tried for quite some time to determine why people do what they do. Librarians, though intimately involved in information-seeking on a professional as well as a personal level, have paid relatively little attention to the psychological sources of this behavior. A look at user studies clearly shows that the focus has been primarily on the demands people make on information systems, secondarily on users and their characteristics, and rarely on the psychological aspects of use. However, as librarianship builds an increasingly strong interdisciplinary base that encompasses theory as well as practice, it is appropriate to explore the contribution that psychological theories can make to our understanding of the sources of information-seeking behavior.

In 1981 T.D. Wilson, a British colleague, published an article in the *Journal of Documentation* that challenged me to take a closer look at the the psychological motivations for information search. In this article he suggests that we shift our emphasis from sources and systems to the user, and that we include in this examination a careful look at the motivational and psychological needs underlying the search for information. Wilson notes that studies dealing with information-seeking behavior often fail to address the core issues. He says, "Such studies may never address the central question of 'information need,' that is, why the user decides to seek information, what purpose he believes it will serve and to what use it is actually put when received." To make the point even stronger, Wilson suggests that "it may be advisable to remove the term 'information need' from our professional vocabulary and to speak instead of information-seeking towards the satisfaction of needs." I decided to follow Wilson's advice and study the needs that information-seeking might satisfy.

THE STUDY

Since I am an academic librarian, I chose to investigate the needs that influence undergraduates to seek information. In addition, I wanted to discover the types of sources they used; and, since students have a wide range of sources to choose from, whether the needs influencing the search also influenced the sources selected. The study is set within the context of "continuing motivation," a term proposed by Maehr to describe the tendency of students to return to and continue working on tasks or ideas away from the instructional setting in which they were initially encountered. The distinguishing feature of continuing motivation is a return to an interest first encountered in class when there is no requirement or external pressure to do so. A basic assumption underlying the study is that undergraduate information-seeking behavior in the context of continuing motivation is an attempt at need satisfaction.

Given the fact that information-seeking as need satisfaction is basically a new area of study within the profession, my work had to be viewed as exploratory. Therefore, the study provides answers to a set of questions rather than support or rejection of hypotheses. To be precise, I investigated the following research questions: 1) what are the psychological needs that motivate undergraduates to seek course-related information outside of class requirements and discussions? 2) what information sources do undergraduates use to satisfy their information requirements? 3) what significant relationships, if any, can be identified between initiating needs and the sources used to satisfy information requirements?

METHODOLOGY

I collected the data according to a method frequently used by psychologists in which one explores the parameters of the problem through a series of interviews and then constructs a questionnaire based on the interviews. Each step in the process builds on the knowledge gained from the previous step.

First, I talked to students in their dorms, on the lawns, in the cafeteria, anywhere I could find them (except the library, so as not to prejudice their response to my probing on sources). The critical incident technique helped them to focus on a particular class and on the particular information they sought. Through discussion, I attempted to discover why they had persisted in seeking this information. This was the first series of interviews, and from them I developed a group of questions to ask a different set of students.

The second interviews were structured in the sense that I now had a list of questions to ask. I probed for needs more overtly, and I asked the questions of a randomly selected sample of students. However, these interviews were still considered exploratory and flexibility was allowed to ask further questions or to change the order of questions in order to elicit more information.

Third, based on the results of the interviews, I developed a six-page questionnaire. The pretested questionnaire was administered to a stratified, random sample of 625 undergraduates on the La Sierra Campus of Loma Linda University. (Study results are actually based on 566 responses because 59 or 9% of the 625 questionnaires collected proved unusable.)

The questionnaire was constructed around three components: 1) 61 operational needs (derived from the interviews) and their intensity, 2) 16 used sources (derived from the interviews) and their importance, 3) demographic data. In the first questions I again used the critical incident technique to focus the respondent's attention on a particular class in which he or she went beyond class requirements in seeking information. Questions dealing with needs and sources were formulated in terms of a Likert-type scale in which the subjects were asked to rate themselves along a continuum of intensity. This provided enough variability in the data to determine the hidden or submerged factors and offered a better estimate of the actual correlation between the items.

I used factor analysis and canonical correlation analysis to analyze the data. Factor analysis is a powerful statistical tool for reducing large amounts of data to manageable and understandable proportions. Canonical correlation analysis maximizes the relationship between two sets of variables and was used to analyze relationships between the previously identified need and source factors.

RESULTS AND DISCUSSION

The first research question concerned discovery of the psychological needs motivating undergraduates to seek course-related information beyond all class requirements. Responses to the 61 need variables were entered into a principle components factor analysis with varimax rotation. Six need factors emerged (table 1): Need for Other-Approval, Need for Success in Chosen Profession, Need for Self-Extension, Need for Self-Approval, Need for Intellectual Stimulation, and Needs Related to a Successful College Experience. As shown in Table 1, factors are typically named according to the variables that load highest on them, in this case, the need variables.

Examination of these need factors shows that they are at one level quite specific to the educational environment; that is, they arise from the people, situations, and expectations that are part of an undergraduate educational setting. Within the limits of the study, it can be said that undergraduates decide to pursue an interest in a problem encountered in class because they seek approval, knowledge, success, and mental and spiritual challenge. These needs are stimulated by the expectation and cultural milieu of the college/university setting and are generally satisfied by the people, situations, and opportunities inherent within it. On another level, the need factors are examples of the more general and basic needs proposed by Abraham Maslow and refined by C.P. Alderfer. Alderfer's E.R.G. theory proposes three basic categories of needs —existence, relatedness, and growth. His theory states that these needs are innate and that they energize and sustain behavior through cycles of desire, satisfaction, and frustration. Existence needs include all material and physiological desires. Relatedness needs center around relationships. Growth needs impel people toward challenge, creativity, and the full expression of their potential.

Existence needs, evident in Need Factor 2 and Need Factor 6, emerge as strong needs to know enough to compete in the job market and to be successful in a profession. These are the expected outcomes of a college experience and they help ensure for the individual an adequate supply of material resource which will satisfy their need for a physically secure environment. Relatedness needs, that is needs for approval, acceptance, belonging, and love are most evident in Need Factors 1 and 3. Growth needs, those concerned with competence, mastery, self-transcendence, and self-actualization, are evident in Need Factors 2, 3, 4, and 5. Relatedness and growth needs predominate in the undergraduates surveyed. This is consistent with Maslow's and Alderfer's view that existence needs are generally satisfied in our culture and that people tend to experience greater needs for love, belongingness, approval, and personal growth.

The second question asked for the sources

Table 1

SUMMARY OF SIX NEED FACTORS

Factor	Variables	Factor Loadings
1 Need for Other-Approval	Need to have classmates think I'm smart Need to have teacher think I'm smart Need to compete with classmates for teacher's approval Need to do more than is required for the class so that I can feel equal to my classmates Need to have friends think I'm smart Need to have teacher notice me Need to prove myself to my husband/wife or boyfriend/girlfriend	.83 .78 .75 .74 .72 .72 .70
2 Need for success in Chosen Profession	Need to be well prepared for chosen profession Need to be successful in chosen profession Need to have broader understanding of the subjects that relate to my chosen profession Desire for more information about my major Need to meet requirements for employment in my chosen profession Need to know wide variety of things so I can feel secure in terms of job market Desire to compete better in job market	.83 .82 .82 .70 .69 .68 .68
3 Need for Self-Extension	Need to learn more about God Need to know more so that when I have children I can do a better job of raising them Desire to have broader outlook toward life and people Need to know more in order to help others Need to become a whole person in terms of the mental, physical, and spiritual Need to understand different people and their environments	.65 .61 .61 .60 .59 .58
4 Need for Self-Approval	Desire to know and understand in order to feel better about myself Need to avoid feeling frustrated by lack of knowledge Need to live up to my expectations of myself Need to feel intelligent A feeling of insecurity when I think I should know something but I don't	.61 .55 .53 .51 .50
5 Need for Intellectual Stimulation	Enjoyment of learning for its own sake Personal interest in subject of class Inner drive to learn more about the subjects that make me curious Need for the excitement and fun of finding answers Personal satisfaction	.71 .62 .61 .58 .51

Table 1 (continued)

SUMMARY OF SIX NEED FACTORS

Factor	Variables	Factor Loadings
6 Needs Related to a Successful College Experience	Need to get my money's worth out of college	.60
	Need to get good grades	.49
	Need to feel that my parent's money is well spent on my college education	.49
	Need to get everything I can out of my college education	.48
	Need to know in order to do better in upcoming classes	.48
	Need to understand basic content of course	.47

undergraduates use to satisfy their desire for information. Responses to the 16 source variables were intercorrelated and the resulting matrix factored by principal-components analysis and submitted to varimax rotation. Five source factors emerged (see table 2): Family, Friends, Libraries, Expert, and Personal Materials.

Many studies make a distinction between formal and informal sources of information and have noted the frequency with which informal, interpersonal sources are used. For the purposes of this study, formal information channels include all printed materials, audio-visual materials, and even formally organized information sessions at conferences and workshops. Informal sources of information are available on an interpersonal basis, center around people, and include conversations, correspondence, etc. Study results suggest that undergraduates make considerable use of

Table 2

SUMMARY OF FIVE SOURCE FACTORS

Factor		Variables	Factor Loadings
1	Family	Friend's library	.53
		Husband/wife	.51
		Boyfriend/girlfriend	.50
		Brother/sister	.49
		Personal library	.40
2	Friends	Friend	.73
		Classmate	.69
		Casual acquaintance	.40
		Boyfriend/girlfriend	.32
3	Libraries	Public library	.57
		Departmental library	.53
		College/University library	.48
		Special purpose library	.43
		Teacher's library	.38
4	Expert	Teacher	.74
		Expert in field	.43
5	Personal Materials	Bookstore	.64
		Personal library	.29

informal, interpersonal sources. Three of the five source factors are composed primarily of informal sources --Source Factors 1, 2, and 4. This is consistent with studies of other groups. However, in an analysis of the 16 sources for their importance in providing information, the library ranked second and personal library ranked fourth (see Table 3). Teacher ranked first. This pattern follows that found in Hardy's study. Authoritative, formal sources are often chosen first, followed by authoritative, informal sources.

Table 3

IMPORTANCE OF INFORMATION SOURCES: MEANS AND RANK ORDER

Source	Mean	Rank
Teachers	1.92	1
College/university libraries	2.18	2
Expert in field	2.35	3
Personal library	2.64	4
Friend	2.78	5
Classmate	3.00	6
Public library	3.13	7
Bookstore	3.15	8
Departmental library	3.23	9
Casual acquaintance	3.41	10
Brother/sister	3.48	11
Special purpose library	3.52	12
Teacher's library	3.56	13
Boyfriend/girlfriend	3.57	14
Friend's library	3.67	15
Husband/wife	3.80	16

Note: The scale runs from 1 to 4. Small numbers indicate greater importance

The third research question was resolved by submitting the six need factors and five source factors to canonical correlation analysis in order to determine what relationships, if any, existed between them. Three significant canonical variates emerged from this analysis (see table 4) which show that there are indeed statistically significant relationships between certain need and source factors. The first canonical variate indicates that individuals with needs for other-approval and self-extension tend to use friends and family as information sources. The thrust of these relationships seems to be that certain needs require people as their primary source of satisfaction and that information-seeking, as well as other activities, can be used as a means to this end. The second canonical variate shows that those with needs for intellectual stimulation and professional success tend to use libraries and experts as information sources. The implication in this need-source relationship suggests that needs based on the acquisition of knowledge and use of intellectual skills predispose undergraduates to the use of libraries and experts --sources that offer the best resources for the satisfaction of these needs. The third canonical variate, though significant, accounts for a smaller share of the relationship in the data than the first two canonical variates and therefore is more difficult to interpret. Basically, this variate suggests that subjects with strong other-centered needs use family as sources of information more frequently than libraries or friends; and that subjects with a strong need to be successful in college tend to seek friends and libraries as information sources rather than family.

CONCLUSIONS

A few others have looked at the psychological factors in information search. However, this is the first study of which I am aware that identifies a group of needs motivating information search in a particular class of people. It is also the only study I know of that finds statistically significant relationships connecting these needs to types of sources. I have shown that sources may not be chosen on a rational basis, but on an emotional basis, a result of motivational factors.

As a result of this study, we now have empirical evidence to assist us in better understanding the motivational factors behind a student's search for information in an academic environment. The needs identified help us to understand the psychological context in which students pursue their studies, and their current as well as future desires. In addition, we now understand that some of these needs influence a student's choice of sources. In view of this, it is not surprising that many

Table 4

SUMMARY OF CANONICAL VARIATES

Canonical Variate	Factors	Canonical Loadings

1
Canonical Correlation .482
Chi-Square 195.278
Significance .000
	With need for:
	  Other-approval
	  Self-extension
	
	Use:
	  Friends
	  Family
		
		-.70
		-.51
		
		-.62
		-.40

2
Canonical Correlation .351
Chi-Square 99.170
Significance .000
	With needs for:
	  Intellectual stimulation
	  Professional success
	
	Use:
	  Libraries
	  Expert
	
	Do Not Use:
	  Friends
		
		-.74
		-.58
		
		-.54
		-.43
		
		.59

3
Canonical Correlation .337
Chi-Square 51.419
Significance .000
	With high need for:
	  Self-extension
	Use:
	  Family
	
	Do Not Use:
	  Friends
	  Libraries
	
	With high need for:
	  Successful College
	  experience
	
	Use:
	  Friends
	  Libraries
	
	Do Not Use:
	  Family
		
		.70
		
		.90
		
		-.50
		-.39
		
		-.65
		
		-.50
		-.39
		
		.90

students do not use the library. A variety of sources is available to them. The library is only one of these, and, for reasons that are now clearer, it is often not their first choice.

These need-source relationships suggest to me that we should continue our efforts to make the library user-friendly. Bibliographic instruction, reference service (along with friendly smiles and a supportive attitude), suggestion boxes, etc., really do help establish our friendship with students as well as our competence as professional information providers. But I would like to suggest that if we want more students in the library, we may have to go beyond this.

We do not have the same level of exposure to students as teaching faculty nor do we participate as frequently in student activities outside the library. As a result of their broader exposure to students, teachers often develop lasting friendships with them. (It is interesting to note that in this study, teachers were considered the most important source of information.) Might it not be possible for us to participate more frequently with students in campus activities. Several things come to mind --join student clubs in which you have an interest, sponsor a college bowl, start a student reading group. There is a larger student body out there that doesn't know we exist, and as long as we stay in the library, they never will.

A final word. Much more research needs to be done in this area. The results of this exploratory study should become hypotheses for future research to be conducted in a similar environment or modified for an entirely different context. Only with additional data can we have confidence in our understanding of the psychological motivation behind information search. In addition, until we have more data on need-source linkages, it will be difficult to design systems that take these relationships into account. Finally, it is of interest to note that the personal computer was not mentioned as a source of information by the respondents to this 1982 study. Personal computers have become more important in the last four years as sources of information and should be considered in future studies of need-source linkages.

REFERENCES

1. Thomas D. Wilson, "On User Studies and Information Needs," *Journal of Documentation* 37:3-15 (March 1981).

2. Wilson, "User Studies and Information Needs," p. 7

3. Wilson, "User Studies and Information Needs," p. 8

4. Martin L. Maehr, "Continuing Motivation: An Analysis of a Seldom Considered Education Outcome," *Review of Educational Research* 46:443-462 (Sept. 1976).

5. J.C. Flanagan, "The Critical Incident Technique," *Psychological Bulletin* 51:327-358 (July 1954).

6. Abraham Maslow, *Motivation and Personality* (New York: Harper and Row, 1954).

7. Abraham Maslow, *The Farther Reaches of Human Nature* (New York: Viking Press, 1971).

8. C.P. Alderfer, *Existence, Relatedness, and Growth: Human Needs in Organizational Settings* (New York: Free Press, 1972).

9. Herbert Menzel, *The Flow of Information Among Scientists* (New York: Columbia University, Bureau of Applied Research, 1958).

10. Janet Friedlander, "Clinician Search for Information," *Journal of The American Society for Information Science* 24:65-69 (Jan./Feb. 1973).

11. H.J.C. Matheson, *Information Seeking Behavior and Attitudes to Information Among Education Practitioners* (Doctoral diss., University of British Columbia, 1979)

12. Andrew Hardy, "The Selection of Channels When Seeking Information: Cost/Benefit vs Least-Effort," *Information Processing & Management* 18:289-293 (Sept. 1982).

13. E.B. Parker and W.J. Paisley, *Patterns of Adult Information Seeking* (Stanford, CA: Stanford University, 1966). (ERIC Document No. ED 010 294).

14. Douglas Zweizig, *Predicting Amount of Library Use: An Empirical Study of the Role of the Public Library in the Life of the Adult Public.* (Ph.D. diss., Syracuse University, 1973).

15. Morell D. Boone, *Expectancies and Values as Predictors of Motivation of Pre-Decisional Information Search.* (Ph.d. diss., Syracuse University, 1980).

REFERENCE BEYOND (AND WITHOUT) THE REFERENCE DESK

Barbara J. Ford
Trinity University Library
San Antonio, Texas

Abstract. Is the reference desk still the contact point where most library users can easily find the services, information and assistance they need? The author proposes that the reference desk as the center of reference service in academic libraries is an assumption that should be examined in light of new technologies and changes in the way people find and use information.

Keywords and Phrases.
Reference desk
Reference services
Alternative models

Everywhere we turn librarians are writing and talking about reference services, their illustrious past and uncertain future. At the 1984 ACRL Conference at the Alternative Format presentation, "A House Divided: Public Service Realities in the 1980's," I realized that an assumption of those addressing the challenges and changes facing reference services was that the reference desk is the center of this assistance. Speakers seemed to support Patricia Swanson's viewpoint that "the reference desk represents the critical mass of resources -- human, printed, and now electronic, so configured for a convenient and predictable location so that library patrons can find the service and can find someone to help them."[1] Even those presentations that were the most questioning and "untraditional" assumed that the reference desk is an important component of reference service.

After returning home and surveying the literature, I found that few authors have questioned this assumption. One of those who has, Thelma Freides, brought up this point in 1983 when she stated, "Equally unarticulated and unexamined is the assumption that the hub of this assistance is the reference desk, where a reference librarian, or surrogate, is available to the reader at all times. The arrangement conveys an implicit promise never to let the reader go unserved, but it also pegs the service at a low level."[2] In 1985, in a symposium about reference work in The Journal of Academic Librarianship, Mary Biggs' proposal to cut the number of desk hours in order to provide other services was met with a less than enthusiastic response.[3] The reference desk appears to be a sacred library tradition that many librarians are unwilling or unable to relinquish or question.

Some authors writing about libraries have begun to address the need to question assumptions relating to library programs and services. Nina Matheson says, "We must ask ourselves some very hard questions. What have we been failing at that we had better stop doing or do differently? How long have we been trying to get people to come to the library, to use the library?... Do our solutions really respond to information access problems?"[4] While not talking specifically about the reference desk, Matheson's challenge is certainly applicable to those of us concerned with the future of reference services. Patricia Battin, in discussing the library as the center of the restructured university, notes, "The weight of our historic traditions is such that we tend to find it very difficult to look at the future in terms of a vastly changed organizational structure."[5] Richard De Gennaro suggests, "Libraries need to develop new goals and new strategies based on new technologies... or risk becoming mere symbols of culture and museums of the book."[6]

I propose that the reference desk, as the center and "given" of reference service, is one of the traditions that should be examined. Those of us working in libraries know that libraries have changed dramatically in collection size, in physical space, and in the heterogeneous nature of collections since the time when the reference desk became a common fixture in libraries. Reference desk service may have been more useful in "simpler" days of smaller collections and buildings. "Renaissance" reference librarians serving all comers at a reference desk may no longer be a realistic solution for providing public services for patrons. Has what happens at the reference desk unnecessarily made general users less self-sufficient and more dependent on library staff? The historic tradition of the reference desk seems to make it difficult for reference librarians and those studying and discussing reference to think of library services without the reference desk as a given for providing service and user interface. On the other hand, much that is written seems to indicate that the reference desk does not seem to work as well as we would like, and therefore we must consider alternatives.

William Miller states, "Objective analyses of reference desk service indicate the cost of pretending that we can continue to do everything for everybody, and do it well. This is an organizational fiction which needs to be discarded. Our success is turning into failure, and we must acknowledge this reality in order to cope with it."[7] The time has come when we must define our clientele and then decide whom we can best assist with various services. Freides says, "The reference desk works best for directional questions and requests for specific factual information. It is not well designed for dealing with questions requiring interpretation or exploration.... Studies of user behavior indicate that users indeed perceive the reference service as intended for simple questions and quick replies.... By establishing the desk as the focal point of reader assistance, libraries not only expend professional time on trivial tasks, but also encourage the assumption that the low-level, undemanding type of question handled most easily and naturally at the desk is the service norm."[8]

We must ask whether our clientele really need a reference desk or whether other services would meet their needs in a more effective manner. Without spending so much time and energy providing service from a reference desk, could we devote our efforts more effectively to developing more appropriate and useful services for our primary clientele? Brian Nielsen has provided a perspective on many of our services, including, in my opinion, the reference desk, when he notes that because reference service "has seen little, if any, design change since its origin in the late nineteenth century, librarians tend not to think of the value choices implicit in that design that they have also inherited. They all accept as a basic postulate that reference service is useful to anyone, at least potentially."[9]

My suggestion is that the reference desk in academic libraries is in need of evaluation based on new technologies and changes in the way people find and use information and the role of libraries in this process. Rao Aluri and Jeffery St. Clair have suggested that "experiments could be conducted to see if much of the information supplied at the reference desk could be made accessible through computers and other means."[10] Much has been written about the importance of user education, bibliographic instruction, point of use aids and other means beyond the reference desk to assist users in libraries. Smith and Hutton report on their successful "use of uniquely developed microcomputer programs to provide reference service to patrons at points throughout the library at all hours, but intended to support service at times when reference personnel are not available."[11] This at least is a beginning. While being hesitant to eliminate face-to-face personal interaction between librarians and patrons, I think we need to begin to think what has heretofore been the unthinkable, exploring alternatives and possibly eliminating the reference desk. In accordance with what is being written and discussed at meetings, the present configuration does not satisfy either librarians or library users. We know there is a problem -- by looking for different models we can begin to explore alternatives.

To assist the development of possible alternative or supplementary models to the reference desk, I propose an alternative model that will be delineated here. I am not disputing that service should continue or that people need assistance in using libraries. The question is whether such assistance is any longer most efficiently and effectively provided from a reference desk.

A theoretical model for future reference service might replace the desk and librarian with a computer terminal where users could log requests and receive answers and appropriate printed handouts. Many questions answered at reference desks could be programmed for quick response; other questions might require interaction with the user, either in person, by telephone or through the computer terminal. For frequently asked questions, such as which source on a bibliography is the best place to begin, annotations and suggestions could be provided on a terminal; and if assistance were still required, office hours of a librarian with expertise on the subject could be provided. Directional and other general questions, such as how to use the catalog or indexes, and how to find periodicals, could be handled through a terminal or printed matter. Librarians could be available much like teaching faculty, by appointment, for certain hours each week in their office.

Articles we read and much that those of us working in reference departments in recent years have experienced indicates that we need a change. What would happen if we closed our reference desks? Would users be terribly frustrated by not having a readily available person to talk to when questions arose or would they begin to answer simple requests for themselves or carefully read written aids and handouts or pay more attention at presentations? Would our institutions be able and willing to cope with the consequences of possible frustration and changed service patterns? Would reference librarians become more productive, respected members of the academic community? Would reference librarians be willing and able to accept the challenge? Should we support a model that takes away the personal communication between librarian and user at a reference desk? Has the reference desk seen its most useful time and will other patterns better meet user needs?

If we closed our reference desks we might be astonished at either how little people missed the service or how terribly frustrated patrons would be in trying to use the library. Faculty accustomed to a traditional library setting would probably be disturbed, as most of us are by changes, but librarians working with faculty in other ways could fill these needs. Librarians could be available for classroom presentations and collaboration with faculty to integrate library use into instructional programs. Students who have grown up playing computer games and solving problems with computers might find new services and models more to their liking. In the academic setting, librarians could work with faculty and provide assistance and guidance for students on which sources and approaches are most useful. With more time librarians could seriously address new ways to meet the needs of the primary clientele.

I propose that as long as the reference desk model is uncritically accepted, librarians are not challenged to respond creatively to changes in materials, formats, and research opportunities for our users, and users are not challenged to use any of a variety of printed or computerized sources or aids. We must come to grips with these disturbing notions and question our basic assumptions. I propose this model and raise these questions to begin to think about alternatives to the reference desk as the center of reference service. I hope other models and possible solutions will follow as we explore the energies for transition to new service patterns beyond and perhaps without the reference desk. The possibilities are many and should be interesting to explore.

REFERENCES

1. Patricia K. Swanson, "Traditional Models: Myths and Realities," in Academic Libraries: Myths and Realities-Proceedings of the Third National Conference of the Association of College and Research Libraries (Chicago: Association of College and Research Libraries, 1984), p. 89.

2. Thelma Freides, "Current Trends in Academic Libraries," Library Trends 31:466-7 (Winter 1983).

3. Mary Biggs, "Replacing the Fast Fact Drop-In with Gourmet Information Service: A Symposium," The Journal of Academic Librarianship 11:68-78 (May 1985).

4. Nina W. Matheson, "The Academic Library Nexus," College & Research Libraries 45:208 (May 1984).

5. Patricia Battin, "The Library: Center of the Restructured University," College & Research Libraries 45:171 (May 1984).

6. Richard De Gennaro, "Libraries & Networks in Transition: Problems and Perspectives for the 1980's," Library Journal 106:1049 (May 15, 1981).

7. William Miller, "What's Wrong with Reference: Coping with Success and Failure at the Reference Desk," American Libraries 15:322 (May 1984).

8. Freides, "Current Trends in Academic Libraries." p. 467.

9. Brian Nielsen, "Teacher or Intermediary: Alternative Professional Models in the Information Age," College & Research Libraries 43:186 (May 1982).

10. Rao Aluri and Jeffrey W. St. Clair, "Academic Reference Librarians: An Endangered Species?" The Journal of Academic Librarianship 4:84 (May 1978).

11. Dana E. Smith and Steve M. Hutton, "Back at 8:00 AM - Microcomputer Library Reference Support Programs," Collegiate Microcomputer 11:289 (November 1984).

AN EVALUATION OF DELIVERY TIMES AND COSTS OF A
NON-LIBRARY DOCUMENT DELIVERY SERVICE

Douglas P. Hurd and Robert E. Molyneux
University of Virginia Library
Charlottesville, Virginia

Abstract. The number of non-library, commercial firms that provide document delivery services to libraries has been rising. It is difficult for librarians to determine what role these services will play in interlibrary loan activities because their performance has not been closely studied. In an effort to gain information about the delivery time and costs for private sector document delivery, a study is being conducted at the University of Virginia. This paper reports on the preliminary results of the study which compares delivery times and invoiced costs for documents ordered from both conventional interlibrary loan sources and the UMI Article Clearinghouse.

Keywords and Phrases. Document delivery, interlibrary loans, costs and performance of document services, UMI Article Clearinghouse.

INTRODUCTION

Document delivery, the article ordering and delivery component of interlibrary loan (ILL), has been the focus of recent discussions on the role that new technologies will play in the interlibrary lending process. Programs sponsored by the Library of Congress Network Advisory Committee[1] and the Association of Research Libraries[2] in 1982 analyzed the current status of document delivery and tried to assess its future. It was apparent in these programs that factors such as improved and more economical electronic document delivery, increased use of express mail services, and the growth of commercial, non-library delivery services could all influence document delivery in the future. The programs also made it clear, however, that more data on the current state of document delivery was needed.

As a result of its program, the Network Advisory Committee recommended to the Council on Library Resources that a study of current document delivery be made. The Council selected Information Systems Consultants, Inc. (ISCI) to conduct a study in two phases--the first phase being what it called a "snapshot" of current activities; the second, an intensive, full-scale study, which ISCI later recommended not be done.[3] The ISCI report on the first phase of the study is the most comprehensive study of document delivery to date, even though it is just a "snapshot."

ISCI's report reaches a conclusion that improvements in document delivery in the near future will probably be accomplished within the conventional delivery framework, supplemented by commercial document services, not as the result of any revolutionary developments in electronic delivery.[4] The growth of commercial, non-library delivery services that might offer better performance at lower costs could offer an immediate and affordable alternative to conventional ILL. There are a large number of commercial document firms--e.g., seventy-five services can now be used through DIALOG's DIALORDER.

These non-library document services are generally operated for profit, do not support on-site borrowers, and are accessible in many ways, including online search services such as DIALORDER, bibliographic networks such as OCLC, electronic mail systems such as ALANET, and by telephone, Telex, and mail. In addition, the cost for these services includes copyright compliance.

The performance and costs of commercial document delivery services have not been adequately studied.[5] The lack of data on these services makes it difficult for librarians to decide what role they will play in their ILL activities. In an effort to determine whether a commercial document service could provide documents in less time at prices that are competitive with conventional ILL document sources, a study is being conducted at the University of Virginia Science and Engineering Library that allows direct comparisons between these two methods of acquiring documents. The study compares conventional ILL with one document delivery firm, University Microfilms International's Article Clearinghouse (UMI) in a manner that provides insight into how document delivery by a commercial firm compares with conventional ILL. The method used, simply, is to order an article from both UMI and a conventional source and then compare the cost and delivery time of the article received from both sources. The preliminary results of this study are reported in the next section of this paper. The third section contains a discussion of the methodology including information on UMI and the Science and Engineering Library's ILL service. The last section contains the conclusions.

RESULTS

This section is in three parts. The first part presents the comparison of delivery time for documents received through conventional ILL at the University of Virginia's Science and Engineering Library with the delivery time for documents received from UMI. The second part presents the comparison of invoiced costs. The third part contains miscellaneous observations.

Delivery Times

In this study, delivery time is defined as the number of days (calendar or business) between the day a request was sent to a supplier and the day it was received from the supplier by the Library. The other elements of "satisfaction time"[6] -- the time it takes to locate a source for the item and prepare a request and the time it takes to provide the item to the requester -- are not measured because they are beyond the scope of this study. Obviously, these elements are important factors in the performance of any document delivery or interlibrary loan system and they demand further investigation, but the purpose of this study was simply to compare direct costs and direct delivery times.

TABLE 1
Mean Delivery Times For Conventional Sources and UMI by Calendar and Business Days

	Conventional Sources		UMI	
	Not Paired	Paired	Not Paired	Paired
Calendar Days	15.0(4.3)	14.9(4.3)	11.3(8.8)	11.1(8.5)
Business Days	10.5(2.8)	10.4(2.8)	7.9(6.5)	7.7(6.3)
N =	30	26	26	28

N is the number of cases per category.
Values in parentheses are standard deviations.

Table 1 gives the mean delivery times for documents ordered from both the conventional sources and UMI. The times are given in calendar days and business days. Note that there are four columns, two labeled "paired" and two labeled "not paired." We are comparing the "paired" values because these 26 cases were received from both sources. For various reasons, some document requests could not be filled by one or the other. It can be seen that documents ordered from UMI were delivered almost 3.6 calendar days and 2.5 business days faster than the conventional sources could deliver them. Thus, UMI is, on the average, faster than conventional sources.

However, note the standard deviations for these mean values which are given in parentheses. The standard deviation is a measure of consistency. If the delivery times for all documents ordered from UMI were, for example, eight days, the mean delivery time would be eight and the standard deviation would be zero, that is, there is no deviation from the mean. In general, consistency would be a positive attribute for any means of document delivery and a problem with ILL is that there is little consistency. If a patron requesting a document wants to know how long it will be before the document is received, it would be difficult to predict. It is reasonable to suppose that ordering from a single source, such as UMI, would result in fairly consistent delivery times but from Table 1 it is clear that UMI is less consistent than the many varied sources that fall under the rubric of "conventional" sources. Most UMI requests were received in five to ten days but some took considerably longer. The requests that took longer than 15 days were apparently lost by UMI and were retrieved by our action. At the time UMI was in the midst of personnel changes according to a phone conversation with a staff member. For this reason, these estimates of time for UMI are low and could have been infinite if there had been no intervention.

TABLE 2
UMI Price per Article
By Size of Deposit Account

Size of Deposit Account	Price per Article	
	Pre-1978	Post-1977
$2000+	$8	$4
1000-1999	8	5
200- 999	9	6

Costs

Table 2 shows UMI's price structure as of July, 1985 for single copies of articles in 8.5 inch by 11 inch format ordered online. Pre-1978 articles carry a $3 surcharge, but at the $2000 deposit account level they cost $8 instead of $7 because there is an $8 minimum for these articles. A document request for a post-1977 article is filled free if UMI does not process the order within 48 hours. Express delivery is offered for an extra fee.

TABLE 3
Costs for Conventional Sources and UMI

	Paired	Not Paired
Conventional Sources	$4.60 (1.21)	$4.40 (1.41)
N=	27	32
UMI Deposit Account Size:		
$200 - 999	7.26 (1.50)	7.16 (1.49)
N=	26	31
2000+	5.69 (2.02)	5.54 (1.98)
N=	26	31
Actually paid	4.69 (3.90)	
N=	23	

N is the number of cases per category.
Values in parentheses are standard deviations.

Table 3 gives the mean costs for documents ordered from both the conventional sources and UMI. As they were in Table 1 for delivery times, "not paired" values are given even though they are not analyzed. The estimated mean costs that would have been paid for the articles ordered during the study if they had been paid for at the lowest and highest deposit account levels are given. The row "Actual Cost" contains the mean cost per article that was actually paid to UMI during the study. This cost is lower than even the high deposit account cost as a result of the fact that fourteen orders were filled free during the study. One of these fourteen was free because UMI did not process it within 48 hours. The rest were free as a result of UMI promotional offers. For this study a $300 deposit account was established, so article prices were either $6 or $9 depending on whether they were post-1977 or pre-1978. Table 3 shows that at this deposit account level, without any free articles, an article cost $2.66 more from UMI than from conventional sources. With a high deposit account an article from UMI was $1.09 more expensive.

Miscellaneous Observations

It was possible to evaluate several aspects of document delivery that were not totally within the focus of the study: (1) Nineteen of the thirty-six conventional requests were sent to the British Library - Lending Division (BLLD) through the Center for Research Libraries' Journals Access Service (JAS)(The other seventeen conventional sources included sixteen academic libraries and one special library). BLLD is one of the Science and Engineering Library's most heavily used sources, so it is useful to compare its delivery times and costs directly to UMI's. For the sixteen cases where a document was received from both sources, BLLD's mean delivery time was 14.5 calendar days; UMI's was 10.1 calendar days. The mean cost for a BLLD article was $5.00 (the standard cost charged to JAS users). The mean cost for a UMI article at the lowest deposit account level was $7.31. It was $5.75 at the high deposit account level. UMI is faster than BLLD, but more expensive--the same as with other conventional sources.

(2) Records were maintained on the total number of document requests processed during the study and it is possible to get an idea of how well UMI's holdings cover the Science and Engineering Library's needs. During the study 212 document requests were processed that had to be ordered. Of these, 41 or 19%, were available from UMI. It should be noted that UMI is increasing its holdings, especially in the sciences and engineering.

(3) During the study each document was inspected on receipt and its photocopy quality was assessed on a simple scale. UMI's photocopy quality was judged to be better than that of the conventional source's in thirteen of the fifteen cases where there was a noticeable difference in quality.

(4) UMI was unable to fill 13.9% (5 of 36) requests for articles even though they were for titles listed in their catalog. Three of these were because of copyright restrictions; the other two were simply "unavailable".

METHODOLOGY

The methodology of the study will be clearer if we first look at ILL services at the University of Virginia's Science and Engineering Library and the non-library document delivery service chosen for the study, the UMI Article Clearinghouse.

The Science and Engineering Library

The Intra-Library Science Information Service (ISIS) of the University of Virginia's Science and Engineering Library was instituted in 1971 and still functions in basically the same way it was described by Pancake[7] in 1973. ISIS is an unusual service for an academic library in that it provides free document delivery services that are similar to those offered in many special libraries. These services are available to faculty, research staff and graduate students in science and engineering departments at the University of Virginia for any item not at their designated branch libraries. Types of items requested include books, conference papers, journal articles, or technical reports. About half of the documents requested through ISIS are located at the University of Virginia and are delivered to the requester. The requests that must be ordered from some other source are sent to a variety of interlibrary loan sources, including other university libraries and the BLLD through JAS.

Since 1971, ISIS has processed an average of 3677 document requests per year. During fiscal year 1983/84, 3524 requests were processed; 44% of these had to be ordered through ILL sources. The Biology and Psychology departments are consistently the heaviest users of ISIS.

The UMI Article Clearinghouse

UMI was chosen for the study for four reasons: (1) it has all of the characteristics of the new document delivery services--it is for-profit, non-library, accessible by a number of ordering methods, and its services include copyright compliance; (2) its subject coverage is comprehensive; (3) it advertises rapid ordering and processing, and competitive prices; and (4) it is highly visible--since the service began in 1983, its marketing efforts have been intensive.

A catalog of post-1977 titles held at UMI is provided free-of-charge to each account. It contains about 8,000 titles. For pre-1978 titles the UMI _1985 Serials in Microform_ catalog was used. It contains about 13,000 titles (including those listed in the post-1977 catalog). The summer 1985 UMI catalog will include all titles from _Serials in Microform_.

Method for Comparing ISIS and UMI

In early April, 1985 a Library Assistant began including a search of the UMI catalogs in all searches for sources for document requests that were not available at the University of Virginia. If an item was available from UMI, whether it was pre-1978 or post-1977, a photocopy was made of the document request form. The item was then ordered from the conventional source chosen by the Assistant. Orders were placed using the method that would normally be used for that source, based on the ILL experience of the Library Assistant. Ordering methods included ALA form, JAS, OCLC, and Telex.

Standard source location and ordering procedures were used during the study. The photocopy of the document request form and a data sheet that included date ordered, sources tried, and ordering method were given to the Librarian, who then ordered the item from UMI on the same day that the conventional order had been sent. All UMI orders were placed through the OCLC ILL Subsystem for two reasons: (1) OCLC offers a fast, convenient, and relatively economical method that would likely be the ordering choice under nonexperimental conditions at most libraries, and (2) it was decided that the initial study should focus on invoiced costs rather than total costs which would have included extra ordering costs (DIALOG connect-hour charges) if documents had been ordered through DIALORDER.

Filled conventional orders were received by the Library Assistant, who gave the document to the Librarian with a note containing the date received, the final source, and the invoiced cost. Filled UMI orders were received by the Librarian, who entered the date received, and invoiced cost on the item's data sheet. All data sheets were maintained by the Librarian so that the staff were unaware of any results that might influence their processing of conventional orders. Whichever copy of each document was received first was delivered to the requester.

CONCLUSIONS

The results of this study indicate that the UMI Article Clearinghouse can deliver documents faster than conventional ILL sources. However, the speed of UMI's service is accompanied by slightly higher costs and some inconsistency. The inconsistency encountered during the initial stages of the study may be temporary because of the personnel changes occurring at UMI at the time. UMI staff were always eager to help when reached through their toll-free telephone number. Most of the problems that developed with orders were eventually solved and reordered documents were received with the average delivery time of ten days.

The higher costs of UMI's service will have to be evaluated according to each user's circumstances. The value of faster document delivery at a higher cost will vary among types of libraries and within types of libraries, depending on budgets, staffing, and priorities. The establishment of a UMI deposit account of over $2000 to qualify for the lowest rate per article could be an advantage for those libraries that can afford it, especially if a large percentage of their UMI requests are for post-1977 articles. However, UMI's holdings covered only a fifth of the total number of document requests made during this study at a large, academic science and engineering library. Of course, the percentage may be higher for other kinds of libraries.

Finally, this study did not compare the indirect costs of the two methods of document delivery. Obviously, staff salaries and the costs of the systems used to order documents are important factors in overall delivery costs. These elements of document delivery must be studied further.

ACKNOWLEDGEMENTS

Special thanks to Ashley Havird and Haynes Earnhardt who helped with the study.

REFERENCES

1. Library of Congress Network Development Office, Document Delivery -- Background Papers Commissioned by the Network Advisory Committee, Network Planning Paper No. 7 (Washington, D.C.: The Library of Congress, 1982).

2. Association of Research Libraries, Minutes of the 101st Meeting: Prospects for Improving Document Delivery, October 13-14, 1982, Arlington, Virginia. (Washington, D.C.: The Association of Research Libraries, 1983).

3. Information Systems Consultants, Document Delivery in the United States: A Report to the Council on Library Resources. (Washington, D.C.: Information Systems Consultants, Inc., 1983), p. 62.

4. Ibid., p. 58.

5. Ibid., preface, p.30, p. 61.

6. Ibid., p. 25.

7. Edwina H. Pancake, "Intra-Library Science Information Service," Special Libraries 64, nos. 5/6 (May/June 1973): 228-234.

USER DEMAND FOR LIBRARY SERVICES: AN UNDERGRADUATE LIBRARY MODEL

Elaine McPheron
Oscar A. Silverman Undergraduate Library
State University of New York at Buffalo

Abstract. Multiple linear regression analysis is used to test the hypothesis that demand for an undergraduate library, as measured by monograph circulation, is a function of these explanatory variables: size of collection, staff, enrollment, and library system; number of serial subscriptions and hours open; quality of students; and year of data. Results include a regression equation with t-statistics for the coefficients and analysis of variance, which together are used to explain the influence of each variable on demand and their combined success in explaining change in demand. Conclusions based on the data, problems with its interpretation, and suggested areas for further development are presented.

Keywords and Phrases. Circulation, Economics, Library finance, Regression analysis, Undergraduate libraries, User demand.

INTRODUCTION

In the early seventies, William J. Baumol and Matityahu Marcus prepared their Economics of Academic Libraries for the Council on Library Resources. It was intended as an aid for librarians, administrators, and organizations that deal with the economic problems of academic libraries. The Council has more recently sought to increase interest in economic analysis of library services and processes by sponsoring seminars in economics. Yet despite a decade of efforts, research literature on the economics of libraries is still scarce. In concluding her 1984 survey of the applications of economic theory to the study of library usage and support, Nancy Van House identified several areas in need of research. One of them, demand for library services, has been studied only by those concerned with public and medical libraries.[1]

The purpose of my research is to analyze the factors that influence demand for undergraduate libraries, defined here as separate collections and services designed to meet the needs of undergraduates in large university settings. In this presentation, I will use the most successful of three models to demonstrate one method of developing and testing a demand function for a library. As background to the discussion, it is useful to consider undergraduate libraries and their use from the economist's perspective.

LAW OF DEMAND

A basic principle of consumer choice theory is the law of demand: consumers buy more of a product as its cost to them is lowered. The product in an undergraduate library is information, and demand for it is reflected in measures such as circulation, in-house use, and reference questions. While there are no fees for library use, the law of demand can be applied in terms of time costs to students. That is, price can be viewed as the amount of time spent for a satisfactory library use (e.g., to identify, find, and check out a needed book). Factors that influence the "price" in an undergraduate library include size of the collection, staff and number of hours open. As the size of the collection increases, the likelihood that needed materials are available should also increase. Similarly, larger staffs imply more people to select the right materials, catalog them, maintain the shelves, and answer questions. The more hours the library is open, the less a student must change plans or sacrifice other activities in order to have satisfactory library use.

In addition to price, other factors that influence demand for a product are tastes and preferences of the consumers, prices of related goods, and the number of buyers; each category is relevant to the study of demand for undergraduate libraries. Tastes and preferences for libraries--or inclinations to use them--are determined by many factors. One, for which comparative data is available, may be the academic quality of the students; that is, as student quality varies, so does their "taste" for or interest in libraries. The related goods are the other libraries in the university. If students are not satisfied for the right price by the undergraduate library, they have alternate libraries to use instead. Finally, as the number of students increases, the total demand is expected to increase; use per student may also change if the size of a university influences the preferences of students for library use.

To summarize, economists view demand as a function of price, tastes and preferences, prices of related goods, and number of buyers. For the undergraduate library model, this is translated to the following hypothesis:

$$Y_{loans} = f(X_{volumes}, X_{serials}, X_{hours}, X_{staff}, X_{enroll}, X_{select}, X_{system})$$

Or, demand, as measured by circulation, is a function of these explanatory variables: collection size, serial subscriptions, hours, staff size, enrollment, student quality, and library system size.

METHODOLOGY

A causal relationship between the explanatory variables and circulation is assumed, and based on this assumption, multiple regression analysis is used to determine the effectiveness of the explanatory variables in explaining changes in demand. In performing multiple regression analysis, data for the variables is input to the computer. It uses the least squares method to find the equation that most closely represents the relationships between the variables. Since the computation is the task of the computer, the major methodological concerns of the researcher are defining the sample and variables and the related compilation of data.

Sample

The number of undergraduate libraries in the United States is too small to do a reliable cross-sectional study, so three years of data are used. This means that the data is both time series and cross-sectional. Those undergraduate libraries that reported the requisite statistical data in the May 1976, January 1977, and January 1984 UGLI Newsletter comprise the sample (table 1).[2]

Dependent Variable

Demand is based on circulation figures, specifically monograph loans per undergraduate. It is the most objective and reliable measure of library use but represents only part of the information disseminated by a library.

Explanatory Variables

Cost. The first four explanatory variables (table 1) are cost factors for the student. As they vary, the time it takes for the student's information needs to be satisfied should change also. Larger values for all except undergraduates per undergraduate library staff (X_{staff}) represent more investments in the library by its parent institution and, presumably, more immediate satisfaction of student information needs. If satisfaction is more immediate, demand should increase as all except X_{staff} increase. Since increased numbers of undergraduates per staff is a decreased service, it should result in less satisfaction and decreased demand.

Tastes and Preferences. There is little quantitative data available concerning students' inclination to use a library or their preferences for different libraries. Two factors used in this study are undergraduate enrollment and selectivity rating. Enrollment is included to check for the influence of the size of the institution on demand for library use. The selectivity rating is based on Cass and Birnbaum's Comparative Guide to American Colleges[3] in which they classify schools according to their selectivity in accepting students.

Table 1
Summary of Statistical Data for Dependent and Explanatory Variables

	Variables		Mean	St Dev	Min	Max
Dependent:	Y_{loans}	monograph loans/undergraduate	5.52	3.79	0.34	17.79
Explanatory:						
	$X_{volumes}$	UGL volumes/undergraduate	7.28	6.13	0.18	28.55
	$X_{serials}$	UGL serial subscriptions	460	285	0.00	1279
Cost	X_{hours}	UGL open hours/week	104.1	18.3	67	168
	X_{staff}	undergraduates/UGL staff	1815	2700	263	18908
Tastes	X_{enroll}	undergraduate enrollment	20051	10291	2146	47038
	X_{select}	selectivity rating	2.75	1.41	1.00	5.00
Related Goods	X_{system}	system volumes/undergraduate	250	301	53	1537
Dummy Variables	X_{76}	dummy variable for 1976/77	0.367	0.486	0.00	1.00
	X_{74}	dummy variable for 1974/75	0.283	0.454	0.00	1.00

Note: For each variable: the mean is the average value; standard deviation (St Dev) is a measure of the dispersion of actual values around their mean; min is the smallest value and max the largest. The sample includes 60 members (n = 60).

The scale is from one to five, with five used for the most selective schools.

Related Goods. An undergraduate library is one of many libraries available to university students. The volumes per undergraduate in the university libraries system (X_{system}) is included to see if variations in the system's size influence the demand for the undergraduate library.

Dummy Variables. These are assigned to 1976 (X_{76}) and 1974 (X_{74}) data to differentiate those years from 1982 data and determine whether significant differences occur because of year. Such differences would suggest change in students' tastes and preferences for libraries over the years.

Data

The source of data for almost all variables is the UGLI Newsletter. Exceptions are X_{system} which is from ARL Statistics[4] and X_{select} from the Comparative Guide to American Colleges. Because the size of undergraduate populations varies substantially at universities that have undergraduate libraries, all variables are presented as per student figures.

RESULTS

The results of the data analysis, performed through the use of the MINITAB statistical package, include a regression equation with t-statistics for the coefficients and analysis of variance.

The regression equation shows the estimated regression coefficients and the t-statistics for each coefficient (table 2). Each variable's coefficient represents the amount that demand for the undergraduate library changes when the variable is changed by one unit while all other explanatory variables are held constant. For example, the coefficient for $X_{volumes}$ is .749. This means that if the undergraduate library's collection is increased by one volume per undergraduate, the number of monograph loans per undergraduate is expected to increase by .749. Note that this is an incremental increase, not a percentage, and in each case the reciprocal also holds. So, if the collection size decreases by one volume per undergraduate, the loans decrease by .749.

The same interpretation is applied to the other coefficients. The addition of one serial title is expected to increase loans by .00023, or it takes 10,000 new subscriptions to raise loans per undergraduate 2.3. Clearly the number of subscriptions does not have much impact on

---

Table 2
Results of Regression Analysis

Regression Equation

$$Y_{loans} = -6.29 + 0.749 X_{volumes} + 0.00023 X_{serials} + 0.0560 X_{hours}$$
$$(3.20)\quad (8.98)\qquad\qquad (.20)\qquad\qquad (3.83)$$

$$- 0.000146 X_{staff} + 0.000050 X_{enroll} + 0.329 X_{select}$$
$$(1.17)\qquad\qquad (1.29)\qquad\qquad (1.31)$$

$$- 0.00861 X_{system} + 1.34 X_{76} + 1.56 X_{74}$$
$$(5.37)\qquad\qquad (2.22)\quad (2.41)$$

Note: Figures in parentheses are the absolute t-statistics for significance tests of the estimated coefficients.

Analysis of Variance

Due to	DF	SS	MS = SS/DF	F(9, 50)
Regression	9	667.716	74.191	20.828
Residual	50	178.124	3.562	
Total	59	845.841		

R^2: 78.9%
75.2%, adjusted for degrees of freedom

circulation of monographs, though the relationship is a positive one.

An increase of one open _hour_ per week increases circulation by .056 monographs per undergraduate; ten hours increases it by .56 loans.

The coefficient for undergraduates per _staff_ is negative indicating that as the number of students per staff person increases, circulation decreases. For every additional 1,000 students per staff person, a decline in loans per student of .146 is expected.

The _enrollment_ variable has a coefficient of .00005. As undergraduate population increases by 10,000, a circulation per student increase of .5 is expected.

Selectivity of students also has a positive relation to number of loans per undergraduate. An increase of one unit on this five-point scale is expected to increase circulation per student by .329.

The _system_ variable, number of volumes per undergraduate in the university libraries system, is negative, so that this "related good" is used as a substitute for the undergraduate library. For each additional one hundred books per undergraduate in the system, a decline of .861 in loans per student is expected.

Both dummy variables (X_{76} and X_{74}) have large, positive coefficients indicating that the year of the data influences the number of loans per student. If all other variables are held constant, the number of loans per student in 1976 is expected to be 1.34 more than in 1982, and in 1974, it is 1.56 more than 1982.

T-statistics are given for each of the coefficients to indicate their statistical reliability. Larger t-statistics mean increased confidence that even under repeated sampling the coefficients would not change much. For the population size used in the undergraduate library model, a t-statistic above 2.01 is extremely reliable. This is the case for $X_{volumes}$, X_{hours}, X_{system}, X_{76}, and X_{74}. The t-statistics for X_{staff}, X_{enroll}, and X_{select} are less reliable, but might be stronger if the unreliable $X_{serials}$ is dropped from the equation.

While the coefficients and t-statistics focus on the effect of each individual explanatory variable on the dependent variable (Y_{loan}) when the other explanatory variables are held constant, analysis of variance is used to evaluate the extent to which the combination of explanatory variables explain fluctuations in the dependent variable. The analysis of variance table provides the necessary figures to calculate R^2 and the F-statistic. R^2 represents the percentage of the total variability of the dependent variable (Y_{loans}) that is explained by the regression equation (table 2). For the undergraduate library model, R^2 is 78.9% (75.2% when adjusted for the number of explanatory variables). This means that the regression equation explains 78.9% of the variation in the number of monograph loans per undergraduate.

The F-statistic tests the significance of R^2. For this model, the F-statistic is 20.828; any value above 2.08 is very good.

To summarize, the regression equation accounts for 78.9% of the variation in undergraduate library monograph loans per undergraduate. Of the explanatory variables previously classified as cost factors, size of collection ($X_{volumes}$) and hours open (X_{hours}) have especially large, reliable influence on the number of loans. The level of staffing (X_{staff}) has smaller weight in the equation and its reliability is less. The number of serial subscriptions is an unreliable factor in predicting monograph circulation and should be dropped from the equation. This combination suggests that the average undergraduate library director forced to make budget reductions should work to maintain collection size and hours, even at the expense of staff, if circulation is considered an appropriate measure of demand. Both measures of tastes, enrollment (X_{enroll}) and selectivity (X_{select}), positively influence the number of loans and are reliable. This implies that cross-sectional statistical comparisons will be more accurate if undergraduate libraries are grouped by size and selectivity. Dummy variables for 1974 and 1976 data show, with high reliability, that the number of loans per undergraduate was larger in each of those two years than in 1982 even with other factors held constant. This signals a difference in tastes and preferences--or perhaps need--for borrowing books between the three time periods and suggests that time series comparisons will be biased by changing use patterns. The factor for related goods, volumes per undergraduate in the university libraries system (X_{system}), shows a highly reliable negative coefficient indicating that other university libraries do serve as substitutes for the undergraduate library.

CONCLUSION

This model of demand for an undergraduate library offers information that may assist directors and demonstrates a method that is applicable to other library situations. It does, however, have two limitations that should be considered, the causality assumption and measure of demand.

The model's hypothesis assumes that demand as measured by circulation is caused by collection and staff size, hours open, and number of subscriptions. It is equally possible that these explanatory variables are themselves caused by circulation. That is, managers may have weighted the factor of circulation when determining the level of support to give a library. A second level of analysis, two-stage least squares regression, can be used to separate user behavior from manager choices. This technique is described briefly by Malcolm Getz in his book, Public Libraries: An Economic View.[5] It would require additional variables other than circulation to represent factors that influence management's decisions about support given for collection, staff, and hours. These factors might include political, curricular, or space concerns, but data is not presently available for a cross-sectional study of this type.

Furthermore, circulation figures may themselves be considered an inadequate measure of demand for an undergraduate library, especially in view of the important role of reference and instruction in this setting. Two other models, for in-house use of materials and reference questions, have been tested but are so far unsuccessful. The limited number of libraries that report in-house use statistics and the inconsistency of their counting methods are the major problems for the first model. The reference model has more potential because the size of the population is sufficiently large, but the regression is much weaker than that of the circulation model. The source of difficulty may be the selection of variables which is, of course, limited to what has been reported, and, unfortunately, this remains quite limited. The statistics of the Undergraduate Librarians Discussion Group are actually unique in their inclusion of reference data. Until the publication of ARL Supplementary Statistics 1983-84,[6] the Association of Research Libraries was not including reference statistics in their compilations. According to the introduction to the supplementary data, the question on reference transactions drew the lowest response rate of any on the form. Improvements in the standardization and availability of reference statistics and other public service measures must continue so that methods such as multiple regression analysis can be better used to aid the study of user demand for library services.

REFERENCES

1. William J. Baumol and Matityahu Marcus, Economics of Academic Libraries (Washington, DC: American Council on Education, 1973); Nancy A. Van House, "Research on the Economics of Libraries," Library Trends 32 (Spring 1984): 419; Kathleen Foley Feldstein, "The Economics of Public Libraries," (Ph.D. diss., Massachusetts Institute of Technology, 1977); Malcolm Getz, Public Libraries: An Economic View (Baltimore: Johns Hopkins University Press, 1980); Cheryl A. Casper, "Estimating the Demand for Library Service: Theory and Practice," Journal of the American Society for Information Science 29 (September 1978): 232-237.

2. "Statistical Issue," UGLI Newsletter [ACRL Undergraduate Librarians Discussion Group] 9 (May 1976); 12 (January 1977); 27 (January 1984).

3. James Cass and Max Birnbaum, Comparative Guide to American Colleges, 7th ed. (New York: Harper and Row, 1975); 8th ed. 1977; 11th ed. 1983.

4. Suzanne Frankie, comp., ARL Statistics 1974-75 (Washington, DC: Association of Research Libraries, 1975); idem, ARL Statistics 1976-77; Carol A. Mandel, comp., ARL Statistics 1982-83.

5. Malcolm Getz, Public Libraries: An Economic View (Baltimore: Johns Hopkins University Press, 1980), 87-88, 190.

6. Robert Molyneux and Kendon Stubbs, comps., ARL Supplementary Statistics 1983-84 (Washington, DC: Association of Research Libraries, 1985).

A LIBRARY RESEARCH APPLICATION OF FOCUS GROUP INTERVIEWS

Meg Koch Scharf and Jeannette Ward
University of Central Florida
Orlando, Florida

Abstract. In order to obtain a direction and set priorities for programs to improve library services, an accepted marketing research method was adapted for library application. The Focus Group is a marketing research method of conducting an indepth interview with a small group to gain insight into consumer needs, problems, attitudes, and behaviors.

The components of a Focus Group interview, and the implementation in an academic setting are described. The results of the interviews were used to gain insights, develop ideas, direct and generate hypotheses, and target areas for more structured surveys and studies.

Keywords and Phrases. Focus Group, Interviewing in Marketing Research, Library Use Studies.

INTRODUCTION

"Energies in Transition" is a phrase that could accurately describe our University Library. Our location in Orlando, Florida ensures us of continued student population growth and increasing requests for service from the business, technical, and professional community. Having spent our energies during the previous years in planning and implementing a physical move that doubled our library's size, we were now ready to direct our energies to improving and increasing our library's services. We wanted input from our users before we set goals and directed our future. Time and budgetary constraints had prevented our library from initiating a user survey in the past.

Many libraries have adopted the marketing concept for planning new services, evaluating existing services, setting goals and priorities, and allocating resources. The marketing concept is simply: "a consumer's need orientation backed by integrated marketing aimed at generating consumer satisfaction and long-run consumer welfare as the key to satisfying organizational goals."[1] This concept strives to meet the users' needs, rather than hoping that the users simply accept services as they are offered. Evaluation of these needs can be a long and costly project. Many librarians are unfamiliar with marketing research and are hesitant about initiating information gathering efforts. After reviewing the marketing literature and examining various survey and research methods, we decided that the marketing research technique called the Focus Group interview might be a viable library research method. Many marketing research firms and advertising agencies use Focus Groups to begin gathering information.

A Focus Group interview is a discussion involving eight to twelve socially and intellectually homogenous participants with a moderator in which various hypotheses about a product, service, or consumer problem are explored in depth. A Focus Group will yield qualitative results that can be used to develop ideas. "To sum up what qualitative research is, the one best brief phrase might be: A chance to "experience" a "flesh and blood" consumer.' It is the opportunity for the client to put himself in the position of the consumer and to be able to look at his product and his category from her vantage point."[2] As such, it is an ideal tool for initiating a research project. In the service industries, Focus Group discussions have had some use in marketing bank services, and Karen Markey, OCLC, Office of Research, has used this method for collecting user opinions on online catalogs for OCLC.[3]

A pilot project using this marketing research technique was implemented during the last half of the spring semester of 1985. Our purpose was two fold: to obtain overall student perceptions of the University Library and to see if Focus Groups would be a useful tool for initiating user research. To minimize costs and ensure the immediacy of the results, the preliminary research, recruitment, physical arrangements and post-interview analysis were done by two librarians.

The components of a Focus Group interview are the setting, the moderator, the participants, the discussion, and the analysis.

SETTING

The setting for a Focus Group needs to create a congenial atmosphere, where the participants feel at ease to express their opinions and feelings. Many universities have facilities that are available for small group meetings. Our setting was an easy-to-reach office in the library where the furniture was arranged to provide comfortable seating for twelve people at a conference table. Refreshments were provided. Indications of a library environment (book trucks, processing materials, etc.) were removed, and conversations could not be heard from other areas of the library. Two tape recorders were placed unobtrusively in the room.

MODERATOR

The moderator should create a relaxed atmosphere, thus keeping the conversation on the topic, and eliciting and balancing comments from all participants. Although the moderator is completely aware of the purpose and objectives of the study, he or she should not demonstrate indepth knowledge of the product or service. Nor should the moderator provide answers or give the impression to the group that he is an "expert" on the topic. The purpose of the discussions should be to raise issues and solicit the opinions and feeling of the participants. Positive as well as negative comments are of equal value and are pursued by the moderator. The moderator should be able to pace the interview so that all topics outlined are sufficiently covered. The library staff were not considered for training to moderate a Focus Group as their presence during the discussion could have considerable influence on the tone and direction of the conversations.

During contact with Dr. M. Joyce of the Marketing Department to see if that department could be of help in suggesting training techniques, we were offered the services of marketing staff and students who had conducted Focus Group sessions during a research project for a nonprofit organization. The moderator was provided with a list of topics such as physical arrangement, staff, hours, and collection. The availability of previously trained moderators enabled us to implement the Focus Group project with very little preparation time.

PARTICIPANTS

The participants must be recruited from the target group of users, and must be made to feel that their comments will be completely confidential. Group participants were recruited from recent library instruction classes in English composition and from health sciences and engineering classes. Limited recruitment was done in the library among known library users by the circulation and reference staff. Library student assistants did not participate in these groups. We found that with a skilled moderator, students who had seldom used library services were encouraged to participate and contributed some substance to the discussion.

Recruitment is the most difficult and time consuming part of arranging a Focus Group discussion. Our experience indicated that twenty people had to be asked to get one participant, and that fifty percent of those that volunteered did not show up. Recruitment efforts could be helped by involving student government and having service clubs, fraternities, and sororities commit to sending two or three participants to each scheduled Focus Group discussion. If funds are available through university or library funding, paying students is the most assured method of ensuring participation. Typically, marketing research firms pay Focus Group participants or offer them a gift as incentive.

DISCUSSION

Groups were given a short time (10 minutes) to take some of the refreshments on hand and be introduced to the moderator and each other. During this time, the moderator made sure that conversation was casual and did not include comments on the subject to be discussed (i.e., the library). This gave the group the chance to grow accustomed to the surroundings and each other, and gave late comers a chance to come in and get settled. All participants were assured that the conversation, although taped, would be confidential. Only library staff directly involved with the project would hear the tapes, and no names or other identifying information would be kept regarding the participants. After these preliminaries, the librarian left before the actual discussion began. The moderator began with several questions designed to demonstrate commonality to the group. Each participant was asked why he or she chose to attend the University, and what each liked about it. After a few minutes, the moderator began asking general questions about perceptions of the library's staff, services and physical facilities. After the interview period (one hour) the librarian returned to the group and offered to answer any questions raised during the discussion.

ANALYSIS

The audio tapes of the discussions are summarized in a written report. Strict quantitative statistical interpretation is not appropriate. The Focus Group method yields qualitative rather than quantitative data, and decisions should not be based on its results. The results of a Focus Group interview are used to form hypotheses when little or nothing is known, to structure questionnaires, to get attitudes and impressions about new and old products, and to evaluate previously obtained quantitative results. "Qualitative research is not a 'quick and dirty' and cheap way for avoiding quantitative research. It serves completely different purposes and does not, in any way, presume to supply the same kinds of answers as quantitative exploration does."[4] Statistical or other empirical data should be collected to support plans and changes suggested by a Focus Group interview project. However, a Focus Group can put the library in touch with its clients (their needs, language, problems) indicate perception discrepancies, generate ideas, and suggest directions for further investigations.

When analyzing the discussion of a Focus Group some points to consider are whether the topic was introduced by the moderator or one of the participants, if agreement among the participants was enthusiastic, and if examples or specific occurrences of the topic were supplied by the group. The report of our pilot project is appended.

Although decisions should not be based solely on the results from a Focus Group, we were given some directions for immediate action. The noise level elicited enough comments that we took action to promote quiet in the library. Duplicate copies of specific reference tools were requested to be put on permanent reserve.

The fact that we were conducting a user research activity in the library was reported in University publications, and this reflected favorably on the library and its administration. We established a closer working relationship with some members of the Marketing Department and other disciplines. In addition, the student participants were made to feel that their needs and opinions are important to the library.

Like most research tools, Focus Groups can be used casually or rigorously. Our purpose in conducting our pilot program was to see if our library research could benefit from an application of the Focus Group technique. We were pleased with the speed of the project, its low cost, and the readily understandable results. We have recommended that our library use Focus Groups as one research method for a variety of special topics on which we need information on user perceptions: the online catalog, library instruction, physical arrangement of study areas, staffing patterns and collection development. We may even consider holding faculty Focus Group discussions on topics relating to specialized services to faculty and staff.

To understand users' needs, and establish priorities before directing energies to expand, create or improve library services, Focus Groups - properly administered and evaluated - are an efficient and cost-effective research method.

APPENDIX

Summary of the Report On Focus Group Discussions

Positive comments were made concerning the library staff in all public service areas. Specific incidents of their friendliness, competency, and helpfulness were described. The online catalog, microfiche catalog, the reserve service, group study rooms, and availability of periodicals in microform elicited positive comments. An isolated but interesting comment was on the condition of the photocopiers in the library - they seem to be better maintained than copiers elsewhere on the campus.

Negative comments included noise control, library hours, availability of appropriate study areas, the physical environment including lighting and temperature, and the online catalog. Specific library tours by junior and senior high school students were given as occurrences of noise pollution. Study areas on the first, second and fourth floors were described as being poorly lit. Bookdrops were mentioned as being difficult to use and poorly located. Comments on the collection covered lack of current periodicals, and lack of multiple copies of heavily used reference titles; specific titles were mentioned by participants. Students stated that some reference titles are not kept back far enough to support case studies, and the arrangement of the periodicals on all floors makes their use cumbersome. Mutilation of materials and missing pages were also mentioned as problems.

ACKNOWLEDGEMENTS

Our thanks to Dr. Mary Joyce of the Marketing Department, University of Central Florida, and Harry Fendt for their assistance.

REFERENCES

1. Philip Kotler, Marketing for Nonprofit Organizations.(Englewood Cliffs, N.J.: Prentice Hall, 1975), p. 47.

2. Myril Axelrod, "Marketers Get an Eyeful When Focus Groups Expose Products, Ideas, Images, AdCopy, Etc. to Consumers," Marketing News, VIII (February 28, 1975), p. 6 - 7.

3. Karen Markey, Online Catalog Use: Results of Surveys and Focus Group Interviews in Several Libraries.(Dublin, Ohio: OCLC, 1983).

4. Axelrod, p. 7.

REDUCTION OF NOISE IN TWO CAMPUS LIBRARIES OF A MAJOR UNIVERSITY

Sally S. Small
The Pennsylvania State University
The Berks Campus Memorial Library
Reading, PA

Maureen E. Strazdon
American International Group
Research and Development Dept.
New York, NY

Abstract. Disruptive social behavior in two campus libraries precipitated increasing numbers of complaints from users who preferred a quiet orderly library environment. This presentation will discuss two library management strategies which attempted to alleviate the behavior problems using the different sets of resources available at the two campuses. The two strategies are described and contrasted with other tactics reported in the literature. Discussion centers on the role of the library as the campus academic/social center; the relationship between the number of users and the disruptive behavior; support of the local administration; and the obligation of the profession to provide a library environment conducive to study, reflection, and research for faculty and changing student populations.

Keywords and Phrases. Discipline in the library; Noise control in academic libraries; Architecture and building - Sound control.

QUIET VS. NOISE IN THE LIBRARY

Noise control in libraries is not a popular topic with many academic librarians. Some seem to equate noise control with the dreaded image of the hushing, spectacled librarian of old; others view noise as appropriate to the more relaxed environment in today's libraries; and still others view user conduct as a problem outside their responsibility. On-line searches, microcomputer applications, and the latest in library instruction techniques are far more absorbing topics than user behavior problems for today's academic librarians. But what happens when a particular mix of circumstances creates a level of noise that is intolerable to one group of users and the library staff is forced to intervene? As distasteful as the problem is, it must be dealt with.

Traditional undergraduate students have varying needs for quiet study. Some want no distraction at all while others are happiest with music blaring in their earphones and/or when arguing with buddies over the best way to solve a math or physics problem. However, traditional students and their potential noise preferences are no longer the sole student force on campus. Many colleges are recruiting older, non-traditional students to round out their enrollments and these students frequently view the library as the quiet place to study on campus. Conflict may develop between the groups with varying needs for quiet and the library staff may be caught in the middle of that conflict.

NOISY LIBRARIES

Recently, disruptive social behavior in two lower division undergraduate campus libraries of a major university precipitated increasing numbers of complaints from users who preferred a quiet, orderly library environment. The purpose of this paper is to report the two management strategies used to resolve the noise problem with each librarian utilizing the varying resources and support available at her location.

Recent articles in both the British and American library literature note the perceived increase in noise in academic libraries.[1,2,3] Reid notes that librarians seem to lack the spine to deal with the issue, but that the reading public, particularly students, have an absolute right to expect traditional peace and quiet in the library.[4] Suggestions to help relieve the noise problem center around building furnishings and arrangement, publicizing the noise policy and staff behavior. Several librarians accept varying noise levels and advocate areas designed to accommodate the variations.[5] One group of researchers suggests separating types of seating,[6] and another author advocates using all carrel seating.[7]

Most authors state that the library should develop and publicize a noise policy to inform users of the behavior expected of college library patrons.[8,9] The policy may be explained during orientation sessions or in a library handbook.[10] It should be positively worded, non-threatening, and should follow the sections on the library services available to students.[11]

Staff behavior and responsibility was also emphasized. The staff should be careful not to hold loud conversations with each other or patrons and should accept the responsibility for maintaining peace and quiet in the library reading rooms.[12]

Two recent studies on noise reduction highlight efforts to make the library quieter. Luyben et al rearranged seating patterns in a college library to break up clusters of seating and to separate the types of furniture.[13] Although measured bursts of noise did not decrease substantially after the intervention, users perceived that there was a significant reduction in noise.

At a two year commuter campus of the Ohio State University, inadequate lounge space for students encouraged the social use of the attractive library.[14] Faculty compounded the problem with frequent assignments that required group effort. The library staff was uncomfortable dealing with the noise. A multi-part intervention helped reduce the noise levels. The intervention included: informing users about the new quiet policy, designating a large room for group study, encouraging small groups to study in group study rooms, monitoring behavior, and insisting that quiet be maintained in the library. The metered sound level declined and patrons perceived the noise level as quieter and less annoying. Most patrons were cooperative, although some lamented the loss of their right to use the library in their own manner. The monitoring took a great deal of staff time.

TWO CAMPUS LIBRARIES

The Pennsylvania State University Libraries include a central collection, several special libraries, and libraries at each of the seventeen Commonwealth Campuses throughout the state. Each of the campus libraries is an independent entity, with the librarian at each location setting administrative policy for that campus. The librarian reports to his or her local Campus Executive Officer as well as the Head of the Commonwealth Campuses Libraries Division at University Park.

Berks and Ogontz are two of the seventeen Penn State campuses, both situated in eastern Pennsylvania. Berks is located in rural Berks County near Reading and serves primarily middle class students, many of whom represent the first generation of college students in their families. Ogontz is located in a suburban area very close to Philadelphia, and has a student population which is predominently middle class. Both offer associate degrees and the first two years of baccalaureate degree programs as well as a variety of formal and informal programs through their continuing education departments. Neither campus has dormitories.

The Berks Campus, with a collection of 38,000 volumes serves a total of 1200 full, part-time, and non-degree students. The new library building was occupied in 1975 and was newly furnished at occupancy. The original seating capacity was 360 seats, 290 of which shared the large public area with the collection. Building use increased steadily from 48,500 the first year of occupancy to 146,000 in 1983-84. Campus enrollments held steady or declined during this period. The staff increased from 4.5 FTE to 5.25 FTE during this time while hours of operation remained constant at 65 hours per week.

The Ogontz Campus Library, which was built and furnished in 1972, has a collection of 60,000 volumes, and is also open 65 hours per week. Since 1972, the library staff has increased from five full-time to six full-time and two part-time staff members. With a student body of 2000 regular and 1500 continuing education students, over 203,000 people used the library in 1983-84. The library has three floors and originally sat 260 users.

The Noise Problems

Both campus libraries have a history of noise problems. Like the situations at several of the locations mentioned in the literature review, both campuses suffer from a lack of adequate space for students to congregate and socialize. The library has been the social center of the campus.

The problems seem to be cyclical, the students being very badly behaved one year and fairly well behaved the next. The "good" years and "bad" years have not necessarily coincided at the two campuses. At both campuses various measures were introduced each bad year in an effort to control the escalating noise.

At Berks, the quiet policy was included in the library handout which was distributed to all incoming students (1975-). Security personnel were asked to walk through the building several times each day (1978-79). Quiet signs were posted and staff members reminded students to lower their voices (1979-80). Carrels, group tables, and lounge chairs which had originally been dispersed throughout the room were regrouped by type and the group tables placed close to the public service staff. In the fall of 1981 a new staff person was hired to monitor student noise and the use and abuse of the study rooms.

At Ogontz, more carrel tops were added and more open tables removed each year. Staff patrols were tried for several years. "Quiet" signs and a letter from the campus CEO asking for cooperation were posted in Spring, 1983.

Each measure was effective as long as the staff reinforced the quiet, but as the year wore on and the staff got busy with other responsibilities, the noise returned. (At Berks, the noise grew worse when the number of users reached 100,000 per year. No such correlation was found at Ogontz.)

During the 1983-84 academic year, the libraries at both locations became particularly popular social gathering places. Student questionnaires administered by university officials at that time rated both libraries very highly. Quiet conversations became loud conversations. Noisy group activities sometimes escalated into mischief. Students who wanted a quiet place to study began to complain.

Complaints started at Berks as early as October when students preparing a persuasive speech advocating weekend library hours received more comments about the excessive noise level than the additional hours. The complaints culminated in a letter in May, 1984 to the Campus Executive Officer from the Organization Assisting Returning Students asking that the library become the quiet study area on campus that it was meant to be. The group shared the letter with the librarian before sending it. Their letter represented the first formal move by students to promote quiet in the library.

Complaints at Ogontz began in February. By May, the noise problem in the library was being discussed by the Student Government Association, the Faculty Senate, sociology classes and the campus administration.

As they had in the past, both libraries tried various small measures in an effort to get things under control. The librarian at Berks tried to interest the campus administration in establishing alternative areas for the students to meet. She asked administrators, staff, and faculty for help in solving the problem. No solutions were generated. At Ogontz, similar attempts proved equally fruitless.

At both locations staff morale declined as staff members had to patrol the library to retain a semblance of order, and other library jobs went undone. Members of the respective security forces took their time in getting to the library when called for major disturbances. A breakdown in reporting procedures for disturbances occurred at both locations. At Berks, the noise situation was viewed as a library problem and the librarian was expected to deal with it. At Ogontz, the administrative support varied from office to office. It was becoming apparent that significant steps were going to have to be taken.

Solutions

Without knowledge of the other's problems, the librarians at Berks and Ogontz worked independently on solutions to the problem over the summer of 1984. The Berks Campus administrators met with the librarian and the head of security. Breakdowns in reporting were identified and the proper reporting procedures reviewed. To ensure that incidents are properly reported to the Business Manager and the Dean of Student Services, the library staff member who calls for security assistance now writes up a brief summary of the incident and forwards it to them. This summary does not replace the security report, but does ensure that each incident is reported. The Dean of Student Services notifies the librarian of action taken on the incident. The staff members no longer feel that they are on their own when dealing with unruly students. Faculty were notified of the plans to maintain a quiet atmosphere and asked to frequent the library building to help lend a more academic atmosphere.

A change in layout was a major component of the intervention. All group tables and twenty-six lounge chairs were removed and placed in storage. Only fourteen lounge chairs remained and these were in a low problem area and used mostly for sleeping. Seating at the index tables was reduced by one third and signs were placed on each tier of tables, noting that area was for index use only and requesting that users not block access to the indexes. Carrels were arranged so users could not sit side by side and were placed far enough apart to discourage seated conversations. The library main room seating was down now from the original 290 seats to 173 seats.

The library no longer provided group study space. Students who wished to study in a group were told to seek space elsewhere on campus. Reserve reading policies were relaxed to permit material to leave the building for group use. At the start of Fall Semester, the librarian and library secretary reinforced the public service staff monitoring by working at carrels in the main rooms during the hours of heaviest use. All staff members asked talkers to continue their conversations outside the library and return later for quiet individual study. The library staff no longer needed to determine whether a group was studying together or holding a social conversation.

At Ogontz, the librarian met with the Campus Executive Officer and the Campus Business Officer. With their cooperation, several physical changes were made in the library. The stacks on all three floors were moved so that there were no longer large areas where groups could congregate. Carrel tops were screwed on to all large tables so that groups could not study together. The only lounge chairs kept were those directly in front of the reference desk. More tables were put outside the library in the lobby area so that students were encouraged to congregate outside the library.

Other changes were also made. Rules and regulations regarding conduct were posted at the door and listed in the student handbook next to the list of services provided. A list of empty classrooms which could be used for group study was posted. The librarian spoke before an assembly of all entering freshmen outlining the services and rules of the library and asking for student cooperation. Group study rooms were no longer available and only individual study was permitted in the library.

Probably the most significant change was that two older males were hired to sit at the entrance of the library and collect student identification cards as students came in, and return them as they left. Since University policy required students to have their ID's with them at all times and surrender them if asked to do so by any University staff member, this was just an extension of University rules. The library staff now could identify everyone in the library and could send the ID's of disruptive students to the Dean if necessary.

Conclusions

Efforts have paid off at both libraries.

Starting in the Fall, 1984, there was a remarkable difference at both libraries. The change has been noted by faculty and students through comments, reports, and editorials in the Ogontz papers. Since so many variables were introduced at one time, it is difficult, if not impossible, to determine what had an effect. Possible considerations are:

1. The physical changes in the library layout help to break old habits and force a change in behavior.

2. The students know the library staff is serious about maintaining quiet and are responding to the efforts.

3. The "troublemakers" have graduated, reformed, flunked out, or no longer come to the library because "it isn't any fun anymore." Some former troublemakers have actually been observed studying.

4. Since students at Ogontz can be identified easily by their surrendered ID cards, and those cards can be confiscated and sent to the Dean, the students are wary of making trouble.

5. Since behavior in general is better, the occasional reminder that is necessary from a staff member has more impact than constant nagging.

6. Furniture arrangements no longer encourage socializing.

The current solutions may no longer work or even be necessary with a new group of students, but for the present they have eliminated a volatile situation. Perhaps librarians have become too interested in making libraries attractive to all users instead of the right user. Perhaps librarians are too enchanted with numbers of users to justify more space, staff, books, etc. We do not advocate a return to the hush, hush days, but we do agree with Reid that we have an obligation to our users to provide a quiet atmosphere for study and reflection.[15]

REFERENCES

1. Nazir Ahmad, "Problem of Discipline in College Libraries," New Library World 76 (Oct. 1975): 203-4.

2. Paul D. Luyben, Leonard Cohen, Rebecca Conger, and Selby U. Gration, "Reducing Noise in a College Library," College and Research Libraries 42, no. 5 (Sept. 1981): 470-481.

3. Charles P. Bird and Dawn D. Puglisi, "Noise Reduction in an Undergraduate Library," Journal of Academic Librarianship 10 (Nov. 1984): 272-277.

4. David Reid, "The Sound of Silence," New Library World 83 (July 1982): 90-91.

5. "Quiet vs. Noisy Patrons: Erecting Noise Barriers," Library Journal 104, no. 2 (Jan. 15, 1979): 145-6.

6. Luyben, Cohen, Conger and Gration, "Reducing Noise," p. 474.

7. Reid, "Sound of Silence," p. 91.

8. Ahmad, "Problem of Discipline in College Library," p. 204.

9. Mary Gregory, Comment on Ahmad Article, New Library World 76 (Dec. 1975): 254.

10. Ibid.

11. Ibid.

12. Bird and Puglisi, "Noise Reduction in an Undergraduate Library," p. 277.

13. Luyden, Cohen, Conger, and Grafton, "Reducing Noise in a College Library," pp. 470-481.

14. Bird and Puglisi, "Noise Reduction in an Undergraduate Library," pp. 272-277.

15. Reid, "Sound of Silence," p. 91.

ROBOT AT THE REFERENCE DESK?

Karen F. Smith
Lockwood Library
State University of New York at Buffalo

Abstract. Libraries seeking to enhance the productivity of reference librarians might consider ways to tap librarian expertise while the librarians themselves are off duty. This paper describes an experimental computer program designed to provide reference assistance for federal documents in a separate government documents department during hours when the regular staff members are not available. By making choices from a series of menus the patron conducts his or her own reference interview and is given a short list of appropriate reference books to consult. Difficulties to be overcome in the development of expert systems for use in reference work are discussed.

Keywords and Phrases. Bibliographic Instruction, Expert Systems, Government Documents, Microcomputers, Reference.

BACKGROUND

"Robot Performs Household Chores,"[1] "Robot Chosen for Commencement Speaker,"[2] "Robot Joins Police,"[3] "Robot Nurse Reacts to Voice Requests,"[4] "Robot Helps Perform Brain Surgery,"[5] "Robot Documents Librarian to be Tested at University,"[6]--these are actual headlines--all, except the last one, probably factual. The robot librarian, unfortunately, is still just a dream.

I say "unfortunately" because a robot librarian might be just the thing to relieve us from overwork, burnout, boredom, and frustration. Academic reference librarians are caught up in a situation where there are too few people to do the work that needs to be done; the job keeps expanding; the reference sources proliferate; information retrieval becomes increasingly complex; and, in spite of all our efforts at bibliographic instruction, naive end users continue to parade through our turnstiles. We are committed to making our users "library literate" but how many times can you explain how to find periodicals in the library without sounding like a robot yourself?

Two years ago our library experienced severe staff cuts and I found myself the sole librarian in the government documents department. The department was open 90 hours per week. We had a collection of 350,000 items classified and shelved by Superintendent of Documents (SuDoc) numbers but not cataloged. Students were coming in day and night seeking assistance. Professors were asking for tours and bibliographic instruction sessions. What could I do? At first I tried to cope by depending more on the clerical staff and the student assistants to provide patron assistance. We hired graduate students to work nights and weekends. But, it soon became apparent that training student assistants to do reference work would be an endless, repetitive, and extremely time consuming task. It just didn't seem like an effective way to increase the productivity of the librarian.

At about the same time, articles about expert systems began to appear in computer journals. Artificial intelligence research was beginning to pay off. Systems had been developed which could do real work and it seemed to me that this was exactly what the library world needed to liberate their experts.

THE PROJECT

If a computer could diagnose bacterial infections and prescribe treatment why couldn't a computer diagnose an information need and prescribe a reference book to solve the problem? Furthermore, the articles said that a secondary function of the expert system was training aspiring but neophyte experts, and I figured it would be easier to teach the student assistants how to tap into a computer system than to teach them everything I had learned during fifteen years of working with documents.

I had no idea how to create an expert system but I gathered from the articles that you needed a person called a knowledge engineer. The knowledge engineer talks to the expert about what the expert knows and how he does what he does. Expert systems are based on the premise that the problem-solving ability of the expert is an outgrowth of his knowledge base. If that knowledge can be identified and transferred to a computer then the computer can also solve problems. It is the knowledge engineer's job to extract the pertinent information from the expert's head and program the computer accordingly.

Not surprisingly, there was a professor in our computer science department who was involved in expert systems research. More amazing was the fact that he was interested in how reference librarians "do their thing" and he was willing to work with me on such a project. We got a small grant, hired a graduate student, and proceeded to investigate the feasibility of developing a computer assisted government documents reference capability. By the end of the summer we had a program written in LISP, designed to be used by an ordinary person, which would lead the person through a decision process to pinpoint the most useful of the fifty or so reference books in the department for that person's particular need.

The system is limited, by design, to just one step in the reference process: the step where the reference librarian chooses a reference book to satisfy the patron's information need. We give the patron the call number of the book and assume that s/he can find it on the shelves and figure out how to use it. The reference interview is handled by providing an overview of government produced information in the form of menus and letting the patron choose the area which most closely matches his inquiry. The basic choice is whether the person is looking for a specific document or looking for information on a topic. (See Sample Search)

PROBLEMS

Grappling with a real project such as this is a good way to experience first hand the problems facing artificial intelligence research. The first problem involves specifying a suitable domain for the expert system. The knowledge based systems that have been developed up to now, even the commercially successful ones, operate on a rather small body of facts as compared to the total body of recorded knowledge which is the domain of the general reference librarian. The ability of the librarian to switch mental gears instantly and place each new inquiry in its proper context is the most difficult feat for the computer to replicate.

Expert systems operate in specialized, well-defined subject areas, whereas government publishing gets into all subject areas. So there was some question about whether government documents librarianship was a manageable domain for an expert system. I reasoned that the bibliographic knowledge of the documents librarian is less dependent on subject expertise than on other factors. Whether the librarian recommends using the Publications Reference File or the Monthly Catalog is not so much dependent on the topic of the inquiry as it is on factors such as the purpose of the inquiry, time period involved, or specificity of information available to work with. Government documents is a specialty area within librarianship. It is an area often handled separately in research guides. Thus it seemed reasonable to try to develop an expert system to handle the types of questions fielded by the documents librarian.

On the other hand, the domain must be complicated enough to make good use of the capabilities of the computer. If you can describe fifty document reference tools on a handout with a chart showing when to use what, why do you need a fancy computerized system? My premise is that people won't read the descriptions of fifty reference books. They want individualized attention. And they don't want to learn about CIS Index when what they need is ASI. Most librarians concede that government documents reference is complicated. You can make do with the Monthly Catalog if you have to but there are times when other tools do the job more quickly. We decided that a system that would direct a library patron to one or more of the fifty most used reference tools in the documents department would be a system worth developing.

After you have specified the domain, the next problem is to identify the knowledge which one must have to operate in that domain. What does the expert need to know before making a decision? What are the facts which lead to a particular conclusion? What rules of thumb does the expert use? Most of us don't think about what we do, we just do it. So, figuring out how we do it can be a time consuming, although valuable, process. There are those who believe that this is the most important aspect of expert systems research. Capturing knowledge which has never before been written down is a contribution in and of itself. However, transferring knowledge from the human expert to the computer system is proving to be the bottleneck slowing down the advancement of expert systems development. If the knowledge engineer is unfamiliar with the field of expertise, the process is even slower.

My knowledge engineer, a graduate student in computer science, had never worked on an expert system before so we proceeded in a rather ad hoc manner. Actually, we were not atypical. This whole field of endeavor is so new that there are few established methods. We had two things to work with: the list of reference tools and a collection of reference questions asked in the department during the previous 18 months. We operated from both ends toward the middle.

From the collection of reference questions we knew that the service we perform most often is helping people locate specific documents already known to them. In the case of federal documents this means identifying the SuDoc number; a relatively straightforward procedure when the title and date are known and easy to program. The more difficult task was dealing with requests for information on a topic, for that required providing a conceptual framework for the government documents domain. Branch of government, type of answer needed, time period, type of reference book...nothing was quite adequate and we never did solve this problem to our complete satisfaction. I felt I was delving into the fundamental mysteries of the universe. I still keep hoping for one of those Ah Ha!! experiences where the big picture suddenly becomes clear and all the pieces fall neatly into place.

However, in addition to the supply of reference questions, we also had our reference tools as a resource to guide us. We asked, "What is this book good for? What does it do?" Library card catalogs, for the most part, do not describe reference books adequately. The people who can benefit from CIS Index are not going to be looking in the subject catalog under Law--United States--Indexes. And how is the card United States--Statistics going to reveal the power of ASI Index? Even reference librarians sometimes have trouble finding sources in the card catalog when they know they exist but have forgotten the exact title. A computerized reference system lends itself to in-depth indexing to bring out the special features of every reference tool. Many reference books have secondary uses, hidden information that only the frequent user is aware of. The computer makes it possible to find those secret gems again because the computer never forgets. When you hand out the U.S. Government Manual do you always remind the patron that the defunct agencies listed in Appendix A are not included in the index?

By working with what the people wanted to know and with what the reference books had to offer, we developed an outline of government information resources which is pragmatic, if not elegant. The next big problem was how to communicate with the computer. Although there are computers on the market that respond to voice commands and there are computers that talk, science is very far from developing a computer system which would listen to a person's voiced request and respond like a librarian. So, a natural language interface not yet being feasible, we limited ourselves to a menu based system. Menu choices have the advantage of being readily understood by both people and computers. Expert systems that demand communication in a specialized language will not be appropriate for libraries.

Twenty years ago, Jesse Shera wrote about automation and the reference librarian. He said, "The important point...is that the machine problems per se are well on the way to solution; the great unsolved problems are those which are fundamental to the reference situation itself. In short, we can now build the machines...but we do not know how to use them intelligently in the reference library environment. The machines are ready for us, or very soon will be, but we are still very far from being ready for machines."[7] Today, I believe, we are ready; not eager perhaps; but accepting of the fact that the computer will occupy a position of importance in the reference setting. Computers never get tired, or cross, or bored. They have the potential to provide a consistent, if minimal, level of service at the reference desk, freeing the librarian to work on problems requiring more creativity or demanding greater intellectual effort.

SAMPLE SEARCH

Welcome to the Documents Department. This system will help you find reference books for U.S. documents. If you need New York State or Canadian documents, please see the librarian. The key to the federal documents collection is the Superintendent of Documents (SuDoc) number. The SuDoc number arranges documents on the shelves by issuing agency, not necessarily by subject. If you have a citation which includes the SuDoc number, you can proceed directly to the shelves. Otherwise you will be directed to various catalogs and indexes in the reference collection where SuDoc numbers can be located. The following are typical SuDoc numbers: EP 1.2:L44/3   Y4.G79/2:M64   LC 1.1:982. Do you wish to continue? Type 'yes' or 'no' and press RETURN.

****

YES

****

Are you looking for:

1. a particular document for which you have a title?
2. a particular document for which you have some number such as a bill number?
3. information on some subject?

Select your choice by entering 1, 2, or 3 and press RETURN.

****

3

****

Do you want:

1. Biographical information?
2. Numeric data?
3. Laws concerning your subject?
4. Regulations concerning your subject?
5. Court cases concerning your subject?
6. Executive orders or presidential statements?
7. Information produced by the Congress?
8. Bills concerning your subject?
9. Names, addresses, or phone numbers?
10. Information contained in treaties?
11. Information in technical reports?
12. Information about grants, fellowships, or jobs?
13. Periodical articles?
14. General information from pamphlets or books?
15. Something not covered above?

Select 1-15 by entering the appropriate number, and press RETURN.

****

1

****

Use the following sources:

1. The Official Congressional Directory located in the reference collection, DOC REF JK1011. See the heading 'Biographies' in the front of the book and the Individual Index in the back.
2. The CIS Index located on the index table, DOC REF Z1223 A22. This reference tool can be used for information covering 1970 to the present.
3. The Congressional Record located in the reference collection and the stacks under SuDoc number X/(session of Congress). See the annual index for the year the person died, was appointed, or otherwise became prominent.
4. The Cumulative Subject Index to the Monthly Catalog located in the reference collection, DOC REF Z1223 A182. See the heading 'Biography' as well as the names of individuals. 5. The Biographical Directory of the American Congress located in the Lockwood reference collection, Ref JK1010 A5 1971. 6. The Congressional Staff Directory located in the reference collection, Ref JK1012 C66.

REFERENCES

1. Los Angeles Times (June 22, 1984).

2. Washington Post (May 1, 1983).

3. Los Angeles Times (January 20, 1984).

4. Buffalo News (April 14, 1985).

5. Buffalo News (April 18, 1985).

6. Library Journal 110:30 (February 1, 1985).

7. Jesse Shera, "Automation and the Reference Librarian," RQ 3:7 (July 1964).

ONLINE SEARCHING AND THE RESEARCH PROCESS

Patricia Tegler
Kirkland & Ellis
Chicago, Illinois

and

Connie Miller
University of Illinois at Chicago
Chicago, Illinois

Abstract. Under the dominating influence of the concepts of recall and precision, online database searches have been evaluated in terms of the characteristics of the bibliographies they produce. This static, product-oriented approach ignores the interactive potential of online files and places online searching outside of the organic and creative aspects of the research process. The relevance of online databases, and of the information specialists who use them or teach others to use them, to the process of research depends upon their ability to contribute to a trial-and-error reformulation of problems under investigation.

Keywords and Phrases. Online searching; database searching; research process; recall; precision; information retrieval.

Despite evidence that researchers seek information in ways which are quite different from a logical linear search strategy model, librarians persist in relating to the information seeking process as if it were static and product-oriented. Even online searching, which is generally considered to be flexible and interactive, is viewed merely as an alternate method of compiling a bibliography. The bibliography is considered a fixed and final product to be measured exclusively according to the limited variables of recall and precision. By having such a restricted view of online searching and its potential benefits to researchers, librarians fail to take full advantage of their role in the academic-research community. If librarians wish to be relevant to researchers, and to offer valuable services to an important constituency, they must fully understand the organic nature of research and the ways that scholars seek information. They must further understand and facilitate the significant way that online searching can contribute to and enhance the research process.

The view of research as a linear, highly structured, logical process has been challenged by studies which indicate that scholars work in ways which can best be described as cyclical, organic, and intuitive.[1] These illogical and intuitive approaches to research mirror themselves in seemingly random, haphazard approaches to locating pertinent information. Rather than following systematic library search strategies, scholars generally employ less structured methods, such as browsing, consulting with colleagues, or tracing footnotes and bibliographies. Printed indexes, by their very nature, tend to limit creative, cyclical interaction between researchers and information. Online systems, on the other hand, have the potential to facilitate highly interactive seeker-information dialogues, just the type of interchange which is integral and essential to the trial-and-error[2] process involved in research. To date, however, this potential for interaction and its corresponding benefits to the scholar have not been fully realized. Further, the limited ways in which online searches have been evaluated have hindered a full understanding of the organic nature of the online process.

A key to exploiting the potential of the online process for researchers lies in understanding the distinction between seeking information on "topics" and seeking information on "problems." Swanson claims that "creative scientific research does not begin with a 'topic' but with a problem -- a researcher must be puzzled, curious, in a sense 'bothered' about something."[3] As scholars research a "problem," the questions they ask and the information they seek shifts and changes. Each new finding alters what follows. "Research," as Maurice Line describes it, "is a process that does not allow for too formal organization."[4] Integral to the loose structure of research is the information seeking behavior of researchers. Stoan states that "scholars...follow no mechanical procedure of thinking up a topic, doing background reading on it..., going through the card catalog..., consulting indexes for articles," etc.[5] Instead they most frequently locate additional information through the bibliographies of previously identified material. This bibliographic tracking technique closely approximates the actual research process. It is organic and cyclical and manifests what Swanson describes as the trial-and-error, problem-oriented process of information retrieval.[6]

This trial-and-error process of information seeking is quite different from a highly structured search strategy approach, and unlike it, does not result in a complete, final bibliography. In trial-and-error searching both the process of the search and its products can lead the researcher to alter the original understanding of the problem, and may lead to additional sources of information. The traditional methods of evaluating information searches, recall and precision, have completely overlooked this generative, creative aspect of a search. By evaluating the product and not the process, recall and precision limit our understanding of information searches and fail to measure them effectively.

Recall and precision measure a specific retrieved bibliography within the context of a particular database. Recall is the percentage of relevant documents retrieved out of all relevant documents in the database. If all possible relevant items are retrieved from the database or databases, the bibliography has achieved 100 percent recall. Precision is the percentage of relevant documents retrieved of all the documents retrieved. If half of the documents in the bibliography are relevant, its precision rate is 50 percent. Let us assume that for a particular topic there are 200 relevant citations in a database. A search for that topic results in a bibliography of 160 citations. Eighty of the citations are relevant. The search has achieved a recall rate of 40%, or 80 of 200, and a precision rate of 50%, or 80 of 160.

Both recall and precision depend on relevance, an extremely difficult concept to measure. Harter summarizes two different types of relevance which have been identified:

> The first type of relevance is "on the topic," which is the kind of relevance that would apply in subject searches. A document is relevant to a topical query if it is on the subject named by the requester. Relevance in this sense can be judged by an individual or by a community of experts; it is objective and involves public knowledge. The second type of relevance is similar to what Kemp and others have referred to as "pertinence" -- it is a subjective, private "creation of new knowledge" by the requester in the context of a personal information need. In this sense, relevance is not a property of a document and a request, but is the property of a document and a requester.[7]

Measurement of recall and precision is generally based on the identification of relevance according to the first, more objective meaning of the term. Search results get high marks for precision when a large percentage of the citations retrieved appear to be "on the topic." The specific information needs of the requester may or may not be met by these highly precise results. Recall and precision, therefore, measure the performance of the database or system. They do not and cannot measure the value of a search to a requester.

The concept of recall itself is a highly questionable one. In the first place, recall cannot be accurately estimated. Using either definition of relevance it is impossible to determine the total number of documents in a database which are relevant to a given request or requester. Secondly, total recall is rarely desirable or valuable. The retrieval of all relevant documents would frequently constitute too much information, and a surplus can be as problematic as a deficiency. Furthermore, recall can only measure a specific bibliography against a hypothetically relevant portion of a database. It measures the value of the search process itself, therefore, only in terms of a quantifiable product.

To be an important part of research, however, the process of an online search and the products of that search must move beyond the restrictions of recall and precision. Hawkins, Bates, Vigil, and others have described heuristic techniques, like title and descriptor scanning, citation pearl growing, the "notting" out of previous sets, and "interactive scanning," which help a searcher make more effective use of online file capabilities.[8] But, the best techniques can still be limited by a topical, recall-and-precision dominated approach. Consider, for example, a search of the ERIC database for citations on end-user searching. Since no thesaurus term, "end-user" currently exists, a searcher could develop a group of synonymous terms using the thesaurus or begin with a free-text approach and locate synonyms by printing several citations in the title-descriptor format. Terms like Online-Systems, Information-Retrieval, or Information-Seeking could be combined with Training, User-Satisfaction, or Surveys to result in high recall. Limiting the combinations to precise user groups, e.g. College-Faculty or Health-Personnel, could increase precision. A systematic process of notting out already examined sets could eliminate needless duplication. Logically, this technique of framing an information request in terms of statically defined synonyms could not be faulted.

Titles and descriptors function, however, as more than static synonyms. Words which name or describe books or articles act as signposts, embodying conceptual approaches to research or indicating directions taken. In this fuller sense, they function as powerful disseminators of information whose importance lies less with their potential for becoming part of online search logic and more with their potential to reshape a research question. A logical combination of topical synonyms for the term endusers is directed toward the development of a final product: a high recall and/or high precision bibliography. Interacting with words as signposts begins the generative process of reformulating an original information request. This generative process depends upon a willing suspension of logic, a leap, that is, into the illogical or intuitive world of pertinence.[9] Harter calls an illogically interactive search a "problem-oriented" online inquiry which is "an integral part of science itself."[10]

How could the search for end-user searching citations have been different? "Full service document delivery: our likely future" is one title that a free text search of ERIC would retrieve. This citation appears minimally relevant at best; none of the logical synonym combinations listed above would retrieve it. By suspending logic, however, and responding to the words in the title, a researcher intent on developing an end-user searching program in an academic library might alter direction considerably, including in the development of the program an online document ordering option.

Whether logically or illogically conducted, an online search results in a bibliographic product. Like the words in titles or descriptors, the importance of this product lies less with its potential to supply information on a topic and more with its potential to alter the direction of research. Each document from the bibliography, while potentially of direct use for its content, also performs the "indirect function...of stimulating a reformulation of (a) request."[11] In addition, each document is a primary source, the bibliography of which provides an entry for the researcher into the literature of the field. Because "the primary literature indexes itself, and does so with greater comprehensiveness, better analytics, and greater precision than does the secondary literature,"[12] whether the bibliography achieves high recall or consists of citations precisely relevant to the researcher's topic is immaterial. The bibliographic product of an online search functions as a gateway into a citation network and, thus, participates in the cyclical, organic process of research.

Viewed statically or as ends in themselves, neither the process nor the product of an online search can be anything but ancillary to research. A logical search based on heuristic techniques with a high recall or high precision bibliographic product will, almost by default, result in articles or books through which a researcher can gain entry into a citation network. The best bibliographic product, however, the one which includes illogically relevant (pertinent) as well as logically relevant citations, will only result from a search in which information disseminated (through words in titles and descriptors) during the process contributes to a reformulation of the researcher's request. Illogically relevant or pertinent sources will open up citation networks of their own. This cyclical organic type of search operates according to what Abraham Kaplan calls its own "logic-in-use, (an) internal logic...(which,) as it germinates and develops...dictates the sources sought out at each stage along the way."[13] By responding to the document delivery concept, the researcher developing the end-user searching program opened a whole new avenue of literature to explore. Because "logic-in-use" is essential to an organic, research-related online search, Harter predicts the inevitability of end-user searching.[14] While his prediction is undeniably correct, the idea that online searches integral to the research process must operate according to a "logic-in-use" seems related less to who performs a search than to how well a search is performed. If librarians who perform online searches for researchers or who offer online training to end-users fail to understand and to communicate the vital and essential implications of the cyclical, organic illogical nature of research for the process and products of an online search they risk becoming irrelevant.

REFERENCES

1. Stephen K. Stoan discusses, in some detail, research on the research process in his article, "Research and Library Skills: an Analysis and Interpretation," College and Research Libraries 45(2):99-109, 1984.

2. Don R. Swanson, "Information Retrieval as a Trial-and-Error Process," Library Quarterly 47(2):128-148; 1977; and Swanson, "Libraries and the Growth of Knowledge," Library Quarterly 50(1):112-134; 1980.

3. Swanson, "Information Retrieval," 138.

4. Stoan, "Research and Library Skills," 102.

5. Ibid., 102.

6. Swanson, "Information Retrieval," 138-139.

7. Stephen P. Harter, "Scientific Inquiry: a Model for Online Searching," Journal of the American Society for Information Science 35(2):114; 1984.

8. Marcia J. Bates, "The Fallacy of the Perfect Thirty-Item Online Search," RQ 24(1):13-20; 1984; Peter J. Vigil, "The Psychology of Online Searching," Journal of the American Society for Information Science 34(4):281-287; 1983; and Donald T. Hawkins and Robert Wagers, "Online Bibliographic Search Strategy Development," Online 6(3):12-19; 1982.

9. D. A. Kemp, "Relevance, Pertinence and Information System Development," Information Storage and Retrieval 10(2):37-47; 1974. Kemp's article includes an excellent discussion and definition of pertinence.

10. Harter, "Scientific Inquiry," 114.

11. Swanson, "Information Retrieval," 138.

12. Stoan, "Research and Library Skills," 103.

13. Ibid, 102, as derived from Abraham Kaplan The Conduct of Inquiry: Methodology for Behavioral Science (San Francisco: Chandler, 1964), 3-11.

14. Harter, "Scientific Inquiry," 114.

LIBERAL ARTS COLLEGES, ONLINE SEARCHING AND ECONOMIC SURVIVAL

Celia Wall
Murray State University Libraries
Murray, KY

Keywords and Phrases. Online searching. Liberal arts colleges. Financial exigency. Economic conditions. Abstracts and indexes.

The private, liberal arts college is the oldest institution of higher education in the United States. For 350 years, it has assumed the responsibility for providing general education experiences for the student wishing not only to prepare for a career but also for the life of an informed citizen.

The last decade or so has seen an economic blight affecting higher education in the United States, and many of the private, liberal arts colleges have been affected more forcefully than have been universities or publically-owned colleges. Indeed, some private colleges have failed and have closed their doors. Others, while not in any immediate danger of economic collapse, find themselves continually faced with unpleasant and difficult decisions dictated by economic conditions. These unpleasant and difficult decisions affect the colleges' libraries and force some unpleasant choices.

This "Idea Brief" is designed to provide some relief for the libraries of small, private, liberal arts colleges. It proposes the substitution of online search capability in the college library for the more expensive indexing and abstracting services.

In many of the libraries to which this "Idea Brief" is addressed, expensive indexing and abstracting services are not in abundance, but two of these, Biological Abstracts and Chemical Abstracts, are of a sine qua non nature to the departments which make use of them. It is the use to which departments in the small liberal arts college put these two abstracting services that will allow the proposal I make here to be successful.

Studies have been done to investigate the substitution of online searching for print subscriptions,[1] but most of these have been conducted in larger libraries, in larger institutions, than the small liberal arts college.[2] In the departments of biology or chemistry in the liberal arts college, the emphasis is overwhelmingly on teaching and these departments use Biological and Chemical Abstracts for two purposes. One of these is to teach students how to access the literature of biology and chemistry. For this purpose, a current subscription to the abstracts is not necessary; last year's volumes will serve this purpose admirably. The other purpose for which the abstracting services are used is current literature searching by faculty. But then, the liberal arts college has little or no research mission and its faculty are expected primarily to teach; little is expected in the way of research and scholarship. Thus, the use of the abstracting services for current literature searching can be expected to be low.

In light of the foregoing, the proposal here is to cancel subscriptions to both Biological Abstracts and to Chemical Abstracts, to retain existing issues for teaching the use of these abstracts, and to establish online search services in the library to allow for searching of current biological and chemical literature. The amount of searching of current literature can be expected to be minimal because of the posture of the college and, thus, the savings can be shifted to other purposes in the library.

REFERENCES

1. Pfaffenberger, Ann, and Sandy Echt. "Substitution of SciSearch and Social SciSearch for Their Print Versions in an Academic Library." Database 3 (March 1980): 63-71.

2. Lancaster, F.W., and Herbert Goldhor. "The Impact of Online Services on Subscriptions to Printed Publications." Online Review 5 (1981): 301-311.

TECHNOLOGY

THE OPEN SYSTEM INTERCONNECTION AS A BUILDING BLOCK IN ELECTRONIC NETWORKING

Richard W. Boss
Information Systems Consultants Inc.
Bethesda, Maryland

Abstract. This position paper discusses the Open System Interconnection Reference Model (the OSI), a framework within which standards are being developed for the linking of computer systems of all types, and being used for different applications. It is the author's contention that the library community should develop its standards within the framework of the OSI so that library systems can link not only with one another, but also with other systems in their organizations.

Keywords and Phrases. Open System Interconnection; OSI; Interfacing; Electronic networking.

ELECTRONIC NETWORKING

No aspect of library automation development appears to have stimulated as much discussion in the past year as networking, or the linking of different computer systems. There were more than a dozen presentations on the topic at the Annual Meeting of the American Library Association in 1985 and at least three vendors have announced networking products in the past year. Several presentations have been scheduled for this ACRL Conference.

This position paper discusses the Open System Interconnection Reference Model (the OSI), a framework within which standards are being developed for the linking of computer systems of all types, and being used for different applications. It is the author's contention that the library community should develop its standards within the framework of the OSI so that library systems can link not only with one another, but also with other systems in their organizations.

The Matheson Model

The Matheson[1] report recommendation that academic health sciences centers and hospitals should take immediate steps to implement a network that facilitates the flow of recorded knowledge can be considered a model for the future of other libraries. The report envisions the interconnection of many computer systems in an institution to that of the library as well as the library's to that of other libraries. However, most academic health sciences centers and hospitals have several computer systems. Political forces are often responsible for a decentralized approach to automation, but an equally significant factor is that practical economics dictate that "off-the-shelf" software be used as much as possible. Such software may require different hardware configurations for different applications. For example, most integrated library system software relies on operating systems and programming languages not commonly used for medical records and financial applications. The creation of a network which spans applications will, therefore, require linkages among different systems.

When one system is linked to another because different functions are on separate machines or because there is a need to accomplish the transfer of information between separate systems, the systems are said to be "interfaced."

Homogeneous and Heterogeneous Systems

The other system to which an interface is sought may be one with nearly identical or "homogeneous" hardware and software, or it may be a "heterogeneous" system which has completely different hardware and software. Interfaces to heterogeneous systems --be they single-function systems or integrated multi-function systems--are more difficult to achieve than linkages to homogeneous systems. This is due not only to the technical differences between the systems, but also because the vendors who supplied the systems involved may not be willing to cooperate in the development of interfaces. Their reluctance may be due to competitive reasons or because there is not enough potential return from future sales to justify the expense of interface development.

Types of Interfaces

For a number of years the only interface available was tape transfer. A magnetic tape produced from one system was loaded into another system. In the case of libraries, the Library of Congress facilitated this interface by developing the MARC (MAchine Readable Cataloging) format for bibliographic records in 1968. However, even today there are systems which can accept MARC formatted records, but cannot retain or output them.

Tape transfer involves considerable delays. It usually takes hours to output and load a tape of several thousand records, and there are set-up costs involved. Organizations which rely on tape interfaces usually schedule tape loading no more than once a week to once a month. While some organizations find this an acceptable way of transferring information, those concerned with timeliness have sought to pursue other types of interfaces.

There are three major types of non-tape interfaces:

- Terminal-to-computer
- Computer-to-computer via ad hoc implementation
- Computer-to-computer via OSI

Terminal-to-computer interfaces permit a terminal to log directly onto a system and perform limited operations. The usual subset of functions supported by a terminal-to-computer interface include: searching the data base, leaving messages and transferring information. With a terminal-to-computer interface, the terminal operator has to know the commands and procedures for using the other system. This can be a challenge when interfaces to several systems are maintained.

Computer-to-computer interfaces involve the physical linkages of computers so that they can exchange information. In addition to supporting data exchange, a computer-to-computer interface enables a terminal on one computer system to access the other system via the computer on the first system, and perform all of the same activities in a manner transparent to the terminal operator.

Interfaces which use the OSI model require that each separate system be able to meet two sets of standards: the internal standards of the particular system, and the common, external, standards of OSI. When the separate systems need to link with one another, they can do so using external networks designed to accommodate the OSI standards.

Linking Homogeneous Systems. Computer-to-computer interfaces, involving homogeneous systems in the same computer room, are well established. They usually involve wiring the machines together. Telecommunications and special networking software, rather than direct wiring, are required to establish computer-to-computer interfaces among homogeneous systems which are at some distance from one another.

Such interfaces are well within the state-of-the-art but they were not achieved in the library environment until mid-1984. Several vendors now offer software which enables a search to be started on the local integrated library system and saved for searching on another remote system from the same vendor without rekeying. Each system that participates in the network is assigned a code which allows users to identify the system(s) they wish to access in a particular transaction. Some vendors provide software that makes it possible for a library to specify a default search for each terminal attached to the local system. The default search list in the local system identifies the other systems which support the data bases to be accessed in the course of processing a transaction initiated from the terminal. When a transaction is initiated at the terminal, the terminal examines the default search list. If it specifies that only the local system to which the terminal is attached should be searched, then no external systems are accessed. If the default search list includes one or more remote systems, then appropriate data accesses to the remote systems are included in the execution of the user's transaction. The user can override the default search and enter in specific instructions for the searching of other systems.

However, even when two homogeneous, integrated library systems are linked at the hardware and software levels, searching may not be easy. This is because the data bases on the two systems may not conform to the same standards. The arrangement of system files may vary considerably even though both systems were supplied by the same vendor. In most situations it will, therefore, be necessary to develop standards for common representation of data before useful computer-to-computer interfacing can be achieved.

Linking Heterogeneous Systems. Libraries seeking linkages between their systems and those of other libraries will have to anticipate that the majority of the other systems will involve the use of different hardware and software. In the library environment, linkages between heterogeneous systems have been achieved between the terminal of an integrated library system and a bibliographic utility, as well as between a turnkey system terminal and the CPU of another turnkey system, but not directly between CPUs. These are, therefore, terminal-to-computer interfaces.

The movement of bibliographic data among heterogeneous systems poses unique technical, economic and political obstacles. Historically, most of the research and applications in the area of computer-to-computer interfacing appears to have been motivated by the desire to fully utilize expensive computer resources rather than to facilitate the movement of large amounts of information. Most of the oldest computer networks in business organizations and academic institutions link large mainframe computers in several computing centers. More recent work has focused on distributed processing; the creation of multi-processor systems for large companies and government agencies that wish to decentralize their computer systems. With few exceptions, these distributed systems continue to have a highly centralized structure with most of the processing power concentrated in one large central installation. The design and structure of the files on such systems is also centrally administered and controlled. The centralized structure has evolved because highly centralized systems have been easier to design, operate and control than decentralized systems. Even though a distributed system might involve more than one hardware type, they have typically been centrally planned systems in which software could be developed for the total system by or for the system's owner. In other words, multijurisdictional problems have been avoided.

What we are seeking to interface or link in the case of libraries are several independently and fully developed library systems, or even library systems and systems committed to other applications in the same institution. Such an effort involves interfacing computer systems with different hardware and different software using various programming languages, some of them proprietary and confidential. There may also be different file structures, operational features, command languages, record access methods, indexing methods, system performance priorities, and so forth. Most important of all, the competing vendors may have little incentive to cooperate with one another.

Computer-to-computer interfaces are particularly difficult to achieve, but such direct communication between or among heterogeneous systems has the advantage of providing full access to and full control of all files, except when restrictions may be imposed for administrative reasons.

The State of Interfacing Library Systems. As of mid-1985, the most common interfaces between independent, heterogeneous, integrated library systems were terminal-to-computer interfaces. They involve the use of a terminal of one integrated library system to access the computer of another integrated library system. Such dial-up access can be readily implemented by individual organizations without depending on vendors to find solutions.

The approach is relatively simple. It is merely necessary to determine: 1) whether a dial-up port is available on the system to be accessed, 2) at what baud rate the system to be accessed transmits, 3) the willingness of the manager of the other system to allow access, 4) the procedures for signing on and off the system, and 5) the search strategies. It is also necessary to add a modem if the terminal being used to access the system does not already have one. Despite the fact that this type of interface works, it is not widely used because it is difficult to access multiple integrated library systems efficiently. Each system requires knowledge of different procedures, and the search results are difficult to use in any form other than as direct displays or printouts.

The Need to Build Networks. It is the desire of most library users to have immediate access to the latest information. Ideally, this involves access not only to an integrated library system and linkages among library systems, but also linkages between integrated library systems and remote bibliographic data bases, full-text data bases of journal literature, knowledge bases, and other information systems. In addition to providing access among such systems, interfaces should also support the use of the results of one search to formulate a search on another system and to combine the results of several searches and manipulate them using text editing, statistical and other software packages.

Obviously neither tape nor terminal-to-computer interfaces provides an appropriate solution to linking such a wide range of systems. The technical, political, and economic problems inherent in developing and maintaining a number of computer-to-computer interfaces appear overwhelming. The answer, therefore, appears to be the adoption of standards for networking. All hardware and software would be required to conform to these standards. Libraries are not the only fields in which this needs exists. Ideally, broad computer-industry-wide standards would be followed to spread the costs of their development and implementation over as wide a base as possible. The standards that currently appear most likely to be widely adopted are those of the OSI model.

Role of the International Standards Organization

The International Standards Organization (ISO) began seeking an alternative to the existing interfaces in the 1970s. The approach of the ISO has been to assume that the number of interfacing combinations among different types of computers could be reduced if it were possible to define the types of linkage required, establish standards or parameters for each category, and persuade computer manufacturers to support at least the minimal common standards for each type of interfacing. The result was the development of a network model based on the concept of an open systems interconnection (OSI).

The OSI Model. The OSI reference model is not a detailed specification for any particular network design, but a conceptual framework within which standard interconnect procedures can be defined. Once defined as protocols and implemented by computer hardware manufacturers and software designers, these procedures would enable users of different computer systems to interconnect their systems and exchange information.

The OSI model is concerned with defining those elements of a computer system that impact upon linkage to external systems. Such elements include both physical entities—such as the plug which connects a computing device to the power supply—and abstract design concepts—such as the way in which an applications program formats data for output from the system. For the purposes of the OSI model, a computing device can be a mainframe, mini- or microcomputer or a terminal which has the intelligence necessary for information processing and communication. The interconnected systems may, but need not be, products of the same vendor. The model's only requirement is that a system be connected to a physical communications medium through which access can be gained to one or more other systems. The medium can be as simple as a point-to-point communications line such as a voice-grade telephone line, or as complex as an interconnected packet-switched network such as TYMNET or Telenet.

The open systems model or concept is based on a layered architecture which segments the problems of systems linkage into different functional layers arranged in a hierarchy. Each layer has unique attributes and interacts with adjacent layers. Each layer defines a discrete task that is essential for the linking of systems, and the layers build on each other to define operations of increasing complexity. The layers defined in the OSI model and their major functions are:

- Physical layer--Permits the transfer of a simple data stream over a physical circuit.
- Data link layer--Responsible for the reliable delivery of data which direct the link, and user information, from one point to another or over a more elaborate multipoint link.
- Network layer--Selects a route from among the available data links in a network.
- Transport layer--Provides the controls to ensure end-user to end-user information transfer; the user does not have to be concerned about validating the actual movement of the information.
- Session layer--Coordinates the communications interchange between application processes which require the interfacing of separate systems.
- Presentation layer--Ensures compatible syntax among the communicating processes by adjusting data structures, formats, and codes to those used by the systems being linked.
- Application layer--Provides a window by which the user of a system gains access to the communications services provided by the OSI architecture.

The OSI layers are often described by their numerical position in the model; for example, the physical layer is Level 1, and the application layer is Level 7. An excellent detailed description of the layers is presented in Auerbach Publishers' Data Communications, a major loose-leaf service available in over 1,000 libraries.

Other communications protocols that have not been adopted as international standards are also based on layered models; for example IBM's System Network Architecture (SNA) and Digital's DECnet. These architectures, however, are homogeneous because total compatibility occurs only within one vendor's family of products. With the open systems architecture, the layered approach is used as a skeleton on which compatibility is built between heterogeneous systems.

Status of the OSI. Significant progress has been achieved in the effort to establish an open systems architecture. The architectural model was officially approved in 1983 as an international standard. Since International Standards Organization includes representatives from users, vendors, carriers, and governments, the consensus on a globally acceptable communications architecture should result in considerable progress.

Open systems compatibility is already widely available at the lower layers (layers 1-3) of the architecture. The CCITT X.25 public data network interface, for example, spans the physical, link, and network layers.

From a communications compatibility standpoint, the transport layer is the most critical. Agreement on this layer ensures that data can be moved transparently and reliably between systems, regardless of their vendors. A great deal of standard development activity has, therefore, focussed on this layer.

Some experts argue that true compatibility will never be achieved above the transport layer. However, there are already several developments for higher layers using the OSI reference model for library applications.

Library Applications of OSI. The Linked Systems Project (LSP) in the United States, which began early in 1980 to support a shared authority file, and the iNET pilot program in Canada are the two most ambitious efforts yet to use OSI for linking heterogeneous library systems. The LSP participants are the Library of Congress, RLG, and WLN. OCLC has recently decided to participate.

The communications link being established will enable the participants' heterogeneous computer systems to exchange data. The link is based on existing and emerging international standards to the fullest extent possible. Each of the institutions participating in LSP uses a minicomputer to interface with the Telenet public data network using the CCITT X.25 protocol for moving data among systems (and between terminals and computers). Software support for the X.25 protocol will be supplied by the minicomputer vendors. At the Session Control layer, the parties collaborated on program specifications based on work in process in ISO and ANSI.

LSP is designed to be extended to additional systems. The shared authority file will support the Name Authority File Service and help to overcome the barrier to effective exchange of bibliographic data caused by the frequent lack of heading consistency across systems. While the computer-to-computer link is being used for the exchange of authority data, it will also facilitate the later development of the sharing of full catalog records, location and holdings data, the transmission of interlibrary loan requests, communication with vendors, etc.

The National Information Standards Organization (Z39) is formulating standards on the basis of the protocols developed by the LSP. Work in progress includes the investigation of a mechanism for maintaining protocol parameter values, a file transfer protocol for library applications, and an intersystem interlibrary loan protocol.

In 1983, a major pilot test of interconnection was undertaken in Canada. The provision of a library network was only one of the aims of the iNET project, which represented a major effort of Canadian telephone companies to manage the commerce between online data bases and a potentially large number of users, including offices and homes. Library participants included the National Library of Canada (NLC) and several other libraries.

The NLC has reported that a network based on the OSI concept seems technically feasible. Diverse bibliographic systems can be made accessible to network users through the standard X.25 interface which governs the linkage of computers to public data networks, allowing access from a single terminal to multiple data bases at minimal up-front cost. The amount of decentralization varies according to the application. For interlibrary loan or cataloging, for example, a composite data base like NLC's DOBIS tends to be searched before a single-institution data base. A limiting factor was identified as the number of data bases which can be searched before manpower costs escalate to a point where it is no longer beneficial to use others' data.

Recommendations of the participants included the suggestion that a system should be able to look at more than one data base in response to the same search strategy, and that there be a common command language structure for accessing different data bases. A need was also seen for specific applications such as interlibrary loans and the online transmission of MARC cataloging records between systems. The Bibliographic Interest Group (BIG) in Canada is currently working on an experiment to transfer batch MARC search results from the National Library of Canada to five Canadian university libraries using the iNET approach.

CONCLUSION

The open system interconnection approach is likely to be adapted to the needs of libraries at least to connect systems at some distance from one another. In addition to the LSP and iNET efforts, OCLC is actively moving toward an open telecommunications system. The first step will be the establishment of a CCITT X.25 standard interface between OCLC and other systems such as the LSP and the various value added networks: Telenet, TYMNET, Uninet, etc. OCLC's announced objectives are to provide greater flexibility in the choice of telecommunications options and to support linkages with other systems. One of the motivations appears to be the desire to develop the OCLC system as a gateway to the various other systems to which utility participants may wish to have access. The organization has the financial resources and the private data communications network to make the concept a reality.

Any network which links libraries and other sources, and managers, of information should be developed around the OSI Reference Model because it is the only international set of standards which is widely supported by hardware manufacturers, software developers, telecommunications providers, and major segments of the library community.

REFERENCES

1. Matheson, Nina, "Academic Information in the Academic Health Sciences Center: Roles for the Library in Information Management," Journal of Medical Education, 57:10, Part 2 (October, 1982).

CD-ROM OPTICAL DISC TECHNOLOGY IN LIBRARIES:
ACCEPTANCE AND IMPLEMENTATION

Nancy L. Eaton
University of Vermont
Burlington, Vermont

and

Julie B. Schwerin
InfoTech
Pittsfield, Vermont

Abstract. A 1984 market survey reported that publishers believe libraries are likely to be early users of optical disc-based information retrieval systems and that CD-ROM technology will dominate in this arena. This paper provides a summary of the state-of-the-art of CD-ROM technology and projects the likely applications of CD-ROM by the publishing industry. It explores the ways in which librarians can make use of this new information medium.

Keywords and phrases. CD-ROM. Optical disc. Optical information retrieval systems. Compact Disc - Read Only Memory. CD-ROM and publishing. CD-ROM and libraries.

INTRODUCTION

In an October, 1984 market survey for its information industry clients, LINK Resources Corporation reported that publishers believe libraries and businesses equally receptive to the early adoption of optical disc-based information retrieval systems.[1] The survey also forecast that CD-ROM would dominate in this arena between 1985 and 1990.[2] A number of new CD-ROM products or prototypes were exhibited at the January and June, 1985 meetings of the American Library Association, signaling that librarians must be prepared to evaluate and use new optical information systems.

OPTICAL INFORMATION TECHNOLOGY OVERVIEW

Compact Disc - Read Only Memory (CD-ROM) describes both an information storage and delivery medium and a retrieval mechanism. The CD-ROM medium is a disc that looks like the compact audio discs which have become successful in the home entertainment field. Essentially they are the same thing, except that CD-ROM is intended for the storage of information rather than of music. The CD-ROM drive is similar to a compact disc player. However, instead of the output being audio signals which are understood by a stereo amplifier, the output of CD-ROM is digital pulses which are understood by a computer.

In many ways, CD-ROM is also similar to the laser videodisc, which stores movies and can be adapted for storage of digital data. Videodiscs store video and audio programming as analog signals or wave forms, whereas compact audio discs store audio programming as digital data code. When videodiscs are used to store digital data, the data must be converted to analog wave forms before the data is recorded onto the disc, and a complex controller must decode the video signals back into digital data before a computer can understand them. This operation is similar to the function of a modem which allows digital data to be carried by the analog telephone lines. However, videodiscs can store pictures as television pictures, which neither compact discs or CD-ROM can do now.

To store a picture or graphic image in digital form takes much more space on a CD-ROM than a picture in analog form takes on a videodisc. Thus, for now, CD-ROM is most applicable to textual, bibliographic, and numeric data bases in digital form; and digital videodisc is uniquely applicable to mixed content requiring both data and graphics.

Other optical disc technologies such as write-once and erasable, which are in development and which should be on the market by 1987, have different market applications and different economic bases. Erasable discs will be used like magnetic memories for active computer storage, but with much greater densities. Write-once discs will be used like Computer-Output-Microform (COM) for archival storage of such things as office correspondence or architectural drawings, with the virtue of being machine-readable, randomly accessible, removable, and (again) very high density storage. Copies of write-once media are made machine-to-machine in real time, however, rather than replicated from a master disc and thus are not as well suited for making copies as are CD-ROM or videodisc.

Digital data are recorded onto CD-ROM discs by making microscopic marks in a track around a master disc that are burned onto the master disc by a laser. Copies of the master are stamped out like records in the replication process. In the disc drive, the marks are read by a tiny beam of laser light focused below the plastic surface; thus the discs do not wear out or "crash" like magnetic discs and can be handled without damaging them. While the cost of creating the "master" disc is expensive, the cost of each copy goes down as the number of copies increases. Philips reports a mastering fee of $3,000 and a per disc cost of $20 in quantities under 50.[3] Studies done by InfoTech suggest a minimum of one hundred copies need to be made for CD-ROM to be cost effective. Thus, CD-ROM has the potential of being a very cost-efficient production system for publishers as a large-volume electronic printing medium.

Optical media in general and CD-ROM in particular have much higher densities than any other media. A typical microcomputer memory or RAM is 256K (256,000 bytes), while the capacity of a CD-ROM is 550MB (550,000,000 bytes). The capacity of a CD-ROM disc is equivalent to 1,500 floppy discs, 100,000 pages of text at 5,500 characters per page, or 5.3 days of online transmission at 1,200 BAUD line speed. The contents of the read-only discs cannot be altered, updated, or erased; to change the content, the publisher sends out an updated version. However, it is possible to print or download the data onto another machine for local manipulation.

ISSUES CRITICAL TO WIDESPREAD USE

There are a number of components necessary to promote the widespread use of CD-ROM discs as a publishing medium: (1) general availability of microcomputers; (2) general availability of CD-ROM players; (3) drivers or interfaces which link microcomputers and CD-ROM players; (4) mastering and replication facilities; (5) retrieval software; (6) standards, so that any disc can be played on any CD-ROM player; and (7) data or content. Each component is at a different stage of development.

Microcomputers

Microcomputers are now so commonly used in libraries and offices that availability or inclination to use them is no longer a major issue. Sales of computer-based workstations exceeded $4,500,000,000 in 1983.[4] The 1985 Bowker Annual reported that an estimated 45,000 microcomputers would exist in academic, public, and special libraries by the end of 1986.[5]

CD-ROM Players and Drivers

Major consumer electronic manufacturers and distributors are producing CD-ROM players, including Philips, Sony, Hitachi, and Panasonic. Digital Equipment Corporation has integrated CD-ROM into their MicroVax equipment line. The fact that major computer manufacturers are producing these players both for the audio market and digital data market increases the likelihood of a stable economic base for future production and availability.

Mastering/replication Facilities

Until the fall of 1985, CD-ROM discs could be produced only outside the United States. 3M recently finished building a facility in Wisconsin which is now in production for mastering and replication, although much of its production is devoted to compact discs. Absence of CD-ROM mastering and replication facilities in the United States has slowed the use of CD-ROM as compared to videodisc for digital data pilot projects during 1985; however, this should no longer be an issue by the end of 1986.[6]

Retrieval Software

Another component necessary to the acceptance of CD-ROM as a publishing medium is software for retrieval of data from the disc. Battelle is interested in the "packaging opportunities" of CD-ROM and the possibility of publishing the search software along with the data files on CD-ROM.[7] Those products demonstrated at the June, 1985 annual conference of the American Library Association utilized proprietary retrieval systems tailored to each application or product line. Companies such as BRS are interested in increased sales of their search software by convincing a significant number of publishers to use their software for accessing the disc content.[8] As the number of products expand, some consistency between packages to aid users would seem desirable. Also, considerable experimentation and refinement of search software will be necessary as these retrieval systems are perfected for CD-ROM applications. Retrieval from CD-ROM can be slower than online retrieval, depending upon the layout of the data on the disc, the index structures used, and the design of the retrieval software. Reliability in speed of retrieval at acceptable levels will be necessary.

Standards

The National Information Standards Organization (NISO) held a meeting in Washington, D.C. on February 25, 1985 to explore the desirability of standards for information to be placed on CD-ROM discs. Response from the group was positive, and a charge to a possible new subcommittee was drafted. The subcommittee has been appointed and it held its first meeting in Washington, D.C. in December, 1985. One of the tasks of the subcommittee is to coordinate with the American National Standards Institute's Technical Committee on Digital Optical Disc (X3B11), which is dealing with hardware standards for some optical formats by means of standardizing such media, its recording and reading systems, and other devices. Many in the industry and library community fear that the slow pace of standards committees will cause producers to forge ahead without standards. Consequently, an ad hoc group called the "High Sierra Group" made up of industry and association representatives from the American Library Association and the Information Industry Association has begun to meet informally to draft CD-ROM standards.

A clear theme at the February 25 NISO meeting was that information producers want standards only insofar as they make the hardware compatible and the location of information on the disc consistent. They appeared not to be strongly in favor of standards for content which would inhibit the proprietary benefits to be derived from the content or retrieval software.

Content or Data

In reviewing the characteristics essential to a successful CD-ROM publication program, a recent Council on Library Resources report summarizes those issues as follows: (1) An application should encompass a large amount of data in the form of a single file or a large number of small files; (2) information which is not volatile--which may require the addition of more information, but little change to existing records; (3) information for which there are many potential users to allow economies of scale to be realized in disc replication; and (4) a product which is marketable for a fixed price.[9] Due to expense of data conversion and the limitation of graphics capabilities, archival and/or graphics applications do not lend themselves to CD-ROM at this point in time. Thus, the content being seen in prototypes are bibliographic or citation data bases; and CD-ROM is being forecast for certain types of reference materials that do not contain large amounts of graphic material and for internal publishing of large-quantity manuals, inventories, company archival data bases, diagnostic software for computer systems, distribution of programs or software, and as a substitute for online storage.[10] The Council on Library Resources report stated that: "Early in 1985 several prototype commercial applications of the videodisc and CD-ROM as digital data publication media began to emerge. None were in sufficiently widespread use to permit in-depth assessment of their performance."[11] However, by the June, 1985 ALA Annual Conference, several in-production commercial systems and several new prototypes were being demonstrated:

1. Silver Platter (previously known as ISIS and IMLAC): Silver Platter was demonstrating a CD-ROM prototype system using samples of five data bases (PsycLit/PsychINFO, ERIC, EMBASE (Exerpta Medica), PAIS, and LISA. A uniform, relatively simple retrieval system aimed at the end user, using Boolean logic, was employed in the self-contained work station for all five data bases. Silver Platter expected to have three test sites by fall of 1985 for its prototype. It expects to be marketing a product by the summer of 1986.

2. LSSI: This company has transferred its MARC cataloging data base to videodisc using the LaserData digital videodisc, with up to four work stations attached to one videodisc player. The president of LSSI indicated that he expected to be using both videodisc and CD-ROM in the future, depending upon which is applicable to a particular content. Lack of production facilities for CD-ROM in the United States had slowed his experimentation with that medium during 1985.

3. Information Access Corporation: Another company using videodisc technology based on the LaserData solution, Information Access (a Ziff/Davis subsidiary) is marketing InfoTrac, available for purchase by libraries since March, 1985. InfoTrac provides access to an index of the contents of over 1,000 business, technical, legal, and general interest publications.

4. Carrolton Press: Carrolton Press, a subsidiary of International Thompson, is demonstrating a prototype videodisc-based file of MARC and REMARC bibliographic records. They also demonstrated DisCon and DisCat at the January, 1985 ALA Midwinter meeting; both are designed for cataloging and retrospective conversion support and utilize CD-ROM as a storage medium.[12]

5. The Library Corporation: This company's BiblioFile system provides the complete Library of Congress MARC English-language cataloging data base on CD-ROM compact discs. Aimed at small libraries with budgets of $50,000 to $2,500,000, this system is priced at under $5,000 (excluding the necessary IBM PC or M300 microcomputer).

6. Ingram: This library book supplier was demonstrating its inventory of titles available from Ingram on a CD-ROM disc.

7. Brodart: A vendor of library Computer-Output-Microfilm (COM) catalogs, Brodart was demonstrating the use of CD-ROM for a library network union catalog.

8. R.R. Bowker: This publisher was showing a prototype software catalog on a LaserData videodisc and drive.

In addition to the above systems, Grolier has been demonstrating the Academic American Encyclopedia using a Philips CD-ROM drive connected to the new Atari microcomputer.

UTILIZATION OF CD-ROM BY LIBRARIES

At present, the manufacturing and replication capability in the United States seems to be the basis for using videodisc rather than CD-ROM more than the attributes of the medium itself. That will change rapidly, however, as new production facilities become available in the United States during 1986. The probability is that both media will be utilized, and the need for graphics within a publication will be the determining factor once production facilities are adequate. Mixed media (graphics and data) is more applicable to videodisc, though limited graphics can be stored on CD-ROM in ASCII format.

While it is desirable for librarians to experiment with these new electronic publications in order to assess their potential, it is also important to protect the library's investment during the early stages of this technology. There are several approaches to consider. The safest approach is to use systems which are being marketed as subscriptions, whereby the publisher furnishes both hardware and software as a bundled product on an annual subscription basis. If technology changes, the publisher owns the hardware and is responsible for upgrading or replacing it for the library. If it seems desirable for the library to purchase the hardware outright, which may be less expensive, look for publications which utilize micro-computers which are plug-compatible with the CD-ROM players and drivers, so that the microcomputer can be used with a variety of players and drivers in the future. When dealing with publishers, insist on standards for disc interchangeability, so that any CD-ROM disc can be played on any manufacturer's CD-ROM player. In that way, the investment in the discs will be independent of the equipment on which the discs are played.

A major attraction of CD-ROM is its ability to house large data bases locally which heretofore have been available only through online services. Local control means unlimited searching at a fixed cost, as opposed to the variable costs of online searching. Several online data base publishers are exploring the combination of CD-ROM discs for older data and online for the most current information. For those combinations, it is desirable to have the workstation so configured that the microcomputer can be used as a dial access terminal to the online services as well as a link to the CD-ROM player, so that both the CD-ROM portion and the online portion of the data base can be searched from the same workstation.

Use of CD-ROM workstations for electronic publications will make the ergonomics of the stations important, since people may have to sit at the units for significant periods of time. Adequate lighting conditions also will be required to minimize glare from the CRT screen. This may involve some renovation or reorganization of library facilities. Above all, these units should be placed in areas and under conditions that will encourage rather than discourage their use.

SUMMARY

CD-ROM is just emerging as a new publishing medium. It has attributes which make it distinct from other optical media such as videodisc, write-once, and erasable. It lends itself to textual, bibliographic, and numeric data bases in digital form; and it is economically cost-effective where more than 100 copies can be sold. It has the virtue of unlimited local searching for a fixed price as compared to online searching. Librarians must be willing to experiment with this and other optical information systems as publishers make information available in these formats. They should also demand standards which allow discs to be played on a variety of players, so that the investment in the disc as the information medium is distinct from the investment in the equipment.

REFERENCES

1. Link Resources Corporation, Optical Disk Strategies for Electronic Publishers. (New York, October, 1984), p.79.

2. Ibid., pp. 2, 79.

3. CD Data Report, 1, No. 6 (April, 1985): pp. 2-3.

4. John Gale, "The Information Workstation: A Confluence of Technologies Including CD-ROM," Information Technology and Libraries 4, No. 2 (June, 1985): p. 137.

5. Bowker Annual of Library and Book Trade Information. 30th edition. (New York and London, R.R. Bowker Company, 1985), p. 427.

6. CD Data Report 1, No. 8 (June, 1985), p. 3.

7. Information Systems Consultants, Inc., Videodisc and Optical Digital Disk Technologies and Their Applications in Libraries (Washington, D.C., Council on Library Resources, 1985), p. 161.

8. Ibid., p. 161.

9. Ibid., p. 161.

10. Link Resources Corporation, pp. 78-87.

11. Information Systems Consultants, p. 140.

12. Ibid., p. 156.

THE USE OF AN ELECTRONIC CONFERENCING SYSTEM
AS A MIDDLE AND UPPER MANAGEMENT TOOL IN AN ACADEMIC LIBRARY

Virginia Gillham
McLaughlin Library, University of Guelph
Guelph, Ontario, Canada

Abstract. COSY, a user-friendly electronic conferencing system with adherents on three continents is employed extensively at the University of Guelph as an internal administrative tool. Because most staff now instinctivley resort first to the system as a method of communication, telephone ping-pong has been virtually eliminated, information transfer has been greatly improved and greatly increased, and meetings are now shorter, less frequent and more productive.

Keywords and Phrases. (Library) Management), Electronic Conferencing, (Library) Administration, Communication, Meetings.

INTRODUCTION

Communication breakdown is probably the most widely cited reason for administrative error or unsatisfactory public service. Poor communication between supervisor and staff, or among colleagues who in theory are working cooperatively, is undoubtedly one of the greatest inhibitors to effective performance. "Too many meetings" is the frequent cry of the beleaguered professional of the 80's. Vain attempts to meet face to face to discuss an issue, frustrated by impossibly busy schedules, are a major deterrent to professional progress. Can there possibly be relief for all of these problems?

There are, by now, few academic librarians who have not encountered electronic messaging. Most commonly, the first use for such a system is as a replacement for the telex, [itself an early type of "electronic mail"] to facilitate interlibrary loan.

In such a situation, one user account per institution (as is generally the case with telex) is the norm. With almost equal frequency, chief librarians or directors of academic libraries are acquiring electronic mail accounts to facilitate personal communication with their peers in other institutions.

These rather tentative, initial ventures into the world of electronic communication are, however, only the miniscule tip of a very large iceberg. Discussion and indeed "conferencing" at a much more sophisticated level than the simple exchange of single messages not only is possible, but opens the door to an entirely new philosophy of professional information transfer. Furthermore, the use within one institution of a large number of separate user accounts makes possible an innovative approach to administrative communication.

THE STRUCTURE OF AN ELECTRONIC CONFERENCING SYSTEM

To understand the potential of electronic conferencing, it is necessary first to understand something of the structure of the more sophisticated systems, and their advantages over such traditional facilities as the telephone, notes on paper, or the more rudimentary messaging systems.

By way of example, reference will be made to the "COSY" system which was developed at the University of Guelph but now includes some 700 users in North America, Europe, New Zealand and the Caribbean. A licence for software which supports COSY has been acquired by Byte magazine to support BIX (The Byte Information Exchange) which will be available to all of the magazine's approximately 450,000 subscribers.

The "COSY" system offers electronic communication at three levels, plus joint editing capabilities. Simplest and least flexible of these levels is "mail", a function intended primarily to facilitate single message transfer from one account holder to another. (Fig.1) While a single message may be directed to several recipients simultaneously, responses are normally only between individual recipients and the originator and general sharing of discussion among several users is not readily achieved (in many ways an electronic analogy to sending someone a piece of paper).

At the second or "conversation" level, the originator of an information exchange may direct his original message to one or several recipients. (Fig.2) Each participant (recipient) in the conversation is able to read the responses from each other recipient and thus multi-participant discussions can occur. Each participant is at liberty to delete himself from a conversation at any time, or conversely to add other participants to whom he feels the discussion may be relevant. The entire discussion remains on (electronic) file for as long as any participant feels the subject is current and may be reviewed in its entirety at any time. New participants added in mid conversation are initially offered all of the messages already contributed, to help them become immediately "au courant". When the discussion is concluded and the last participant deletes himself, the file effectively disappears (and eventually is removed from the system).

The third and perhaps most interesting level offers "conference" facilities and a permanent record of the proceedings. (Fig.3) One person becomes the "moderator" and includes in the conference group any other users to whom the discussion may be relevant.

The difference between the "conference" and the "conversation" level is partly a matter of

MAIL

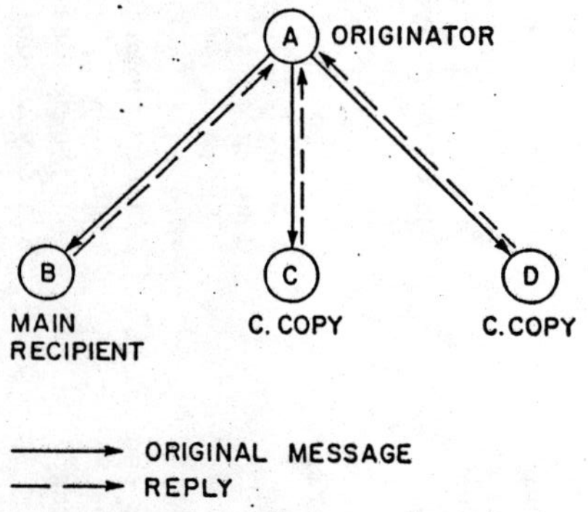

→ ORIGINAL MESSAGE
--→ REPLY

B,C & D ARE UNAWARE OF EACH OTHERS' REPLIES

Fig. 1

CONVERSATION

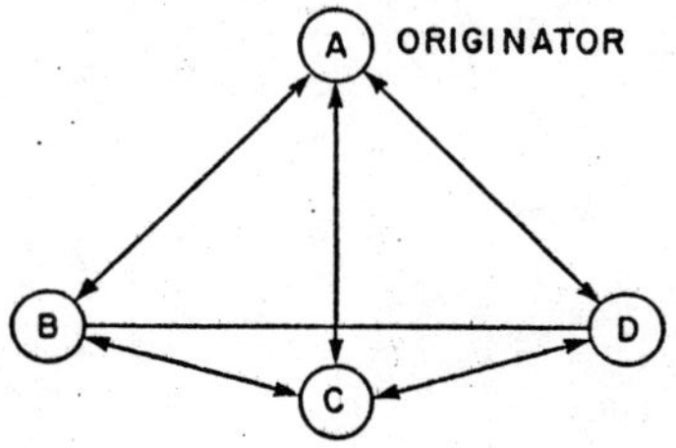

MULTIPLE RECEIPT OF ALL MESSAGES IS AUTOMATIC AND ACHIEVED FROM ONLY ONE INPUTTING OF THE TEXT. EACH PARTICIPANT SEES ALL MESSAGES AND REPLIES FROM EACH OTHER PARTICIPANT.

Fig. 2

CONFERENCE

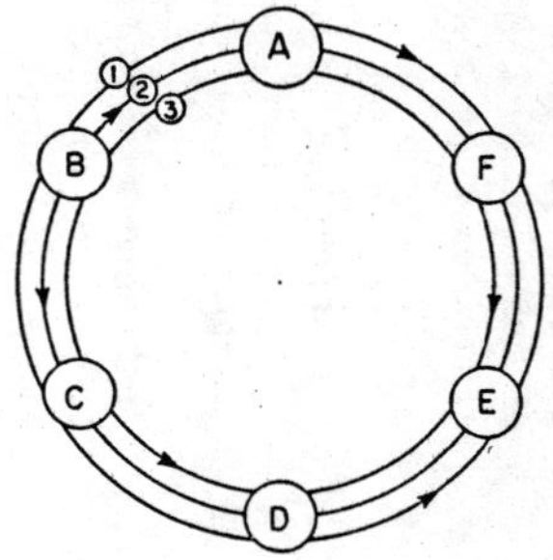

A - MODERATOR
B,C,D,E,F - PARTICIPANTS
1,2,3 - SUBTOPICS

ANY PARTICIPANT MAY INPUT AT ANY TIME, IN ANY SUBTOPIC, AND ALL OTHERS WILL SEE THE MESSAGE

Fig. 3

degree of permanence. In addition, conference may have several sub-topics, while a conversation is directed toward only one, narrowly defined issue.

A "conference" can be likened to a computer-mediated round table discussion that is unlimited by time and distance, where, because of the medium, it is more difficult for one person to dominate the discussion. Unlike audio teleconferencing, (conference calls) or video teleconferencing, computer conferencing does not take place in "real time". Communication is conducted in an asynchronous mode.

The conference level is chosen for discussion topics which are likely to continue indefinitely, such as, for example, the subject area of a standing committee. Members are less likely to delete themselves from a conference and the record of discussion is stored permanently on line where it can be reviewed at any time without using precious office space for paper files.

Conferences can be open, closed or confidential. Open conferences tend to be of very broad general interest, such as, for example, the three which presently exist for discussion of music, Commodore 64 micro computers, and suggested enhancements to the COSY system. Anyone with a COSY account can join an open conference simply by asking the system to add his name.

Closed conferences are usually more specialized. They are listed publicly so potentially interested users can become aware of them; however, they can only be joined by applying to the moderator who may wish to keep the group small or the audience to the discussion restricted. Closed conferences will often include those of standing committees or other carefully chosen, special interest groups.

Private conferences are often very small, even frequently including only two people. Though they may, in fact, be somewhat larger, they are not listed publicly and therefore only their participants are aware of their existence. Standing committees may avail themselves of this type of conference, or a confidential conference may be simply the on-going communication between two colleagues whose professional responsibilities generate considerable discussion.

For any of these three types of conference a record of the discussion is maintained permanently on line without fear of misplacing a memo or report.

Finally, colleagues who are geographically separated, even by a continent or an ocean, can share access to an on-line file and thus co-edit a writing project without ever depending upon a federal mail system.

ADMINISTRATIVE USES OF ELECTRONIC CONFERENCING

What is the role for such a system in modern administration?

The advantage of the discussion modes over single message transferral are obvious. Even institutions with only a single account for the director can participate in inter-institutional discussions much more meaningfully than with single message systems.

Most interesting of all, however, is the potential for institutions where all members of a logical group, such as all professional or management staff possess separate user accounts.

Such a situation has evolved in the library of the University Of Guelph. Fifty-seven professional and supervisory staff members have individual access to the conferencing system. Each user also has very ready access to a computer terminal, and has developed the habit of checking it at least twice each working day. As a result, most users have grown to consider the electronic conferencing system as the library's first line of internal communication, before either the telephone or paper memos.

The advantages are many. As indicated earlier, unlike teleconferencing or telephoning, the system is asynchronous. Participants in a discussion need not be available simultaneously, thus precluding both the frustration of telephone ping-pong (two people repeatedly missing each others' returned calls), and the agony of trying to mesh busy schedules for a meeting.

Message originators can send information quickly and easily at their most opportune time. An audience of one or many can be reached with one message creation, and messages can be replied to at the various conveniences of the recipients. The danger of unrelayed messages is eliminated. If a multi-part discussion ensues, neither the time nor the expense of face-to-face meetings is involved. Furthermore, colleagues travelling with portable terminals, or located at a distance, can participate equally in discussions and decisions.

The existence of standing conferences among cohesive groups is a constant encouragement to communicate. A fact can be conveyed immediately, in one exercise, to the entire group - a marked improvement over individual telephone calls or memos.

Applications at Guelph have included document preparation, such as the situation when a dean, a department director and two senior library staff were required to produce on the university's behalf a submission to the parliamentary committee to revise the Canadian copyright law. Despite the other commitments of all four, this project had to be completed within ten days. Only one face-to-face meeting took place.

On-line group problem solving was demon-

strated when a conference of about ten participants, active intermittently over about two weeks, succeeded in redefining the five levels of performance review ratings without ever gathering in the same room.

At the operational level, an on-going conference moderated by the building manager includes a sub-topic for noting needed repairs and the like, and one for swapping furniture and equipment.

An informational function is performed by the conference wherein staff note their research activities and interests, and the one called "B'Board" which displays items of broad general interest which do not fit elsewhere.

Using electronic conferencing as a preliminary, an adjunct and frequently a substitute for face-to-face meetings results in fewer, briefer and more productive meetings. Furthermore, any one person can take part in several on-going conferences using much less time than would be required for even one face-to-face meeting. It also enables those senior library staff who must be away from their office or the campus to maintain an active, ongoing presence in all essential policy discussions and decision-making situations.

It is an established fact that the average person talks faster than he writes, or types, but listens more slowly than he reads. Since the average person spends more than 90% of his time in a meeting listening and less than 10% speaking, and since in addition to reading more quickly than he listens, he can skip around and read selectively, electronic discussion is clearly much more economical of time than face-to-face meetings. When the cost of getting people to meetings - especially from long distances, and the actual salary value of their time are totalled, the potential savings are enormous.

The consensus at the University of Guelph is that while meetings are now fewer, and shorter, communication in general is better because it is so very easy and convenient and because both formal and casual but productive discussions are much more numerous than they were previously.

The secret to successful electronic administrative communication is frequent, regular system use by all participants. Just as not opening mail defeats its purpose, infrequent reading of electronic mail will sabotage its potential.

In turn, the secret to frequent, regular use is very easy access to a terminal - preferably in the office of each user reachable without moving the desk chair.

While the cost of multiple terminals and user accounts for many individuals may seem prohibitively expensive upon initial consideration; correct use, resulting in improved communication and reduced meeting time, will realize savings in staff time which far outweigh the capital expenditure. Furthermore, the general improvement in morale, performance and service, and the reduction in staff frustration, justify significant costs.

REFERENCES

1. Black, John B. One User's Perspective of Electronic Messaging: (or Confessions of a Terminal Addict) Proceedings of the 10th Annual CAIS Conference, May 2-6, 1982.

2. Gillham, Virginia. Electronic Conferencing in a University Library. Paper presented to the WNY/ONT ACRL Workshop, September 28, 1984.

3. Pearson, Ellen. From Mail to Conferencing: Experiences of a Middle Management Group. Proceedings of the Conference on Computer Conferencing and Electronic Messaging, University of Guelph, 22-23 January, 1985.

A POPULIST APPROACH TO AUTOMATION: DEVELOPING LOCAL SYSTEMS IN A MAINFRAME CONTEXT

David F. Kohl
University of Illinois Library
Urbana, IL

Abstract. The increasingly mature automation environment of the 1980's provides new possibilities for dealing with large, shared mainframe systems such as LCS and WLN. By using microcomputers as an interface to the mainframe system, library patrons can be provided with customized access and services designed for local conditions and under local control. Such systems can be developed locally by use of off-the-shelf hardware and software and by the use of increasingly widespread automation expertise. Examples of such piggyback systems at the University of Illinois-Urbana are provided and the evolution of large, shared mainframe systems into providers of generic services with local microcomputer interfaces providing specialized local services is considered.

The increasingly mature automation environment of the 1980's, and in particular the advent of relatively cheap, relatively powerful personal computers, has given rise to two promising developments. The first is the use of increasingly powerful and sophisticated microprocessors to access large mainframe systems and the second is the dramatic widespread growth of computer literacy.

In such an automation environment it is possible to look at mainframe automation from a new perspective and, perhaps more importantly, to solve, what to date have been regarded as inherent problems of large, shared mainframe systems such as WLN or LCS. The two major problems to which I refer are: 1) such systems have to fit the local needs of a variety of library types and so fit no one library's needs particularly well, and 2) changes in such shared systems are difficult, time consuming and expensive.

In the first case, joining a large, shared automated system is still a lot like buying a suit off the rack. Financially it may be a good deal but such a system is simply not going to fit local needs as well as a customized system. A shared mainframe system may not allow for multiple local fine schedules or it may not include a circulation period you need. In the second case, many of the large, shared systems are made up of largely independent constituencies with the result that governance, particularly when it comes to making changes and modifications in the automated system, is a complicated, slow and therefore expensive and frustrating decision-making process. Contrary to what many of us may think in the heat of passion, this difficulty is not really the product of incompetency and pig-headedness on the part of our colleagues whose institutions share the system, but rather it is the legitimate process of many different voices with many different agendas, priorities and local needs being forced into an agreement on decisions which have to be implemented in a single, shared mainframe system. The remarkable aspect of this process, reminiscent of Dr. Johnson's dog, is not that it works with such difficulty but that it works at all.

One solution to this problem is the concept of piggyback automation, i.e. using a microcomputer to access a mainframe system. More technically, the piggyback idea is to use microcomputers to provide a distributed front end to the large, shared system. This basically simple idea provides the potential for users of large, shared mainframe systems to reestablish local control and local individuality to their automated system without sacrificing the clear benefits of participating in the large, shared mainframe system.

At the University of Illinois-Urbana/Champaign, we are putting this concept into practice with considerable success. We have successfully implemented a number of such projects including a user-friendly interface which allows patrons to use our command-driven LCS (Library Computer System, a brief record circulation system which allows patrons, among other things, to determine if the library has an item and, if so, whether it is checked out). One of our most ambitious projects in the use of piggybacking, however, has been the development of a local Reserve system.

The Reserve system represents the development of a whole new component to the automated system but one which is added on as a front end system rather than as part of the mainframe system. As in the case of the interface we were very much interested in having a system designed to meet local needs and which would remain under local control but which would use the LCS system as a host so that, in the case of the Reserve system, we would not have to duplicate the massive collection or patron files of LCS.

Our overall goals for this Reserve system were twofold. Not only did we want to end up with a workable Reserve system which we and others could use but we wanted to demonstrate as well the feasibility of grassroots automation. In terms of this second goal this meant we wanted to be able to use off the shelf hardware, off the shelf software and make any customized changes with local, non-programmer talent. We have, I believe, been largely successful in achieving both goals.

SYSTEM DESCRIPTION

The Reserve system which we have designed is best described in terms of three elements; record entry (and deletion), circulation and management data. For any Reserve system the most important element is record entry and deletion. Each semester the old Reserve records must be purged or updated and a large number of new records added. Further, this all must take place in a relatively short period of time. The constant re-creating of the Reserve collection is the most complex problem which the Reserve manager faces.

In order to simplify this constant re-creation of the Reserve collection, records are input by use of a series of menus. First a course menu gathers data on the course (course name, number, first instructor, second instructor, etc...) and then a materials menu allows input of data on the specific item (title, first author, second author, call number, copy number, status, notes, etc...)

Once material has been entered it may be accessed in dozens of ways. You may search each semester's Reserve database by author, title, course, status, call number or various combinations of these. Records may be deleted or updated by course or individually. Records may also be entered manually or downloaded from the LCS system. It is also possible for the Reserve staff to begin creating the databases for several semesters in the future while continuing to use the present semester's database.

The Reserve circulation system is absolutely minimal and based on the fact that most of the material circulated is in fact returned and returned on time. We merely associate a student's ID number with the bibliographic record of the specific item which the student wishes to check out. Each record has a circulation code, generally two hours, and the system's internal clock records the time out and the time back in. The vast majority of items which are returned on time simply have the associated circulation information deleted except for a circulation counter. Items which are overdue have their bibliographic record, the patron ID, time out and in and the calculated fine read into a separate file which is printed out once a day. The student ID is checked on LCS to get the student's name and all the information is reported to the University Accounts Office. Since we seldom have over ten overdues a day, this is an acceptable procedure.

The management information generated by the system is also spare but critical. The system automatically counts and displays with the appropriate menus the number of courses in the data base for a given semester, the number of items in the data base for a particular course in a given semester and even the status of a particular item, e.g. on reserve, recalled, purchase order generated, etc... We are able to generate a printout of all the items which a particular professor has on reserve and even, at the end of the semester, to indicate how many times each item on the list circulated. We have the capacity to add more management information bells and whistles at a later date but for the time being we think that this should suffice.

TECHNICAL DATA

The system consists of 5 IBM personal computers each with 192 K of memory and one IBM XT with a 10 MB hard disk drive. The units are linked with the Orchid networking system which is a multiuser, multitask system. We also use an Epson FX 100 printer in the configuration. Two of the IBM units sit at the circulation desk and are used primarily for circulation although it would be possible to use them for record entry and manipulation, one unit sits back of the circulation desk and is used both for circulation checkin and record entry/manipulation depending on need, and two units sit in work areas and are used primarily for record entry/manipulation. The cost of the hardware will vary depending on the kind of purchasing agreements which an institution has but our equipment costs ran about $18,000.

Our software was developed by a local UIUC professor of Chinese linguistics who has an interest in library automation and wanted to find a way to support one of his Graduate Assistants who he used to assist him with the project. He began writing the program in BASICA but quickly shifted to the network version of BTRIEVE which vastly simplified the problem of creating the necessary indexes and files. The out of pocket personnel costs to the library (i.e. excluding time spent on the project by library staff) ran about $11,000. The project has been underway for two years but the amount of time spent on it is difficult to estimate since there have been constant interruptions for higher priority projects. A rough guess would establish the programming time at approximately 2-3 months full time for a professional and a Graduate Assistant.

The one weak link in our argument about grass roots automation is clearly C. C. Cheng, the professor of Chinese linguistics. Although he is not a trained programmer he clearly has a gift for automation software. The degree to which expertise such as his is generally available is not at all clear and probably is, in fact, somewhat unusual.

SIZE OF SYSTEM

We have not had enough experience with this Reserve system to know its upward limits. The size of operation which we are now supporting with this system involves a daily checkout rate ranging between 100 and 600 + circulations. Each semester we add or update records to create a database of around 3,000 items. In addition there are also approximately 200 permanent reserve items which serve as part of the database in any given semester. So far, even with complete file backup on the harddisk, the program and data files take up less than half of the ten megabyte hard disk.

SUMMARY

What we set out to show was a new approach to solving library automation problems in today's automation environment. The key features of this maturing automation environment are the possibilities offered by piggyback hardware configurations and a grassroots approach to automation development.

In the particular instance of large, shared mainframe systems, grassroots automation can use a piggyback configuration to re-establish local control and customization without giving up the benefits of the large, centralized systems. Futhermore, in the two years that this project has been underway, the possibilities for grassroots automation seem to be increasing. Microcomputers continue to get cheaper and more powerful, the variety and sophistication of software continues to grow and computer literacy is increasing dramatically.

I think that it is not at all unlikely that large, shared systems may well try to take advantage of these developments by reducing their attempts to be all things to all users from a central mainframe environment and instead turn their attention to providing generic services associated with large files. This should make the large mainframe systems both faster and more reliable. Microcomputer systems will then be used to massage the data provided by the mainframe systems and provide whatever ideosyncratic or customized data is most appropriate to the local user. This may be as simple as user-friendly interface or as complex as separate Reserve component.

CONSERVATION, PRESERVATION AND DIGITIZATION

Clifford A. Lynch and Edwin B. Brownrigg
Division of Library Automation, University of California
Office of the President and Universitywide Services
Berkeley, CA

Abstract. Considerable attention has been focused recently on the problems of conservation and preservation of library materials. Particularly daunting are the scale of the problems and the enormous ongoing investment that will be required to address them. Currently proposed approaches include extensive microfilming of material, deacidification, and other repair measures.

We argue that microfilming, one of the most commonly used methods for conservation and preservation, is inappropriate to the needs of libraries, which increasingly are offering online access to catalogs from home and office and eventually should provide access to the holdings themselves. A conservation and preservation program is an investment in the future, yet the end product of microfilming represents a deterioration in the usability of library holdings.

We propose that digital technologies be used to accomplish simultaneously the aims of conservation and improved access to materials, and we review the various technologies that are necessary. Such an approach to conservation would form a natural extension to the current growth of electronic publishing, online catalogs, and online databases of journal abstracts. Furthermore, it would provide the greatest return for the massive investment that will be needed to save our deteriorating collections.

Keywords and Phrases. Conservation, Preservation, Electronic Imaging, Library Automation.

INTRODUCTION

Conservation and preservation present serious problems for the library community today. However, these problems are generally considered in isolation, without much reference to major trends in the development of library service or to the impact of library automation, widespread access to computers, and telecommunications on both the nature and delivery of library service. In fact, conservation and preservation issues are often the province of people in the library who have been least affected by developments in technology and library automation: archivists, collection management specialists, etc. These people have always dealt with books as artifacts, and historically their concern has been the preservation and management of the printed word. This orientation is clearly reflected in classic works on conservation and preservation, such as the book by Cunha and Cunha entitled *Conservation of Library Materials* [1].

Thus, the approach to conservation and preservation has been to try to save what exists — where possible, to save the physical artifacts themselves, and where this is not possible, to create and save surrogates for the physical artifacts in the tangible form of microfiche. Up to a point these efforts obviously have been worthwhile: a beautifully produced book is a thing worth saving in its own right, and books as artifacts have considerable historical interest.

However, the nature of library services is changing. In times past, the library has been a repository for artifacts of the printed word. Today, it is taking on a more dynamic role as both a repository and a distributor of *information* (as distinct from artifacts) [2]. This transformation raises some difficult questions about the wisdom of current approaches to conservation and preservation.

THE ACCESS REVOLUTION

The advent of the online catalog has made it possible to provide remote access to the bibliographic holdings of libraries from computer terminals. This permits the identification of materials of interest from a patron's home or office, and provides a superior means of searching the library's holdings.

In spite of their advantages, however, online catalogs still have limitations. In general, they contain only monographs, providing little access to journal literature, which is critical, for example, in scientific research. Automated access to the latter is offered today by systems such as DIALOG and BRS, although the user interfaces for these systems are so complicated that use is largely limited to trained searchers or inveterate computer users. Fortunately, these two sources of information should converge over the next few years, providing the end user with the ability to readily identify journal literature of interest.

From the user's point of view, an even more serious limitation is that online catalogs can only provide references to information, not the information itself. Thus, online catalogs simply form the backbone for far more extensive electronic publishing and document delivery systems to come. They deal with identification of material; the next challenge is to deliver the *material* electronically to the end user. Meeting this challenge requires complex technologies in the areas of telecom-

©Clifford A. Lynch and Edwin B. Brownrigg 1986

munications, computing, and electronic imaging [3,4]. For any activity that affects a library's collections, such as conversion to microfilm to save space, acquisition of new materials, preservation and conservation, or migration of little-used material to dense storage, the library must look ahead to the new world of information delivery and begin the lengthy and costly conversion of collections to a form amenable to such delivery.

CURRENT APPROACHES TO CONSERVATION AND PRESERVATION

The current strategies for conservation and preservation of library materials includes restoration, bulk deacidification, repair and microfilming [5].

For rare and valuable works of great significance, elaborate restoration and repair techniques have been developed. These techniques have been used to wonderful effect on illuminated manuscripts, early books and the like. Only a relatively small number of threatened works justify such treatment, as is consistent with the handling of works of art in museums.

For books that are rotting because of the use of acid paper, various mass deacidification schemes have been proposed. Experience with these techniques is limited, however. If they work, and if they prove to be cost-effective, they will preserve the status quo for the books that are treated.

Many books are in disrepair due to hard use or deterioration of their bindings. In some such cases, rebinding the work gives it a new lease on life, and, when this is cost-effective, it also preserves the status quo.

Books that are extremely fragile are being microfilmed page by page. These microfilms are then copied, and the master copies are stored in central, environmentally-controlled repositories while copies replace the damaged book on the shelf. Although the contents of such books are preserved, access is greatly reduced. In general, it is impractical to circulate microfilm, and microfilm is almost universally loathed by library patrons, who have demonstrated that they will go to almost any lengths to avoid using it. Finally, microfilm is expensive to copy, which inhibits resource sharing, and it does not hold up well under heavy use.

In no case is the end product of these strategies converted to a form more hospitable to delivery over telecommunications media. Leaving aside rare works (the works of art), deacidification and rebinding leave the patron neither better nor worse off. However, microfilming greatly reduces access to the microfilmed material, and the patron is far worse off.

DIGITIZATION FOR CONSERVATION AND PRESERVATION

Capture of a work in digital images is an attractive alternative to microfilming. Since in both cases a book has to be scanned page by page, the predominant cost will be labor. Any extra expense of digitizing is marginal and is far outweighed by the value of the end product. Moreover, digital scanners and image storage devices are dropping rapidly in price.

Depending on how the economics and effectiveness of rebinding and deacidification turn out, digitization may prove to be an alternative to these strategies as well. In the next section, in fact, we argue that even if digitization costs more than deacidification it is still worth considering since it represents an investment in the future and prospectively protects the work. In the case of works of art, where the cost of preservation is a secondary issue, digitization may provide an attractive supplementary activity since access to the work can then be provided through the digital copy without any further threat to the original artifact. Thus, digitization could provide wide access to rare books that today are protected from use by any but the most serious and trustworthy scholars.

Consider the following attributes of digital images:

- They do not deteriorate with use. In fact, each use of a stored digital image causes the data to be read, validated, and corrected via error-correcting codes, thus permitting early detection and automatic correction of any deterioration in the storage media.

- They can be copied quickly and at virtually no cost. Any kind of digital information can be duplicated endlessly with no loss in quality, without human intervention, and at high speed and low cost. Although legal questions in regards to copyright must also be considered [6], they are often irrelevant for older works that are being preserved since the copyright has expired.

- Copies can be transmitted over a network at high speed and low cost. This attribute makes archives of digitized works possible; they can be duplicated and sent across the country to the requester via automated systems in a matter of minutes, or perhaps a few hours if the system is busy. Consequently, resource sharing becomes more practical, and it is not necessary for each library to retain copies of the microfilm for each work or to call for copies of these to be shipped (perhaps weeks later) from a central clearing house.

- Digital data are much less vulnerable to disaster and environmental threats. Digital information, especially on optical disks, does not deteriorate rapidly. When deterioration occurs, the information can be copied easily. Since digital information is easy to copy, it is feasible to store copies at several geographically diverse repositories, removing the threat that a natural disaster will destroy the only available copy.

Thus, digital images solve not only the immediate conservation and preservation problem but also the problem in the long term. In addition, they are easier to use, deliver, and share.

ECONOMIC AND POLICY QUESTIONS

Given, then, that digitization is a desirable objective, the following economic and policy questions have to be addressed:

- What books are valuable as *artifacts* and thus require the kind of treatment accorded works of art?

We would argue that the answer to this question is to preserve liberally. Books as artifacts have considerable value, and wholesale elimination of examples of publishing from certain presses, countries, or historical periods would be a tragic loss.

- How should material from a collection be selected for digitization?

We might decide to digitize a book for one of three reasons:

1. Because it is disintegrating and needs to be copied. In this case we must act to preserve the work, and, if the cost of digitization is competitive with other techniques (such as microfilming), it should be used. In cases in which digitization is more costly than other approaches, such as deacidification or rebinding, we must decide if the extra benefits of digitization justify the extra costs.

2. Because it is rare or delicate and, although not in immediate danger, we want to protect the book prospectively and permit its contents to be widely used.

3. Because it is often requested and we want it in a form appropriate for digital delivery via a network. Note that this has nothing to do with conservation and preservation. In fact, the parts of a collection that are most endangered today probably receive relatively light use overall.

Balancing the importance of these three criteria for digitization, particularly in the face of widespread deterioration of the collection and insufficient funding, is difficult. To a certain extent, this amounts to finding a balance between funding priorities for preservation and access.

In addition to these policy questions, there are a variety of more technical and operational issues that must be addressed. One such issue is the development of appropriate standards for the storage and transfer of images. Some of the standards under development for Group IV digital facsimile devices will be applicable here, as will some of the standards being developed for optical disk storage (particularly since optical disks are the natural storage medium for digital images). Other issues that must be addressed include the creation of links between bibliographic records and digital images of a book; research in appropriate technology for displays and user interfaces to integrate the online catalog with document delivery; and the development of a repository system for digitized material to encourage resource sharing and eliminate duplication of effort on a national basis. In addition, effective use of digital images will require the installation of low-cost, broadband telecommunications networks. Packet switching and satellite technology are ideal for these purposes.

CONCLUSIONS

Conservation and preservation will demand substantial sums of money during the remainder of the century if library collections in America are to be saved. At the same time, the library in the year 2000 will be radically different than the library of 1960. This transformation, which is well underway, has been costly since it has required the introduction of a massive amount of computer and telecommunications technology into the library — and the change is far from complete.

Saving the collections and revolutionizing access to them can be treated as independent problems competing for funds. In our view, this would be a major error since these two apparently disparate problems are in fact closely related. Conservation and preservation can become an investment in an increasingly obsolete status quo, or it can become an investment towards the future.

ACKNOWLEDGMENTS

We would like to thank Mary Jean Moore for editorial assistance.

REFERENCES

1. George M. Cunha and Dorothy G. Cunha, *Conservation of Library Materials: A Manual and Bibliography on the Care, Repair and Restoration of Library Materials*, 2 vols. (Metuchen, NJ: Scarecrow Press, Inc., 1971).

2. Edwin B. Brownrigg and Clifford A. Lynch, "Online Catalogs: Through a Glass Darkly," *Information Technology and Libraries* 2 (March 1983): 104-115.

3. Clifford A. Lynch and Edwin B. Brownrigg, "Library Applications of Electronic Imaging Technology," (Paper presented at the SPSE Electronic Imaging Conference, Boston, October 1985).

4. Clifford A. Lynch and Edwin B. Brownrigg, "Document Delivery and Packet Facsimile," *Proceedings of the 48th ASIS Annual Meeting* 22 (1985): 11-14.

5. University of California, Office of the Executive Director of Universitywide Library Planning, *Con-

servation of the Collections: A Supplement to the University of California Libraries: A Plan for Development, 1977-88 (Berkeley, CA: University of California, 1983).

6. Edwin B. Brownrigg and Clifford A. Lynch, "Electrons, Electronic Publishing, and Electronic Display," *Information Technology and Libraries* 4, no. 3 (September 1985): 201-207.

The Library of Congress
Optical Disk Print Pilot Project
Staff Evaluation

Victoria Ann Reich
Melissa Ann Betcher
Office of Planning and Development
Library of Congress

Abstract. This project was conducted April-May 1985 and involved 62 public service librarians. The evaluation goals were to involve the staff during the implementation of this new technology and to collect data on these objectives: to measure satisfaction with training, documentation, equipment, printing, and system reliability; to identify materials to be scanned; and general satisfaction. Terminal logs, a message phone, three questionnaires, and group interviews were used to collect data. Staff were generally satisfied with the system, with some interesting exceptions. Staff suggestions, once implemented, will ease the incorporation of the optical disk into the Library's environment.

INTRODUCTION

The Optical Disk Pilot Program, begun in late 1982, is a four-year (1983-1986) program designed to assess the applicability of digital optical disk and analog videodisk technologies to library materials. The Library of Congress embarked on this project as a means to preserve high-use and rare materials and to provide rapid access to them. (1) The optical disk is being used to store printed materials, and the videodisk is being used to store visual materials.

This study focuses on the digital optical disk system. At this time, selected articles accessed via BIBL, one of the Library's online bibliographic files, are available on the optical disk system.

Patrons search the BIBL file by author, title, or subject. When the citations from a particular search are displayed, those which have the text available are noted. The user can then request the text. The black-and-white image of the document appears on the screen at a video resolution of 150 lines per inch by 300 lines per inch. Users can page forward and backward through the images of text.

Reader stations are located in four of the Library's reading rooms: Law, Main, Newspaper and Current Periodical, and Science. A fifth station is in the Congressional Research Service (CRS). Users have the option of reading the document on the terminal or printing it. The Newspaper and Current Periodical Reading Room has a Xerox 2700 convenience printer, and patrons in all stations can use a remote Xerox 5700 to generate offline prints. The quality of the printers is identical, the differences are speed and convenience. (2)

Because of the nature of the Optical Disk Print Pilot Project and the evaluation objectives, this study is a description of the specific environment surrounding the project. (3) Since the focus is not on theoretical research, statistical manipulations were not included, for they would not enhance the data. Although this study is practical and not theoretical, it is hoped that it will encourage staff participation in the development of library systems and technologies.

OBJECTIVES

The major goal of the staff evaluation was to involve all levels of Library of Congress staff with the project and elicit their opinions on how the system can be improved before it is released to the public.

The staff assisted in providing quick and early feedback on possible hidden problems within the system. Further, it allowed the staff to become fully familiar with the system in order to assist the public user better. Within this framework, there were seven specific evaluation objectives of the Optical Disk Print Pilot Project:

(1) to identify satisfaction with training,
(2) to identify satisfaction with documentation,
(3) to identify satisfaction with equipment,
(4) to identify satisfaction with printing,
(5) to determine system reliability,
(6) to identify potential groups of materials for scanning onto optical disk, and
(7) to determine general satisfaction.

METHODOLOGY

Following installation of the optical disk terminals in late March, each staff member received approximately one half hour of individual training, a group tour of the optical disk operations center, and an opportunity to hear welcoming remarks by William J. Welsh, The Deputy Librarian of Congress. All areas except the Law Library participated in the staff evaluation. Logs were placed near the terminal, and a message center phone was instituted. During March and April, informal opinions of the staff were collected as they began to use the system. When staff members signed onto the system, they were asked to note the time and date on the log as well as any impressions of the system. In May, the staff participated in a more formal evaluation of the system by completing three questionnaires. (4) The questionnaires, entitled <u>Training and Documentation</u>, <u>Equipment and Software</u>, and <u>Printing</u>, were designed to address the objectives of the pilot program and the concerns of the senior managers of the project. Each questionnaire included a log. People were asked each time they accessed the optical disk system to note the system's status. The questionnaires were pretested, revised, and distributed to all professional staff from the Science and Newspaper and Current Periodical Reading Rooms. All staff from the Main Reading Room, Telephone/Correspondence/Bibliography, and Automation and Reference Collection Sections of the General Reading Rooms Division were also queried. Staff in the CRS participated voluntarily. System trainers in the reading rooms distributed and collected the surveys. Respondents' identities were anonymous to the evaluation team. The distribution and return rate for the questionnaires are given in Tables 1-3.

Table 1
Distribution and Return
Training and Documentation Questionnaire

Department	# Distributed	# Returned	% Returned
Main Reading Room	25	25	100
Science Reading Room	20	18	90
Newspaper and Current Periodical Reading Room	17	17	100
Total	62	60	97
Congressional Research Service	20	9	45

Table 2
Distribution and Return
Equipment and Software

Department	# Distributed	# Returned	% Returned
Main Reading Room	25	25	100
Science Reading Room	20	18	90
Newspaper and Current Periodical Reading Room	17	17	100
Total	62	60	97
Congressional Research Service	20	6	30

Table 3
Distribution and Return
Printing Questionnaire

Department	# Distributed	# Returned	% Returned
Main Reading Room	25	24	96
Science Reading Room	20	18	90
Newspaper and Current Periodical Reading Room	17	17	100
Total	62	59	95
Congressional Research Service	20	4	20

In early June, three one-and-a-half hour blocks of time were scheduled for group interviews with librarians from the Main, Newspaper and Current Periodical, and Science Reading Rooms. Participation was voluntary, with a total of 18 of 62 librarians attending. Along with a discussion of how they perceived the system, the librarians were asked their opinions on certain key policy issues.

RESULTS

The questions below do not reflect the format of the questionnaires. They have been rearranged to facilitate clear presentation of results, and some instructions and all open-ended questions have been omitted. The instructions which are needed to understand the results are in Boxes A-F. Comments from open-ended questions are summarized at the end of each objective. The percentages were rounded to the nearest whole number, with "N" being the number of people who answered each question. CRS is not included in these tabulations.

OBJECTIVE 1:
TO IDENTIFY SATISFACTION WITH TRAINING

How often do you use the BIBL file?

N=50
20% rarely
54% moderately
26% extensively

Was the orientation and training you received sufficient to make you feel comfortable about trying the system?

N=51
81% yes
13% partially
6% no

Approximately how long was your training?

N=51
59% 0-30 minutes
29% 31-60 minutes
8% 61-90 minutes
4% 91-120 minutes

During the training period, did you have an opportunity to "play" with the system?

N=50
86% yes
14% no

Would you have liked further instruction?

N=51
45% yes, (check all that apply)
52% using information screens
48% moving from citation to text
39% moving from text to citation
35% moving from page to page of text
39% printing online
52% printing offline
52% creating sets
61% using limit commands
52% other
55% no

Staff were pleased with their optical disk training. System down time was the cause cited by those saying they were only partially satisfied. No trends could be established among respondents desiring further instruction. There was an even split between those interested in specific optical disk manipulation and those needing assistance in accessing software.

OBJECTIVE 2:
TO IDENTIFY SATISFACTION WITH DOCUMENTATION

Box A

Imagine that you are approaching the Optical Disk terminal for the first time. Use the printed manual "Searching in the Optical Disk Information System..." to guide your steps and search the term "China." (You may wish to limit this set by "text.")

Display the first document in your set. Page forwards and backwards. If your terminal is connected to a printer, copy the second and last page of the document and attach it to this questionnaire. Print offline the fifth document in your set, instead of your name type "test" as the requester.

Did you have any problems completing this task. (See Box A)

N=51   27% yes
       73% no

What kinds of problems did you experience? Check all that apply.

N=17   24% signing on
       18% creating a set
       35% display text
       18% paging forwards/backwards
       6% copying the pages online
       18% printing the document offline
       6% ending the search
       0% limiting
       24% other

Does the manual cover all the current and/or potential uses you can envision of the Optical Disk System?

N=44   75% yes
       25% no

Do you think a patron coming to the OD terminal could successfully use this manual to retrieve text?

N=46   57% yes
       43% no

Box B

Please END your previous search, and return to the menu screen. Choose menu option 2, for information about searching the BIBL file and viewing the full text of documents.

Would this information enable a patron to do a search online? (See Box B)

N=50   40% yes
       44% partially
       16% no

Box C

Choose menu option 4, for background information on the Optical Disk Pilot Program.

Do you have any suggestions for improving these screens? (See Box C)

N=47   74% no
       26% yes

Does the "Gone to the Stacks"[1]/ message help you feel comfortable while waiting for the text to appear on the screen?

N=45   62% yes
       31% partially
       7% no

---
[1]/ This message appears between the time text is requested and the text is displayed. In several paragraphs, it explains how the system displays an image on the screen.

A large number of respondents (12 of 22) felt that a patron's previous knowledge of The Library of Congress databases would effect how successfully they could conduct a search. It was believed by four staff members that the manual should provide standard search information or that search instruction flipcharts be attached to the Optical Disk Manual. When comparing the manual and menu option 2, a majority of respondents (eight) felt that a hardcopy version is more useful, particularly for the naive user. Three suggestions to improve on the information screens appeared consistently: to shorten the screens, write them with less jargon, and be consistent.

Two-thirds of the respondents felt comfortable with the "Gone to the Stacks" message; however, there was some feeling that the message is fine the first time, then becomes repetitious and boring. Ten respondents believed that some indication of length of time before system response, potential time delays, and what one should do after a certain amount of lapsed time would be beneficial.

OBJECTIVE 3:
TO IDENTIFY SATISFACTION WITH EQUIPMENT

3.1 Work Station

As you sit at the Optical Disk Station, do you have adequate writing space?

N=52   75% yes
       25% no

Do you have sufficient light to read printed materials near the work station?

N=52   100% yes
       0% no

Clearly, staff felt the work stations are acceptable. The writing space was adequate in Science and Newspaper and Current Periodical Reading Rooms. In the Main Reading Room, approximately half the people reported that the writing space was cramped and awkward for right-handed persons.

3.2 Screen Displays

What is the longest approximate time you have read text from the screen?

N=48   60% 1 - 5 minutes
       32% 6 - 15 minutes
       8% 16 - 30 minutes
       0% 31 - 60 minutes
       0% more than 60 minutes

For how long do you think you would be able to read text comfortably from the screen?

N=47
- 15% 1 - 5 minutes
- 34% 6 - 15 minutes
- 30% 16 - 30 minutes
- 8% 31 - 60 minutes
- 13% more than 60 minutes

Have you encountered problems while trying to read text from the image screen?

N=46
- 57% yes, check all that apply
  - 38% screen image flickers
  - 23% images too bright
  - 4% images too dim
  - 46% surface glare
  - 27% blurry image
  - 35% unable to read very small print
  - 42% other
- 43% no

Have you encountered problems while looking at graphic or picture images?

N=45
- 56% yes, check all that apply
  - 24% needed color to interpret display
  - 40% halftones were indistinct
  - 28% blurry image
  - 44% fine detail missing
  - 16% screen flickering
  - 32% surface glare
  - 8% other
- 44% no

Box D

Please compare the screen image from LRS80-15568 image 4 with attachment D. (Attachment A had small print and foreign text.)

Do you think a patron would ever need to look at the original page or a copy of the original page in order to fully utilize the information presented? (See Box E)

N=44
- 70% no
- 30% yes

Box E

Please compare the screen image from LRS84-1110 image 2 with attachment B. The caption for this map is on images 1 and 2. (Attachment B was a color map, where the color eased interpretation of the data.)

Do you think a patron would ever need to look at the original page or a copy of the original page in order to fully utilize the information presented? (See Box E)

N=44
- 32% no
- 68% yes

Of those people citing problems while reading from the screen, four people complained of lines through the text, and three stated there was a loss of print, or blank sections on the screen. Another four staff members suggested that the screen be tiltable in order to eliminate some of the difficulties in reading. A tilting screen might have assisted those respondents who felt that the angle and glare on the screen contributed to the difficulties in reading small print. Staff had difficulties viewing color images, with 30 respondents stating that the screen's approximation of gray scale was insufficient to delineate the colors, thus making interpretation difficult. Three persons commented that it was difficult to read letters originally imposed on color.

3.3 Software

While viewing images on the Optical Disk System, have you encountered incomplete or incorrect documents?

N=45
- 47% yes, please check all that apply
  - 29% missing pages with no message
  - 86% "image unavailable" message
  - 52% "portions missing" message
  - 67% "technical problems" message
  - 14% article/BIBL citation mismatched
  - 14% other
- 53% no

Can you move back and forth between the bibliographic citation and the text?

N=45
- 87% yes
- 11% somewhat
- 2% no

Respondents are generally satisfied with the optical disk software. About half have encountered incomplete or incorrect documents.

3.4 Keyboard

Are the function keys arranged so you can find the one(s) you need?

N=47
- 83% yes
- 15% somewhat
- 2% no

Do the function keys perform the action expected, based on their labels?

N=45
- 93% yes
- 7% somewhat
- 0% no

What new keys would you like to see?

N=46
- 54% sign on
- 49% sign off
- 69% display text
- 38% display citation
- 51% limit text
- 8% other(s)
- 15% none

Are there any superfluous keys?

N=39
- 41% yes
- 59% no

Although the arrangement of function keys met overwhelming approval, four respondents in the "somewhat" category felt that the enter key was too far right. Suggestions for new keys ranged from "display text" to "return from text" to "citation set" and a "cancel command" key. Seventeen people identified more than a dozen different keys as superfluous, many of which are essential to system usage. A detailed explanation of the keyboard is necessary, perhaps in the manual.

OBJECTIVE 4:
TO IDENTIFY SATISFACTION WITH PRINTING

4.1 Remote Printer

Box F

Choose an article, preferably one which has pictures or other fine details, and examine the images on the screen. Please order offline the entire article, entering your name as the requester.

Did you receive the article you ordered? (See Box F)

N=41
- 80% yes
- 20% no

How many days did it take for you to receive your offline printout?

N=37
- 52% 0 - 1 day
- 38% 2 - 3 days
- 8% 4 - 5 days
- 2% more than 5 days

Would this turnaround time be adequate for your average patron's needs?

N=38
- 53% yes
- 47% no, please comment:

Are any pages missing?

N=35
- 71% no
- 29% yes, specify which ones

Are you satisfied with the overall quality of the image?

N=38
- 69% yes
- 31% no (check all that apply)
  - 27% text blurred
  - 45% black lines
  - 18% too dark
  - 9% too light
  - 45% top chopped off
  - 18% bottom chopped off
  - 73% poor contrast
  - 18% other

To the best of your knowledge, are the fine details legible?

N=36
- 53% yes
- 42% no
- 5% not applicable

Eighty percent of respondents received the article they ordered, 51 percent within a day. Staff were evenly divided on whether this turnaround time would be adequate for patrons. Fourteen of 16 people commenting in the questionnaire felt that same-day service was essential, particularly for out-of-town users. The majority of those participating in the interviews believed next-day service would be satisfactory. Fine details which tended to be illegible included bar graphs, some photographs, characters on multicolor images, and fine details such as cursive writing on old documents. Twenty-nine percent had pages missing from their document, and 31 percent were not satisfied with the quality of the image, thus prompting the comments that print reliabiilty must be improved before charges are installed. The administrative procedures for printers was discussed at the interviews. Staff tended to feel that the cost for offline printing should be less than convenience printing, thus encouraging patrons to use the batch method. A serious concern arose about maintaining convenience printers; changing paper, making change, and the like are annoying with the current photocopiers and will only increase with the advent of convenience printers.

4.2 Convenience Printer
Newspaper and Current Periodical Staff Only:

In your experience are the copies made by the convenience printer legible?

N=13
- 92% yes
- 8% no

How would you rate the printer's reliability?

N=13
- 8% poor
- 77% adequate
- 15% excellent

Are you satisfied with the overall quality of the image?

N=13
- 69% yes
- 31% no (check all that apply)
  - 75% text blurred
  - 25% black lines
  - 0% too dark
  - 25% too light
  - 0% top chopped off
  - 0% bottom chopped off
  - 0% poor contrast
  - 0% other

To the best of your knowledge, are the fine details legible?

N=12
- 58% yes
- 42% no
- 0% not applicable

How does your printout compare to the image on the screen?

N=11
- 18% more legible
- 64% same legibility
- 18% less legible

Staff members in the Serial and Government Publications Division were asked to comment on the convenience printer. Percentages on overall quality and fine detail legibility were comparable for convenience printing and offline printing, although difficulties with the images varied. The legibility was felt, by the majority, to be the same as that on the screen, prompting two commentors to say the copies were as easy to read as photocopies.

OBJECTIVE 5:
TO MEASURE RELIABILITY OF SYSTEM

For Objective 5, data from CRS was incorporated into the results from other reading rooms. The logs from March and April indicate that half of the recorded attempts to access the system were successful. Table 4 shows the data recorded in May as people approached the system to complete their questionnaires. These data are hard to substantiate as BIBL system problems are difficult to separate from optical disk system problems. When BIBL is down the optical disk system cannot be accessed. Use of both the terminal and questionnaire logs was sporadic and any findings are inconclusive. Scheduled stress tests and data from the questionnaire logs indicate that the system works well when multiple users (up to five, the current maximum) are signed on.

Table 4

System Reliability -- May

	8:00-9:00	9:00-10:00	10:00-11:00	11:00-12:00	12:00-1:00	1:00-2:00	2:00-3:00	3:00-4:00	4:00-5:00	5:00-6:00
5/6							▽			
5/7	▼		▽̇	▼			▼	▼		
5/8	▽̇	▼	▼	▽̇▽	▽	▽	▽̇ ▽	▼		
5/9	▽ ▽	▼		▼			▼		▼	▼
5/10	▼	▼	▼			▼		▽̇		
5/13	▽̇	▽̇	▼	▼		▼	▼	▼		
5/14	▽	▽̇▽	▼	▼		▼				
5/15		▽	▼		▼	▼		▽̇	▽̇▼	
5/16						▼	▼	▼		
5/17				▼	▼		▼			
5/20	▽̇	▼	▼	▼		▼				
5/21	▽̇	▽̇ ▼	▽̇	▼		▼			▼	
5/22		▽̇ ▽̇	▼			▽̇	▽̇▽			
5/23	▼▽̇	▼	▼	▼		▼	▽		▼	
5/24		▽̇ ▼	▼	▽		▼		▼	▼▽̇	
5/27		▽				▽				
5/28							▽̇			▼▽̇
5/29		▽̇ ▼		▼	▽̇	▼		▼	▼	▼
5/30		▼		▼	▼			▼		
5/31		▽		▼	▼	▼				

▼   BIBL and Optical Disk System Up

▽̇   Optical Disk System Down

▽   BIBL Down

Note: Two symbols within a box separated by a dotted line indicates that the system's status changed within that time period. Two symbols within a box without a dotted line indicate that conflicting data for that time period was reported by the reading rooms.

OBJECTIVE 6:
TO IDENTIFY POTENTIAL GROUPS OF MATERIAL FOR SCANNING ONTO OPTICAL DISK

As part of this pilot project, the Library is determining how best to use the optical disk technology for preservation and access. At the interview session, staff were asked, "What kinds of materials are best suited to this technology?" Staff felt that the optical disk was not suited for high-use current periodicals unless many more terminals were installed, for example, 20 in the Newspaper and Current Periodical Reading Room. High-use periodicals, however, are the next format scheduled for scanning onto optical disk. One alternative was to scan specialized high-use items such as the SAMS Photofact Service (appliance repair), the Physicians Desk Reference, and other items that are hard to control such as the Congressional Record and Federal Register. Other suggestions that met with general approval were items locked up for their own protection--issues of Playboy, the comic book collection (color was not seen as a major problem), and the pulp fiction collection. United Nation and foreign documents on disk also met with approval as these items are hard to control. U.S. Government documents on disk met with mixed reaction since many librarians felt the problem here was access through indexes and not to the item itself. Other suggestions were the "x" collection,* the sample file,+ association newsletters, foreign language technical materials, BIBL items listed as not in the Library of Congress and Tracer Bullets.#

OBJECTIVE 7:
TO DETERMINE GENERAL SATISFACTION

User satisfaction is always a difficult item to measure, particularly with staff who may feel that they are evaluating their own abilities. In general, the questionnaires and interviews show the staff is interested and satisfied with the optical disk system. They realize that as the system enters into production, system bugs will be worked out. One respondent wrote, "In spite of minor complaints, all in all, I think the whole idea of this system is wonderful," which seems to characterize overall feeling for the print pilot project.

DISCUSSION AND CONCLUSION

The staff did not uncover any major flaws in the technology, and their feedback gave the Library useful information about how to change the environment to make the technology easier to use. The evaluation project offered the staff a chance to be involved formally in the implementation of a new technology. This was important both for data collection and for the staff's acceptance of new responsibilities.

A half hour of individual training appears to be the minimum time needed to integrate a new system into the workflow. When the system is ready for public access, "refresher" training sessions should be scheduled. Staff offered many specific suggestions for improving the printed and online documentation. Work stations are adequate. Some of the problems experienced while reading images from the screen may be alleviated by altering the work station, as by installing tiltable screens. However, until the technology can affordably provide color, or enlargement of details on the screen, the Library may wish to use discretion in choosing materials for scanning. A large percentage of people has experienced problems viewing documents on the screen: however, the source of these difficulties is often unclear. The data under Objective 3.2 will help the technical people to assess the magnitude of each of the problems and to determine how to allocate resources for their correction. Comments about the keyboard clearly point to the need for a labeled chart with explanations in the manual.

---

*Pamphlets having a call number beginning with X.
+Serials not in the collections, of which the Library has only one sample issue.
#Four to eight page handouts designed to assist users in finding information on high interest topics

Many necessary keys were listed as superfluous. The wide range of suggestions for new keys also points to the need for mock keyboards to be made up and tested before final keyboards are ordered. Most users of the optical disk system will use the offline printing facility. Current procedures require that printouts are delivered the next day. This may cause problems for some of our clients, especially those from out of town. The impact of this limitation will be strongly affected by the materials chosen for inclusion on the disk--for example, are copies available more quickly from elsewhere in the Library? The problems experienced with print quality can be alleviated somewhat by a judicious choice of materials to be scanned. The staff's opinions about good candidates for inclusion were materials that are hard to access. Library staff members look forward to the time, not too far from now, when a patron can sit at a terminal and search and access the Library's resources easily.

REFERENCES

(1) Ellen Z. Hahn. "Library of Congress Optical Disk Pilot Program: A Report on the Print Project Activities," Library of Congress Information Bulletin, October 31, 1983, p. 374.

(2) Joseph Price. "The Optical Disk Pilot Program at the Library of Congress," Videodisc and Optical Disk, Nov.-Dec. 1984, p. 429.

(3) Michael Stuart Freeman. "The Simplicity of His Pragmatism: Librarian and Research," Library Journal, May 15, 1985, p. 28.

(4) F.W. Lancaster. The Measurement and Evaluation of Library Services. Washington, D.C.: Information Resources Press, 1977, p. 301.

MOVING FROM A FIRST GENERATION TO A SECOND GENERATION ONLINE CATALOG DATABASE

Judith Sessions and William Post
Meriam Library
CSU, Chico

Abstract. California State University, Chico is currently involved in a demonstration project to move from an operational FIRST GENERATION online catalog to an enhanced SECOND GENERATION online catalog. The purpose of this paper is to discuss the migration path chosen by CSU, Chico for this transition, and particularly to illustrate how this transition is being made in a manner transparent to the users of the current first generation system. As always, the data base and maintaining its integrity is the crucial element in this transition. The methodology used at Chico to create, load and index a "clean" MARC data base which has been synchronized with the current system's non-MARC database is discussed in detail.

Keywords. Online Catalog
Migration Path
MARC Data Base
File Processing

Background

In 1982 the Meriam Library at California State University Chico installed a vendor (C.L. Systems) designed online catalog/circulation system as part of a California State University systemwide pilot project. This first generation system provided access to catalog records which previously had been available only in the library's card catalog.

Although the system met most users' needs and was found preferable to the card catalog, it did have certain limitations which prevented the library from abandoning the manual catalog system. The most important of these limitations were the lack of cross referencing structure (authority control), of a full range of search functions (e.g., it did not support keyword or full Boolean searching), and of a MARC-based bibliographic file to support these features.1

Unless these problems were addressed, it would not be acceptable for the California State University system to move forward with systemwide implementation, and thus the strategy of a continuation of the pilot with a new enhanced PAC (Public Access Catalog) II product developed by C.L. Systems was decided upon.

THE TRANSITION PROCESS

The PAC II second generation online catalog pilot project was intended to demonstrate an online catalog acceptable from both a public and technical perspective. Such a catalog must provide for sophisticated information retrieval, must be user friendly even for a novice patron, must support national standard data formats (e.g., MARC). It was planned that the PAC II system being developed at Chico by C.L. Systems would meet all of these criteria using a strategy combining microcomputers, super micros, and minicomputers. An essential criterion for the system in Chico's environment was that the system be designed to allow a simple migration path from the PAC I non-MARC environment to the PAC II MARC-based system. A crucial part of the Chico demonstration project was to prove that this move to the new system could be achieved with minimum impact on the current operational system, and viewed by the user as a simple evolutionary change. To accomplish this transition to a second generation catalog the first problem faced by Chico was to create a "clean" MARC database which was also "in sync" with the current operational non MARC database.

CREATION OF A CLEAN AND SYNCHRONIZED MARC FILE

At first glance obtaining a MARC file for Chico's move to a second generation online catalog appeared a simple matter. The original source of cataloging data for Chico's first generation online catalog was the OCLC bibliographic utility, with a full retrospective conversion of all records in the main shelflist having been completed in 1980. All new records added to the initial online catalog system were also obtained from OCLC, thus Chico was in the enviable position of having an archival tape record in MARC format for its entire main collection. However, these original tape records were anything but clean, as was graphically demonstrated when they were initially loaded into the first online catalog system. For example, a summer cleanup project of just the subject headings on the non-MARC bibliographic file (which had been derived from the "raw" OCLC archival file) resulted in some 40,000-50,000 heading changes. These changes were not reflected on Chico's archival tapes since the changes would then have had to been made through OCLC, a process which would have required a higher level of staff and five to ten times the amount of time, due to OCLC's inability to store a local record and its primitive editing capabilities at that time. In order to meet our goal of a relatively painless transition to the next generation of an online catalog, we had to develop a methodology for transition which would avoid repeating these cleanup projects which required staff intervention. We approached this problem by breaking the process into two stages; the first was to provide a bibliographic source file as correct as possible and the second was to develop synchronicity between the source file and our current live non-MARC online catalog.

The first step in the bibliographic cleanup of our archival MARC file was to develop a program to perform certain types of edit checks on the file such as; checking for abbreviations; checking for a small "l" in fields which are supposed to be numeric only; and removal of leading articles from MARC fields which are indexed and have no nonfiling character indicators (these kind of checks are now available through vendors).2 On a file of 370,000 records this process resulted in approximatly 19,000 changes. More than half of these changes were simply changing "U.S." to "United States" and "Gt. Brit." to "Great Britain". All of these search and replacement activities were specific to the field and subfield code level. The removal of leading articles from the subfield "t" in 600 and 700 fields was viewed as a priority change as we had already seen the results in browsing author/title headings in the first generation catalog, where erratically appearing articles left users with an unintelligible sort.
For example:
    700 =a Dickens, Charles, 1812-1870.
#t A Christmas Carol.
Files before
    700 =a Dickens, Charles, 1812-1870.
#t Barnaby Rudge

After preprocessing our archival MARC file as described above we continued our bibliographic cleanup process by sending the file to a vendor to be run through an authority control system which would provide us with two products: an authoritized bibliographic file in MARC format, and an authority file in MARC format. Our specifications for this process included a detailed list of those fields which were to be run against their authority control file, and a requirement for a human edit check of every heading which did not find a match in the authority file. This human edit check examined the headings for a variety of problems such as obvious typos, indirect subject headings, abbreviations, etc. If a manual correction to the records could be made, the record was sent back through the authority loop one more time looking for a match. The result of this process was a substantially "cleaner" bibliographic file. However, although we now had a "cleaner" file of bibliographic records, we had to bring it "into sync" with the already implemented live non-MARC first generation catalog file.

In analyzing the divergence between the cleaned up MARC file and the live non-MARC file we found that the possible differences lay in three main areas; the fields changed by the non-MARC system and thus not reflected on the OCLC archival tapes; and the actual existence of a matching record on the live file for every cleaned-up MARC record. The first of these areas of divergence was handled in almost all cases by accepting the cleaned up heading as the new correct heading. This meant that the new form might vary from the orginal archival record, the live non-MARC record, and/or any associated manual files (a problem for serials). The second area, where the local changes to the non-MARC database were not reflected on the cleaned up MARC file, was more significant. This area of divergence exists as a problem not only for a library in Chico's position of upgrading from one online catalog to another, but also for any library which is attempting to bring its online circulation database "into sync" with a catalog database.

In Chico's case, information as to location or holdings may have been added to the non-MARC bibliographic record, and as a result this information had to be transferred to the corresponding MARC record. This problem was resolved by loading a copy of our non-MARC database off of our C.L. System computer onto the campus Computer Center's CDC 170/20 mainframe computer and matching the new clean MARC records against the non-MARC file using as the matching criteria the OCLC number which had been preserved in the non-MARC record. The result of this process was not only the transfer of local data to the new clean MARC file, but also a verification that such a MARC record still had a corresponding record in the existing non-MARC file. The matching process was designed so that if information in specific fields differed, local information which Chico decided was essential was written in to the MARC record. This information included such information as the local notes (field 590), call number, and a holding summary statement for serials. Some information, such as the serials summary statement, required special processing routines as it had been nicely formatted for display on the non-MARC system using embedded carriage returns which are not expected in the MARC structure. In order to avoid any rekeying of these fields we created a new repeating subfield in the MARC record for each line in the non-MARC record which then, for display purposes, could be broken back into separate lines. The object of the process was again to make the transition to a MARC-based system transparent to the user.

Once the reconciliation of the clean MARC file to the non-MARC was completed, there remained one last aspect in the new second generation online catalog database to be completed. This was the creation of MARC records for records in the non-MARC database which never went through OCLC and thus never had an archival MARC record created. These records were identified as those which did not have a corresponding MARC record and were then simply mapped into a MARC structure. These records were then added to what was now the MARC load file for the new system. It should also be noted that the one final piece of information transferred from every non-MARC record to the new MARC record was the unique system identification number (in Chico's case the Author/Title ID plus uniqueness digits). It was this number which was used to establish absolutely that the new incoming MARC load file could be linked to the correct current live non-MARC file during the load process.

SWITCHING OVER TO MARC BASED SECOND GENERATION CATALOG

Once Chico had a clean and synchronized MARC database, the challenge became how to load this file onto a system currently in use by patrons as an online catalog and a circulation system. Our goal was for this transfer not only to be transparent for patrons, but also to be relatively painless for the staff. Downtime during the transition was planned to be zero. In fact there were several days of downtime due to hardware failure, but no extended downtime was required for the transition. Since up to a year might pass while the indexes and files, such as the authority file, were built, the system had to maintain all of the old catalog/circulation files and services while building the new catalog access system. The strategy for this transition period was to set up a separate processor and storage system linked to the original system. This separate system would have the task of loading in the new MARC file and performing all the tasks related to the new catalog access system based on the MARC record while maintaining synchronicity with the old non-MARC based catalog and circulation system. This was accomplished by taking each new MARC record and from it deriving a new non-MARC record to overlay the old online catalog system public record. This process took months, but since these overlayed records looked like the old records with the exception of some headings corrections, the change was unnoticed by the public. Once the separate system finished overlaying the old record structure, it began building a new index structure for PAC II. These indexes would support the enhanced searching capability (ie. keyword and Boolean searching, as well as a syndetic structure of cross references) and an authority control system. This lengthy index building process could continue on the separate but linked system without impacting service on the operational system. New records added to the system during the transition period were loaded and stored in a MARC format. From this MARC record a non-MARC record was immediately generated and transferred automatically to the "live" system for current operations. The new MARC record was then added to the queue of records waiting to be indexed for PAC II. This strategy allowed new records to be added to the growing PAC II access system while keeping the "live" system up to date for patron use.

At this point California State University Chico has proven that it is posssible to migrate from a first generation online catalog database to a second generation online catalog database with relatively little impact on current operations. This transition required very careful planning especially in the file building stage. Our experience in this transtion process applies not only to a move from one catalog system to another, but also to the shift from a non-MARC based circulation system to a MARC based circulation/catalog system, as many of the problems of file synchronization are the same.

REFERENCES

1. William Post and Peter Watson, editors, Online Catalog, the inside story: a planning and implementation guide. Chico, California: Ryan Research International, 1983.

2. Dan Miller, "Authority Control in the Retrospective Conversion Process." Information Technology and Libraries, 3, 3 (September 1984): 286-292.

ACCESS TO INFORMATION IN THE ONLINE LIBRARY

Joe Santosuosso
CLSI
West Newton, MA

Keywords and Phrases. Dissemination of information, electronic information, end user searching, gateways, information access.

ELECTRONIC INFORMATION

Soon the academic library may no longer play a role in the dissemination of information. Electronic information providers such as BRS and DIALOG are bypassing libraries to distribute online information to homes and offices to users with personal computers. The number of software interfaces designed to facilitate online information retrieval by end users is increasing.

A small but growing volume of information is published only in an electronic format. For example, some Bureau of the Census information is only accessible by electronic means. There is a charge each time this information is accessed, so that even browsing to determine the value of the information incurs a cost. The fact that this information is public information makes the issue more problematic, but the same situation exists with respect to private sector publications. As the volume of this information increases, the need to use it increases proportionally. Researchers may choose to access electronic information directly or to have the assistance of library intermediaries. Those unfamiliar with complex information retrieval techniques normally use library intermediaries. As more sophisticated software interfaces for information retrieval are developed for end users, this will no longer be true. When researchers using direct access can obtain the same results as intermediaries, most will choose the convenience of non-library related end user searching, unless incentives such as lower costs are associated with using the library.

ISSUES

How may academic libraries play a role in the dissemination of online information? Software interfaces exist which allow libraries to serve as electronic gateways capable of switching both on and off campus users through the library computer to remote computer systems. Libraries can use these interfaces to deliver online information to researchers directly and through intermediaries. One way for academic libraries to budget for this is to devote a portion of the materials budget to information access. Another tactic is to negotiate lower prices from online vendors, based on high volume.

College and research libraries need to move to an orientation where access to information is more important than ownership. In the online environment the physical location of an item is no longer important; access and timely delivery are. Transition to an access orientation will be facilitated if library standards are developed to place more emphasis upon the availability of information than upon volume count. Can quantifiable standards be developed which will require access to information and which will express this requirement in relation to the materials budget, the size of the collection, the number and level of degree programs, the number of terminals in the library, or in some other way? How will technological change such as CD-ROM technology affect these standards? Librarians need to consider these issues now so that libraries will continue to play a vital role in the dissemination of information.

THE EFFECT OF AUTOMATION ON THE RATE OF CHANGE IN PROCEDURES

Pat Weaver-Meyers and Nedria Santizo
University of Oklahoma Library
Norman, Oklahoma

Abstract. The continuing change in procedures that are part of new software development by vendors require constant retraining of personnel and may not always be changes which your institution deems desirable. Realizing that the vendor's goals may not be consistent with your library's goals is basic to deciding whether to adopt, alter, defer or reject new capabilities. Some strategies are recommended to help librarians, in their increasing role as trainers and procedure manual developers, cope with the constant change which seems to accompany automation.

Keywords and Phrases. Automation, Procedures, Change planning, Training for automation, Software problems.

In the past, a dust-covered three-ring binder in the back of a desk drawer was often a realistic description of an office procedure manual. Revamping such a manual usually came from a turnover in personnel. Now, it is more likely the result of automation. In fact, automation is nothing short of revolutionary in its influence on office procedures and on the middle manager in charge of seeing that procedures are properly followed. Once in place, an automated system can even become a dictator of office conventions. The rapid proliferation of automated systems in libraries today make a closer examination of their influence on everyday procedures an interesting exercise.

AUTOMATION EFFECTS

What are the effects of an automated system and software changes on procedures? It seems that four generalizations apply:

1) Automation, due to software enhancements, bugs, etc. speeds up the rate of change in procedures.

2) Automation tends to remove procedures and their formulation from the individual library's locus of control.

3) Automated system designers incorporate other institutional goals in their design which may or may not coincide with your institution goals or procedural preferences.

4) Automation, due to rapid changes, increases the demand for continued training of personnel.

Most libraries prepare adequately for the major change associated with the implementation of an automated system and the literature is loaded with advice about staff training upon conversion. We maintain though, that the subsequent changes associated with automation continue at an increased pace long after adoption of a system. This continuing change in procedures and the demand it places on middle managers and operational staff is often overlooked by administrators.

MIDDLE MANAGERS/TRAINERS

The rate of change in procedures is clearly illustrated by what happens when new software is released by a vendor. How many of you have eagerly awaited a software release from your vendor because you needed a new capability contained in that software? How many of you have then spent the next several months coping with software bugs that accompanied the long heralded release? Well, if you haven't yet experienced this, you probably will. This kind of occurence is very common in software changes, because no new software is perfect. This also demonstrates the proliferation of changes in procedures that can accompany a release. The librarian may find that he/she will be in the midst of informing staff about how to use a new function, while they must also train them to deal with a problem. Two weeks later, the trainer may be in the position of advising staff of a correction to the problem, which forces yet another change in procedure. What does this mean? It means the middle manager may often find him/herself in the uncomfortable position of training personnel to implement new procedures for new capabilities that both enhance and detract from their everyday productivity. It also means that the middle manager should expect the accelerated role of trainer, which they assume upon implementation of an automated system, to continue indefinitely[1]. Administrators should expect this of their middle managers and realize that trainers will need to be freed from other duties to meet this continuing responsibility. It has even been suggested that many newly created future positions in libraries will be solely responsible for coordination of training[2].

In the design of an automated system, somebody's assumptions are built in[3]. Whose assumptions? If you haven't been involved intimately with the vendor, or designed your own system, they're probably not yours. This means that you are not in total control of how the system dictates your procedures or in how the system's design may influence your workers' attitudes and effectiveness[4]. In fact, changes in system software may actually be brought about by other, more demanding subscribers. This brings to mind a software release we waited for

last year, which was touted by the vendor as a
fix for our overdue notices. We were not having
any particular problems with our notices, but
many of the other clients the vendor serviced
were having problems. The release came, and lo
and behold, we began having problems. We had to
change our procedure for processing the notices,
because the computer was now generating overdue
notices for books that were not overdue.
Incidentally, the release had several other
changes in it, which did fix some problems, but
somehow I can't seem to recall them. I guess it
isn't surprising that needed changes are readily
incorporated into office procedures, and
unneeded changes are so resisted that they
become the most memorable part of the change.

UNNEEDED CHANGES

A good illustration of the problem with
unneeded change can be seen by examining a standard model of change[5]. In most models of
change, the change process begins with a need or
lack of satisfaction. The problem with the kind
of change we are discussing is that the need may
originate with another subscriber or with the
vendor. It is not the result of any need within
your organization. During implementation of a
system, staff are often willing to undergo
unneeded change in order to obtain the other
needed changes that the system offers. Once
staff have incorporated and learned the new procedures in a new automated system, they will
naturally resist further change. In part, this
is due to the fact that they have invested
effort in learning the new procedure and are not
ready to give up what they have spent so much
time assimilating. This is particularly true if
they and you do not see any clear need on the
part of your institution to adopt the new procedure. It is at this point, that the middle
manager may find rejection of the new procedure
a legitimate, cost effective solution.
Rejection also may be valuable because adoption
of some procedures may detrimentally affect some
long-held standards designed to protect the
quality of your database. For example, the
online bibliographic record transfer capability
on our system, which interfaces with OCLC, is
currently unreliable and does not consistently
transfer the complete MARC record. As a result,
we have rejected that function and do not intend
to implement it until we are assured of its
accuracy.

Besides actual rejection of a procedure,
there are other effective solutions to the
problem of maintaining control over what procedures your institution selects to use. Active
involvement in a user's group can help in
insuring that your institution's interests and
goals influence the vendor's decisions. In
addition, a network of communication with other
user's helps too. Many times an institution
will solve the same problem you have in-house.
If it is applicable, you can borrow their strategy and alter the procedure. In-house development of training materials which supplement what
the vendor provides is, of course, an absolute
necessity and can provide a kind of "history" of
the alterations in a procedure over a several
year period. Altering a procedure can be
accomplished both manually by the operator and
with in-house programming.

So far we have talked about rejecting or
altering a new procedure. Deferring the adoption of a procedure is also an effective strategy and it supports our earlier assertion about
unneeded change. Deferring can be good for two
reasons. It can prevent your institution from
going through the more difficult transition of
adopting an unneeded change, until your
library's needs in this particular area rise to
a level at which implementation of this function
is required (needed) by the staff to operate at
highest efficiency. Secondly, deferring adoption in some cases will allow your library to
avoid some system bugs in new releases until
those bugs are worked out, thus saving both time
and stress.

ADVANTAGES OF UNIFORMITY

Lest everyone conclude that we favor too
much the continuance of in-house procedures, we
should at this point, mention some of the advantages of uniformity with other institutions.
OCLC, RLIN, and other bibliographic utilities
are classic examples of automation's effect on
local procedures. The uniformity in local versus systemwide procedures brought about by
bibliographic utilities have justifiably found
strong support. Definitely, this is a cost
effective approach. Training manuals,
workshops, etc. are also handled in large part
by the utilities because uniformity makes it
possible. However, we maintain that not all
procedural uniformity adequately meets the needs
of the various concerns represented by different subscribers (public vs. academic for
example) of some vended systems. Librarians
should closely examine a new system capability
and feel comfortable rejecting it if the
library's needs are not compatible. Cost
effectiveness is not the only important measure
of efficiency or appropriateness. It is important to be cautious in terms of future networking concerns, though, and not sacrifice the
compatibility of your database with others.

SUMMARY

In conclusion, the strategies we recommend
include:
1) Realize your role as trainer includes
interpreting changes and interceding between the
change and your staff, if necessary.
2) Higher level management must understand that
automation means a <u>continuing</u> training commitment for middle managers.
3) On all levels, the subscriber should be aware
of the vendor's orientation and feel comfortable
"editing" software that does not fit their
needs.
4) Legitimate ways of dealing with changes in
procedures brought about by new software
include: altering, deferring, rejecting, or

adopting. ADOPTING DOESN'T HAVE TO BE AUTOMATIC.

REFERENCES

1) Homer J. Hagedorn, "After the Information Revolution: Training as a Way of Life for Line Managers," Management Review 73:8-13 (July 1984).

2) Dennis Reynolds, Library Automation: Issues and Applications (New York: Bowker, 1985), p. 275.

3) Shoshana Zuboff, "New Worlds of Computer-Mediated Work," Harvard Business Review 60:142-152 (Sept-Oct 1982).

4) Lewis M. Branscomb, "The Computer's Debt to Science," Library High Tech 7:7-18 (1984).

5) Ronald G. Havelock, The Change Agent's Guide to Innovation in Education, (Englewood Cliffs, N.J.: Educational Technology Publications, 1973), p. 7.

AUTHOR INDEX

Adams, Judith A. 63
Adams, Marjorie E. 23
Anderson, David G. 3
Atkins, Stephen E. 8
Bausser, Jaye 27
Belanger, Sandra 159
Bentley, Stella 146
Betcher, Melissa Ann 229
Borgendale, Marilyn 165
Boss, Richard W. 209
Brownrigg, Edwin B. 225
Burlingame, Dwight F. 99
Carey, Kevin 168
Chiang, Katherine S. 67
Comes, James F. 117
Cook, Colleen 70
Cooper, John M. 101
Corey, Constance 122
Coutts, Mary Carrington 63
Creaghe, Norma S. 76
Davis, Douglas A. 76
Davis, Jinnie Y. 27
Demas, Samuel 11
Dunn, Kathleen 172
Easterbrook, David L. 80
Eaton, Nancy L. 214
Fink, Deborah 49
Ford, Barbara J. 179
Gamble, Lynne 82
Gillham, Virginia 218
Gleim, David 27
Griffin, Mary Ann 105
Haeuser, Michael 13
Hafter, Ruth 30
Hays, Kathleen M. 130
Herman, Edward 86
Hitchingham, Eileen E. 133
Hood, Elizabeth 15
Hsueh, Daphne C. 23
Hurd, Douglas P. 182
Johnson, Carol A. 108
Kathman, Michael D. 108
Kelley, Carol Marie 34
Kemp, Barbara E. 52
Kenyon, Sharmon H. 55
Knutson, Gunnar 35
Kohl, David F. 222
Lagana, Gretchen 90
Landram, Christina 3
Lynch, Clifford A. 225
McPheron, Elaine 186
Miller, Connie 202
Molyneux, Robert E. 182
Montanelli, Dale S. 18
Morita, Ichiko 44
Neal, James G. 139
Nofsinger, Mary M. 52
Piele, Linda J. 56
Pinzelik, Barbara P. 141

Post, William 236
Pryor, Judith 56
Reich, Victoria Ann 229
Robinson, Judith G. 59
Santizo, Nedria 240
Santosuosso, Joe 239
Scharf, Meg Koch 191
Schmidt, Karen A. 93
Schwerin, Julie B. 214
Sessions, Judith 236
Shaw, Julia R. 59
Small, Sally S. 194
Smith, Karen F. 198
Snyder, Carolyn A. 146
Spitzer, Alice M. 52
Steel, Virginia 122
Stenstrom, Patricia F. 18
Strazdon, Maureen E. 194
Tegler, Patricia 202
Thorne, Rosemary 159
Timko, Georgene A. 112
Tuckett, Harold W. 56
Wall, Celia 205
Ward, Jeannette 191
Weaver-Meyers, Pat 240
Welch, Jeanie M. 152

SUBJECT INDEX

Abstracts and indexes 205
Academic libraries 30, 67, 76, 82, 93, 99
Academic librarians 3, 18, 133, 152
Academic library personnel 139
Academic status see also faculty status 18
Access points 35
Access to serials in micro-reproduction 23
Acquisitions systems 70
ACRL see association of college and research libraries
Added entries 35
Alternative models 179
Approval plan 93
Architecture and building--sound control 194
Area studies 80
Articulation, educational 52
Artificial intelligence see also expert systems 44
Assessment see evaluation
Association of College and Research Libraries standards 101
Automated access facilities 76
Automated library systems 70
Automatic quality control 44
Automatic validation 27
Automation see also library automation 34, 108, 222, 240
Automation of library processes--book storage 76
Bibliographic control of serials in micro-reproduction 23
Bibliographic instruction 49, 52, 56, 59, 198
Bibliographic records 35
Bibliographers 82
Book selection policy statement 15
Branch libraries 146
Browsing 76
California State University, Northridge 76
Career development 117
Career and performance 117
Catalog maintenance 27
Cataloging 30, 35
Cataloging of micro-reproductions 23
CD-ROM see compact disc-read only memory
Censorship 15
Change planning 108, 240
Circulation 35, 186
Classification and pay plans 152
Collection development 67, 80, 82, 90, 93

College and university librarians see academic librarians
College and university libraries see academic libraries
Communication 218
Compact disc-read only memory 214
Computer bibliographic searching see online searching

Computer end-user training 168
Computer literacy 56
Conservation 225
Continuing motivation 172
Cooperation 34
Cooperative programs 52
Copyright and machine - readable formats 11
Costs 101
Costs and performance of document services 182
Curriculum clearinghouse 63
Curriculum reform 13
Database searching see online searching
Developing-world scholarship 80
Development team 99
Direct transmission 70
Discipline in the libraries 194
Dissemination of information 239
Document delivery 165, 182
Economics 186
Electronic access to reference services 165
Electronic conferencing 218
Electronic imaging 225
Electronic information 239
Electronic networking 209
Employee turnover 139
End-user 55, 59
End-user searching 239
Enrollment 101
Error detection 27
Evaluation 59, 82
Expert systems see also artificial intelligence 198
Faculty 55
Faculty governance 8
Faculty status see also academic status 8
"Fair use" of computerized information 11
File processing 236
Financial exigency 205
Focus group 191
Freedom of access to information 11
Fund raising 99
Funding 101
Gateways 239
Goals and objectives 3
Governance 8
Government documents 198
Government information 86
High school/college cooperation 52
Information access 239
Information literacy 56
Information retrieval 202
Information-seeking behavior 172
Information processing 49
Instruction see also bibliographic instruction 55
Integrating online search services 159
Interactive library systems 70
Interdisciplinary research 63
Interfaced library systems 70
Interfacing 209

Interlibrary loans 182
Interviewing in marketing research 191
Job design 130
Job enlargement 130
Liberal arts 13
Liberal arts colleges 205
Library administration 218
Library automation see also automation 70, 76, 165, 225
Library of Congress Optical Disk Project 229
Library directors 8
Library finance 186
Library management 218
Library of Congress 229
Library research 8
Library school courses 3
Library skills 52
Library use studies 191
Linking systems 70
Local microcomputer interfaces 222
Lockwood Library see State University of New York (SUNY) at Buffalo Lockwood Library
Management see also library management; middle management 105
Managerial interventions 117
Managers 139
Manuscripts 90
MARC data base 236
Medical ethics 63
Meetings 218
Merit evaluation 122
Microcomputers 55, 56, 67, 108, 198
Microcomputer labs 56
Microforms 86
Microcomputer software 67
Micro-reproduction 23
Middle management 141
Migration path 236
Myers-Briggs Type Indicator Test 108
Need-source linkages 172
Noise control in academic libraries 194
Non-print materials 90
Objectives see goals and objectives
Obsolescence of library materials 76
Off-site access 165
Ohio State University Libraries 23
Online catalog 44, 108, 236
Online catalog maintenance 27
Online networks 30
Online search services 59, 159
Online searching 168, 202, 205
Open System Interconnection 209
Optical disk technology 214, 229
Optical information retrieval systems 214
Organization 82
Organizational values 105
OSI see Open System Interconnection
Peer review 30, 122
Performance evaluation 122, 141
Personnel 152

Personnel evaluation see performance evaluation
PERT see Program Evaluation and Review Technique
Plateauing 117
Photocopy services 165
Popular culture 90
Precision and recall 202
Preservation 225
Procedures 240
"Pro-Search" 55
Professional roles 56
Program Evaluation and Review Techniques (PERT) 108
Psychological motivation 172
Public services 112
Public services staffing see also reference services staffing 146
Rare books 90
Recall see precision and recall
Reference desk 179
Reference interview process 168
Reference services 168, 179, 198
Reference services staffing 159
Regression analysis 186
Research see also library research 3, 18, 49
Research process 202
Research time 133
Resource development 99
Salaries 152
Selectors 82
Serials in multiple formats 23
Service time 133
Shared mainframe systems 222
Sociotechnical model of job design 130
Software problems 240
Source linkages 172
Space problems 76
Special collections 90
Special libraries 63
Staff allocation 165
Staff utilization 146
State University of New York (SUNY) at Buffalo Lockwood Library 86
Statistical methods 3
Stress 130
Subject headings 35
Syllabus exchange 63
Tape processing 27
Team Evaluation and Management Systems (TE*MS) 122
Technical services 112
Time analysis 133
Training for automation 240
Triangle Research Libraries Networks (TRLN) 27
University Microforms International (UMI) Article Clearinghouse 182
Undergraduates 172
Undergraduate libraries 186
University governance 8
User demand 186

Values articulation 105
Video Display Terminals (VDT's) 130
Videodisk technology 229
Workload 133